Miriam Coles Harris

Rutledge

Miriam Coles Harris

Rutledge

ISBN/EAN: 9783742897503

Manufactured in Europe, USA, Canada, Australia, Japa

Cover: Foto ©Thomas Meinert / pixelio.de

Manufactured and distributed by brebook publishing software
(www.brebook.com)

Miriam Coles Harris

Rutledge

NEW YORK:

DERBY & JACKSON, 498 BROADWAY

1860.

RUTLEDGE.

CHAPTER I.

"Heavily hangs the broad sunflower,
Over its grave i' the earth so chilly;
Heavily hangs the hollyhock,
Heavily hangs the tiger lily.

TENNYSON.

IT was the gloomy twilight of a gloomy November day; dark and leaden clouds were fast shutting out every lingering ray of daylight; and the wind, which moaned dismally around the house, was tossing into mad antics the leaves which strewed the playground. The lamps were not lighted yet; of visible fires the *pensionnat* of St. Catharine's was innocent; a dull black stove, more or less gigantic, according to the size of the apartment, gloomed in every one, and affected favorably the thermometer, if not the imagination. We paced untiringly up and down the dim corridor—Nelly, Agnes and I—three children, who, by virtue of our youth, ought to have been let off, one would have thought, for some years yet, from the deep depression that was fast settling on our spirits. In truth we were all three very miserable, we thought—Nelly and Agnes, I am afraid, more so than I, who in common justice ought to have participated deeply in, as I was the chief occasion of, their grief.

My trunk was packed and strapped, and stood outside the door of my dormitory, ready for the porter's attention. In it lay my school-books, closed forever, as I hoped; and souvenirs innumerable of school friendships and the undying love of the extremely young persons by whom I was surrounded.

From them I was to be severed to-morrow, as was ex-pected, and

"It might be for years, and it might be for ever,"

as Nelly had just said, choking up on the last sentence. I *did* feel unhappy, and very much like "choking up" too, when I passed the great windows, that looked into the play-ground, and remembered all the mad hours of frolic I had passed there; when I took down my shawl from the peg where it had hung nightly for five years, and remembered, with a thrill, it was "the last time;" when the lid of my empty desk fell down with an echo that sounded drearily through the long school-room; when I thought "where I might be this time to-morrow," and when Agnes' and Nelly's arms twined about me, reminded me of the rapidly approaching hour of separation from those who had repre-sented the world to me for five years—whom I had loved and hated, and by whom I had been loved and hated, with all the fervor of sixteen. The hatreds now were softened down by the nearness of the parting; all my ancient foes, (and they had not been few), had "made up" and promised forgiveness and forgetfulness entire; and all ancient feuds were dead. All my friends now loved me with tenfold the ardor they had ever felt before; all the staff of teachers, who had, I am afraid, a great deal to forgive, of impatient self-will, mad spirits and thoughtless inattention, were good enough to forget all, and remember only what they were pleased to call the truth and honesty and courage, that in the years we had been together, they had never known to fail.

They little knew how their unlooked for praise humbled

me; and how far more deeply than any reproach, it made me realize the waste of time and talents that I had to look back upon.

So, most unexpectedly to myself, I found that I was going off with flying colors; that all were joining to deplore my departure and laud my good qualities; and that, from being rather a "limb" in the eyes of the school, and a hopeless sinner in my own, I was promoted, temporarily, to the dignity of heroine at St. Catharine's.

It was with a very full heart that I remembered all this; and deeper feelings than I had known since my childhood were stirred by the kindness I was certain was as undeserved as it was unexpected. But such a future dawned before me, that tender regret struggled hard with giddy hope for the mastery. In almost every girl's life, leaving school is a marked and important event; and imagination has always a wide, and generally well-cultivated field for its powers, even when home and future are as certain as things mundane can be. But in my case there was so much room for dreaming, so much raw material for fancy to work up, that a tamer and less imaginative child than I was, would have been tempted into castle-building. The sad event that five years before had placed me, a stunned, bewildered, motherless child, in the midst of strangers, had largely developed the turn for dreaming that such children always possess. The sympathy and love that God provides for every child that is born into the world, withdrawn, they turn "not sullen, nor in scorn," but from an instinct He has himself implanted, inward, for their sympathy and counsel. So it happened, that though Nelly and Agnes, and a dozen merry girls beside, were my sworn friends and very firmest allies, none of them knew anything of the keen wonder and almost painful longing with which I pictured the future to myself. They knew, of course, the simple facts, that as I had no father or mother, I was to go and live with my aunt, who had been in Europe until this summer and whom I had not seen since my mother died; that she had three daughters, one older, two younger than myself; that she had sent me some pretty things from Paris, and was, probably, very kind, and I should have a very nice time.

They knew only these bare beams and framework of the gorgeous fabric I had reared upon them; they little knew the hours of wakefulness in which I wondered whether I should be happy or miserable in that new home; whether my aunt would love me as I already most ardently loved her; whether the new cousins were at all like Nelly and Agnes; and whether they were prepared to value the wealth of affection I had in reserve for them. But time would soon settle all this into certainty; and my aunt's last letter, containing all the final arrangements for my journey, I at present knew by heart. The only possible shade of uncertainty about my starting, lay in the chance of the gentleman who was to be my escort, being detained by business a day or two longer at C——, and not arriving to-night, as had been considered probable.

Nelly built greatly upon this possibility, and as the twilight deepened, and the moaning wind and growing darkness pressed more and more upon us, we turned to that as our only chance of comfort. Nelly had said, for the twentieth time, "I am sure he will not come till to-morrow, it is too late for him now," when a sharp ring at the bell made us all start, and sent the blood swiftly enough through *my* veins, and, I suppose, no less swiftly through my young companions'; for Nelly convulsively clasped me round the neck and burst into tears, while Agnes said, in a choking voice, "I'm certain of it!" And for three dreadful minutes of suspense we stood motionless, holding our breath, and watching for the first token of the approach of the messenger who should confirm or confute our forebodings.

At last, steps echoed along the hall, and bearing a dim candle, which blinked nervously at every step, appeared the

Biddy who officiated as waiter at St. Catharine's. She had a card in her hand, and our end of the corridor seemed her destination, and our party the party she was in search of.

"Well?" said Agnes, making a distracted effort to break the silence, as Biddy groped stupidly and slowly toward us. "A gentleman," she said, "a gentleman to see you, miss," and she handed me the card. "I knew it," said Agnes, with a deep sigh, as, per favor of the blinking candle, the three heads, clustered over the card, made out the name, "Mr. Arthur Rutledge."

"Oh, I am so frightened!" I said, sitting down on the lowest step of the stairs. "Girls, what shall I do?"

Nelly shook her head; she did not wonder I was afraid; for five years I had encountered no gentlemen more alarming than the professors, and no strangers more intimidating than occasional new scholars; and knew no more how to conduct myself on this occasion, than if I had not received Miss Crowen's valuable instructions on deportment. I had been taught to swim, theoretically, on shore, and now was to be pushed suddenly out into deep water, to make the best use I could of my scientific knowledge. As was to be supposed, I found myself not much the better for it.

"He's not a young gentleman though," said Agnes, "and I shouldn't mind it much if I were you."

"Oh, of course he's not young, or Aunt Edith would not have had me go with him. He's as old as the hills, I know but that makes it so much the worse; and then, he wa abroad with my aunt and cousins, and knows them all so well; and Aunt Edith calls him 'an accomplished gentleman of high standing;' and oh! I am sure I shall blush and act like a fool, and disgrace myself; and aunt is so particular."

Nelly condoled, Agnes counselled, and I stood shivering in an agony of apprehension and dismay, when the heavy tread of Miss Crowen on the stairs, gave an impetus to my faltering steps, and sent me parlor-wards with emphasis.

"If you don't hurry," whispered Agnes. "Miss Crowen

1*

will drag you in, and make one of her horrible speeches about educational advantages and mental culture, and put you through a course of mathematical problems, and make you show off on the piano, if not sing."

The wily Agnes had touched the right chord. Threatened with this new horror, I grew reckless, and without a moment more of hesitation, bolted into the parlor, and stood confronting the object of my terror, before I had had time in the least to prepare my line of conduct. I stood for a moment with burning cheeks and downcast eyes, unable to articulate a word, and saw nothing, heard nothing, till I found myself seated on the sofa, and being talked to in a kind manner by the dreaded stranger, who sat beside me. If my "Yes sir," and "No sir," came in in the right places, I can claim no sort of credit for it; for neither then nor now, had or have I the faintest apprehension of anything he said By and by, however, under the influence of that steady unmoved voice, my alarm began to subside, and my scared senses, after fluttering hopelessly about, like a dislodged prood of swallows, began at last to collect themselves again, and resume their proper functions. By degrees I began to comprehend what he was talking about, and in process of time, commanded my voice sufficiently to answer him audibly, and before the interview was over, had the courage to raise my eyes, and satisfy myself as to the personal appearance of this my destined protector in the three days' journey we had in prospect.

And the result of this investigation was, the instant establishment, upon a firm basis, of ease and confidence. For few men or women, much less children or girls, ever looked into Mr. Rutledge's face, without feeling that they saw their master, but withal so firm and kind a master, that all thought of resistance to his will, or stubborn maintenance of their own, together with all foolish vanity and consciousness, vanished at once and forever, or returned but seldom, and was soon conquered. If I had

cherished any romantic hope that this " accomplished gentleman " might prove anything out of which I could make
that dearest dream of schoolgirl's heart, a lover, I likewise
relinquished that most speedily, for nothing in the person
before me, gave encouragement to such an idea. Rather
below than above the medium size, and of a firm, well-proportioned figure, Mr. Rutledge gave one, from his com-
manding and decided carriage, the impression of a much
larger man. His dark hair was slightly dashed with grey,
his eyes were keen and cold, the lines of care and thought
about his brow were deep and strong. If his face could be
said to have an attraction, it lay in the rare smile that
sometimes changed the sternness of his mouth into winning
sweetness and grace. But this was so rare that it could
hardly be called a characteristic of his habitually cold stern
face. That it wore it that evening however, I knew then
as now, was because I was a child, and a miserable, frightened one besides. I never doubted that he knew how I
felt, and read me thoroughly.

The interview was, according to the prim little clock on
the mantelpiece, by no means a long one; and after intro-
ducing (with but indifferent grace) Miss Crowen, who entered the room with elephantine tread, to my visitor, he
took leave, having arranged to come for me the next morning at six.

That last evening, with its half-strange, excited novelty
of leave-taking, and last messages and last thoughts, is still
distinct in my memory; and the start with which I
answered Biddy's call in the darkness of the November
morning, the dressing with cold hurried hands that were
not half equal to the task, the wild way in which everything
came dancing through my mind, as I tried to say my
prayers, the utter inability to taste a mouthful of the breakfast Miss Crowen herself had superintended, the thrill with
which I heard the carriage drive up to the door, are as vivid
as recollections can well be. And I am in no danger, either

of forgetting the moment, when, with half a dozen of my schoolfellows who had been allowed to see me off, I descended the steps toward the carriage, the door of which Mr. Rutledge was holding open. The kind good bye of Miss Crowen, the warm embraces of the girls, Nelly's tears, Agnes' wistful look, are memories I cannot part with if I would.

The carriage door shut to with a snap, the horses started forward at a brisk pace, and we were off, and I had left school and childhood behind me forever. I did not cry at all, though I felt desperately like it; but the consciousness that Mr. Rutledge looked sharply at me to see how I took it, made me struggle harder to keep back my tears, and seem womanly and composed. In this I succeeded beyond my hopes, and before half an hour had passed, the bracing air of the fine autumn morning, the rapid pace at which we rolled along, and the new delight to my cloistered eyes, ot farms, and villages, woods rich in the many colors of the fall, and meadows and uplands basking in its sunshine, made me feel as if I had been months away from school, and as if the melancholy of last night were some strange distant dream. Seventeen never dreamed more fantastic dreams than I did that morning, however, as I leaned back in the carriage and idly watched the gay landscape past which we were hurrying. It was quite a relief to me that my companion, after attending to my comfort in every necessary way, settled himself in his corner of the carriage, and taking a book from his valise, devoted himself to its perusal, and left me to my own thoughts the entire morning. He did not put it up till we reached the town where we were to dine and wait for the cars.

Dinner did not prove a very animated meal; my companion, after asking me about school, and whether I felt sorry to leave it, and a few more questions of the same nature (such as people always put to school-girls, and by which they unconsciously give great offence), seemed to consider his conversational duty performed, and fell into a state of abstraction, which made his face look harder and colder than ever; and as I stealthily regarded him from under my eyelashes, some of last night's alarm threatened to return. But I tried to overcome it, and endeavored to reassure myself by remembering how kind he was when I was so much embarrassed, and how well he had helped me through the interview that he might have made so terrible; and that he did not talk to me—why, certainly it was not strange that a gentleman of his age should not have much in common with a girl of mine.

By and by the cars came tearing through the town with a whoop and a shriek, that seemed to excite everybody wonderfully, considering the frequency of the occurrence. Passengers, porters, newsboys, in one mad crowd, rushed toward the depot, each emulating in his own proper person, the noble rage of the snorting, impatient monster, upon whose energy we were all depending. The only individual entirely unexcited, was my escort, who never for a moment lost the appearance of sang froid and indifference that an earthquake would not have startled him out of, I was convinced. Though we did not hurry, we were, before many of our fellow-voyagers, in possession of the best seats, and most commodiously, because most deliberately, settled for the journey. Mr. Rutledge was emphatically a good traveller, carrying the clear-sighted precision and deliberation of his mind into all the details of travel, and thereby securing himself from the petty annoyances that people often think unworthy of attention, but which do more than they suspect, toward marring pleasure and destroying comfort. I aptly followed his manner, and was a marvel of unconcerned deliberation in the matter of securing my seat and arranging my shawls, books and bags; which drew from him the remark, with an approving glance, that he perceived I was used to travelling. That observation, either from the fact of its being so absurdly incorrect in its premises,

or from the stronger fact of its being the only one addressed to me until 7 P.M., when we stopped at F—— for
purposes of refreshment, impressed itself very much upon
my mind.

After the wretched meal, called by compliment tea,
which we were allowed twenty minutes to partake of, had
been dispatched, and we were again settled in the cars in
which we were to travel all night, commenced the trials of
the journey—to me, at least, for I was an entire novice,
not having been twenty miles away from St. Catharine's
since I was first taken there, and having but a dim recollection of that, my first and last journey till the present
time. Being also subject to the most unbearably severe
headaches upon any unusual excitement, it is not very wonderful that on this occasion I was attacked with one, and
before night had actually set in, was as completely miserable, as in the morning I had been completely happy.
Excitement and weariness began to tell most painfully upon
me. Not a bone but ached, not a nerve in my whole body
but throbbed and quivered. It was as impossible to think
quietly as to sit quietly. Homesickness, for the home I had
been longing to get away from for five years—all the
miserable things I had ever suffered or dreaded—all the
fancied and real trials of my life, then and there beset
my aching head, and made sleep or composure an impossibility.

If there had been a soul to speak to, a human voice to say
a single word of sympathy, however commonplace, I
thought it would have made the night endurable. But
among the sleepy, senseless crowd around, the only one I
had a right to expect attention from, or to whom I was
entitled to address a word, was as regardless of my existence as any of the rest. Mr. Rutledge occupied the seat
before me, and the imperfect light of the lamp that rattled
and flickered above us, showed me more plainly than any
other object, his fixed, unsympathizing face, as he leaned

against the window of the car, his lips compressed and his brow knit. He did not sleep any more than I did, nor do I think he was a whit more comfortable; but he had his impatience under better control, and never moved a muscle or uttered a sound for hours together.

It was the most torturing thing to watch him, so entirely unmoved by the discomforts that were, I was firmly convinced, driving me mad; and in my jaundiced eyes, his profile took a thousand wizard shapes. It would have been a relief if he had moved in ever so slight a degree to one side or the other; but a painted face upon a painted window could not have been more rigid than the one before me. I was dying of thirst, was smothering for want of air, ached in every limb, and there were hours yet to morning! The monotonous motion of the cars, and their accompanying noises, harsh and shrill, made to my perfectly unaccustomed ear a frightful combination of discord; and this all coming upon my excited and sensitive nerves, worked me up into a state of wretchedness that naturally resulted in that climax of woes feminine, a fit of crying.

I could no more have helped it than the wind could have helped blowing, and never having learned to control myself, could not suppress the indulgence of an emotion which, an hour afterward, I remembered with acute mortification. I tried to smother my sobs, but they reached at last the ear of my silent companion, who started, and turning toward me, asked, with a shade of impatience in his tone, what was the matter? Was I ill?

That question, so put, in the indescribable tone that shows to a sensitive ear a want of sympathy the most galling, was the best cure that could have been devised for my tears. They were done, altogether; but in their place, the angry blood flew to my face, and I inly vowed, in accordance with school-girl notions of right, never to forget or forgive the insult. Angrily averting my head, I declined any assistance or attention whatever, and pride having thus stepped in to the rescue, I was able to maintain as rigid a demeanor as Mr. Rutledge himself. For a moment he looked at me with an expression that I could not quite make out, then with the slightest possible shrug of the shoulders, turned away, and seating himself again in the corner, resumed his former attitude. That was enough; all my spirit was roused; I had always been good at hating, but the present crisis brought out powers I had never been aware of before; and there was a great deal in the fact of my having made a fool of myself in the presence of Mr. Rutledge, to help me along in detesting him; and not being in a particularly reasonable or well-governed frame of mind, the aversion I had conceived increased with alarming rapidity. It was wonderful how powerful my resentment was to keep my weariness and impatience in check. I did not move an inch nor utter a single word; I would have borne the rack and torture rather than exhibit, after that shrug, another shade of emotion.

When at last, morning being broadly awake, we were released from our prison for an hour to breakfast and rest at a way-station that seemed most utterly repugnant to those two ideas, Mr. Rutledge asked me if I would not prefer, on account of my fatigue, waiting there till the next train, which would arrive at noon?

I answered, "*Decidedly* not," with so much emphasis, that he only bowed and turned away; with what opinion of my temper it is not pleasant to think. Before the day was over, he had, I presume, concluded, that he had taken under his charge about as willful and disagreeable a young miss as ever tried the patience of parent or protector.

The day wore on, much after the manner of yesterday. That night at twelve, we expected to arrive at C—— where we were to rest till morning; and thence taking the boat, were to reach our journey's end about noon.

It was toward evening of that weary day; I was sitting listlessly looking out upon the dreary suburbs of the town which we seemed approaching, and thinking, by way of diverting myself, of Nelly and Agnes and school, and what they were doing now, and whether they missed me ; when there came a sudden jar, then a horrid crash, a shriek that rent the air, a blow upon my head that made a hideous glare of light, then darkness absolute, and I knew no more.

CHAPTER II.

" The brightest rainbows ever play
Above the fountains of our tears."

MACKAY.

How long after it was that consciousness returned, I cannot tell ; if indeed that bewildered dizzy realization of things present that gradually forced itself upon me, can be called consciousness. I was lying on the ground, and looked, upon opening my eyes, up at the clear evening sky. It could not have been long after sunset, and all the scene around me, when at last I tried to comprehend it, was distinct enough. Some distance from where I lay, there was a bridge and an embankment, perhaps thirty feet high. Between that and me, a horrid mass loomed up against the sky, black and shapeless, one car piled above another in an awful wreck. Dark figures lay around me on the ground, some writhing in agony, others motionless and rigid ; groans and cries the most appalling smote my ear. But my ear and all my senses were so stunned and bewildered, that to see and hear was not to feel alarm or awe or pity, only dull stupor and discomfort. I did not feel the least desire to move or speak, the least solicitude about my fate. Half unconsciously I lay watching the fading light in the sky, and the dark figures that soon were swarming around, bending over and raising up the wounded, and thrusting lanterns into the faces of such as lay stiff and still and did not heed their ejaculations.

At last two men came up to where I lay, and one, from the exclamation of recognition he made as they bent over me, I knew to be Mr. Rutledge. The effect of the lantern glaring so suddenly in my face, was to make me start up,

13

with some broken exclamation; but the words had hardly left my lips, when an acute pain and then a giddy blindness rushed over me, and I sunk back, and with a horrible sensation of falling down, down, to unfathomable darkness, I was again insensible.

I suppose I must have remained in that state all night, for it was daylight when I was again sufficiently conscious to know what was going on around me. Mr. Rutledge was sitting by me and was saying to the physician, whose entrance had, I think, first aroused me, that he considered me doing very well, the fever was evidently abating, and that he thought the doctor would agree with him that I might soon be moved to more comfortable quarters.

"If any such can be found," the doctor answered; "but every house in the town, as well as both the hotels, are crowded with the sufferers, and I think your chance of comfort is as good here as it will be anywhere else; for, sir, it is a wretched little town at the best. I wish we could boast better accommodations for strangers."

"Then doctor," said Mr. Rutledge, "I am sure you will consent to what I have been thinking of as the most feasible plan. You know it is but eight miles to Norbury, and my country place is only three miles beyond. The house, to be sure, is closed for the winter; I little expected to be visiting it so soon. But there are several servants in it, and it can quickly be made comfortable, and Mrs. Roberts, my housekeeper, is an excellent nurse. Don't you agree with me that any or all of these reasons are sufficient to make it wise to try to get there as soon as possible? For it is not going to be any joke to stay in this dingy place for a fortnight, and that child will not be fit to travel any sooner; and this arm of mine does not feel much like bearing the motion of those accursed cars again very soon."

Mr. Rutledge's arm was bound up, and an occasional expression of pain crossed his face, though that was the only

time he alluded to it. The doctor made an unequivocal
opposition to Mr. Rutledge's proposition, and raised innumerable objections to it, all of which he quietly put aside and
overruled. It was easy to see who would carry the day;
but the doctor did not give over for a long while. When
at length he had been unwillingly brought to say that it
might do no harm to be moved in the course of the morning
to Rutledge, he started another unanswerable objection—a
suitable vehicle could not be obtained in the town for love
or money, he declared.

"I will manage that," said Mr. Rutledge, and left the
room.

The doctor shook his head as the door closed, and said,
partly to himself, and partly to the woman who seemed to
be officiating as nurse :

"He goes at his own risk; it may do or it may not."

"He's a gentleman what's used to doing as he wants to, I
guess," remarked the woman, "and don't think any too much
of other people's opinions."

"You are very correct," said the doctor, with importance.
"A little learning is a dangerous thing, and Mr. Rutledge
knows just enough of medicine to be confident of his own
judgment. I only hope his imprudence may not be
visited upon this poor child. So young!" he continued,
shaking his head.

The woman shook hers, and looked at him with reverence,
while he went on to describe my case at great length, and
in such alarmingly long words, that I was in danger of being
frightened back into a high fever, had not the return of Mr.
Rutledge saved me from any further display of Dr. Sartain's
scientific knowledge.

Mr. Rutledge saw in a moment the state of the case, for
he looked at me attentively as he came in, and I heard him
mutter in a low tone as he felt my pulse, "This won't do."
Then aloud, he told the doctor that the carriage he had been
fortunate enough to engage would be at the door in about

an hour and a half, and that he would not detain him any longer at present, but would recommend his taking a little rest, for he should be obliged to ask him to accompany his patient during the drive; it would be safer, he thought, and as he could return in the carriage, it would involve no great loss of time; though he well knew Dr. Sartain could hardly spare a moment from the demands of his extensive practice, etc.

The doctor, somewhat mollified, consented and retired. Mr. Rutledge then sent the woman off, and telling me, cheerfully and kindly, that I was doing very nicely, and that he thought a little sleep would strengthen me for the journey, darkened the windows, and throwing himself into an easy-chair, seemed inclined to set me the example. The lounge or settee on which I was placed, had been made as comfortable as the circumstances would permit, but still was painfully far from easy; and I tossed about, excited and restless, for some time. But, gradually reassured by Mr. Rutledge's quiet composure and cheerfulness, and soothed by the stillness of the room, I fell into a very refreshing sleep.

It was about noon when we started, the doctor being in the carriage with me, Mr. Rutledge, I am sorry to remember, going in a much less comfortable vehicle. It did not trouble me seriously at the time, however. Dr. Sartain's opinion to the contrary notwithstanding, I was by no means injured by the ride, and when we drove under the gateway that conveyed to my listless intellect the knowledge that we had reached Rutledge, besides a little increased languor and weariness, I felt no worse than when we left the town.

Mr. Rutledge, who was in advance, reached the house first, and in a moment the excitement that our arrival had produced became apparent; two or three maids rushed out from a side-door as Mr. Rutledge ascended the steps, and, overcome with alarm at the sight of two carriages, and their master with his arm in a sling, rushed back again wringing

their hands, and displaying many symptoms of consternation.
Mr. Rutledge in the mean time had entered the house, and
soon appeared at the door accompanied by a tall, elderly
woman, in a black bombazine dress, and a lace cap with
white ribbons, to whom he was explaining, in a concise and
forcible manner, the state of affairs, and what was to be done.
They came down to the carriage, and Mr. Rutledge introduced " Mrs. Roberts" to the doctor and to me, and then
assisting me to alight, we ascended the broad stone steps to
the piazza, and thence into a wide hall.

Mr. Rutledge told the housekeeper that it would, he
thought, be best for me to go immediately up to her room,
where I could lie on the sofa till my apartment could be
made ready.

Accordingly I went upstairs, and took possession of Mrs.
Roberts' sofa and Mrs. Roberts' room, both sombre and stiff
enough, but infinitely more easy and prepossessing than the
lady herself. I cannot imagine that at that very early stage of
our acquaintance, she could have entertained any personal resentment toward me, and yet I was entirely possessed of that
belief from the first moment that I saw her. But I have
since discovered that she invariably impressed all strangers
with a similar conviction, and from that, and from subse-
quent knowledge of her character, I have concluded that it
was merely " a way she had," and was by no means to be
regarded as an expression of her sentiments toward any one.
Unhappily, I did not have this light upon her, and soon began to feel myself in the hands of a grim tyrant, whose only
motive in exertions made ostensibly for my benefit, was to
get possession of me, soul and body, and render. me, if possible, more wretched than she found me.

I lay quietly on the sofa where she had placed me, with
no ungentle hand to be sure, but without the slightest relax
ing of her blue lips, or the smallest indication of pity in her
uncompromising eyes; and watched her as she pursued her
plan of operations, steadily and energetically. She cer

tainly knew what she was about, and for precision and
promptness must have been a treasure in Mr. Rutledge's
eyes. There was an incredible amount of work accomplished in that house within the next hour; rooms were
opened, fires were lighted, beds were aired; sounds of
sweeping and dusting and beating of mattresses, filling of
pitchers, and crackling of fires, reached my indolent ears.
Mrs. Roberts, standing before a huge open wardrobe, dealt
out sheets, pillow-cases, towels, table-cloths and napkins to
the maids, who bustled about with distressing activity, not
unfrequently goaded on by a few sharp words from their
mistress, who ruled them, I could see, with a rod of iron.
The threat, however, that stirred up their flagging energies
most effectually, seemed to be, the wrath of Mr. Rutledge.
I began to feel myself drawn sympathizingly toward the
maids, and could not help wondering whether they were as
much afraid of the master, and as much averse to the mistress of the house as I was, and whether they wished themselves away as much; and if they did, why they didn't go;
or whether, indeed, people ever got away who once came
in it. The gloom of the great hall, with its broad, stone
staircase, on which the servants' steps echoed drearily, and
the dark glimpses of shut-up rooms that I had caught on
my way up, seemed to favor this latter idea—I would write
for my aunt to come for me immediately; I would ask the
doctor to take me back with him. I should die if they left
me in this gloomy place. Perhaps I might die here—who
could tell? The doctor had said I was very ill.

Tears came but too easily in those foolish days, and burying my throbbing temples in the pillow, I cried as if my
heart would break, or as if it had indeed broken. My
emotion was none the lighter because it was imaginary, nor
none the easier to bear because it was absurd. Children's
troubles and terrors are only less severe than those of
maturer minds, as they are shorter lived; while they last
they are, if possible, more violent and less bearable. And

at that time I was, to all intents and purposes, a child, and a sick, nervous, excited one besides.

By and by Mrs. Roberts came up to where I lay motionless with my face hidden in the pillows, and, leaning over me, said in her chilling tones, "Are you comfortable? Will you have anything?"

I did not move. She listened for a moment, then going to the door said to some one outside:

"She's asleep, sir, and doing well. You had better take some rest yourself."

The door closed, and I suppressed my sobs to listen. In a few minutes Mrs. Roberts came again to look at me, then noiselessly left the room. I could endure it no longer, and throwing back the blankets, raised myself and sat upright. I cried for a long while; every minute the prison feeling seemed to grow stronger, till at last it drove me to that climax of desperation which, in actual prisoners, results in knocking down turnkeys, and (according to the newspapers) doing many frantic and atrocious acts, to reach "the blessed sun and air," from which they have been "banned and barred."

I had reached that climax, I say; I had dried my tears, and sat still, with clenched hands, some wild plan of escape arranging itself in my brain, when the door suddenly opened, and Mrs. Roberts reappeared.

"Oh, you're awake, are you? I'll call the doctor; he's got through setting Mr. Rutledge's arm, and was just going."

I hurriedly pushed the hair from my flushed face, and tried to look composed as the doctor entered with Mrs. Roberts, and followed soon by Mr. Rutledge, who came, he said, to get the doctor's directions, and to see if Mrs. Roberts was doing everything for me that I required. The doctor sat down by me, and taking hold of my wrist, asked me if I felt better for my sleep.

Mr. Rutledge, looking at me, said, "Not much sleep, I am afraid. How is it?"

I pressed my lips very tight together to keep from crying, and shook my head. Mrs. Roberts, who did not probably notice the gesture, said, "Oh, yes, she's slept nicely for three-quarters of an hour."

Then she and the doctor talked about me as if I were in the next room, and no way interested in the affair. After many directions given and received, and many injunctions and much emphasis, the doctor rose to go, saying that he should not be able to come again until the day after to-morrow (unless, of course, I should be taken with any unexpected symptoms); in the mean time he hoped he left me in safe hands (with a look direct at Mrs. Roberts). Mr. Rutledge smothered a smile, accompanied him to the door, and parted from him very courteously, then returned to me. He hoped, he said, that I did not mind trusting myself to him during the doctor's absence, and Mrs. Roberts would, he knew, take as good care of me as the doctor himself could. He then went on to say that he had telegraphed my aunt last evening to prevent her feeling any alarm on hearing of the accident, and that he had written to her more fully by mail to-day, telling her of my improvement, and assuring her that it would not be necessary for her to come on, as I could have every care here.

"In two or three weeks," he continued, "I trust you will be perfectly well and entirely fit to travel."

Two or three weeks! The thought was too dreadful. and bursting into tears, I exclaimed:

"I am well enough to go now! I had rather go home with the doctor!"

Mr. Rutledge was silent for a moment, then sitting down beside me, in the doctor's vacated seat, said, as if he were speaking to a very little child:

"You are not well enough to start now; it might do you a great deal of harm. Possibly you may be able to go much sooner than the doctor thinks; only be patient a day or two, and depend upon it, I will let you go the very minute you can bear it."

I shook my head and sobbed convulsively.

"My dear little girl," he said, "you are too nervous now to be reasonable, but you must try and be quiet and not cry, for that is the very worst thing for you, and will keep you here longer than anything else. Your head aches, doesn't it?"

"Yes, dreadfully," I sobbed.

"Well, the more you cry, the more it will ache, and the more it aches, the more fever you will have, and that is just what you must get rid of before you can be fit to start for home. You will feel very differently, I assure you, to-morrow morning, after you have had a good night's sleep."

"I can't sleep!" I exclaimed.

"Oh yes, you can! The doctor has left you some powders that will make that all right, and I will give you one now."

He mixed it in a glass that Mrs. Roberts had brought for the purpose, and I drank it, then followed his advice and lay my hot and throbbing head on the pillow. He sat down again, and continued, speaking soothingly, and in a manly, kind voice, still as if I were about eight years old.

"Your room will be ready in a few moments, and I think you will be more comfortable there than in this old-fashioned retreat of Mrs. Roberts'. Hair-cloth and mahogany are rather dismal for sensitive nerves, it must be acknowledged," glancing with a smile around the apartment. "The room you are to have is on the other side of the hall, and looks out on the park, and is quite cheerful and pleasant. And if you do not like to be alone, Mrs. Roberts shall come and sleep on the sofa by you."

The expression of my face was probably unmistakable; much as I dreaded solitude, I dreaded Mrs. Roberts more, and was immensely relieved when my companion added, "Perhaps, though, on the whole, Kitty had better come and wait on you. Kitty is one of the maids, and is very pleasant, and I think you will like her. I will send her to you now. She will give you your medicine, and sit by you for company. You must send her to me if there is anything more I can do for you to night. I hope the headache will all be gone by to-morrow morning."

And with a few more kind words the master left me, and the maid soon appeared, whose bright face and cheerful care helped along very considerably the cure that was already begun. It was a pleasure to be waited on by Kitty; it was a pleasure to hear her clear young voice and to be served by her strong young arms. She must, I think, have had strict orders not to leave me; for after everything in the way of arranging the pillows and smoothing the blankets, and adjusting everything in the neighborhood of the sofa, had been accomplished, she still lingered beside me, asking if I was comfortable, if she shouldn't get me a glass of water, if I wouldn't like the curtains drawn back a little, etc.

Mrs. Roberts, who had returned, was sitting by the window, a huge basket of work beside her, over which she was straining her eyes, economical of every ray of the rapidly fading daylight. She was too utilitarian in her turn of mind to submit quietly to the sight of Kitty's idleness, and very soon suggested to her that she had better go downstairs to her work. Kitty said, " Yes ma'am," but didn't go. Again Mrs. Roberts suggested, and again Kitty cleverly evaded. The third time, the mistress laid down her work, and any one less stout-hearted than the young person before her would have trembled at the sharp tone in which she repeated her order. If it had been addressed to me, I am sure I should have submitted in trepidation ; as it was, I trembled for Kitty, who, however, was nothing daunted, and turning round, said, in a tone just one remove from pert :

" Mr. Rutledge, ma'am, sent me up, and told me to stay with the young lady, and to wait on her; and, also, he says that's to be my duty while she's here, ma'am."

A genuine thundercloud lowered on Mrs. Roberts' face, but a portentous "Umph" was all the rejoinder she made to this decisive speech. Kitty reassured me with a little nod, and I quite rejoiced in our apparent victory.

Before long, a servant knocked at the door, and announced that my room was ready. Then succeeded a pleasant bustle and excitement incident to my removal to it. Kitty insisted upon considering me a perfectly helpless invalid, and would have carried me, if I had not remonstrated, and Mrs. Roberts had not sneered at the idea. As it was, she wrapped me up so that I could hardly move, and supporting me with her arm, preceded by Mrs. Roberts, we crossed the hall, and stopped at the door of the apartment assigned to me.

"Oh, what a pretty room!" I exclaimed, as we entered it. Kitty was charmed that I liked it, and proceeded with great satisfaction to do the honors. Wheeling toward me an easy-chair, and settling me in it before the bright fire that blazed on the hearth, she said with animation:

"Isn't it a pretty room, miss? I've always said, that though the others were bigger and finer, there wasn't one that had such a sweet pretty look about it as the blue room had. It's just fit for a young lady like you."

Kitty was not wrong about its being a pretty room; I never saw a prettier myself. It was not large, but well-proportioned and airy. Opposite the door there was a bay window, with white curtains trimmed with blue, and the same at the other two windows. The bed at the end of the room stood in a recess, curtained in the same manner. The walls were papered with a delicate blue paper, the woodwork about the room was oak, and all the furniture was oak and light blue. The carpet, which was in itself a study, was an arabesque pattern of oak upon a light-blue ground. The slender vases on the mantel, the pictures in their carved oak frames, had an inexpressible charm for eyes so long accustomed to the bare walls and wooden presses of a boarding school dormitory. And even to a maturer taste, I think it would have been pleasing; for I do not remember ever to have seen a room more entirely in keeping, and in which there was less out of place and inharmonious. Indeed, this impression was so strong, that I involuntarily begged Kitty to put away my dark plaid shawl, the sight of which, upon the delicate blue sofa, annoyed me exceedingly; and I thought with satisfaction of a certain blue morning dress in my trunk, that I could put on to-morrow, by way of being in keeping with the room. And the white lava pin and earrings, Agnes' parting gift, which I had never worn yet, and admired beyond expression, would come in play exactly.

While Kitty made herself delightfully busy in unpacking my trunk, which stood in the little dressing-room at the right, and bestowing my modest wardrobe in the drawers and closets thereof, I lay nestling in the soft depths of that marvellous Sleepy Hollow of a chair, that holding me lovingly in its capacious arms, seemed to perform every office of a good old nurse, even to the singing of lullabies. Though that kind attention, I think, really emanated from the glowing, merry fire, which sung, crackled, and blazed most hospitably at my feet.

The headache that an hour ago had seemed so insupportable, had now subsided to a dull throbbing that was comparatively ease and comfort; and to lie there, and look at the fire, and think about nothing, and speak to nobody, and be sure that Kitty was near me, and Mrs. Roberts and "the master" very far away, was all I asked or desired.

This negative sort of bliss found a temporary interruption in the necessary departure of Kitty to the kitchen, to procure my tea and bring up candles. I felt rather babyishly about it, and nothing but shame kept me from telling Kitty that I had rather do without my tea, and go to bed by firelight, than have her leave me. She did not stay away very long, however, and the nice cup of tea and crisp thin slice of toast, that she brought back with her, quite compensated me for the self-denial I had had to exercise in letting her go. These edibles, Kitty, with all the pomp and circumstance of war, arranged upon the little table beside me, placing the tall wax candles in the centre, and distributing the diminutive pieces of the dainty little tête-à-tête set in the most advantageous manner. The tea tasted very nicely out of the thin china cup, that felt like a play-thing when I lifted it, accustomed as I was to the heavy bluish-white crockery of boarding-school, and though I lacked the vigorous appetite, that had made the primitive meals of that establishment enjoyable, still, the delicate food before me had a decided relish. Kitty very much enjoyed my appreciation of it, and was very sorry she could not go down and bring me another slice of toast, but Mr. Rutledge had said I must not have any more.

"I couldn't eat any more, thank you," I said, rather haughtily, though Mr. Rutledge, and not the kind Kitty, inspired the hauteur. Mrs. Roberts made us a call soon after this, and said it was high time I went to bed, and told Kitty sharply, she knew it was her work, keeping me up so long, and hurried up the preparations for retiring, with energy. Kitty looked saucy, but did not dare to rebel, and only indulged in defiance after the door was closed behind the intruder. She again returned, however, on a final tour of inspection, after I was comfortably arranged in the fair white delicious bed, that seemed to be a special partner of tired nature's sweet restorer, who was good for any amount on its demand. She "poked in every corner" as Kitty expressed it, and found a dozen things to object to in her arrangements, pulled open drawers, and set Kitty poutingly at work to settle them properly, and made my temples throb again with alarm lest she should find something objectionable among my clothes, some rent in my school frock, or an undarned stocking smuggled through the vigilant scrutiny of last week's wash. She sent Kitty for her

mattress and blankets, and superintended the arrangement
of them, though I could see she did not enter cordially into
the plan; but as Mr. Rutledge had ordered that Kitty
should sleep beside me, I was sure she would not dare to
oppose it.

At last there was no excuse for a longer tarry, and she
withdrew; Kitty, with a triumphant gesture, slid the bolt
upon her, and we "settled our brains for a long winter's
nap." A nap not altogether uninterrupted on my part, by
troubled dreams, and sudden starts, and foolish fears; but
my waking was always met by Kitty's ready care and
soothing sympathy; and toward morning quieted into a
long refreshing sleep.

CHAPTER III.

"O Time! thou must untangle this, not I,
'Tis too hard a knot for me to untie."

Whex I awoke, it was to the pleasant reality of morning
and sunshine, that had found their way through the light
curtains of my pleasant room, and made it pleasanter than
ever. Kitty was at my side in an instant, and a brighter
fresher face to greet one's waking vision could not be desired. She managed, by prompt and clever measures, to
keep off Mrs. Roberts till I had had my breakfast, and risen
and been dressed. It was matter of great astonishment to
me to find myself so absurdly weak, my strength and spirits
at school having passed into a proverb. This sudden illness
had reduced me extremely, however, as I found whenever
I attempted any exertion, and all Kitty's services were required.

While she was dressing me, she chatted very confiden-
tially, though always with a tone of deference that counter-
balanced the liberty she took in talking at all. Our distaste
for Mrs. Roberts was potent in putting us on as good terms
as young lady and young lady's maid could well be, and
there is a sort of freemasonry in youth that sets at defiance
the restrictions of rank, and that drew us, the two youngest
things in the stately old house, together, naturally and irresistibly.

I call it an old house, because it impressed me at first as
such. It was solid and dark, and excepting my room and
one or two others on the same floor, had very little that was
light and modern-looking about it. It had been built, Kitty
said, in the time of Mr. Rutledge's father, and was called the

finest house in the country. Loads of money, she informed me, he had spent upon it; workmen had been sent for, hundreds of miles, to do the carving and paint the walls, and no money and no labor was spared to make it a fine place, and indeed there was none like it anywhere around; and now to think of its being shut up like a prison half the year, and sometimes all the year; it was a shame, Kitty thought, upon her honor it was.

I asked her why Mr. Rutledge did not live there?

She did not know; she supposed it was lonesome; he never stayed home for over a couple of months, and then would be off, for no one knew how long. Sometimes he went to Europe, and was gone two or three years at a time. And such dull times as it was *then* at Rutledge, if you please! Nobody but Mrs. Roberts, and the cook, and dairy-woman, besides the farm hands. Nothing to do but stand Mrs. Roberts' preaching from morning till night. She only wished she'd lived in the old times that her father talked about, when Rutledge was the gayest of the gay. (Her father, she explained, had been gardener there for thirty years, and had lived on the place from a boy.) Such fine doings! Ah! if Mr. Rutledge would only take it into his head to have such times now! It was when he was very young, and Mr. Richard and Miss Alice, and there was nothing but balls and picnics and pleasure-parties all the time, company staying in the house, and visitors from the neighborhood for miles around. Ah! it was mighty different now!

"What has become of the others? Is Mr. Rutledge the only one left?"

Mr. Rutledge, Kitty told me, was the youngest of the three. Mr. Richard died when he was just twenty-four—a month after his father—and so Mr. Rutledge came into the property when he was a mere lad.

"But the daughter, Alice, what became of her?"

"I don't know exactly," said Kitty, lowering her voice, and looking anxiously toward the door. "They never talk about her; something must have happened very strange, for there's always a mystery about Miss Alice. The old servants on the place will never say a word about her; and though I've teased father again and again, I never could get anything out of him."

"But, Kitty," I exclaimed eagerly, my curiosity thoroughly excited, "what makes you think she isn't dead?"

"Oh! that much I know, that she didn't die then, and that she didn't die at home in this house, and isn't buried there below in the churchyard by the others; and I know she was away when old Mr. Rutledge died; because once father said it was an awful thing, when he lay so ill, and out of his head, to hear him call upon her to come home. AL that night before he died, he would call 'Alice! Alice!' til you could hear it all over the house. And father says," continued the girl, in a still lower tone, "that sometimes of wilt dark nights, when he's coming past the house late from hi work, he could swear for all the world that he hears the old man still calling 'Alice! Alice!' till it makes his blood freeze to listen to it. And then, when I say 'Where was she, father, all the time, and why didn't she come to him?' he always says, 'that's not for the like of you to hear about; it's none of your business, child, nor mine,' and sends me off about something else."

"But, Kitty," I persisted, "is that all you know of her? Tell me all you've ever heard; was she pretty?"

"Oh, so pretty! You can't think how white her skin was, and her eyes like violets, so large and blue, and curls all over her head—loose, shiny curls."

"How do you know," I said quickly; "surely you never saw her, did you?"

Kitty blushed and stammered, and said, "No, not exactly; but there was something she had seen she'd never told anybody about; she didn't know whether she ought to;" but the result was, she at last imparted to me the fol. lowing:

"When Kitty was about twelve years old, it appeared, from her account, the demon of curiosity was stronger in her even than it was now, and her keen young eyes had detected long before that time, what had escaped many maturer observers, viz., that at the end of the upper hall there was a room, that was ignored in all descriptions of the house, and might well, indeed, have been overlooked. A huge wardrobe stood in the middle of the space between the corner room on the east, and the corner room on the west, of the hall; and none but a very inquiring mind like Kitty's would have investigated the exact dimensions of these rooms, whether they met and were separated but by a partition, or whether a distinct room, the width of the hall, and corresponding to Mr. Rutledge's dressing-room at the opposite end, existed between them. Kitty crept down on the lawn and looked up on the outside, and discovered a large window, the shutters of which were closed and dusty; and on exploring the corner rooms, they corroborated her suspicions—they did not extend across the hall. Behind that wardrobe, Kitty knew, then, existed a door; and night and day the insane desire to penetrate beyond it, haunted the child.

At length, circumstances seemed to favor the fulfillment of her wishes. It was a beautiful, mild May day, and the untiring energy of Mrs. Roberts was enjoying a full swing in the pursuit of her favorite *divertissement* of house-cleaning. Doors and windows were thrown open; all manner of scouring and scrubbing was going on in all parts of the house. Step-ladders and water-pails graced the hall; the odor of soap-suds and lime filled the air. Serene amid the confusion, Mrs. Roberts applied herself to the overlooking and rearranging the identical wardrobe in the hall, that had so long been the fascination and torment of little Kitty, who, it may well be supposed, was " on hand " during the operation. Demure and useful, she made herself very officious in assisting Mrs. Roberts in her labors, standing, for hours together, to be loaded with the heavy piles of rich old curtains from the shelves, faded long ago, and anti- quated table-covers, heavy Marseilles coverlets, that must have made the sleepers of old time ache to turn over under; great packages folded up in linen, through the ends of which Kitty's eager eyes caught glimpses of satin and bro- cade, and the tarnished buttons of military clothes. Kitty never thought of her aching arms, or her tired little feet; she never took her eyes away, and never lost a movement of Mrs. Roberts, nor a sight of anything before her; and after dinner, following like a kitten at the housekeeper's heels, came back to the fascinating business of disinterring the faded glories of the past.

By three o'clock, the shelves were all emptied and the drawers all taken out; and Mrs. Roberts was just begin- ning the important business of dusting and wiping them, and restoring their precious contents, when a man from the fields came posting up to the house in the greatest haste, with the intelligence that a pair of the farm-horses had run away, and done no end of damage to themselves and to the man who was driving them, who was now lying below the barn in a state of insensibility, and Mrs. Roberts' assistance was instantly required. It was not a case that admitted of a demur, and the housekeeper bustled off, leaving Kitty with orders to stay where she was, and take care of the things left about till she came back, and, taking the only woman who was upstairs with her, left Kitty in possession of the field.

She did not mean to move the wardrobe, but it was so natural just to try how heavy it was, and if it would really stir! And to her surprise and guilty pleasure, the ward- robe, lightened of its weighty contents, yielded to her touch, and moved a little—a very little—way forward; but enough to show to her eager eyes, in the dark wood-work, a door, over which generations of painstaking spiders had spun their webs unchecked, and where the scourge of Mrs

Roberts' eye had failed, or feared to penetrate. Kitty, holding her breath for fear, turned the knob; it resisted; it was locked, of course, possibly on the outside, and the key might have been taken out. An expedient struck the child's fertile brain; and she darted across the hall, and, possessing herself of the key of the corresponding room, darted back again and applied it to the lock. It fitted, and turned in it; the knob yielded to her eager grasp, and, too near the completion of her wishes now to pause, she wound her lithe figure through the narrow aperture, and pushing open the door, stood within the mysterious room! For a moment, Kitty's heart beat quick; an awe crept over her; for a moment she longed to be out in the sunshine again. But her elastic spirits and indomitable curiosity soon triumphed over the transitory dread inspired by the darkness and solemnity of the deserted chamber, and the close, dead atmosphere, and the unearthly stillness; and, gaining courage every moment, she made her way, with what caution she might, toward the window, undid the fastening, and, pushing up a very little way the heavy sash, turned the blind, and let in a ray of God's blessed sunlight, dim and dull enough, though, through the dusty panes, into this strange room, deserted these many, many years, it would seem, both of God and man. Kitty was a bold child, little given to nervousness or timidity, or she would have shrunk in terror from the weird, fantastic shadows that the dim light showed about the room. But that was not Kitty's way; and, sitting down on a divan by the window, she rested her elbows on her knees and her chin upon her hands, in contemplative fashion, and proceeded to look about her.

What a strange sight it must have been! the slow sunbeam creeping over the faded carpet, and lighting up the dust-covered furniture and the dusky walls. Kitty's glance first turned, naturally enough, to the bed, which, richly curtained and spacious, stood on the left of the door. The curtains were swept back and the bed was made, but it was

apparent that some one had occupied it, lying on the outside; the pillows were displaced and crushed, and the
coverlet was deranged. That, since the occupation of that
some one, the room had never been arranged or touched,
seemed evident, from the confusion and disorder that prevailed. The door of the wardrobe on the right was partly
open, and a dress was hanging out from it. A shawl, faded
beyond recognition, hung upon the chair near Kitty, and
at her feet lay a slipper—such a slim, pretty little slipper!
while on the toilette table, you could have sworn, a hasty
hand had just dropped the stopper in that odor-bottle, and
pushed back the glove-box that stood open under the glass.

Pins rusted in the embroidered cushion; dust inch thick
on the mirror and over all, told of a dreary space since any
human face had been reflected there. Upon a little table
by the window stood a work-box and some books, and in a
slender vase, the ghosts of some flowers that fell to dust at
Kitty's touch. But what most excited her wonder, was a
picture, that, with its face to the wall, was placed on the
floor near the door. It evidently did not belong to the furniture of the room, and had been put there hastily, and to
be out of the way. Kitty surveyed it from her seat
curiously, and at last crept up to it, and turned it around,
then slipping down on the carpet before it, was soon lost in
admiration of the lovely face it presented to her.

The lustre of the dark-blue eyes, and the delicate outline
of the oval face, from which large wavy curls of fair hair
were pushed back with girlish freedom, stamped themselves
indelibly upon Kitty's retentive memory. It must have been
an odd sight; the eager child, in that dark, uncanny room,
upon her hands and knees before the picture, watching it in
utter fascination, forgetful of the passing moments, and
of all save the sweet face so strangely banished from the
light.

But the heavy shutting of the hall door, and the sound
of voices in the hall below, put a sudden period to these

fancies, and brought her to her feet with a desperate start and a pang of genuine fear. This was a tangible terror, and as such, Kitty's common sense succumbed to it. With nervous haste, she restored the picture, flew across the room and drew down the window, and made the best of her way back toward the door. But in her haste, her feet became entangled in something, and tripping up, in an instant she lay at full length on the floor. She disengaged her feet from the impediment that had caused her fall; it was a long ribbon, and a locket was attached to it; hastily thrusting them into her bosom, she picked herself up, and sprang toward the door. Steps were already mounting the stairs; a voice she knew too well was already audible; the unused lock grated and creaked cruelly under the nervous hands that struggled with it; but, with the strength of terror, she mastered it at last—locked it, dropped the key in her pocket, slipped through the narrow space between the wall and the wardrobe, with an eager push restored the latter to its place, and before Mrs. Roberts reached the landing, stood, a pallid, trembling, but undetected culprit, among the piles of valuables she had been left to guard. The habitual darkness of that end of the hall, increased by the near approach of twilight, screened her white cheeks from the scrutiny of Mrs. Roberts' searching eyes, and the haste that lady was in to restore the wardrobe to its ancient and uninterrupted order, further favored her escape.

But she fully paid the penalty of her crime—she acknowledged, in the dread she felt lest it should be discovered, and the unaccustomed alarm she endured, when on dark nights, her ruthless mistress sent her candleless to bed; and she, with suspended breath and strained ear, would creep past the mysterious chamber to her own little loft above, to lie whole hours awake and trembling. Her fertile imagination had supplied the wanting links in the chain of fact; and the fair-haired Alice, the banished daughter of the house, was her dream of beauty by day and her haunting terror by night.

"But Kitty," I exclaimed, breathlessly, 'does no one else know of the room? Does no one ever go in it?"

"Oh yes! Mrs. Roberts must know of it, for she lived here long before the present Mr. Rutledge was master; she knows all the family secrets, I'll warrant. But neither she nor any one else ever troubles *that* room, I'm pretty sure. I've watched it close enough, and the wardrobe never has been stirred since that day I did it, six years ago last spring. Hardly any one goes to that end of the hall; the corner rooms are shut up and not used, and Mr. Rutledge's own rooms, and Mrs. Roberts', and this one for visitors, being all on this side of the house, there's very little occasion for anybody to go near the others in the rear."

"What was in the locket you picked up?" I asked.

"It was a miniature, tied by a long narrow blue ribbon, and that night, when I got upstairs, I bolted the door and looked at it; it was the picture of a gentleman, young and so"——

CHAPTER IV.

"The deeds we do, the words we say—
Into still air they seem to fleet:
We count them ever past—
But they shall last—
In the dread judgment they
And we shall meet!"

LYRA INNOCENTIUM.

BUT our antiquarian researches were brought to a sudden conclusion by the appearance of Mrs. Roberts at the door, whose cold eye seemed to say, she comprehended at a glance that we were in mischief, and no effort should be wanting on her part to thwart our further confidence. That much she *looked*, the following she said:

"Mr. Rutledge desires to know how the young lady is, and whether she is ready to see him?"

"She'll be ready in one minute," said Kitty, hurrying nervously the retarded business of arranging my hair. Mrs. Roberts stationed herself at the fire, and threefold increased Kitty's nervousness, and my trepidation, by the stony gaze she fixed upon us. At last, however, the operation was concluded, and Kitty helped me to the sofa, and regulated the light from the window, put away my dressing-gown, and gave the last touches to the room; while Mrs. Roberts looked on sardonically, and then told Kitty to go and call her master. I had hoped this order of things would have been reversed, and that Mrs. Roberts herself would have gone to summon my dreaded visitor, leaving me a moment's time to recover my composure, under the genial influence of Kitty's sturdy courage, which to do her justice, she had not long been disarmed of. As it was, the housekeeper's efforts at conversation were not of an enliven

41

ing character, her first remark being, "that Kitty was much of a chatter-box, and she should speak to the master to give her altogether downstairs work to do, where there would be nobody to be hindered or bothered by her tattle."

I tried to remonstrate, but, for my life, could not say an audible word, and nervous and trembling to an absurd degree, I listened for the approaching footsteps in the hall. The door opened, and Mr. Rutledge entered. Walking up to me in his firm quick way, he said, extending his left hand:

"Well, my young friend, and how's the headache?" I stammered something about its being better, while he sat down beside me, and with wonderful tact and patience, tried to amuse and draw me into conversation.

Now it was an inexplicable thing to me at that time, that I, who had never known the first emotions of awe before, in presence even of the imposing dignitaries of St. Catharine's—I who had pulled the wool alike over the eyes of governesses and professors—I, who had enjoyed, if ever any did in that establishment, the privilege of doing as I pleased, by reason of the inability of anybody to prevent me —that I should, I say, be so utterly subdued and humble, before this quiet stranger, was an inexplicable thing to me.

I had yet to learn, that those, clothed in a little brief authority, and holding temporary sway over young minds and wills, are not always and inevitably so far exalted, in intellect and in character, above those they are supposed to govern, as were to be wished, and as they sincerely desire to appear. Narrow-minded pedantry and injudicious igno- rance often rush in, to responsibilities and duties that angels might well tremble to assume—the moulding for good or evil, the flexile souls of children during the most vital years of their lives.

Be this as it may, I quailed for the first time before a superior, and not without a stubborn feeling of resistance, owned myself in the presence of one I feared. I suppose

I must have looked very childish, with my hair brushed down simply and knotted low on my neck, and a tiny linen collar turned over my plain blue merino frock; the lava pin and earings having been unavoidably omitted in the hasty completion of my toilette. These circumstances of dress, I comforted myself, might account in part for the manner in which Mr. Rutledge continued to treat me, and which was very galling to my pride, for being at the most sensitive period of adolescence, nothing could have been more humbling than to be regarded as childish and immature. Such considerations did not add to my ease of manner, or grace of deportment, and all Mr. Rutledge's well-selected topics of conversation fell to the ground for want of a sustaining power on my side. At last relinquishing the attempt, he turned to Mrs. Roberts, and gave her minute instructions in regard to my medicine and diet, felt my pulse, and pronounced me very much improved; but he judged it, he said, very much better for me to lie on the sofa pretty quietly all day. Perhaps by to-morrow, I might be well enough to come downstairs for a little while, he continued, looking attentively at me, to see, I suppose, how I bore the intelligence of my prolonged captivity. He did not see any expression of impatience in my face, however, firstly, because I did not feel any, and secondly, because, if I had, I would have concealed it to-day. He rose to go, first turning toward the bay window, where he stood for some minutes thoughtfully, attracted by the beauty of the landscape it overlooked.

"After all," he said at length, addressing Mrs. Roberts more than me, and his own thoughts, perhaps, more than either, "the view of the lake is finer from this window than from any other in the house. The slope of the lawn is beautiful, and that opening in the pine grove on the left, through which you see up to the head of the lake, is very fine. Mrs. Roberts," abruptly, "do you remember when that opening was cut?"

"Yes sir," said Mrs. Roberts (she was never known to have forgotten anything), "it was during Mrs. Rutledge, your mother's last illness; she sat a great deal in that window, and your father had it cut to suit her fancy. I remember the very morning that the workmen began it; she was so interested, and quite tired herself with watching them, and sending them orders."

"Ah! I think I remember something of it. I must have been "——

"Just eight years old, sir," said Mrs. Roberts with precision. "She died the next spring, when Mr. Richard was in his sixteenth year; there was just four years between you and "——

"Yes, I know."

A dark frown contracted his brow; a forbidding compression of the lips renewed the dread that had begun to lessen under his patient kindness. During the five minutes that he stood thus by the window, we were, I suppose, as entirely forgotten as one of us, at least, desired to be. The trivial Present fell back into insignificance and oblivion before the iron domination of some stern memory, that touched with ruthless hand, his tenderest affection, that humbled his pride, and baffled his indomitable will. This much I could see, in the restless light of his dark eye, as it wandered over the familiar scene; child as I was, I could not but see the suffering in his face. At last, with an effort, he threw off the tyrant memory, and abruptly turning, quitted the room. Something almost as human as a sigh escaped from Mrs. Roberts blue lips, as his steps echoed across the hall, and his door closed heavily.

With me, the day passed quietly and pleasantly enough; Mrs. Roberts took the precaution to leave Kitty alone with me as little as possible, always managing to come in, when Kitty had got nicely fixed with her sewing at the furthest window, and find some excuse to send her away for half an hour or so. But as Kitty had brought me some books from th: library, and as I felt too lazy and indifferent to object to anything, I did not much mind her surveillance.

The chicken soup that Kitty brought me for my dinner, was the very nicest ever administered to hungry convalescent; and after the meal was concluded, and the afternoon sun shut out, I made up for all deficiencies in last night's repose by a very satisfactory sleep; from which I awoke with a start, to find that I had slept "the all-golden afternoon" quite away, and that twilight was stealing over the quiet lake, and the rich autumn woods. I smoothed back the tumbled hair from my face, and leaning against the window, looked thoughtfully out. The sun had but just gone down, and left the horizon still glowing with his light, without a single cloud to break the unruffled calm of sky and lake. Not a breath of wind stirred the dead leaves that lay thick beneath the trees in the park—not a sound broke the stillness. How hushed and silent the dark house was! How much more to the past did it seem to belong, than to the living actual present. And turn my eyes or thoughts whichever way I might, they still reverted to something that would remind me of the strange story I had heard that morning, still brought before me the desolate room, where the dust of years lay on all traces of her, who, banished, or wronged, or fled, had darkened forever the home she left. With her, it seemed, had vanished the gaiety, the life of the house; following fast upon her absence had come death and desolation; and the sole survivor of this, her ancient race, grew stern and silent at the merest allusion to her.

My young brain grew feverish and impatient at the baffling mystery, and refused to entertain any other thought or interest. A vague dread and superstitious awe crept over me as the twilight waxed dimmer and greyer, and the dying fire smouldered on the hearth, and the stillness remained unbroken. Where was everybody; or had I slept over a few years, and were they all dead? And was I the only living thing in the great house—another Princess in another Day-dream, only wakened without the kiss, and the prince gone off in a huff?

I laughed aloud, but my laughter had a very hollow sound, and only made the succeeding silence more ghastly; it was very foolish, but I was exceedingly uncomfortable. Why didn't Kitty come? I could not find a bell. I searched in vain for matches; the fire was past service, and could not for its life, have raised flame enough to light a candle. Every minute the room grew darker and chillier, every minute the silence grew more and more oppressive. I began to think of what Kitty had said of the voice that still called "Alice" through the vacant halls; and then I wondered whether this were not the very room in which the father died; and then I tried not to listen or hear anything, and the next moment found myself with strained ear, watching for the lightest sound.

At last I could endure it no longer, and groping my way to the door, opened it, and held my breath, as I listened for some sound to indicate that I was not the only thing that breathed and lived within the gloomy walls. But such sound was wanting; a more vacant, drearier silence reigned without than within the room; through the long hall and distant corridors, not a footfall, not a motion; the rustle of my own dress awoke the only echoes. I dared not look toward the end of the hall that I had learned so much to dread; but starting forward and leaning over the balusters I called "Kitty," in a voice that would fain have been stentorian, but was in actual fact a whisper. No answer, of course, and the faltering whisper seemed to float down the dreary vacancy with mocking lightness and unconcern. I called again, this time desperation overcoming the choking terror.

Then there was a sound of some one moving, a door opened on the opposite side of the hall, a light appeared, and Mr. Rutledge's voice said, "What is it?"

What was it, indeed; it would have been difficult to say just what it was, and so I found it.

"Oh! it is you. I beg your pardon. Do you want Kitty?"

I said yes, and that I had been asleep, and just waked up a little while since, and could not find any matches. My white cheeks told the rest. Mr. Rutledge explained that Kitty had been sent to the post-office, and had not returned yet; he was very sorry she had not been at hand to attend to me, and coming across the hall, brought a light to my door. Very much ashamed of my fears, I went in to get my candle.

"Why," he said, looking in; "your fire is all out, it looks dreary enough; I am afraid you will take cold. You had better come down to the library and have tea with me. How will that do?"

"It will do very well," I said decidedly; for as to stay ing up there all alone till Kitty came back, it was not to be thought of, and folding my shawl around me, I stepped out into the hall, and with great satisfaction, shut the door of my room, and followed Mr. Rutledge through the hall and down the stairs. I kept pretty close to him, as we de-scended into the vast chilly-looking lower hall, but the coldness of its marble pavement, and the darkness of its heavy panels, only made the library, as we entered it, doubly attractive. The fire that would have made any other room uncomfortable at that season of the year, only warmed pleasantly the wide and lofty apartment. As Kitty said, "those great windows let in no end of air, and it took a power of wood to make it fit to stay in." And a "power of wood" now lay, "a solid core of heat" upon the hearth, casting a warm glow over the book cases that lined the walls, and the huge windows with their-crim-son drapery. The room delighted me; there was such an air of comfort and elegance about it, and the warm fire and bright lamp took from it the look of old-fashioned grandeur that is so comfortless, but so universal, in houses that have remained unchanged for a generation or so.

"What a delightful room!" I could not help exclaiming, as my eyes wandered eagerly over the long rows of books, that stood one above another, from floor to ceiling, in every variety of binding, from the dusky calf of a hundred or so years ago, to the elegant morocco and gilt of to-day.

"Yes, it is quite a delightful room for any one who likes books," said Mr. Rutledge, seating himself by the fire; "do you like them?"

"That's rather a general question, sir," I said, walking up to the case on the right side of the fireplace, where some more modern-looking volumes tempted my curiosity.

"So it is," answered my companion, pushing his chair a little further from the fire, and leaning back, shading his eyes with his hand. "It *is* rather general, I admit; but to reduce it to a more particular and answerable shape, are you fond of reading?"

"Some sort of books I like to read, sir."

"What is the sort you like?"

"Why," I said, rather puzzled, "I like—why I can't tell you exactly—but I like books that amuse me, that are not dry and stupid."

"There are so many different criterions of dryness and stupidity," said Mr. Rutledge with an amused smile, "that your answer, I must confess, doesn't give me much light; some people might consider as highly interesting, you know, what you and I might look upon as hopelessly dry and stupid."

I thought, as Mr. Rutledge said, "you and I," that it was very polite in him to put it so, but that he probably knew as well as I, that we had very different tastes, and that my favorite books were as unknown and indifferent to him, as his literary proclivities were, in all probability, elevated above, and incomprehensible to me.

"For instance," he said, "I like natural history. Now, a great many persons think it very dull. How is it with you?"

"That's just a case in point," I answered, with an effort not to care what he thought of me, "I never could get interested in it at all."

"I am not surprised; it is not very often attractive to those of your age and sex. Now, leaving off the 'natural,' perhaps you're fond of history?"

I reflected a moment; but while "White's Universal," and "Esquisses Historiques" were so vividly fresh and hateful, how could I honestly say I liked history? Yet I knew there were some historical works that I had as soon read as novels, but I did not know how to explain it; so I said, "I don't like all history, by any means."

"Neither do I," said Mr. Rutledge; "we agree on that point, and I am certain we shall on many others, if we can only get at them. Suppose you take any shelf, for instance, the lower one on your right, and let us see what we think of the contents. What's the first volume this way?"

I stooped down and read off the name, "Hallam's Middle Ages."

"Ah!" exclaimed my interlocutor, "we have stumbled upon history in earnest. How do you stand affected toward 'Hallam's Middle Ages'?"

"I like it exceedingly, sir." I responded very concisely, very much afraid of being pressed to give my reasons, which would have involved me in utter dismay and confusion, for in common with most very young persons, I liked because I liked, and disliked upon the same discriminating principle.

"What comes next?" asked Mr. Rutledge, to my great relief.

"'Goldsmith's Animated Nature.'"

"Ah! you don't like that. What follows?"

"A long row of 'Buffon,' sir, and then 'Tytler's Universal History.' I haven't read 'Buffon,' and I think Tytler—well—very nice, but tiresome, you know."

"Try the shelf above."

"The first book, sir, is 'Irving's Goldsmith.'"

" Did you ever read it ?"

I said Miss Crowen had given it to me to read, last vacation.

" You found it tiresome ?"

" Tiresome! why, sir, I think it is the nicest book in the world. I can't help thinking how Goldsmith would love Mr. Irving, if he knew about it! Next, sir, comes a very pretty copy of 'Macaulay's Roman Lays,' and five volumes of his ' Essays.'"

" Did Miss Crowen give you Macaulay to read ?"

" I took it from the library, and she did not mak ? any objection."

" And what do you think of him as a writer?"

I did not need to look in his face to know how much diverted he was at the idea of extracting a criticism of the great historian from such a chit as I ; and summoning all my courage to the aid of my pride, I answered steadily.

" If one of my ' age and sex,' sir, can be considered to have an opinion, I should say, that though Mr. Macaulay is probably the most brilliant writer of the century, he is the one who has done the least good. I don't think any one who has the least faith, reverence, or loyalty, can read him except under protest."

" Which means," said Mr. Rutledge, " that you and Mr. Macaulay are so unhappy as to differ on some points of politics and theology, *n'est ce pas ?*"

" I know very little about politics, and less about theology; I only know how I feel when he calls King Charles the First 'a bungling villain,' 'a bad man,' and says even prettier things about Lord Stafford ; I know it vexes me when he elevates Cromwell 'into a man whose talents were equal to the highest duties of a soldier and a prince,' and never omits an opportunity of sneering, with a mixture of contempt and pity, at that slow old institution, the Church of England."

"And you do not agree with him?"

"Agree with him!"

"What sentiments," exclaimed Mr. Rutledge, "what sentiments for a young republican! Do you mean to tell me that *you* don't look upon the death-warrant of Charles as the 'Major Charta' of England? Do you mean to say that you don't regard it as the first step in that blessed march of liberty that is regenerating the world?"

"A blessed march indeed!" I cried indignantly, "over the dead bodies of honor and obedience, faith and loyalty! A blessed march, to the tune of the Marseillaise and murder!"

"But, my young friend, how do you make that view of the subject agree with your patriotism as an American, and your veneration for Washington? Were there no carcasses of deceased obedience and loyalty under his chariot-wheels?"

"*Grâce à Dieu!*" I cried, eagerly, "it was Liberty, but Liberty with a different cap on, and marching under very different colors, that Washington fought for; no more the same deity that Cromwell and Robespierre acknowledged, than the idol of the Hindoo is the God we worship!"

Mr. Rutledge shrugged his shoulders, and begged me to explain the difference to him. And with a vehement mixture of enthusiasm, ignorance and anger, I tried to explain my meaning to him, but, as was not difficult to foresee, made but little headway in my argument, every moment adding to my adversary's coolness and my own impatience. I altogether forgot my diffidence and alarm; I was too angry and excited to think who it was I was talking to; I only knew he was opposing and tripping me up, and saying the most hateful things in the coolest way, and exasperating me to the highest degree, and not being a bit exasperated with all my saucy replies; and it was not till I had exhausted all my combined wrath and logic, that I caught a lurking smile about his mouth, that flashed upon me the conviction that I was entirely the victim of his wit, and that he had just been arguing on the wrong side for the sake of argument and amusement.

"After all," I exclaimed, " I believe you think just as I do, and have only been talking so, to draw me out!"

" Why, mademoiselle! How can you suspect me of such duplicity?" he said, with his peculiar short laugh.

And seizing a book, I sank down on the sofa to hide my burning cheeks behind its pages. How angry, frightened and mortified I felt, no words can tell, and every stealthy glance I obtained of my neighbor but added to my vexation. Wholly absorbed in his paper, he seemed to have forgotten all about me and my indignation; and having furnished him with half an hour's amusement, I was to be pushed aside to make way for a more serious train of thought, such as was now knitting his brow, and fixing his attention over some political debate or Congressional transaction. I might smooth my ruffled temper at my leisure; no danger of interruption or observation; I might solace myself with what consolation was to be found in the reflection, that whatever I had said savoring of exaggeration or absurdity, was by this time doubtless entirely forgotten by my companion. But it was a slim comfort, and could not displace the angry thought—what business had he to catechise me so; make me stand there, and tell him what books I had read, and then lead me on to say all manner of foolish things? My cheeks glowed at the recollection. There was one comfort; I knew enough now, never to let him have the amusement of making me angry again; he should never hear anything but monosyllables from me henceforth; I would be ice and marble when he was by.

Presently there came a low knock at the door, and Kitty appeared, very fresh and rosy from her walk, and entering, laid upon the table some papers and a couple of letters.

"Ah!" said the master, in a tone of satisfaction, reaching out his hand for them, "the mail is late to-night. You may send tea up; we will take it here this evening."

Kitty looked in great astonishment to see me downstairs, but the etiquette of the place forbade anything more on my part than a glance of recognition, and Kitty retired to order tea sent up. Till that refreshment arrived, and was arranged upon the table, Mr. Rutledge devoted himself to the newly-arrived papers, of whose contents he possessed himself with surprising celerity; and before the servant announced that tea was ready, I had watched his eyes scan rapidly every column of every paper; and looking up from the last one as Thomas made his announcement, he laid it aside, and turned toward the table, asking me, with a smile, if I should mind the trouble of pouring out tea. It was an attention, he said, that he was generally obliged to pay to himself, but it would make it much more agreeable if I would take the trouble.

I took my place behind the heavy silver service, and with fingers that trembled very visibly, proceeded, for the first time in my life, to fill that womanly office. Mr. Rutledge looked on silently, and without note or comment received and drank his tea. The toast and cake were unpatronized; Mr. Rutledge, I am inclined to think, forgot them, so absorbed did he appear in his own thoughts; and I, for my part, shrinking behind the urn, considered myself sufficiently taxed in swallowing a cup of tea, which almost choked me, as it was. It was not till the tea-things were removed that Mr. Rutledge allowed himself to open his letters, doing this, as everything else, at great disadvantage, and with some effort, with his left hand. I resumed my book, and did not raise my eyes, till some time having elapsed, Mr. Rutledge, rising, handed me a letter, which he said had come inclosed to him in one he had just received from my aunt. I opened it with considerable interest, and looking up from the reading of it with a smile, met Mr. Rutledge's eye, who said

"Mrs. Churchill seems to be very much alarmed about you. I think it's quite lucky that she was prevented from coming on in person, for she would have considered herself basely deceived, I am afraid, if she had dropped in upon us this evening; the two objects of her solicitude taking tea comfortably downstairs, in the apparent enjoyment of uninterrupted health. My bandaged arm, I believe, is the only visible reminder of the accident."

"How is it to-day, sir?" I asked, rather faintly.

He looked a little inclined to smile, remembering, no doubt, that this was the first time I had vouchsafed an inquiry concerning it; but he answered very civilly, that it was rather painful: whether old Sartain had made some blunder in setting it, or whether he had not kept it sufficiently quiet, he could not tell. However, he had no doubt it would soon be all right, etc.

Therewith he dismissed the subject; but I could not dismiss so easily, a little feeling of remorse for my selfishness and thoughtlessness; and he had been so careful of *my* comfort, too! Perhaps from that reflection, I was very prompt to drop my book in my lap, and be very attentive to his first remark, as, pushing away the pile of letters and papers, he leaned thoughtfully back in his chair, and said:

"You have not seen your aunt for a long time, have you?"

"It is rather more than five years, sir, since I have seen her."

"Have you been at school all that time?"

"Yes, sir; I have been there vacations and all. Aunt Edith went away the year after I was put there, and only came back last spring."

"Josephine is considerably older than you, is she not?"

"Just two years, sir; Josephine was nineteen last month, and I shall be seventeen the 28th of December, and Grace is eighteen months younger."

"I suppose you remember them quite well?"

"Not very, sir; I have never seen a great deal of them,

We lived in the country, and excepting when we went to town for a visit, we were not together. You met them abroad, did you not, sir?"

"Yes; we travelled through Switzerland together, and I saw them very frequently last winter in Paris."

"Oh!" I exclaimed, eagerly, quite forgetting my dignified resolutions, "do tell me about them. Is Josephine taller than I, and is she pretty? They say she sings so beautifully! Does she?"

"Where shall I begin?" he said, with a smile. "Such an avalanche of questions overwhelms me. First, as to height; well (thoughtfully), let me consider. It is difficult to judge. Stand up, and let me see how tall you are."

I sprang up, in perfectly good faith, and stood erect before him for three full minutes, while, with a critical eye, he surveyed me from head to foot.

"I should say," he continued very deliberately, while I resumed my seat, "I should say that there was not the difference of an eighteenth of an inch between you."

"Really?" I exclaimed. "Why, isn't that odd! It's very nice, isn't it, for us to be so near alike?"

"I did not say you were near alike."

"Oh, but in size I mean. I know we don't look alike. Josephine used to be such a thin, dark, old-looking little girl, that I cannot imagine her tall and grown-up."

"I think," continued Mr. Rutledge, "that she is still rather slighter than you are; though your additional shade of health and robustness will, I fancy, soon be lost, under the influence of town habits and constant dissipation."

"Are they very gay? Does my aunt go a great deal into society?" I asked.

"They did in Paris, and I fancy it will be the same in New York. In fact, there is little doubt of it."

"I wonder," I said, leaning my cheek on my hand, and looking thoughtfully into the fire—"I do so wonder whether I shall like it."

"Ah! my child," he said rather sadly, "you need not waste much wonder upon that; you will like it but too well. Wonder, with a shudder and a prayer, how you will bear the ordeal."

He sighed, and pressed his hand for a moment before his eyes; then catching my wistful look, he continued in a lighter tone:

"But I do not mean to frighten you; people, you know, are very apt to preach against what they are tired of, and inveigh against the world after they have 'been there,' and have seen its best and its worst, and tasted eagerly of both; and have spent years in its service, and are only disgusted when they find that it will yield them no more. They have no right to discourage you young things, just on the threshold, eager and impatient for you don't know what of glory and delight."

"Why, yes; I'm sure they have a right to warn us, if they see our danger. I am sure it is their duty."

"Oh!" he said, with one of his quick laughs, "it would be a thankless task; they would not be heeded. You all have to go through it, and how you come out is only a question of degree—some more, and some less tainted—according to the stuff you're made of."

"I don't want to believe that."

"You want to believe, I suppose, that you can go into the fire and not be burned; that you can go into the world and not grow worldly; that you can spend your youth in vanity, and not reap vexation of spirit; that you can go cheek by jowl with hollowness, and falsehood, and corruption, and yet keep truth and purity in your heart! You want to believe this, my little girl, but you must go to some one who has seen less, or seen it with different eyes from me, to hear it."

"I want to believe the truth, whether it's easy or hard, and I had rather know it now, at the beginning, if I've got to know it, than when it is forced upon me by experience."

"Wisely said, *ma petite;* self-denial, hard as it is, is easier than repentance; but there are few of us who would not rather take our chances for escaping repentance and 'dodge' the self-denial, too. Is not that the way?"

"I don't know; I suppose so. But, if the world is really as dangerous as you say, why should kind mothers and friends take the young girls they have the charge of, into it? Why should my aunt, for instance, take Josephine into society, the very gayest and most brilliant?"

An almost imperceptible smile flitted across my companion's face at my question, but he answered quite seriously:

"A great many different motives actuate parents; the principal, I suppose, are such as these: The children, they reason, are young, and they must have enjoyment; and so they cram them with sweets till they have no relish for healthier food. Sorrow, they say, comes soon enough; let them be happy while they may; and so they fit them for bearing it by an utter waste of mind and body in a mad pursuit of pleasure. And then, they must be established in the world; their temporal interests must be attended to. And the myriads offered up on that altar, it would freeze your young blood to know of! And then," he continued, with an amused look at my perplexity, "then there is another very potent reason why they cannot be kept in the nest—for before they are well fledged, the willful little brood will try their wings, and neither law nor logic will suffice to keep them back. Now, even you, sensible and correctly-judging young lady as you have this evening discovered yourself to be, would, I fear, not bear the test of a trial; I am afraid your courage would droop before the self denial of the first ball or two, and you would soon be drawn into the vortex without a struggle."

"I don't think so," I said. "I am pretty sure that if I resolved not to go into society—being convinced that I ought not—I should be able to keep my resolution. And even if I should see that it was best for me not to go out till I am older, but to stay at home and study and improve myself, this winter, at least, I know I could do it. If I thought that balls and parties were wrong, I am certain I should never go to one."

"That would be carrying the thing too far. Do not suppose that I mean anything like that. What I condemn is the wholesale worldliness—the unwearied career of folly that I have seen so much of, utterly excluding all cultivation of heart or intellect—utterly ignoring all beyond the present. That's the snare I would warn you of, my little friend. I know perhaps, better than you do, the trials that lie before you; so when I tell you that you will have need of all the courage, and self-denial, and resolution that you are mistress of, to keep you from that darkest of all lives—the life of a worldly woman—you must remember, I have seen many plays played out—have watched the opening and ending of more careers than one, the bloom and blight of more than one young life."

A pause fell—a long and thoughtful one—while my companion, shading his eyes from the firelight, gazed fixedly upon vacancy, and some time had passed before he shook off the momentary gloom, and resumed, in a lighter tone:

"That accident was a miserable business, was it not? Keeping you a prisoner in this dull old place, and knocking I don't know how many plans of mine in the head. And it is impossible to tell how many days it may be before I am able to travel, even if you should be. ·Perhaps, however, I may succeed in finding an escort for you, as I suppose you are impatient to be in New York."

"Oh, I beg you will not take any trouble about it; I like it here very well. I am not in the least hurry, and I hope you will not go a moment before you are fit, on my account."

My effort at civility was rewarded by a smile to which no one could be indifferent; and in reply, Mr. Rutledge said that he was glad to find me so philosophical ; that I must amuse myself as well as I could, and he should tell Mrs. Churchill, when he wrote, that I was in a fair way of being made a strong-minded woman ; between Mrs. Roberts' austere example in the conduct of the household, and his own invaluable moral lectures, my mind would be in no danger of rusting during my captivity. " Not to mention," he added gravely, " very able and improving mental exercise in the criticism of the most eminent living historians."

I hung my head at this last cut, administered, however, so daintily, that it was impossible to resent it ; and being on. the rack till he should get away from the subject, I quickly reverted to his letter to my aunt, asking when he should write, and desiring permission to inclose a note to her at the same time. He should probably write to-night, he said, glancing up at the bronze clock, which pointed to nine.

" Writing, however, with my left hand, is a business requiring much time and application, and possibly I may not attempt it till to-morrow morning."

Blushing very much, I said I wished I could be of service in writing that or any other letters for him; it would give me great pleasure. He thanked me for the offer, but considered it, he said, entirely too much to ask of me. I must remember I was still an invalid. I laughed at the idea, and the result was, that in five minutes I was seated at the library table, with a portfolio before me, writing a letter to my aunt at Mr. Rutledge's dictation.

I was in high spirits at the idea of being useful, and the pen flew over the paper almost as fast as the words were uttered. I rather writhed under the necessity of writing without demur of myself as " the little girl," and " your young niece ;" but there was nothing to be said, and after finishing it, and adding a few lines of my own, I enveloped and directed it. I asked if there was any other I could write for him.

He said there was one he was anxious to dispatch in the morning; so taking another sheet of paper, I began another letter. It was one on business, full of law terms and dry details, but fortunately not very long, and writing it as rapidly as possible, in my boldest, freest hand, I soon laid it ready for dispatch beside the other.

"What else?" I inquired, taking a fresh sheet ot paper.

"You are not tired?"

"Not in the least, sir," and I rapidly wrote the date, and with my pen suspended over the paper, awaited his dictation.

Without a word of explanation, he began to dictate as quickly as before, in French. For a moment my heart failed me, as the teasing French verbs rushed on my bewildered ear; but rallying instantly, without raising my eyes or giving the least evidence of my discomfiture, I began to write.

Thanks to Mademoiselle Céline's drilling, I was pretty ready at "dictée," and after the first surprise, got along very well. It was quite a severe exercise to keep pace with his rapid language, feeling all the while as if an error would be irreparable. I would not appear to read it over, of course, for purposes of correction, any more than I would have done the English ones. I managed, however, while looking for an envelope, and wiping my pen, to glance hurriedly and anxiously through it, and was somewhat comforted to meet no fault apparent, at least, on such a rapid scrutiny. I folded and addressed it, not, though, without some misgivings, and after receiving thanks, and a refusal of further services, glanced at the clock, and rose to go upstairs.

Mr. Rutledge lit my candle, and as he handed it to me, said I must do as I found it most agreeable about coming downstairs to my meals. He should be most happy to have a companion whenever I felt well enough to come down; but Kitty, he hoped, would make me comfortable whenever I preferred remaining upstairs.

I bowed, and said, "Yes sir," rather unmeaningly, and passed out of the door, which he held open for me, and which he was charitable enough not to shut till I was safe in my own room.

Kitty, active and pleasant as ever, awaited me there, and I threw myself in the easy-chair before the fire, while she unbraided and combed my hair, with a feeling of great comfort and complacency. She congratulated me upon going downstairs; and indirectly and respectfully endeavored to ascertain whether I had found master as formidable as I had anticipated. I did not wish to commit myself on this point; but finding that Kitty herself stood in a little wholesome awe of him, I was tempted to acknowledge that I did not feel altogether at ease downstairs; upon which she said, she guessed I wasn't the only one; nobody on the place, from Mrs. Roberts down, dared say their souls were their own when Mr. Rutledge was by.

"But then, he's a kind master, is he not?" I asked.

"Oh, yes! None better; that everybody knows. He's as liberal as can be; but then he expects everything to go on *just so;* and every man on the place knows that he won't put up with a bit of laziness or shirking. And so, whether he's here or not, things go on like clock-work, and the Rutledge farm is a perfect garden, everybody says. Better a good deal, I guess, than it used to be in old Mr. Rutledge's time, though there were twice as many men on it then, and twice as much money spent on it; but there was too much feasting and company for anybody to attend much to work, and I suppose the old gentleman was what they call a high liver, and cared more for his hounds and horses, and dinner-parties and wine, than for looking after his farm."

"How old was Mr. Arthur Rutledge when his father died?"

"Oh, a mere lad, sixteen or so; and for a time, I've heard them say, things went on bad enough, nobody to look after anything, the farm just going to destruction. For, the trouble all coming together, his father's and Mr. Richard's death, and whatever it was about Miss Alice, it was too much for Mr. Arthur, and brought on a dreadful fever, and for weeks they couldn't tell how it would go with him. Mrs. Roberts nursed him day and night; I guess she was the best friend he had, for he was the last of the family, you see, and hadn't a relation in the world, and though he had plenty of fine folks for his acquaintance, fine folks don't seem to think they're needed when people are in trouble and come to die; and I don't know but what they're right; they would be rather in the way. However, they didn't have much to do for Mr. Arthur that time; and at last the fever turned, and he began to get better."

Kitty had an attentive auditor, and she only too willingly talked on, and gave me all the facts she was possessed of. I had nothing else to think about just then, and so it was not to be wondered at that I made the most of them, and gave many an hour to the working up and embellishing of Kitty's story. I pictured to myself the lonely boy, coming back to life with no one to welcome him in the changed house. I fancied him pale and melancholy, wandering through the deserted halls and empty rooms, finding at every turn something to remind him of his grief. I could not blame him when, as my informant said, he grew to be morose and gloomy, and to hate the very name of home; for, going abroad, he did not come near it for years, and seemed to have lost all interest in it. The estate, during this time, was managed by an agent, who neglected it shamefully, and in whose charge it was fast going to ruin.

But suddenly, the young master returned, and to the surprise of all, took things into his own hands; dismissed those who had been living in idleness at his expense so long, only retaining such as were willing to conform themselves to the new *régime,* and by industry and faithfulness to regain what had been lost during this long period of neglect. It was a reform which required great energy and perseverance, but these the young heir possessed, and before a year was over, things wore a very different aspect; the house was repaired and the grounds put in order; the farm began to show the presence of a master. The reform did not stop here, however. For more than fifty years, there had been no church nearer than Hilton, a distance of six miles, which the family at Rutledge nominally attended, when the weather was fine; but, unhappily, Sunday and Sunday duties were by no means of paramount interest at Rutledge; and, naturally, master and tenantry fell into a criminal neglect of all the outward duties of religion. In the village which lay about a mile to the south of Rutledge, there had once, before the Revolution, been a church edifice, but long since it had fallen into ruins, and only a neglected graveyard remained to attest its former site. Here, Mr. Rutledge had built a church, and repairing a cottage that lay at the southern extremity of his farm, and not a quarter of a mile from the church, had turned it into a parsonage, where he had established a clergyman, who had labored very faithfully and very successfully among the almost heathenish inhabitants of the place, and had immeasurably improved its character.

"But still you say, Kitty, Mr. Rutledge does not live here much of the time. I should think he would be happy in a place where he had done so much good."

Kitty shook her head. "There is too much to remind him of old times, I suppose, for him to like it here; besides, it's very lonesome. He does his duty by it, but I don't believe he'll ever stay here more than he thinks he has to, to keep things straight."

I reminded Kitty, by and by, of the miniature of which we had been talking when Mrs. Roberts interrupted us in the morning.

"Should you like to see it?" Kitty asked.

"Of all things," I replied; and Kitty, laying down the

brush, said she would run up to her room and get it. She stopped a moment, after she had cautiously opened the door, to listen if Mrs. Roberts was still awake, then leaving it ajar, stole quietly up the stairs. My heart beat guiltily as I listened to her retreating footsteps. What business had I to be prying into family secrets? I was involuntarily ashamed of myself, but how could I help it? How could I resist the temptation? It could do no harm; I should only just look at it, and should be no wiser after all. It seemed an age before Kitty's returning footsteps rejoiced my ear, and I did not feel safe till, again within the room, she slid the bolt behind her, and put into my hand the old-fashioned locket, with its faded blue ribbon. I started up, and going to the light, bent down to examine it.

"It's like none of the family," Kitty said. "Their pictures are in the dining-room, and I've compared them all."

It certainly, I saw myself, was not in the least like Mr. Rutledge. It was a face I could not altogether understand. The eyes were dark, and perhaps tender in their light, but about the mouth—and a handsome well cut mouth, too—there was a something I could not define, that suggested coldness and insincerity; something that repelled me when I first looked, but seemed to disappear after a longer scrutiny. The features were regular and strikingly handsome, the skin a clear olive, the hair dark and wavy. As far as my limited knowledge of these things went, what was visible of the uniform appeared to me to be that of a French officer, and the letters, in tiny characters, engraved on the back, "à Paris, 1830," seemed to confirm the probability.

"Twenty-four years ago," I said.

"That was the year before old Mr. Rutledge died," said Kitty.

I kept it in my hand while she undressed me, and only returned it to her as she was leaving me for the night. But she said,

"You'd better keep it, Miss, if you will, to-night. I am

afraid to go to my trunk to put it away, for Dorothy, the cook, sleeps ·in the room where we keep our trunks, and she's just gone upstairs."

I consented, and for safety put it under my pillow. I wished it anywhere else, however, after the door had closed ; and Kitty departing,

———" Left the world to darkness and to me."

CHAPTER V.

"Girls blush, sometimes, because they are alive,
Half wishing they were dead to save the shame.
The sudden blush devours them, neck and brow
They have drawn too near the fire of life, like gnats,
And flare up bodily, wings and all. What then?
Who's sorry for a gnat—or girl?"

                                    E. B. BROWNING.

THE question, whether I should breakfast downstairs or
alone, was settled by the ringing of the bell before Kitty
had half done my hair, and as I would not for worlds have
been two minutes late at any meal that Mr. Rutledge was
to share, I determined to "take the benefit of the act," and
remain an invalid till dinner-time.

"What a dismal day, Miss!" remarked my maid, as she
made herself busy in removing my breakfast from the table.
"How shall you manage to amuse yourself?"

"I don't mind the rain in the least," I answered, wheeling
my admired chair up to the window, and throwing myself
into it, with a lapful of books and work. "I think a rainy
day is splendid."

And so, indeed, I found it for a while. I read till I had
extracted all the honey from the pile of reviews and maga-
zines before me, and then pushed them away, and leaning
against the window, gazed out on the dreary landscape. A
sheet of rain and mist hid the lake, the pine grove looked
black and sullen, the trees in the park tossed mournfully
about their naked branches, as showers of yellow leaves fell
in gusts upon the ground ; the wind moaned dismally around
the house, and dashed the rain, by fits and starts, against
the windows with a heavy sound. It was very nice to feel
that it could not get in, and that there was stout glass and

stone between me and the pitiless autumn storm, and a snug
and cosy shelter from its fury. But by and by I grew
rather tired of watching the rain and the leaves, and yawn-
ing, began to cast about for some more attractive occupation. This I found for a short time in my worsted work,
which I disinterred from the depths of my trunk, and applied myself to in great earnest for half an hour. But the
motive for exertion was wanting; I could not help thinking
wearily, that there was not the least hurry about finishing
it, and those roses would blow, on demand, any time during the next six years, with as much advantage as at present.

And so I laid it down and took to the window again,
wondering, with a sigh, whether all young ladyhood were
like this; and if it were, how it happened that we did not
hear of more early deaths—deaths from utter ennui and exhaustion. I had for so long been used to having every half
hour in the day filled up with some unavoidable exercise of
mind or body, that I felt entirely lost without the routine,
and firmly resolved, as soon as I should be settled at my
aunt's, to begin a course of study which should fill up all these
idle moments, and give some vigor to my faculties. "I
should die of this in a month," I thought; and seizing one
of the rejected Reviews, the only literature at hand, I resolutely set myself to read the longest, driest paper in it.
And really, after the task was accomplished, though I am
sorry to say I was not by much the clearer in my views on
the particular branch of science of which it treated, still I
felt decidedly better satisfied with myself for the effort, and
experienced less compunction in taking, after lunch, a short
nap.

Kitty had been absent all the morning, having been
detailed for some pressing laundry work by the practical
Mrs. Roberts, for which I was still owing her a grudge,
when, just as I awoke from my nap, she walked in, and
accepting the chair I offered her, made me quite a little

visit. I exerted myself to appear amiable, and was con-
gratulating myself on the success of my efforts, and on the
absence of all disagreeable topics, when, just as she was
going, her keen eyes having made the circuit of the room
many times, she detected something amiss in the bed, and
walking across to the recess where it stood, began to
examine the manner in which it was made.

"That Kitty," she said, "was not to be trusted to make
even a bed by herself. She was sure I did not lie comfortably."

And stooping down, she began to dissect it. My heart
gave a spasmodic thump, and then stood "stock-still for
sheer amazement," not to say consternation, when it flashed
across me that I had left the guilty miniature between the
mattresses, where, in the sleepless nervousness of last night,
I had put it, in order to have it as far out of the way as
possible. It was the strangest thing that I should never
have thought of it since I waked up. "And now," I thought,
with a cold chill, "now it is probably under Mrs. Roberts'
very nose, and Kitty and I are undone." I hardly breathed
as I watched her throwing back blanket and sheet, and
making sad havoc among the bolsters and pillows, giving
the one a contemptuous shake, and the other an indignant
poke; all the while most animatedly anathematizing the
the unlucky Kitty. I had already pictured Kitty and
myself dragged by the hair of our guilty heads, before
Mr. Rutledge, for judgment, and terrified into confession by
that awful look of his, when to my unspeakable relief, Mrs.
Roberts stopped just short of the mattress, and coming
indignantly across the room, rang for Kitty, who promptly
answered the bell. She looked somewhat blank to find that
the summons was not to dress me, but to stand one of Mrs.
Roberts' tirades.

Mrs. Roberts was, I believe, troubled with rheumatism,
"the worst kind," and the cold storm and east wind had
aggravated these long-tried enemies to an unbearable pitch,

and it was well known in the house that there was but one
remedy that succeeded in the least in allaying the irritation
of her nerves, but one soothing panacea, and that was, a
thorough and satisfactory "blow-out" on scolding; the
raking fore-and-aft some adversary's craft with the unerring
fire of her indignation, the entire annihilation, soul and
body, for the time being, of the victim that happened first
to cross her path. And tradition pointed to Kitty as the
favorite scape-goat on these occasions. She knew her fate,
I am certain, from the moment she caught the dull glare of
Mrs. Roberts' eye, and doggedly tossing her pretty head to
one side, stood ready to confront her.

Did she call that bed *made*, Mrs. Roberts would like to
know? Kitty considered it made—yes.

She did, did she? Then she would please to come
across the room and try if she could do it as well the
second time.

I made Kitty an agonized gesture, which she promptly
understood, but which Mrs. Roberts also caught sight of,
and was at her elbow in an instant. It was a pretty severe
contest of skill between the veteran rat-catcher and the keen
little mouser; Mrs. Roberts knew there was *something*, and
inly vowed to scent it out; Kitty was as determined to
elude her vigilance, and as is not unusual, youth and dex-
terity triumphed. From under the very eyes of Mrs.
Roberts, Kitty, under cover of a zealous shake of the
mattress, bore off the miniature, and smuggling it in her
apron, passed by where I was sitting, and threw it into my
lap. I thrust it down to the lowest depths of my pocket, and
looked with admiration at Kitty's unshaken composure, as
she continued her work under the galling fire of Mrs. Roberts'
sarcasms.

The bed at last was made irreproachably; even Mrs.
Roberts could find no fault with its unruffled exterior;
though to my unpractised eye, it had looked much the same
before its revisal. It seemed a long time before the antago

nists withdrew, and a longer still before my tranquillity of temper was restored. How I wished the miniature safely back in Kitty's trunk, in the furthest corner of the attic! That came of doing what I was ashamed of! I did not feel as if I could look any one in the face till it was out of my hands. I did not venture to ring for Kitty, for I felt certain Mrs. Roberts stood with the door of her room ajar, ready to pounce upon her if she came in sight again; so I exerted myself to perform the duties of my *toilette* unaided. They were not arduous, and I was soon dressed, and vainly trying to interest myself in my embroidery till the bell should ring. It was still an open question whether I should go downstairs; I half inclined to playing invalid a little longer, and taking this one more meal in my room. But then the dreary prospect of my solitary dinner, and the long dull twilight, with nothing but my own thoughts for entertainment, and the longer, duller evening, with nothing to amuse but what had failed of that object during the day, weighed down the balance in favor of a change of scene, and I was on my feet in an instant, as my watch pointed to three, and the bell announced dinner, simultaneously. I pushed the worsted into my workbox, and putting the miniature hastily into a drawer, essayed to lock it, but the key was defective, for some cause, and would not turn, and not daring to run the risk of being late, I again put it into my pocket, and hurried down.

As I reached the lower hall, I remembered that I had not the least idea which door led into the dining-room, and so had to try three or four which gave no evidence of being inhabited, furniture being covered and windows closed, before I hit upon the right one. I entered hesitatingly, not discovering, till I was fairly in the room, that I was the only occupant of it. The table was laid for two, and the dinner was already served, but the master was not yet down. As some minutes passed and he did not appear, I had time to look around, and get acquainted with the *salle à manger.*

It was a fine room, old-fashioned though it was; and modern architecture has still to produce its rival in my eyes. The ceiling was very high, the fireplace wide, with tiled jambs; the wood-work carved in stiff but stately patterns; the windows were deep, with enticing window-seats, and the walls were covered with pictures. Pictures, I imagined, of people who had once owned Rutledge : some of them, perhaps, lived in this very house, ate and drank in this very room. There were several portraits, that I rather hurried over, of pompous-looking people in very old-time style, but I knew in a moment the handsome picture over the mantel-piece. It was the late Mr. Rutledge, like Mr. Arthur, but infinitely handsomer, on a larger scale, with a jovial, pleasant face, but I thought, less intellectual in the expression. Then I was certain that the picture on the right represented Richard, the heir, who had died so soon after his father. Ah! But, I thought, what a handsome, gentle face! What soft eyes! If Mr. Arthur had only looked like him, what a nice thing it would be to be dining *tête-à-tête* with him. *Quel dommage!* If he had only lived! But I felt inclined to laugh when I remembered that his younger brother might easily, as far as age was concerned, have been my father, and the handsome Richard himself could almost, well, yes, quite, have stood to me in' the relation, more reverend than romantic, of grandfather.

So, with a wistful look at the pensive, delicate face that never had grown, never could grow old, I glanced at the empty panel that intervened between this picture and the the next. That space surely once had held a portrait, and with a rapid transition of fancy, I thought of the picture with its face to the wall, in the deserted room upstairs. That was it, I made no manner of doubt, that had once hung here. Beyond it was the mother's portrait, fair, gentle, and sad : beneath this picture, and depending from its frame, hung a little crayon sketch, that I examined with interest, thinking to find it identical, possibly, with the miniature, which I pulled from my pocket to compare. But a glance refuted that idea; not the faintest likeness between them, nothing in common but human features. It represented (the sketch I mean) a boy of about my own age, with such a fine, glowing, ardent face as made "new life-blood warm the bosom," only to look into his truthful eyes, only to catch the merry smile that lingered about his handsome mouth. It had, however, such a likeness to Mr. Rutledge, that I should, despite the difference that time had wrought, have imagined him to be the original of the picture, had I not found, written hastily and faintly in one corner, " Obit. 1830," and some words in Latin that I could not make myself mistress of.

I was so intent upon it, that I did not notice Mr. Rutledge's entrance till he stood beside me. I pocketed the miniature, which I still held in my hand, in hot haste, and turned to meet his inquiring eyes.

" Are you making acquaintance-with my ancestors?" he asked.

I answered that I had been looking at the pictures. " But this," pointing to the crayon head, " this is not an ancestor, is it ?"

" No," he said, with a half smile, " not exactly an ancestor; a relation."

I asked him if it was not considered like him.

He had been told, he said, that there was some resemblance. I looked at it with a critical eye, and then remarked that the resemblance lay, I thought, in the contour of the face, and perhaps something about the eyes; but the expression was as different from his as it was possible for an expression to be.

" That's true," he said looking at it sadly; " that face expresses what no man's face can express after thirty: hope and courage, and an unshaken confidence in the honesty of his fellows."

I did not fancy that doctrine very much, so I began

talking of the other pictures. Of the older ones, Mr. Rutledge gave me some slight sketches, passing briefly by those that I knew he could have told me most about. But I turned admiringly back to the sketch that had so much taken my fancy.

"After all," I said, "this is the finest face among them."

Mr. Rutledge shook his head dissentingly, and looked sadly up at Richard's portrait.

"No indeed," I exclaimed, "that's not near so good a face as this; handsomer, perhaps, dreamy and poetical, but not so brave and spirited. Look at the impatient fire in those eyes! And his smile is truth itself. There is something so determined in the attitude too."

"He was, I believe, an honest, truthful lad," said Mr. Rutledge, unenthusiastically.

"He was more than that I'm sure," I exclaimed, "or would have been, if he had lived. With that high spirit he would have made everything bend to him; and if fair fortune hadn't smiled upon his humble birth (which, however, I suppose she did, being a Rutledge), he would have conquered her, you may be sure. I am certain he wouldn't have known the meaning of the words despair and doubt; but come what might, would have hoped and believed to the end."

"But perhaps," said my companion, "perhaps a hand of ice might have been laid upon his youth; a cruel blow might in one day have dashed from him all that feeds hope and faith; perhaps disgrace, grief, illness, coming all together, might have crushed out of him all energy and spirit. What would have become of your hero then? Would he have hoped, when death and the grave had all that he loved? Would he have believed, when what from his cradle he had most trusted in had proved false and worthless?"

I was a little startled at the bitterness of his tone, but persisted, "All that wouldn't have happened to him. 'Fortune favors the brave.'"

4

"Not always, *petite*, not always," he said, with an iron
ical laugh.

"Nevertheless, I wish he had lived," I said; "I am sure
he would have been my hero."

"Why," said Mr. Rutledge, looking at me, "why, if, as
you say, that boy had lived, he would have been—let me
see—nearly forty years old: and that, you know, would
have made it out of the question for you to love him."

"I never thought of that," I said naively. "Well then,
I wish I had lived when he did, and been born thirty years
ago."

"What! Your youth all over? No, little simpleton,
whatever you wish, don't be wild enough to wish that!
Make the best of your youth, and freshness, and spirit, for
they'll take themselves off some fine day, and leave you nothing to do but to look back."

"That's according to the use I make of them, I suppose,"
I answered, a little ungraciously. "I am not at all afraid
that I shall be bitter and misanthropical when I am old, if I
spend my youth as I ought."

Mr. Rutledge laughed very much as if he thought I meant
it for him; yet the laugh was not altogether a happy one,
and he continued:

"See to it then, child, that you use them right. I do
not mean to discourage you. I have no doubt you will be
very happy and contented when forty comes around on the
string of birth-days. Always being and provided, of course,
that the hero, or one as near like him as possible, has come
in at the right time to realize your dreams."

"But I don't believe," I said, perversely, "that I shall
ever have any lover that I shall like as much as I should
have done this one."

"He would have made you an earnest lover, certainly, if
that would have won you, with perhaps a dash of impetuosity and tyranny in his love; but that is what you women
like, is it not?"

"How can I tell?" I said, very demurely.

"I forgot," he answered, laughing, "I forgot that you were just out of school, and could not be supposed to know anything about love and lovers."

"Of course not," I said, putting my hands in the pockets of my basque, and looking at the ground over my left shoulder, after the manner of a French print I had seen in Mademoiselle Céline's room. "Of course not."

Mr. Rutledge seemed to take in such good part my saucy ways, that I began to feel much more at my ease, and laughed quite like myself, when on going to the table we found the soup very unattractively cold; "glacée," Mr. Rutledge said it was.

"While people moralize they are very apt to forget the realities; and so we have let the soup get cold, and the dinner get burned, very likely, and shall have to wait for it as it has been waiting for us."

Mr. Rutledge rang, and a servant and hot soup promptly appeared, and dinner was soon in progress, and a very pleasant dinner it proved. For the time, my companion forgot abstraction, and I forgot timidity, and both forgot the dismal storm without. Mr. Rutledge condescended to be entertaining, and I deigned to forget all former slights, and be entertained. Unluckily, however, at dessert, I made some allusion to the loneliness in which he usually took his meals, and that seemed to raise some disagreeable recollection, for his face darkened, and he said, after a short pause:

"Yes, young lady, it is long since I have seen any face, and most of all, a woman's face, opposite me at this solitary table."

Then he fell into a fit of musing that made me feel uncomfortably sorry for my mal-à-propos speech. I could not help wondering who had last sat where I did, and the thought was anything but genial; my eyes wandered involuntarily to the empty panel; and it was with a feeling of relief that I arose from the table and followed my host

toward the library. As we passed the crayon picture, however, I paused a moment, and Mr. Rutledge, turning, said :

"You're not tired of it yet ?"

I said no, I liked it better all the time, and to-morrow
I meant to bring my drawing materials down and make a
copy of it, if he was willing.

"You are welcome to the picture itself, if you'll accept
it," he said, indifferently, proceeding to unhook it from the
frame of the picture above, to which it hung.

I was mute with amazement for a moment, and hardly
found breath to exclaim:

"How strange that you do not value it !"

He replied that there were two or three sketches of the
same face about the house, and he did not care particularly
for this one. It gave him great pleasure to give it to me,
if I fancied it.

I hope I thanked him, but I am not at all certain that I
did. I seized the picture with great *goût*, and ran into
the library, and up to the lightest window, to enjoy it by
myself.

Mr. Rutledge threw himself into a chair, and his hand
being before his eyes, I could not see whether he slept or
not. I looked long and earnestly at my favorite in every
light, and from every point; then got up on a chair and
reached down a Latin Dictionary to help translate the sentence written below the date. But I could not get it right,
and gave up in despair.

That amusement exhausted, and no other presenting, in
the course of time the unavoidable weariness, and want of
elasticity consequent upon my three days' confinement to
the house, began to make themselves felt, and at last, I
thought, to become utterly unbearable. I conceived the
mad plan of getting my shawl and hood, and escaping to
the piazza for a little exercise, though the rain had beaten
furiously upon almost every part of it. I got up, and was
stealing noiselessly toward the door, when Mr. Rutledge,

whom I had fancied asleep, said uneasily, without altering his position:

"Why do you go away?"

"I am so tired of the house, sir, I am going to wrap up and walk up and down on the piazza for a little while. It will not hurt me," I continued, pleadingly; "mayn't I?"

"On no account," he said decidedly; "it would be absurd, after the fever you have had."

"I am positive it would not hurt me, sir."

"And I am positive it would."

As Mr. Rutledge had not turned toward me at all, I suppose he did not see how very angry I looked, and how very red my face was. Perhaps his thoughts had gone off to something else, for he did not say anything more; and I stood drumming on the table, waiting for him to continue; determined, *determined* not to go back and sit down, till, exasperated beyond patience by his silence, I said, moving toward the door:

"I suppose then, sir, you have no objection to my going to my own room."

"Why, yes," he said, "I have, decidedly. I think it would be much more sensible for you to amuse yourself down here."

"I've failed in doing that, sir, already."

"Well, then, stay and amuse me."

"That's entirely beyond my power, I am afraid, sir," I answered, shrugging my shoulders.

"You cannot tell till you have tried," he said; "I have a wretched headache. Don't you feel sorry for me?"

"Of course, sir, exceedingly. But unluckily, I don't see how I can help you."

"Oh, it's of no importance. Pray go."

I stood irresolute and very uncomfortable.

"If there's anything you'll have for your head, sir"——·

"No, there's nothing, thank you."

This was the way in which I repaid his indulgence and

attention! This was a nice return for the care he had taken of me during my illness. I would have given worlds for a good excuse to stay, but Mr. Rutledge seemed determined not to give me any. At last, after everything else had failed, I said, hesitatingly:

"Would it annoy you to have me read aloud to you, sir?"

He would not trouble me on any account, he said.

"But," I answered eagerly, "it is not the slightest trouble. I should like to do it, I assure you."

He would not think of putting such a task upon me.

"But do say," I exclaimed, "whether or not you like reading aloud."

He liked it very much, but begged me not to trouble myself.

That was enough, and in a moment I was by the fire.

"What shall I read, sir?"

"Anything you fancy."

"You are the most provoking man," I thought, as I looked up and down the shelves in search of a book. I shrewdly concluded that I might as well please myself in the choice, as it was not probable that Mr. Rutledge would attend to three words of what I read, even if he did not go to sleep. So recognizing an old friend in "Sintram," I took it from the bookcase, and sitting down in the window-seat, opened its familiar pages with some pleasure. Familiar, that is, they had been to my childhood, but it was some years since I had seen the book. It was not long, however, before I forgot myself and my auditor over the strange, wild, touching story. The dreary storm without, the growing gloom within, all added to the charm of its wild pathos. I read on, bending forward to catch the last grey light from the window, till, baffled by the rapidly-deepening twilight, I left it, and sitting down on a low seat by the fire, read on by its flickering light. If I had not been sure that no one was attending, I should have stopped for shame at the trembling of my voice, which I could not control, as I read the lines that tell to Sintram his release from terror and temptation:

> "Death comes to set thee free—
> O meet him cheerily
> As thy true friend;
> And all thy fears shall cease,
> And in eternal peace
> Thy penance end."

A low, quick-drawn sigh told me that I was not alone in my interest in the tale. I finished it, and dropping the book in my lap, sat resting my head on my hand, and gazing dreamily into the fire. Presently steps in the hall interrupted my revery, and I rose to put the book away. As I passed Mr. Rutledge, he held out his hand, and, as I laid my own in it, he said, "thank you," and looked at me with the most mournful expression in his eyes. The tears rushed involuntarily into mine as I met his glance; I did not know which to pity most, Sintram or my companion. He saw the pity in my look, and remembered it, long after the emotion had passed.

A servant entered at that moment, with the brightest of cheerful lamps; Mr. Rutledge ordered more wood on the fire, which presently blazed and crackled genially; the curtains were drawn, and the conquered twilight and moaning wind were banished the room.

Mr. Rutledge roused himself from his abstracted mood, and I said to myself, "What can I do to keep him from thinking of the things that trouble him?" And, woman enough to like the task, I set myself to make the evening a pleasant one, and to keep all dullness and ennui away. And it was a very happy evening to me, and not a dull one, I am certain, to my host. I made tea with much less trepidation than on the evening before, and it proved almost magical in curing Mr. Rutledge's headache. I could hardly believe the clock was right when it struck ten, the evening had seemed so short. I took my picture from the mantel-piece, and bidding my companion good night, ran upstairs two steps at a time, not remembering till I reached the top, that Miss Crowen had condemned the practice as unlady-like. "I hope Mr. Rutledge wasn't listening," I thought with mortification. If Mr. Rutledge wasn't, Mrs. Roberts was, though, for I heard her door shut softly soon after I had reached my room, and presently she found an excuse for coming in upon me, which she did rather suddenly, as I was standing before the new picture, looking at it very earnestly, as I leisurely unbraided my hair. I went over to the glass, however, very quickly upon her entrance; and after her errand was over, she quite inadvertently, it would seem, glanced up at the picture, but *I* knew she had seen it the first thing when she came in.

"Why," she exclaimed, looking surprised, "how came Mr. Rutledge's picture up here? It has always hung under his mother's in the dining-room. There must be some mistake," she continued, looking inquiringly at me.

An alarming truth began to dawn on my mind, a vivid blush spread over my face, and Mrs. Roberts never once took her eyes off me.

"I fancied it, and Mr. Rutledge said I might have it," I stammered. Mrs. Robert's blue lips parted for an instant in a contemptuous curl; then, looking stonier than ever, she said:

"Yes, it is a good likeness; or was, at least, when he was a young man; he's sadly changed since then; he's an old and an altered man now, is Mr. Arthur Rutledge."

The housekeeper, saying this with emphasis, and having no excuse for staying longer, was obliged to withdraw.

"Yes, ma'am," I muttered, as I locked the door after her, "I know he's an old man, I know he's nearly forty years old: who better? for he told me so himself." And my cheeks scorched with blushes, as one by one, I recalled my foolish speeches. How stupid, how blind I had been. Why, as I looked at the picture now, there wasn't a feature in the face that could possibly have been mistaken for any one else, not a shade nor outline that was not characteristic. I could have cried with vexation. How should I ever dare to look him in the face again? "My hero!" And I covered my face with my hands, and started up guiltily, and put it out of the way before I unlocked the door for Kitty.

4*

CHAPTER VI.

"The Sundays of man's life
Threaded together on time's string,
Make bracelets to adorn the wife
Of the eternal glorious King.
On Sunday, heaven's gate stands ope;
Blessings are plentiful and rife;
More plentiful than hope."

HERBERT.

"MR. RUTLEDGE'S compliments, Miss, and he begs you will breakfast without him this morning; he isn't well enough to come down," said the servant, as I entered the dining-room next morning.

"Is his arm worse?" I asked.

"It pains him a good deal, Miss; and he's had a very bad night. Michael has ridden over to get the doctor."

That was bad news, certainly; I wished very much I could do something for him; but as I couldn't, the next best thing was to eat my breakfast; which, however, was rather choky and unpalatable in all that grand solemnity, with the tall Thomas (Mr. Rutledge's own man, temporarily supplying the post of waiter) looking down at me. I broke down on the second slice of toast, and concluded to give it up and go into the library.

It seemed incredible that it had stormed yesterday; such splendid sunshine, such a clear sky, I thought, I had never seen before. I would have given anything for a race down the avenue in that keen, bracing wind, but I determined heroically that I would not stir out of the house till Mr. Rutledge gave me permission. But about eleven o'clock my reading was interrupted by the abrupt entrance of Kitty, who, with her face all aglow with pleasure, an

82

nounced to me that Mr. Rutledge had ordered the carriage for me to take a drive, if I felt like it; and sent word, that if I was willing, he thought Kitty had better accompany me. I tossed away my book, exclaiming, "it was grand," and, followed by Kitty, ran upstairs.

"How odd," she said, as in breathless haste she prepared me for the drive, "how odd that Mr. Rutledge shouldn't have sent word for Mrs. Roberts to go with you, miss, isn't it?"

"Odd, but very nice, Kitty," I answered, with a grimace that made her laugh; and as the carriage drove to the door, we ran down the stairs, Kitty putting on her bonnet and shawl as we went. I am sure it would have eased for a moment Mr. Rutledge's pain, if he could have known the extent of the pleasure he had conferred on the two children who so delightedly occupied his carriage that morning. All Kitty's knowledge of it, I suspect, had hitherto been speculative, and I think one of the dearest wishes of her heart was gratified when she tried experimentally the softness of its new dark green cushions, and in her own proper person occupied the front seat, an honor whereof she had only dreamed before.

It was a perfect autumn day; the air was exhilarating, the sunshine brilliant, the scenery picturesque, and a great deal less than that would have sufficed to make me happy in those days; and before we reëntered the park gate, three hours had slipped away in the most unsuspected manner. Kitty having gathered, at my request, an armful of the few gay autumn leaves remaining after yesterday's storm, I entertained myself, during the drive home, with arranging them in a bouquet. The glossy dark laurel leaves, and the varied and bright hues of the maple and sumac, with some vivid red berries, name unknown, made quite a pretty and attractive combination. As we reached home, I was seized with an audacious intention, which I put into execution before allowing myself time to "think better of it"

"Kitty," I said, "take this to Mr. Rutledge's door, and give it to Thomas for him, and say I hope he is better, and I am very much obliged to him for sending me to drive, and that I enjoyed it very much."

I was rather alarmed when Kitty had accomplished her errand, but it was too late to retract. That evening was a very long one; I went upstairs at nine o'clock, wondering at its interminable length.

The next day was Sunday. Mr. Rutledge was no better, and I went to church alone in the carriage, with only Kitty to attend me, Mrs. Roberts, she said, not being able to leave "the master." It was a beautiful little church, Gothic, and built of stone, with nothing wanting to render it church-like and solemn. When I looked at the tablets on the wall, that recorded, one after another, the deaths of Warren Rutledge, and Maria, his wife, and Richard, their son, I could not help thinking it must be sad for him to come here, Sunday after Sunday, and see that; but then it's easier to think of such things in church than anywhere else; somehow, quick and dead do not seem so far separated there.

Why, I could not tell, but there I remembered a great deal more thoughtfully and thankfully than I had done before, the evening, not a week ago, when I had lain, living and unhurt, among the dead and dying. It was strange, in the humored nervousness of the first day or two, and the returning health and spirits of the following, how little I had thought of it. And when Mr. Shenstone read his text: "Were there not ten cleansed? But where are the nine? There are not found that returned to give glory to God, save this stranger," my heart smote me. I indeed had forgotten, and had taken carelessly, and without much thought, my preservation from a terrible death. I indeed had gone on without giving glory to God, without acknowledging the mercy by which I yet lived.

Mr. Shenstone's sermon was one that those who recognize only as eloquence, pathos and fire and passion, would have pronounced very far from eloquent. His manner was quiet, and not particularly impressive, his language simple and unostentatious. But he possessed the true kind of sermon eloquence—keen perception of spiritual things, and the clearest knowledge of the Christian life. He had learning and talents; but it was not by them alone that he gained so deep a reverence from his humble parishioners, so strong an influence over them. It was because his own hope was high, that he could elevate theirs. It was because learning and talents and fame were things indifferent to him, save as aids in the service he had entered, that he could descend to their level, to raise them more nearly to his own. They could grasp what he taught them, for it was "a reasonable religious and holy hope," a rule of life, sober, practical, and simple, that led to high things, but began with low. It was because his heart was in his work, that his work prospered; because the World, the Flesh, and the Devil, were his sworn and baffled enemies, and not his half encouraged and secret allies, that in his little flock he made such headway against them; because "through faith and prayer" he kept his own heart and life pure, he could see more clearly to guide them.

Thus it was, that though Mr. Shenstone hardly took his eyes from his notes, and used very few gestures, and those few awkward ones—though he preached quietly and unenthusiastically—though there were no ornaments of rhetoric, no efforts at oratory, it was a sermon that, to this day, I distinctly remember, and never, I fancy, shall forget. Keen, pithy, conclusive, no one could help acknowledging its power; kind, earnest, sincere, no one could doubt its spirit; full of a devotion the purest, a faith that pierced to heaven itself, a love that cast out all fear and slothfulness, no one could listen and not be better for the listening. He put old truths in new lights, and gave to the familiar Gospel story a vivid interest, that often reading had made tame and unimpressive. He brought distinctly before the imagi nation the Samaritan village, through which the Saviour was passing on his way to Jerusalem ; the sad company of leprous men, cut off from the sympathy and society of their fellows, who attracted his notice. That they " stood afar off," not daring to approach him, was no obstacle to him ; no distance could put them beyond the pity of that watchful eye, beyond the attention of that ear, ever open to the prayers of his people. They were marked, miserable, suffering men, and as such they cried with all their hearts and humbly, " Jesus, Master, have mercy on us !"

It was their one chance for restoration to home and kindred, no doubt they cried with all their hearts. They were considered beyond the reach of human aid ; no doubt they cried humbly. And He " who hath never failed them that seek Him," had mercy on them and heard their cry and helped them. Sending them simply and unostentatiously to the ordained means of cure and cleansing, they, obeying eagerly and unquestioningly, were cured and cleansed. On their way to the priests, the hated disease left the bodies it had so long degraded and afflicted, and with the glow of returning health, they felt they were men once more, men without a curse and a reproach upon them. And with returning health came the pride, the self reliance that had been only slumbering, not dead, under the weight of the punishment laid on them. Without a thought of Him to whom they owed the power to do it, they hurried forward, one perhaps to his farm, another to his merchandise, long denied, absent, but unforgotten idols. Among the crowd, but one remembered to be thankful, but one returned to give glory to God. And he was a Samaritan, but another name to Jewish ears, for infamy and contempt. No doubt he had been in a good school to learn humility among these proud Jews, who, even in their degradation, had probably never forgotten to revile and to persecute. And on him alone, of all the ten, rested the blessing and commendation, beside which the bodily cure was but a paltry gift. These things were written for our admonition; they had called for mercy in their extremity, they had been heard and their prayer granted, and they had forgotten whence came the mercy, and had used it only to harden themselves in worldliness and sin. Had this case no parallel in Christian times? Was Jewish ingratitude the last that had been offered to Divine love? Were there none, among the Congregation of Christ's flock, who in time of peril and temptation, had with all their hearts and humbly cried for mercy, which when sent they had forgotten to be thankful for? The vows made in a time of terror and despair, fade in the sunshine of returning prosperity, the blessing is used, the Giver is forgotten. Must not such a sin look black to Him who is of purer eyes than to behold iniquity? Will it not provoke Him more surely than any other, to leave the ingrate forever to the idols of his choice, to let him see, when next comes peril and perplexity, how worthless and how frail they are, and how fearful a thing it is, to forfeit forever the protection of a God that can save.

If any such there were, let them repent while there was yet time, let them wash out the ingratitude that stained their souls, with penitential tears, and purify themselves with prayer and fast, and daily self-denial. Let them remember that mercy was not yet withdrawn, that a period was not yet put to His forgiveness; but how near the time might be, how short the term of their probation, none could tell, not even the angels in heaven.

Ah! I thought, as we passed out of church, If I could always come to this little church, and hear Mr. Shenstone preach, there would not be much danger of my caring more than I ought for that wicked world Mr. Rutledge talks about.

I had not yet learned that there is not much merit in doing well when there is no temptation to do evil, and that, though there was no harm, but great propriety, in wishing to be kept away from all chance of temptation, still, if my station in life lay in the world, the safest prayer would be, not to be taken out of the world, but to be kept from the evil.

In the afternoon, I went to church alone, and this time on foot, Kitty pointing me out a path across the fields that shortened the distance very considerably. I recognized Mrs. Roberts in the pew in front of me ; and began to feel somewhat ashamed of my unreasonable aversion, as I caught sight of tears on her wrinkled cheeks, and heard a slight trembling in her usually harsh voice. Who knows, I thought, how much she may have suffered, and what heavy cares may have worn those wrinkles so deep, and made her so harsh and exacting? I really determined to be more charitable and patient, and that very evening, by way of bringing good desires to good effects, I went softly to Mrs. Roberts' door and knocked. Now it was one thing to feel the beauty and power of Christian charity and forbearance, under the influence of Mr. Shenstone's earnest voice, and in the solemn stillness of the dusky church, and another to realize it brought down to fact, before the door of Mrs. Roberts' sitting-room, and under the influence of her grim "come in."

My courage was beginning to fail, and I felt tempted to make a precipitate retreat, letting the good resolutions evaporate as good resolutions too often do, in pretty sentiment. But remembering how very contrary this was to Mr. Shenstone's practical directions, after a moment's hesitation, I opened the door and entered. Mrs. Roberts was sitting by a small table with a small lamp upon it, reading a Bible, which, upon my entrance, she shuffled away, very much as if she were ashamed to be caught at it ; then turned toward me with a look of surprise that was anything but agreeable. She could not avoid asking me to sit down, which I did, slipping into the first chair I reached, and stammering out something about thinking she was lonely, and that she might be glad of company for a little while. She stiffly replied she was too much used to being alone, to mind it at all, and thereupon ensued an awkward silence. The mahogany and haircloth looked dismaller than ever by the feeble light of the little lamp, and Mrs. Roberts' face looked colder and harder. How I wished myself out again! What possible good could my coming do? What could I talk about? Mrs. Roberts did not make any attempt to relieve my embarrassment, but sat rigidly silent, wondering, in her heart, I knew, what brought me. I at last hit upon what seemed an unexceptionable topic, and said, what a nice day it had been.

Rather warm for the season, it had appeared to Mrs. Roberts. Then I rung the changes upon the lateness of the fall, the beauty of the woods, my admiration for the little church, the goodness of Mr. Shenstone, but all without producing the slightest unbending in my auditor. She simply assented or dissented (always the latter, I thought, when she conscientiously could), and beyond it I could not get. By and by, I said quite warmly, feeling sure that I should strike the right chord this time:

"What a fine old place this is! I like it better every day."

She gave me a quick, suspicious look, and replied quite snappishly:

"I shouldn't think it would be very pleasant to a young lady of your age."

"What does she mean by being so cross about it?" I pondered. "Is she afraid I am going to put it in my pocket and carry it away with me when I go. Really I think I've done my duty; she won't let me be kind, and now I can, without any scruple, say good night."

As I rose to go, my eye fell on a book on the table, the title of which I stooped to read.

"Ah!" I cried, "'Holy Living and Dying;' how familiar it looks!"

And with a mist of tears before my eyes, I turned over

its well-remembered pages. Rutledge, Mrs. Roberts, were all faded away, and I was in a dim sick-room, where, on a little table by the bed a Bible and Prayer-book and Taylor's "Holy Living and Dying," had lain day after day, and week after week, the guides and comforters of a dying saint. Again I was a child, half frightened at I knew not what, in that tranquil room, half soothed by the placid smile that always met me there. Again the choking sensation rose in my throat, the nameless terror subdued me, as when longing to do something loving, I had read aloud, till my tears blinded me, in this same book. I had never seen it since then; since I had been away at school; but those five years of exile were swept away at a breath as I opened it. I sat down, and, shading my eyes with my hand, glanced over paragraphs that I knew word for word, and that made my heart ache to recall. After a while, however, the bitterness of the first recognition passed away, and it became a sort of sad pleasure to read what brought back so vividly the love and grief of my childhood.

"Shall I read aloud to you?" I said, looking up.

"I shall be very glad to hear you," she answered, in a softened tone.

I do not know whether she divined the cause of my unsteady voice, but it is not unlikely that she did, or the book may have had some similar association for herself, for after I had read nearly an hour, and closed it, she said, with a voice not over firm:

"I am very much obliged to you, young lady; that is a book that, for whatever cause we read it, is good for young and old."

"I shall be very glad to read in it again to you whenever you would like to hear me, Mrs. Roberts," I said, as I rose to go. She accompanied me to the door, and held the light till I had crossed the hall to my own room.

If I had not done her any good by the effort I had made, at least I had done some to myself.

CHAPTER VII.

"He that knows better how to tame a shrew,
Now let him speak; 'tis charity to shew."

It was a lovely afternoon, milder than November often vouchsafes, and perfectly clear. The sun was pretty low, and its slanting beams lighted the smooth lake and threw long shadows across the lawn and over the garden, through the winding paths of which I was now sauntering. The last two days having been marked by no improvement in Mr. Rutledge, he had, of course, not been out of his room, and I had been left pretty much to myself, and had improved the time in perfecting my knowledge of the out-door attractions of the place, and from stable to garden, I now knew it thoroughly. Delightful days those were, saving the occurrence of a little loneliness and ennui that would creep over me as evening approached; delightful days, when, without a thought of care for present or future, I wandered unchecked over the loveliest spot I had as yet seen. A long avenue led from the house to the gate; the lawn on the right sloped down to the lake, a lovely sheet of water surrounded on three sides by woods; and around as far as the eye could reach, stretched wide fields, rich with cultivation, and woodlands where one could almost fancy the axe had never resounded. Further, however, than the gate, and the lake, and the boundaries of the lawn, I had never dared to venture. Dared, though, is not exactly the term; for if I had even thought of the word in that connection, I should probably have gone miles in an opposite direction, to prove that, as to that, I *dared* go anywhere. But I had a sort of chivalrous respect for what I was certain would be the wishes of my protector, now *hors de combat*, and determined, therefore, to stay within the grounds.

Which were ample, enough to satisfy any reasonable young person, certainly, and picturesque enough, and well kept enough for the most fastidious. That particular afternoon, as the declining sun lighted up the dark massive house, and the fine old trees, nearly bare though they were, and the winding paths of the garden and broad fields beyond, Rutledge seemed to me the realization of all I had ever dreamed or read, of beauty and of stateliness. I walked slowly down the garden; the faint smell of some lingering grapes on the arbor overhead perfumed the air; the dead leaves rustled under my feet, alone breaking the stillness peculiar to an autumn afternoon, unprofaned by the many murmurs of insect-life, or the animating song of summer bird. You might listen for hours, and a nut dropping off the tree among the dry leaves, or the tinkling of a cowbell, acres off across the fields, or the letting down a pair of bars somewhere about the farm, would be all the sounds that would break the serene silence.

But just when I was speculating on this, I heard another and a very distinct sound, and looking whence it proceeded, discovered it to be the shutting of the hall door, and presently some one descended the steps and walked leisurely toward the garden. "Hurrah!" I exclaimed aloud, "it's Mr. Rutledge!" And I ran down the path, followed closely by a little terrier, who had introduced himself to my notice at the barn, and not being unfavorably received, had attended my movements ever since. It was not till I was within a few yards of Mr. Rutledge, that the recollection of that unlucky "hero" business brought me to a sudden stand-still, and took all the cordiality out of my greeting He had seen me coming, and was waiting for me, evidently, however, somewhat at a loss to account for my sudden shyness, putting it down, it is probable, though, to the score of

childishness and folly along with the rest of my short-
comings and absurdities.

" I see," he said, extending his hand, " that you've been
getting better as industriously as I have been getting worse.
You begin to look quite like the little girl I brought away
from St. Catharine's."

" I am as well as possible, sir. How is your arm ?"

" It isn't *my* arm! it is Doctor Sartain's. I don't take
any of the responsibility of it. I do not think, however, it
could possibly be much worse, as far as I can be supposed
to judge."

He spoke lightly, but I perceived in a moment that he
was looking very much paler than when I had last seen him.

" Ought you to be out, sir, if you still suffer from it ?"

" I suppose not," he answered, as we walked slowly
down the path; " but to tell you the truth, I was tired of
the house, and *coûte qui coûte*, determined to get a breath
of fresh air."

I couldn't help remembering a certain scene in the library
not many days ago, and giving him rather a wicked look,
made him remember it too.

" I had nobody, however, you see, to make me stay in
and by showing a little firmness at the risk of putting
me in a bad temper, keep me from doing an imprudent
thing."

" I should have supposed, sir, that Mrs. Roberts would
have been in her element on such an occasion. I thought
she always adopted the opposition ticket."

" By the way," he said, laughing, " how do you and Mrs.
Roberts get on ? You weren't very much charmed with
her at first sight, were you ?"

" I do not adore her yet, sir, but I don't think she's quite
as dreadful as I did."

" You thought, poor child," he continued in the same
tone, " that you were in a dreary prison. Absurd as it was,
I could not help feeling dreadfully sorry for you; and ought

to feel so yet, I suppose, only I've had no time lately to feel sorry for anybody but myself."

"Indeed, sir, I think you are the fittest subject," I said a little nettled. "I am as contented as possible, and shouldn't mind staying here a year."

"You like Rutledge, then?"

"Yes," I returned, "but I hardly dare say so, after the way in which Mrs. Roberts snapped me up about it the other night."

"How was that," he asked, with some curiosity.

I related the peculiar manner in which she had received my admiration of it, and ended by asking him if he could imagine what was the cause of it.

"Oh," he said, carelessly, "you must not mind what she says, and make all excuses for her. She has had a great deal of trouble, and is naturally of a nervous and irritable disposition, and living here alone has increased all her pecu liarities in a very great degree."

"In a very uncomfortable degree," I said; and Mr. Rut- ledge was continuing, when his further remarks were cut short by the desertion of two of the party, to wit, the terrier and myself. Now I had no intention of being rude, but looking down at that moment, I discovered that Tigre had possessed himself of one of my gloves, and was gnawing and shaking it with unspeakable *goût*. I made a motion to take it from him, whereon the rascal darted away down the path, then paused an instant, and before I could reach him, was away again toward the barn. I could not surrender so, and forgetting everything but the chase, tore after him at the top of my speed. To see the way in which that little object "streaked" along, looking back at me out of the corners of his eyes! Four legs naturally get over the ground faster than two, and Tigre had the start of me besides, but I had graduated in running at St. Catharine's, and was not to be beaten by such an antagonist as this. It was a steeple chase of no unexciting character.

"We staid not for brake, and we stopped not for stone."

A ditch intervened, but proved no obstacle, and on we tore, till we reached the low fence that separated the grounds from the outbuildings. Tigre shot under it—I took it at a flying-leap. He was making for the barn, and once there, he would baffle me; some favorite hole or inaccessible cranny would shelter him from my pursuit, and hide forever from human gaze my ill-fated glove. This goading thought sustained my flagging energy in the same proportion that the nearness of the goal reanimated that of Tigre. On, on, with desperate resolve! Stephen leaned on his spade to witness the issue of the race, Michael paused, the currycomb in his suspended hand, to see the result; and both involuntarily ejaculated, "Pretty well done!" as on the very threshold of the barn, I sprang upon my opponent and wrested the glove from his determined teeth! And in a frantic romp, we rolled together over and over on the hay, Tigre's active paws and nose in my very face, his excitement carrying him beyond all bounds of decorum, and mine, alas! making me as forgetful of all proprieties; till an approaching footstep recalled me to my senses.

Throwing down Tigre, I sprang up, and hastily shaking the hay from my dress, and pushing back my disordered hair, prepared myself for the lecture I knew I deserved, and "cut and dried" a very impertinent rejoinder. I might have saved myself the trouble; Mr. Rutledge did not take any more notice of me than if I had been Tigre's four-legged and shaggy compatriot. Passing through the barn, he called up one of the men, and gave him orders about the storing of some grain; sent for another upon the question of supplies; talked with Stephen about the state of the grape-vines; with Michael about the condition of the colts; inspected the poultry-yard; pronounced upon the cattle; equally a connoisseur, and thoroughly at home on every point.

During this time, I leaned thoughtfully against the barn door, and reviewed my own conduct, and that of Mr. Rutledge. Of course, I had been unladylike and all that—I knew it as well as anybody; but then, I was old enough to do as I liked, and who had a right to reprove me? Well, nobody *had* reproved me. But then, I knew just as well what he thought of me; I knew he considered me rude, disrespectful, childish; and it would have been ten times less hateful of him to have been angry and done with it, than to have taken no notice of me in any way, just as if he had at once dropped me out of his esteem, consideration and recollection altogether. Angry, humbled, but rebellious, I lingered a long while near him, with a hope that he would say something that I could resent, but no such chance was afforded me. Mr. Rutledge's whole mind was given to his business; and sullenly enough, I called to Tigre and turned toward the house. It was unlucky that I did not know now to whistle—I longed to whistle a tune, and put my hands in my pockets with a jaunty and defiant air as I passed Mr. Rutledge on my way to the house. As it was, I was obliged to content myself with the significant attitude alone, that was meant to convey tones of don't-care sauciness and indifference.

I did not feel at all like going indoors when I reached the house, though it was growing dark very rapidly; and with Tigre at my heels, paced for a long while up and down the stone walk before the steps of the piazza. The sound of Mr. Rutledge's approaching footsteps, far from checking my walk, quickened it considerably, and calling to Tigre, just as he reached the terrace, I started at a brisk pace down the avenue. Mr. Rutledge stopped and called me; I went on, pretending not to hear. He called again, and this time there was no avoiding it. I turned sharply round and said:

"Did you speak, sir?"

"It is too late for you to be out; you will take cold."

"I am not afraid, sir, I shall soon be in;" and I turned away.

"But it is too late," repeated Mr. Rutledge, in a voice I could not mistake. "You must excuse my interference, but I should prefer your coming in now."

I looked down the avenue, the moon was just rising, though day had not quite faded in the west; I wondered what would be the result if I dared rebel; I almost determined I would. But I glanced toward the house; Mr. Rutledge stood holding the door open for me with a resolute quietness that made resistance impossible. With a bad enough grace I turned back, ran up the steps, and passed through the doorway without raising my eyes, and never stopped till I had gained the second story, and locked myself into my own room. Most bitter and most extravagant tears I shed of course, very angry and very implacable resolves I made; and finished off by a violent fit of contrition and humility under the influence of which I started to my feet, anc remembering that it was long past tea-time, hastily smoothed my hair, and followed by my little favorite, ran quickly down the stairs and paused a moment at the library door. All contrition, I half opened it, and looking in, with a most April-like face, whereon smiles and tears contended, said humbly:

"May Tigre and I come in, sir?"

Mr. Rutledge sat reading by the fire; tea was on the table. He looked up a moment, then resumed his book.

"Without doubt; tea is waiting."

I came up to the fire, and stood leaning against the mantelpiece. If he would only look up, and not be so hopelessly cold and indifferent! My penitent speeches fled at the sight; I could never tell him how ashamed and sorry I felt, while he looked so. He did not look any otherwise, however, all through the uncomfortable meal, that I thought never meant to end; nor during the uncomfortable hours that succeeded the uncomfortable meal, that seemed

to stretch out, like a clown's leg, indefinitely and inter
minably.

I had time to realize and become very well acquainted
with the fact, that I had forfeited the newly-acquired position
of companion, and had sunk to the capricious child again.
He had just begun to treat me like a reasonable creature,
and to talk to me for something besides the kindness of
amusing me, and now by my own folly, I had made an end
to all this, and compelled him to see in me nothing but childishness and self-will."

Mr. Rutledge, after tea, had taken up his book again,
and pushed across the table to me some new reviews that
had come that day, saying, perhaps I might find something
amusing in them. That meant I was to amuse myself.
That meant there was to be no talking, no reading aloud, no
dictating of letters.

"It's all Tigre's fault, the little villain!" I ejaculated,
mentally, pushing him angrily down from my lap, as I took up
the literature assigned me. The discarded favorite uttered
a low whine, looked pleadingly up in my angry face, then
walked over to his master, and putting his paws on the arm
of his chair, wagged his tail, and looked imploringly for
permission to spring up. But an impatient "Off, sir!" made
him withdraw abashed, and, standing on the rug between
us, he gazed wonderingly from one to the other. If it had
not been for the precedent of "the dog in the manger,"
and the proverbial comparison of all cross people to "Hall's
dog," I should have been certain that such scenes were
entirely new to Tigre, and that in the bosom of his family
bad tempers were unknown. As it was, he looked very
much mystified and considerably shocked; and at length con
cluded to lie down where he was, at an equal distance from
both antagonists, to whose movements, however, he lent an
attentive eye and ear. But there was not much to repay
his watchfulness; for beyond an occasional symptom of
fatigue on my part, and the periodical turning of the

leaves of Mr. Rutledge's book, dire and entire quiet reigned.

At last, at half past nine, I sprang up, determined to put an end to such an evening; and with a firm resolution not to say more than the one necessary word, "good night," I looked furtively toward my companion. He had closed the book, and leaning his face on his hand sat looking into the fire. Just so he had looked the other night when I had felt so sorry for him; and perhaps I felt the least bit sorry now. To my good night, he replied, carelessly, "Good night;" then, looking up at the clock, said:

"It is early yet."

"But I am very tired," and I moved toward the door.

"I forgot to ask you, sir," I said, turning back, whether you had any letters you would like to have answered?"

"No, thank you; none of any importance. You need not stay."

Contrition, pity, good resolutions, etc., all rushed over me; making three steps back into the room, and swallowing down the rebellious pride and temper, I came out with—

"If I am a child, sir, I am old enough to know when I have done wrong, and not too old to be willing to acknowledge it. I am very well aware that I have been rude and disrespectful to you, and I hope you will have the goodness to excuse it."

He looked at me for a moment with a puzzled air, as if he had not quite expected the sudden humiliation; though I am not sure that my attitude implied so much of humiliation as it did of determined conscientiousness. After a moment's quiet scrutiny, which I bore unflinchingly, he said:

"I am not quite sure that I understand to what you allude, nor how I come to be entitled to pass judgment on your conduct. Pray explain."

The blood mounted to my temples as I answered:

"I acknowledged my faults to you, because they were

committed against you; because to you I owed respect, attention, and courtesy, which I failed to show. I owed this to you as my elder, my host, and the person who, in a manner, had charge of me."

"You seem to have analyzed your duty pretty thoroughly, I must acknowledge! You have stricter views of duty than most persons of your age."

"I don't resent the sarcasm, sir; I know it is well merited."

"I did not intend it sarcastically. I say again you have shown a habit of mind, that, if persevered in, will lead you to a high standard of excellence."

"My failures in duty, since I came here, sir, have been too conspicuous to let me understand you literally."

"You judge yourself severely; I cannot recall any very flagrant offences."

"They would not," I said, as steadily as I could, "be likely to make the same impression on you as on me; with me they were matters of conscience; with you they were, I hope, only occasion of momentary surprise, or better, of indifference and inattention."

"On the contrary," said Mr. Rutledge, "I have watched you attentively since you came here, and have taken quite a strong interest in all you have said and done."

"You are kind," I exclaimed, nettled more at the tone than the words. "Then I shall have to be doubly careful while I have the honor to be under your eye."

He went on, as if he had not heard me: "It has appeared to me that you are in most respects "——

"I must beg," I exclaimed, with an impatient gesture, "that you will defer your summary till I am in a better frame of mind to bear it. Just now, it wouldn't be as profitable as you, no doubt, desire to make it."

"I should be sorry," he replied, "to spoil the humility you have taken such pains to get in order for the occasion, and will not say a word to interfere with it."

"Do you know humility when you see it, sir?" I could not help saying under my breath.

"I learned a good deal about it when I was young," he answered, "and thought, till I came to years of discretion, that I knew all that could be taught in regard to it. But I have since discovered that there is more spurious coin bearing that stamp than almost any other; false pride, wounded vanity, morbid self-love, all get themselves up under the title of humility, and pass current very readily."

I bowed. "Wounded vanity fits me, I think. May I retire, sir, if you have nothing further to say?"

"But I have," he exclaimed, suddenly changing his tone. "I have a great deal more to say." And, taking my hand, he drew me down into the chair beside him, and looking at me with a mixture of kindness and mirth, he said:

"So you are beginning to feel ashamed of yourself, are you? You are such an absurd child, it is impossible to be angry with you, or tired of you, for you are never two minutes alike. Upon my word you're quite a study!"

He did not let go my hand, and though I turned my face away, I could not escape his eyes.

"The uncertain glory of an April day," he exclaimed. "Why, a minute ago you were angry, then you were pleased, now you are frightened, and I suppose you will wind up with a burst of tears. How is one to take you?"

For this style of lecture I had not any retort ready, so I only hung my head, and was silent.

"One moment you are a woman, intelligent and sensible, the next a pettish child. One day you show a sympathy, a tact, a depth of feeling, that go to one's very heart; the next, capricious, silly, and childish, you destroy it all. Sometimes you amuse yourself with Tigre, sometimes with me. And," he continued, after a pause, "sometimes you talk too much, and sometimes, as at present, for instance, too little. Well?" he went on, interrogatively, having elicited no reply. "Well? Have you nothing to say for

yourself? Then go!" he exclaimed, throwing my hand
from him. "I am tired of you; you've been one thing too
long; you've been silent exactly two minutes."

I got up very quickly, and retreated toward the door.

"What?" said Mr. Rutledge, rising and standing by the
fire. "You are going? Why, we have but just made
up."

"I am not quite positive that we have," I answered,
lighting my candle. "It's rather a one-sided make-up, it
strikes me."

"How so? You surely haven't any complaint to make
of me, after all my unexampled goodness to you?"

"Of course not!" I exclaimed; "nothing to say about
your treating me like a baby, and expecting me to behave
like a woman, making me talk to make you laugh, and putting my French and my temper to the hardest tests you
could think of; and then, after I've vexed you by a little
inattention, pushing me aside, as if I weren't capable of
understanding a reproof, and turning your back on me for a
whole evening. *I* have nothing to complain of, of course!
Good night, sir."

"Stay a moment! You take away my breath with all
that catalogue. *I* tease you! *I* laugh at you! Impossible!"

"So I said, sir; and now, if you please, good night."

"Ah! I see I must get you away to your aunt; I shall
spoil you if I keep you here much longer. You are getting
very saucy; Miss Crowen wouldn't own you."

"I am afraid you are right there," I said, with a little
sigh; "I don't think I am improving very much."

"Well, then," he said, seriously, "suppose we determine to do better for the future, and instead of trifling
and teasing, be good sensible friends. Will that suit
you?"

"I think it would be about as one-sided a friendship as
the reconciliation was."

" Why ? Are you not willing to be my friend ?"

" Of course I am; but friendship implies equality, and all that sort of thing, and the power to help each other. Now, you know the absurdity of my being your friend, as well as I know it, and you are laughing at me."

" Do I look as if I were laughing at you ?" And indeed he did not.

" Well, but," I continued, "you know perfectly well I like you, and would do anything in the world to serve you, but that cannot make up for my inability to do it, you see."

" You can do a great deal to help me," he answered. "There are a hundred ways in which you can prove yourself my friend."

I laughed incredulously.

" You doubt it ?" he said. "Listen, little girl. I have not many friends. 1 do not choose to believe in many people. I choose to believe in you; therefore you can do me a kindness by keeping alive in my heart a little faith in human nature. I have many cares to harass me in the present ; much that is sad to remember of the past. By your youth and cheerfulness you can brighten the one ; by your gentleness and sympathy you can soothe the recollections of the other. Youth is gone from me forever, but you can be the link between it and me, and keep it in sight a little longer. You can show me what I once was, earnest, hopeful, and trusting, and so keep me from forgetting what I should be. Above all, you can be honest, and never deceive me ; and faithful, and never withdraw from your allegiance. This is what you can do for me : now, what can I do for you ?"

I tried to speak, but the words wouldn't come, so he helped me to them.

" You find it difficult to enumerate my duties ? Something like this, perhaps, is what you will require of me. I must be careful not to wound the sensitiveness of one naturally much more susceptible to unkindness than myself. I must bear patiently with childish faults, and not forget the indulgence due to youth. I must be just and unflattering, and when my maturer judgment suggests amendment, it is my duty, is it not, to point it out? For having been over the same ground that you are to travel, I can give you many hints that will make your path an easier one, if you will but receive them. And finally, I am to have your interest always at heart, and to observe the same faith and truthfulness toward you that I expect you to maintain toward me. Will you subscribe to that? Is it what you would require of me?"

"Yes, that is fair, I think."

"Well, then, give me your hand upon it, and remember the compact is sealed; we are friends henceforth! Stay, what shall we have as a reminder of this promise? Some pledge, some security is necessary, for we might forget, in the lapse of years, you know."

He went up to an escritoire in a distant corner of the room, and unlocking it, took from a secret drawer two or three little boxes, and from these selecting one, replaced the others, turned the key, and came back to the table. The box contained a bracelet of curious foreign coins, handsomely mounted—a very unique and elegant ornament. This Mr. Rutledge proceeded to fit around my wrist, and with my assistance (having the use of only one hand) clasped.

"Are you willing to wear it always," he said, "*in memoriam?*"

"Yes."

"Well, then good bye to liberty!" and he turned a tiny gold key that I had not noticed in the clasp, and took it out. I must confess to a feeling not unlike bondage when the lock was snapped and the key withdrawn; and involuntarily exclaimed:

"But what if I want to take it off?"

"You must not want to, the thing is irrevocable," he said coolly, fastening the key upon his watch-chain, "help me with this. I have but one hand, you know."

"I don't altogether like the idea," I said obeying him nevertheless, and arranging the little key on his chain.

"You should have thought of that before," he said with a laugh. "It is too late to retract. You may well look serious," he continued noticing my expression. "You forgot, when you made it, what a solemn thing a promise was; but now you'll have something to remind you of its weight, and of the impossibility of getting rid of it. There's no danger now that you'll forget you promised to be my friend; you are bound, irrevocably, solemnly, forever!"

"I thought you weren't to tease," I exclaimed shaking my arm. "It's a very pretty thing, but I shall hate it if I feel that I must wear it always, and that I can't take it off when I want to."

"That's exactly what I meant to guard against. If you could take it off whenever you were tired of it, you would of course soon throw it aside, and there would be an end of compact, friendship and all. I hope you know me better than to suppose I would be satisfied with such an arrangement! *Now*, no matter how many little obstacles in the way of oceans, mountains, and other imbecile contrivances of Nature for the separation of friends, intervene, I shall feel as if I had a check upon your conduct, a guardian of my place in your affections that will make me quite easy about it. For you know of course, the legends that are related of such gifts. I hope you are not superstitious, but you remember the power attributed to them; how such a pledge will surely take the giver's part, and grow tighter and tighter till the pain is unnedurable should the wearer, in her inmost heart, harbor a thought of treachery or faithlessness."

"I suppose, sir, having my arm amputated in case I

changed my mind, would free me from the obligation of wearing it, would it not?"

Mr. Rutledge shook his head gravely.

"I am not of the opinion that it would; but I hope we shall not have to proceed to any such extreme measures."

"Oh, it's my left arm, I shouldn't mind very much. You manage so well with one, that I should feel encouraged by your example, if my handcuff should grow too unbearable."

"Still there are advantages in possessing the use of both, that I would not advise you to give up unnecessarily. For instance, if you wanted a cigar from the case on the top of that étagère, which cannot be reached down without two hands, your temper would be severely tried in having to ring for Thomas to get it for you, or having to depend upon the uncertain charity of a most capricious friend who might or might not, be in the humor to serve you."

"But I shouldn't be likely to want a cigar," I said as standing in a chair I lifted down the case, and took out one.

"There are matches on the mantelpiece," he said nonchalantly as I handed it to him. I brought the matches, drew one, and held it for him, as he lit his cigar.

"Anything more sir?"

"Nothing but the evening paper, which you interrupted me in reading, half an hour ago."

"I beg your pardon, sir, but you haven't had a paper in your hand since tea," I said, hunting among the piles of books and papers on the table for it. "Here it is. Good night."

"Doesn't common kindness suggest your staying to read it for me."

"No sir, it hasn't suggested it as yet," I replied as I took up my long neglected candle. "It suggests 'goodnight,' sir," and the door closed between us before he could answer.

The moon was making my room so bright, that I soon put out the candle as superfluous, and wrapping my dressing gown about me, sat in the bay window for a long, long while, watching the soft shadows on the lawn, and the silvery smoothness of the lake. Ah! how hateful it would be to leave this quiet place, and go among strangers again! The idea of city life had never been altogether attractive, but now seemed most distasteful. Altogether, my new home in New York did not to-night attract my errant fancy, neither did the old school life draw it back regret-fully, from a Present so sufficing that I did not ask myself why it was better than Past or Future; nor why my fancy, usually so eager on the wing, should lie so contentedly in so calm a nest.

CHAPTER VIII.

"Be good, sweet child, and let who will be clever,
Do noble things, not dream them, all day long
So shalt thou make life, death, and that vast forever,
One grand, sweet song."

             KINGSLEY.

"No one who aspires to the honor of writing my let ters," said Mr. Rutledge, as I entered the breakfast-room, "can indulge in such late hours as these. Twenty minutes to eight, Mademoiselle, and the mail goes at ten. You are getting in shocking habits.

"Why sir!" I exclaimed, "I've been up two hours at least."

"And what have you been doing all that time, I should like to be informed?"

"I've been to the barn and fed the kittens, and to the stable and fed the dogs; and then I went to the garden for some flowers, but the frost had been there before me and there wasn't one worth pulling. So to get warm (it's very chilly out this morning) I ran down the avenue, and across to the chestnut wood, and so home by the lake. And here are all the chestnuts those rascally village boys have left!" I exclaimed, throwing a couple of handfuls on the table. "I do wonder, sir, you allow them to commit such trespasses, so near the house too. I would keep at least that grove for my own use. I never saw finer trees, and a week ago they were loaded, Stephen says. Yesterday morning there were two boys up threshing one of the largest trees; I heard them, just as I came under it; the nuts were falling down nicely, so I began to pick them up as unconcernedly as possible, and got my pockets and

109

apron full, while the young vagabonds up in the tree didn't dare, of course, to breathe, for fear of being discovered and had to see me carrying off their precious nuts without a word. I didn't leave a shell, I assure you; I never enjoyed anything more and went down this morning in hope of another adventure."

"I hope," said Mr. Rutledge very seriously, "that you will never do such an imprudent thing again. You should never go into the woods without taking Kitty with you, least of all, when there are such marauders about."

"I took Solo and Dash with me, and I would have kept them up there till noon, if I had caught them at it again, the rascals."

"You are very thoughtless, not to be aware of the danger of provoking such lawless fellows."

"I cannot see the danger; not half a mile from the house, and with two great dogs to back me. And 'if the worst came to the worst,' I know I could outrun the longest-legged loafer among them."

The words were hardly out of my mouth, when I remembered that this latter accomplishment had not appeared to win me any favor from Mr. Rutledge in the unlucky affair of the glove yesterday; and, with a blush, I hastily, by way of effacing the impression, continued:

"But if you don't approve, of course I will not do so again; and when Kitty can't be spared to go with me, I will stay nearer the house."

"Kitty always can be spared, and though I am sorry to insist upon your taking her, I shall be much better satisfied to know you are not alone."

"Very well, sir. May I trouble you for another biscuit?"

"You have a fine color this morning. Rutledge agrees with you."

"Famously," I replied, applying myself with great satisfaction to my breakfast; "and as I have so much to do before ten o'clock, there's no time to lose."

"Not a minute; but I should be uncomfortable to think you were starved; don't hurry so frantically."

"There! I'm ready now," I exclaimed, in a few minutes following him into the library with a light step, and singing snatches of a gay tune.

"I see you do not dread work," he said, as I sat down before the writing-table, and took up a pen with alacrity.

"Not when I can see daylight through it, sir, and a reasonable prospect ahead of getting it done. Now, sir."

And Mr. Rutledge dictated, and I wrote for an hour, without the slightest intermission. At the end of that time he said :

"Do you think you are equal to the task of answering those two letters by yourself, of which I will give you a general idea, while I look over those accounts with Maurice and Ruthven, to be added to the New Orleans letter? It is important that they should all be dispatched to-day."

"If you are willing to trust me, I am willing to try."

And I immediately began the task. It was by no means an easy one; but by referring to the letters to be answered, and by keeping before my mind the synopsis Mr. Rutledge had briefly given me, I was able to finish them to his satisfaction ; added the memoranda he had been making to the other letter, sealed and addressed them all, and had the package ready for Michael when he appeared at the door at ten o'clock.

"You have worked pretty well for two hours," said Mr. Rutledge, as for a moment I leaned my head on my hand. "I am afraid you are tired."

"Not in the least," I said bravely, looking up.

"Then get your bonnet and come out with me. It is too fine a day to stay in the house."

As I followed him through the hall, Mrs. Roberts encountered us at the dining-room door. Her greeting to me was stiffer than ever. To Mr. Rutledge she said:

"If you can spare the time, sir, you would oblige me very

much by looking over the 'household expenses' this morning; Dorothy has got her account with the grocer in a great snarl, and hasn't done much better with the butcher, and I can't make them all come out right."

"My good friend," said Mr. Rutledge, "if you had appealed to me any other time, I might have helped you, but I have been doing quite as much this morning as I think prudent; to-morrow I will attend to the books."

"I am sorry," said Mrs. Roberts, uneasily; "but to-day is the day the grocer brings in his account, and I don't like those sort of people to suppose there's any irregularity in the accounts we keep. They're always ready enough to take advantage."

"Couldn't I help you, Mrs. Roberts?" I asked. "I should be very willing to."

She gave me a look which plainly said, " *You* help *me!*" but she merely answered:

"Thank you, Miss, but Mr. Rutledge understands the books better than any one; and if he felt able "——

"But he doesn't," said the gentleman in question. "The grocer can come to-morrow with his bill. It will not signify for once."

Still Mrs. Roberts demurred, and I saw there would be no peace till she worried Mr. Rutledge into it, so I renewed my offer of assistance. This time it seemed to strike her in a more favorable light.

"If I didn't mind the trouble, perhaps I might help her reckon it up. She wasn't as quick at figures as she used to be."

I would do my best, I said, untying my bonnet. But Mr. Rutledge peremptorily interfered.

"By no means, Mrs. Roberts. She has been writing two hours already for me; she must have nothing more at present," and he walked on toward the door.

But the housekeeper was by no means vanquished, and clung tenaciously to my offer. She was sure, she said,

the young lady would be glad to oblige an old woman.
And duty so plainly pointed that way, that I wavered no
longer. I had made up my mind to be kind to Mrs.
Roberts; here was the chance to carry my good resolutions into effect. Throwing my bonnet into a chair, I
said :

"If you will excuse me from walking with you, Mr. Rutledge, I will see what I can do to help Mrs. Roberts."

"I cannot excuse you," he replied, with decision. "I
do not think it best for you to be confined to the house any
longer at present."

"Oh," I exclaimed, while Mrs. Roberts looked on anxiously, "I have been used to studying and writing nine
hours out of the twenty-four at school, and this morning's
business has been mere play. I shall not think of feeling
tired for hours yet, so please do not make any objections.
Come, Mrs. Roberts," I continued, going toward the stairs,
and giving her a little nod.

She hesitated, and I saw her glance uneasily at Mr. Rutledge. I now perceived that he was more than vexed; but
I was strong enough to dare even that, when I was as cer
tain as I now was about what I ought to do. He naturally,
I thought, didn't like to have his wishes interfered with ;
but that could not alter the right for me, "and he cannot
help but see that when he thinks it over." So again summoning Mrs. Roberts, I excused myself to him, and ran upstairs, followed lumberingly by the housekeeper, while the
hall door closed, with no gentle emphasis, between us and
the sunny autumn morning.

I am only doing Mrs. Roberts justice, when I say that on
that particular occasion, she manifested diplomatic talents,
which, in another sphere of life, would have won her no
inconsiderable place. I had not given her credit for the
tact and acuteness that developed themselves that morning,
and which, added to her well-known decision and unalter-
able devotion to the one idea that happened to be upper

most, formed the elements of a character I had not sufficiently looked up to. This, of course, I did not appreciate at first, and went at my task with the kindest desire to get Mrs. Roberts out of her perplexity, and unravel the tangled threads of Dorothy's arithmetical inaccuracies.

It was the greatest effort of self-denial that I could well have attempted, for besides the heroism required to give up my walk with Mr. Rutledge, on this splendid day, and spending the morning instead with the only person I sincerely disliked in the house, and in the room of all others that I was most averse to, was added my unconquerable detestation of mathematical calculations of all kinds. From the multiplication table up, I held all such exercises in abomination. But Miss Crowen, with her usual discrimination, having detected this weak point in my character, bent her whole mind to the strengthening of it, and night and day, labored to instill into my unwilling brain the rules and methods it was constitutionally unfitted to receive. Other studies were made to bend before it; favorite pursuits were sacrificed to this one object; passionate tears had washed the distracting figures from the hated slate; high tragedy had been enacted before the blackboard, and stormy scenes in the study had only strengthened Miss Crowen in her determination to enforce obedience, and her pupil in resistance to what she looked upon as tyrannical injustice. The result of this continued struggle was, that after nearly five years of drilling in that branch of study, to the exclusion of more congenial pursuits, I left St. Catharine's with about the amount of mathematical knowledge usually acquired by girls of ordinary application in a year and a half. I was too fresh, however, from such exercises, not to be quite competent to master the difficulties presented in the Rutledge "Household Expenses," and before an hour had passed, had reduced the "snarl" to a very comprehensible state, and calling to Mrs. Roberts to come and look over it, I began to explain the errors I had found, and the manner in which I had corrected them, in as lucid language as I could command.

But Mrs. Roberts was hopelessly obtuse; she put on her glasses and fumbled among the loose papers on which Dorothy registered her financial transactions, with agonizing bewilderment. In vain I assured her I had copied them off on the book, and they would give her no light on the subject; she could not give them up, and again and again looked them over, and bemoaned Dorothy's inaccuracy and her own stupidity. She hoped I would excuse her, but she could not really get her mind quite clear about that last column; would it be asking too much of me to run it over again aloud. I tried to be patient, and again went over it, and explained the case in all its bearings. I resolutely kept my back to the window, and would, if I could, have forgotten that there was such a thing as sunshine in the world; but, however I may have succeeded in that attempt, I could not help hearing Mr. Rutledge's step on the stone walk outside, as he returned from the direction of the stables; nor could I help being aware that he entered the house, paused a moment in the library, then came upstairs. The fragrance of an Havana penetrating the keyhole, told he had passed this door, and gone into his dressing-room. My fingers flew over the columns; in proportion as my patience diminished Mrs. Roberts' dullness increased; she fretted, she groaned, she bewildered me with questions, and almost crying with vexation, I exclaimed, as I heard the horses coming up from the stable:

"Oh, Mrs. Roberts! Won't you please understand! Can't you see the only mistake was in that second figure, and that I've put it all right? Can't you see it balances?"

But Mrs. Roberts couldn't see, and her obtuseness redoubled, as Mr. Rutledge's door opened and closed again, and his steps echoed down the staircase and across the hall. I could not help leaning back, and glancing out of the window, while tears of disappointment and vexation rushed to my eyes, as I saw Mr. Rutledge drive off with Michael in the light waggon, and the identical pair of fast trotters that I had made admiring acquaintance with a few days since at the stable. As their hoofs clattered rapidly down the avenue, I could have thrown the account-books at Mrs. Roberts' head, for in truth it began to dawn upon me that that worthy person had had some ends of her own to serve in keeping me so long at the work of elucidation, and that something besides natural dullness of comprehension had been in the way of her understanding my calculations. I began to reflect on the absurdity of supposing that a woman who had for years had the charge of such an establishment as Rutledge, could be in reality so dull and ignorant as she had appeared this morning. There could be no doubt but that she had intended to keep me in the house; for what cause, I could not yet determine.

The mists that had obscured her intellect, began now, however, to clear away; and it was not long before she pronounced herself quite satisfied on all points, even on the vexed and tortured question of that "last column," and I was released from my task. I did not doubt the sincerity of Mrs. Roberts' rather meagre thanks, nor the truthfulness of her slight commendation of my patience. It was not in her way to flatter, and I knew that for some cause she distrusted me, and that whatever praise she awarded me, was fairly wrung from her by her stubborn sense of justice. Though I knew Mrs. Roberts had been generalling this morning, there was that about her that forbade my doubting her habitual truthfulness. I merely replied that she was welcome to the assistance I had been able to give her, and with a weary step I left the room.

At the door I found Tigre waiting for me with wistful earnestness in his erected ears and attentive eyes. I took him in my arms, and carried him into my own room, where I tried to enter with spirit into the frolic he seemed to desire. But it proved a miserable failure; I could not enjoy that or anything else; my head ached "splittingly," and the sunshine streaming in at the window made it worse, and playing with Tigre made it worse, and reading, writing, thinking, all made it worse. What should I do? I hadn't even the spirit to go out into the fresh air; but, leaning wearily on the dressing-table, counted the heads on my bracelet, and wondered that I could have been so happy this morning.

By and by, I summoned sufficient energy to smooth my hair, and bathe my head with eau de Cologne; then, calling Tigre, I concluded to go to the library for a book. I found that apartment rather more endurable than my own just then, as the sun did not come in there at that hour of the morning, and the light was very subdued, and the room was quietness itself; so, taking a book from the table, I arranged the cushions of the sofa alluringly, and motioning Tigre to his place beside me, sat down to reading. It would have been a thrilling book that could have riveted my wandering thoughts that morning; and unluckily the book I had chosen was very far from that stamp; it was a third-rate novel of the highly wrought order, into whose pages characters, incidents, scenes, were crowded in such bewildering profusion, that one's appreciative powers were fagged out and exhausted, before the first chapter was accomplished, and, like a restaurant dinner, where all the dishes taste alike, there was but one flavor to the whole array of dramatis personæ from heroine to *bête noire;* but "one gravy" for roast, bouilli, and ragout. The wearying tide of adjectives and interjections stunned my senses; the book slipped from my hands, and, leaning my head on the cushions, my eyes closed, and with one arm round Tigre and the other under my head, I slept, realizing even in sleep that the bracelet touched my cheek.

The precise duration of my nap I could not tell; but when I awoke, it was to find Mr. Rutledge standing by me. I started up, and he said:

"I meant to be angry, but you look so pale and tired I think you are punished enough already. Does your head ache still?" he continued, laying his hand on my shoulder. "You would have done better to have followed my advice. I knew you would repent."

"I don't repent, though," I said, quite decidedly. "I haven't even thought of repenting, and would do it all over again, if the same circumstances occurred."

"You begin to relent toward Mrs. Roberts, then," he said, coolly. "I thought yesterday you didn't particularly affect my worthy housekeeper."

"My liking or disliking her doesn't alter the question of my duty. And, Mr. Rutledge, I don't think it's kind in you to pretend not to understand my motive. You must know that in all reason, I could not prefer staying worrying in the house over some tiresome accounts, to going out on such a splendid day; and you must see that there was no way for me to refuse her conscientiously. You yourself say she is old, and particular, and fixed in her ways; and I am certain you often put yourself out to humor her; how can you blame me for not leaving her to fret and worry over something that I could do for her in half the time?"

Mr. Rutledge looked down at me, but said nothing, while I briefly concluded my defence, adding at the end, a concise request that he'd please not say anything more about the matter.

"We will consider it amicably adjusted, then," he said, "and direct our attention to something else. What, for instance, do you propose doing with yourself this afternoon?"

"I haven't thought anything about it. Take a walk, perhaps."

"You are so fond of being useful," he said, rather wickedly, "would you like to go down to the village for the letters?"

"Yes, I should like it very well, only I don't know the way exactly; but I suppose I can inquire."

"Will you ride or walk? Michael can drive you down, or Kitty can walk with you."

"I think I'll walk, if it makes no difference," I said, indifferently.

"I suppose," said Mr. Rutledge, "you don't like riding on horseback?"

Like it! There was no need to answer; my face told fully my enthusiastic preference for that mode of travel.

"I do not know if there is any horse in the stable that I would venture to let you ride. Madge I am afraid of. How long since you've ridden?"

"Not since I've been away at school; but I'm not a bit afraid. I used to ride constantly at home. I had the dearest little pony; but he was spirited enough, and I always managed him. I don't really think you need be afraid to trust me," I went on, pleadingly.

Mr. Rutledge shook his head; Madge was only fit for an experienced rider; she was too full of spirit for such a child to manage. Now, Madge had been my secret admiration ever since I had had the entrée of the stables, and I felt that life offered, at that moment, no more tempting honor than a seat on her back; and it may be supposed I was not lukewarm in my pleading. I urged, coaxed, entreated; I appealed to his generosity, I promised everlasting gratitude.

"Dear Mr. Rutledge," I cried, "you know I go at my own risk; it will be my own fault if anything happens to me. And oh! it will be *so* unkind if you refuse me the very first favor I ever asked of you!"

I am not sure about the tears at this point of the petition, though I was quite in earnest enough to have cried, and I had begun to appreciate the availability of tears as a weapon sufficiently to have used them if they had occurred. Certain it is, however, that Mr. Rutledge began to relent, and at last, though evidently much against his better judgment, gave the desired permission.

"But remember, I don't approve it."

"Oh! but you will," I exclaimed, "when you see how quiet she'll be with me!"

"And you have no habit," he continued.

"I'll manage that. Kitty's a host in herself; I'll press her into the service."

My companion half sighed as I flew out of the room and upstairs, where, in two minutes' time, I was deep in consultation with Kitty on the subject of the habit. She entered into the plan with great ardor, and racked her brains to devise something feasible. I sat on the bed and waited breathlessly for the bright thought that I was sure would come, sooner or later, to Kitty's clever brain.

"You say you have a jacket that will do," she said, meditatively.

"Yes, the very thing—black cloth, trimmed with buttons and all that; and now, if I only had a long enough skirt. Oh, Kitty! can't you think of something?"

Kitty knit her brows, and, after a moment, said, thoughtfully:

"There's a whole piece of black bombazine, that was left over from the last funeral, upstairs in a trunk I know of. Sylvie and I could run up the breadths in no time. Would you mind?"

"Oh, Kitty! I couldn't quite stand that!" I exclaimed, between a shudder and a laugh. "Can't you think of anything else?"

"I have it!" cried she, with a sudden illumination of countenance. "I have it!"

"What!—how? Oh, do tell me!"

"Why," said my artful maid, with mischief in every line of her bright face, "why, Mrs. Roberts, by way of keeping me busy this morning, gave me her best bombazine dress to rub off and press out, and it's downstairs this minute; and you see, she always has a wide hem to her dresses, and a great piece turned in at the top; so by letting out all this,

and putting on a piece around the waist, where it'll come
under the basque, it will make you the very nicest riding-
skirt in the world." And Kitty's eyes danced.

"Capital!" I cried. "But then, Kitty, I'm afraid it
wouldn't be right; I'm afraid "——

"Don't disturb yourself, Miss; it'll be ready before you
want it," and my conscientious scruples were cut short by
the abrupt exit of my maid, who was out of hearing before
I could remonstrate.

The dinner-bell rang at the same moment, and I ran down
at the summons, too much excited, and too nervous, however, to do more than go through the ceremony of a meal.
Mr. Rutledge was rather thoughtful; he called me a foolish
child for being so much excited about such a trifling affair.
As I rose to leave the table, he asked me if I had succeeded
in improvising a habit. I said yes, and that my present perplexity lay only in the matter of a hat. He proposed to see
if he would help me, by a review of his chapeaux, past and
present; and after trying on at least a dozen caps and hats,
beaver, straw, cloth, and velvet, I decided upon a little
black jockey cap, that was the trimmest, nattiest thing imaginable, and I knew, from Mr. Rutledge's approving
glance, vastly becoming. So I bounded off to my room,
to submit myself to Kitty's hands for the next twenty minutes.

Very pretty, she assured me, I looked, as, the last touch
bestowed, she stepped back to take a survey of me.

"So slim and elegant, Miss, in your black clothes, and
that jaunty little cap, and your hair so smooth and tight to
your head; nothing in the way, nothing flying," said Kitty,
with a gesture signifying her aversion to the decorated style
of equestrian costume, so popular with our contemporaries.
"And that skirt!" she exclaimed, smothering her laughter,
"who would think it was the very one Mrs. Roberts had
on, day before yesterday, when she was all dressed to go
to the Parsonage! Wouldn't her hair stand on end, Miss,

if she could see it trailing along the floor! The precious dress she always takes off before she'll go down to the kit-chen, even to give an order!"

"Oh, I'm really sorry, Kitty! Indeed, I've a great mind not to wear it."

"Why, Miss," she said, in alarm, "don't think anything about it. It won't hurt it a bit; I'll have it just as good as when she gave it to me, if I sit up half the night to fix it!"

And Kitty buttoned my boots with great *empressement*, and as Madge's hoofs struck on the stone walk below, she hurried me off, thrusting my gloves and handkerchief into my hand, and wishing me a very nice time.

CHAPTER IX.

" Thy steps are dancing toward the bound
   Between the child and woman,
And thoughts and feelings more profound,
   And other years are coming."

                         SIDNEY WALKER.

IF I say that my heart beat a little quicker, as I came in sight of the group before the steps, I shall acknowledge to no inexcusable weakness. Mrs. Roberts stood a little at one side, with a darker, more gloomily prophetical cast of countenance than ever, and seemed to be giving some unwelcome advice to Mr. Rutledge, who, saying briefly, " I cannot disappoint her now," turned uneasily to Michael, who held the horses, and who was to accompany me, and appeared to give him some emphatic directions, to which the man, from time to time, nodded assent.

And the mare herself! Michael's whole strength was but sufficient to control her under the unaccustomed restraint. She was a beautiful animal, glossy black, clean-limbed, and delicately made, with a head and neck that told " she came of gentle blood," as plainly as aristocratic lineaments ever spoke. The insane absurdity of my controlling such a fiery, powerful thing as she, rushed sickeningly over me, but I never for a moment entertained the idea of giving up. If I had been ten times surer than I was, that I should be thrown within the first half mile, I should have rejected with scorn the advice of Mrs. Roberts, who now came forward and favored me with her views on the subject of the proposed expedition. I had more than one reason for desiring to keep her at a distance ; so raising my skirt as carefully as I could, I ran down the steps to where Mr. Rutledge stood. When he saw me, he immediately cleared his brow of the shade of anxiety that had been contracting it during his conversation with Michael, and said, smilingly:

"Madge Wildfire is as impatient to be off as her mistress."

"Pretty creature!" I said, patting her neck with a hand that trembled visibly; then, with a voice that was meant to be very cheerful and unconcerned, I added:

"What a perfect afternoon it is! I wish you were going."

"I wish I were," he said, taking in at a glance the unsteadiness of the hand that patted Madge's neck, and the direful whiteness of the lips that spoke. After a moment of reflection he turned to Michael and gave him some order that sent him rapidly toward the stable, while Thomas was summoned to hold the horses, and telling me to wait a moment, Mr. Rutledge hurried into the house. I did not rightly comprehend the reason of this delay, till I saw him reappear, with riding gloves on and a whip in his hand followed by Mrs. Roberts, whose astonishment and anxiety were undisguised.

"It's madness sir! With one hand you can hardly guide your own horse, let alone that creature she's to ride; and if you'll forgive me for being so plain, you may have to pay dearly for it! You are humoring a foolish girl at the risk of your life!"

Mr. Rutledge stopped short, "My old friend," he said in a tone of decision, "you know I will always bear with more from you, than from almost any one else; but you must remember, there is such a thing as going too far. I cannot be interfered with in this way, even by you," and he descended the steps.

Mrs. Roberts groaned, and turned away, silenced temporarily. Michael reappeared with Mr. Rutledge's horse, Madge was soothed, and brought to where I stood, and Michael tossed me up on her back. Before I could realize

the dizzy height, or get the reins fairly in my grasp, she
was off with an eager bound that showed how great had
been her impatience at the delay. I kept my seat—more I
did not attempt to do, as at a tearing pace she darted
down the avenue. The reins were in my hands, but
they might as well have been around her neck, for all
the use I made of them. Fortunately the gate was
open, but before we reached it Mr. Rutledge was by my
side.

" To the left," he said, as we dashed through it. It was,
however, because Madge's fancy lay that way, that she
took it; I cannot flatter myself that my faintly suggestive
touch on the left rein had anything to do with influencing
her decision. And *on* we flew, Michael clattering behind
us. It was a pretty clear straight road, bordered on both
sides by trees, and slightly descending ground. In a
moment, Mr. Rutledge spoke, but so quietly and unexcitedly that I felt soothed even by the tone.

" You sit very well; don't lean forward quite so much ;
that's better," and in a few minutes he added, " keep a
steady rein, don't pull suddenly or hard, but just firm.
She is perfectly kind, and you can manage her very nicely
after you get used to her."

A confidence in Madge's good disposition, certainly was
encouraging, and as Mr. Rutledge didn't seem to feel any
alarm or discomposure of any kind, but on the contrary, an
assurance that I was equal to what I had undertaken, per
haps, after all I was ; and under these influences, something
like composure began to return to my startled nerves and
something like strength to tighten my hold upon the reins.
Still we were tearing onward, Michael now left far behind,
and the question of *stopping* began to exercise me painfully. I knew from the pull upon the bridle, and the eager
bounds of the animal beneath me, that as yet, it formed no
part of *her* intention. Presently Mr. Rutledge said, quite
nonchalantly—

"I think, when we begin to ascend that hill on our right, we'd better pull up a little. Keep a steady rein till we get there. Let Madge know who's mistress; the lower one's the curb; now, pull; whoa, Madge!"

And Madge *did* whoa, that is, she slackened in a slight, a very slight degree, her frantic pace, checked perhaps by the new determination of her rider's rein, and the startling emphasis of that decided "whoa."

It was but a very slight symptom of irresolution on her part, but it gave me the advantage; from that moment I determined to be mistress, and before we reached the brow of the hill, Madge had quieted to a walk. I was as white as a ghost, and shook all over, but my companion was considerate enough not to notice it, and checked with a look, Michael's exclamations of alarm, as with open eyes and mouth, that attendant galloped up.

Several miles of country had been got over, before I began, in any degree, to realize that I was out for the purpose of enjoying myself, or before I was able to think of anything in heaven or earth, save the beast I rode.

At last, however, I began to feel, with a sense of exultation the more elating in proportion to the struggle I had had to gain it, that I had my horse under entire control, and with that consciousness, color came to my cheeks, and warmth to my numb hands and feet; I could laugh and talk then, could see that the sky was clear and sunny, and the country we were crossing, the very prettiest and most picturesque imaginable; could feel the wind blowing fresh against my face, as we galloped rapidly over the open road; or listen, with an ear keenly awake to every phase of pleasure, to the rustling of the dead leaves beneath our horses' feet, and the clear ringing of our voices in the still air, as we sauntered along woody passes, or threaded our way through unfrequented bridle-paths.

"How delightful it is!" I exclaimed, and my exclamation was echoed in my companion's look of intense enjoyment. There was a freedom from restraint, an abandonment to the pleasures of the present, that I had not seen in him before. Ten years of care and trial seemed lifted from his brow; a glow of health on his face, and a clear light in his eye, made him almost handsome; and for the time, it was easy for me to forget the differences of age and circumstances; it was an involuntary thing to look upon him as the companion whom most I liked of all I had ever found; the readiest, the keenest, the kindest; one who understood me, himself, and all the world; who could govern me, but whose very tyranny was pleasant; who was, in fact, so far and unquestionably my superior, that it pleased him to lay aside all differences, and be, for the time, the companion and equal of a child, whose very youth and ignorance, appeared the passports to his favor.

For the first time, during this ride he talked to me of himself, and of his past life, but a past far separated from all association or connection with Rutledge. He recounted, for my entertainment, travels and adventures, that had the most exciting charm to my crude ear, at least. And indeed I doubt whether an older and more critical taste could have found anything but pleasure in his vigorous sketches of scenes and incidents that had impressed themselves upon his memory. He was, indeed, an excellent *raconteur*, and had, beyond any one I have ever known, the power of bringing up, in bodily shape and presence, the places and characters he chose to recall. Whether it was a sunrise among the Alps, or a scene in a French café, it was equally distinct and life-like; I saw the glittering of the sharp cloud piercing icy peaks, as, one by one, they caught the rosy sunlight; or, the men and women in their foreign dress and eager manner, lived and spoke before me, gesticulated, rattled off their voluble absurdities, and vanished from the scene, to give place to pictures of quiet English villages, with sunny meadows and long green lanes, grey churches and mossy gravestones, or quaint old Flemish towns, with their "cathedrals vast and dim," and tall, gloomy houses overhanging the narrow streets; or the rich warmth of some Italian landscape; or the vastness of the illimitable plains of Granada, that stretch away on all sides from the ruined Alhambra; Constantinople, with its mosques and minarets; the Holy City, with its mongrel population and half profaned associations, all were distinctly realized by me, as if I had in very deed been there. Mr. Rutledge rarely exercised his talents for description, and my enraptured attention seemed to surprise him.

"You are an admirable listener," he said, laughingly; "no flattery could be subtler than that attitude of interest. I should grow positively garrulous if you were with me much. I must send you away! I hate a talking man; with such an eloquent face before me, I shall learn to talk hours at a time."

"I won't look at you if you don't want me to, only don't stop talking. Ah! please!" I exclaimed, as he pointed to the rapidly sinking sun, and turned his horse's head toward home. "I cannot go home yet."

"But it will be dark before we reach it, as it is," he said.

"There's a moon!"

"I shall never let you come again, if you are not 'good' about going home. Come!"

His tone wasn't alarming, and I said: "I've just got in the spirit of it; and that's the best piece of road we've seen yet. I couldn't think of going back under another mile; indeed I couldn't."

Mr. Rutledge still persisted in refusing permission, though, as I said, his tone was not alarming; not, for instance, as it had been last evening, when he called me in from the terrace. Though his face was perfectly serious, there was a look of smothered merriment about his mouth, that quite recalled the crayon sketch in my trunk. He was a good horseman, and no attitude could have been more advantageous to him than his present one, sitting easily and gracefully on his fine horse, and indicating with a turn of his head, the direction which he desired, nay, commanded me to take. We were just on the summit of a hill; the sunset was lighting up the woods behind, the road stretched smooth and broad before us. I turned my head as decidedly in that direction, saying:

"There's another road turns off to the left of that bridge toward Rutledge, I know, for we drove there the other day; and it isn't more than two miles further. That's the way *I'm* going home. 'They'll have fleet steeds that follow.'"

And, touching Madge, I was off, without a look behind. It was, indeed some minutes before I turned around to see how near Mr. Rutledge might be; but what was my chagrin on finding myself alone, Michael only visible descending the hill at full speed. I paused to wait for him with ill-concealed impatience.

"Where's your master, Michael?"

"Gone back, miss."

"Are you sure?"

"Yes, miss. I think he's going home by way of the village, and that he's going to get the letters from the office on his way."

"Couldn't we overtake him possiby?"

"I'm afraid not, miss; we've got two miles further to go, and the horses are not as fresh as when we started, miss."

That was a very palpable fact; indeed, both Michael's arguments seemed equally invincible; but I evaded them by exclaiming:

"Isn't there any shorter way back to the village? Think quick, Michael, I know there must be."

Michael thought, as quickly as he could, no doubt, but very slowly, it seemed to me.

"Yes, Miss," he said, meditatively, after a moment's

pause, "yes, Miss, there is another; but it's but a wild road for the like of you to be travelling—so late too."

"Which way is it?" I said, with an impatient wave of the hand.

"To the right, Miss, about a quarter of a mile further on; it strikes off through Hemlock Hollow. It's a lonesome road, though, Miss, and there may be one or two pairs of bars to take down before we get to the end."

"You're sure, however, that you know the way, and that it's shorter?" I asked.

Michael thought he was sure.

"Then, my man, we'll try it; and keep as near to me as you can."

And turning Madge's head, I gave her liberty to do her best. Michael had much ado, I fear, to keep in sight of me; but I cared very little for his guardianship, or indeed for any other circumstance or occurrence whatsoever, so long as I reached the village and the post-office before Mr. Rutledge quitted them.

Michael was nearer right than he generally had the good fortune to be, when he described the Hemlock Hollow road as a wild and lonesome one. It was an unfrequented wood road; the trees met above it; there was neither foot-path nor fence on either side; it was just a way hewn down and cleared for one wagon to pass. Lying in a hollow, it was always damper, and colder, and darker, than anywhere else, and as I pressed on, I couldn't help being struck with the chilliness of the air, and "the rich moist smell of the rotting leaves" that lay thick upon the road. How fast the light had faded! I never knew twilight to come on so rapidly.

"Never mind," I reasoned, "it cannot be long before we are out of this hollow, and then we shall be so near the village that I shall not mind the dark, and after that Mr. Rutledge will be with us. He will not be angry, I know; there was too much laughing about his mouth, when he

motioned me homeward. I am sure he won't be angry;
but I almost wish——Michael!"

"Yes, Miss," called out my attendant in the distance.

"How long before we are out of this wood?"

"I don't rightly remember the length of it, Miss," gasped
the panting esquire, as he reached me.

"Well," I said, "its growing dark so fast, you must
whip up, and make all the haste you can."

"Saving your presence, that's exactly what I've been
doing for the last three hours; and though I'm as anxious
to get on as yourself, Miss, my horse is just a bit *exhausted.*"

I had to suppress a laugh at his dejected looks. Melancholy had marked for her own both horse and rider.

"Well, Michael," I said, encouragingly, "it cannot be
very long before we reach the village, and then you shall
have time to rest. Keep up as well as you can, meantime."

And unable to control my own impatience, I rode on,
and in a little while was again out of sight, or rather out
of hearing, for sight was fast becoming a useless gift, so
rapidly had night descended, and so effectually did the
thick trees shut out what of light might have been still left
in the sky. I again called to Michael, who again was far
behind, and again had to be waited for. I was certain we
had gone three or four miles, and yet there was no sign of
an opening, no change in the monotonous, narrow road.

"Are you quite positive, Michael," I said, "that this is
the right road? Are you certain it leads to the village?"

He had never been over it but once, he said, and that
was two years ago, but he thought he knew it; it didn't
seem so long to him before, though, he must confess.

A genuine pang of fear crossed me as I saw the man's
bewilderment and uncertainty, and as I realized that I must
depend on myself, for he knew no more about the road than
I did, it was plain, and seemed, indeed, fast losing his wits,
from sheer fatigue and terror.

" Think a minute, Michael," I said, in a firm voice, " how ought the road to terminate? Does it come directly out on the turnpike, or do we have to cross any fields before we reach it?"

If he remembered right, there was a field to cross—no—he couldn't be sure, on the whole, that the road didn't open right into the turnpike, after all. Perhaps it didn't, though; it was two years since he had been over it, and how could he remember—so dark as it was, too!

A moment's reflection told me that there was no use in going back till we had tried a little further, for the turnpike could not be very distant. I thought I had a general idea of where the village lay, and that we were going toward it. So cheering up my attendant as well as I could, and suiting my pace to his, I endured another half mile of pretty uncomfortable suspense before an opening in the trees, and a patch of cloudy sky, sent a ray of comfort to my heart.

" Courage, Michael!" I cried, " here's the end of our troubles—here's an opening in the woods. Is this the way the road looked, do you think?"

Michael sprang down from his horse with great alacrity, to let down the bars that retarded our progress. Ah, yes! This was all right—just as he said; he knew we had to cross a field.

Quite reassured, I told him to ride on in front, as he seemed to know the way now, and he valiantly led on, along the edges of what seemed to me a ploughed field; but Michael being positive that there was a beaten road along it, I submitted to his judgment. By and by, we came to another pair of bars, which Michael confidently took down, and conscientiously put up after we had passed through, and again led the van.

In the meantime, I watched the sky with anxiety. The wind was rising, and swept cold across the fields; the clouds, though broken and flying, obscured the light of the

moon, yet low in the east. I had no way but to trust to
Michael, and I tried to do it without any misgivings, as he
seemed so confident; but it was not long before he began
to waver again. After a pause, and a moment's bewildered
gaze around, he struck his hand upon his forehead, and exclaimed :

"Upon my honor, Miss, it's my opinion we're in a dreadful fix! I know no more than the dead where we are!"

"Fool!" I cried, starting forward in an agony of apprehension, "why didn't you say so before?"

Michael gave a miserable groan, and seemed utterly con-
founded.

"Let us go back as fast as ever we can!" I exclaimed.

"That's just what I can't see how to do," whined my
hopeful guide, "for between letting down, and putting up
bars, and crossing backward and forward, I can't seem to
to remember where we did come in."

It was too true ; the place we had entered seemed a wild
open common, fenced on two sides, while on the others, it
stretched away into woods and hills ; but since we had
entered it, we had ridden so irregularly, that I was, as well
as Michael, at a loss to tell on which side we had come in,
and if there was a wagon track, it was too dark to see it.
I made a strong effort to command myself, and said concisely, " The best way, Michael, is for me to ride along the
fence here, and see if I can't find something that will direct
me to the place where we came in, while you ride across
the fields, there, on the left, and see if you can't find a
road through the woods, and come back as soon as you've
found any, and tell me."

Michael obeyed, and spurred off toward the woods, while
I picked my way back along the irregular fence, which in
some places was quite hidden by the high bushes, that
grew thick on either side, while in others, it was quite
open and unobscured. But the uncertain light, the similarity of one pair of bars, and one side of the common to

another, completely baffled me, and I was as much bewildered as Michael himself. I tried, however, to be brave
and keep up my courage, trusting momentarily that
Michael would return and report favorably of a road on
the other side, which would lead *somewhere ;* anything was
better than this pathless common.

I tried to be patient as the moments passed without any
signs of his return. I walked my horse up and down
beside the fence, and struggled manfully to be calm.
There was not light enough left to see him till he got near
me; all I could do was to wait: And I did wait; hours, it
seemed to me, till every nerve throbbed with fear, and the
nameless horrors that night and solitude always bring to
those who brave them for the first, crowded so upon me,
that I would rather have ridden into certain danger, than
have waited there another moment; and I dashed across the
common, toward the dark woods that skirted it. I halted
and called as loudly as I could, but no answer came. Then
riding along the edge of the wood, I called again, with all
my strength, and waited for the reply as if my life hung
upon the sound of a human voice. None came, and half
wild at the dawning of this new terror, entire isolation, I
whipped Madge to her utmost speed, and flew along the
whole length of the wood, then back again, shouting
Michael's name.

At that moment the moon came out from behind the
shifting clouds, and halting suddenly, I looked around me;
the common, as far as I could see, was bare; the woods
were before me; I had halted at the entrance of a road
that led into them. Perhaps Michael was wandering there,
and calling once more, I waited in vain for any answer but
the swaying of the boughs in the night wind, and the panting of my tired horse. At this renewed disappointment,
all my firmness gave way, and all the perils and horrors
that fancy suggested rushed upon me; dropping the reins
upon the horse's neck, and covering my face with my

hands, I uttered a cry of despair. Startled by it, and by
the sudden relaxing of the reins, the horse gave a bound
forward, and dashed terrified into the woods. That I was
not unseated, is the strangest part of all my strange adventure; but conscious of nothing, save an agonized fear of
losing this my only living companion, I clung tightly to her
neck, as brushing against the overhanging boughs, and
swaying from side to side of the narrow road, she tore onward in her headlong race.   Of the length of time that
passed before, spent with fatigue and shuddering in every
limb, she paused suddenly before a fallen tree that block-
aded the road, I can form no idea. It was all, as then in
acting, so now in recalling, one wild dream of terror. It
may have been moments, or perhaps only seconds, before,
raising myself from my crouching attitude, I looked
around, and saw the position of the horse, and the fright
that she was in. The moon was shining fitfully through the
naked branches of the forest around us, and right across
the road, lay the giant trunk of a fallen tree; while the
only sound except the moaning of the wind, was the brawl-
ing of a stream that ran beside the road. Madge shook
violently, while I tried to soothe her, but in vain.

I slipped down from the saddle, still holding the bridle
over my arm, and almost fell, from the dizzy feeling on first
touching the ground after being so long in one position. I
regained my feet, and approaching her, patted her neck,
and tried to urge her to make the leap; it was unbearable
to think of staying an instant here! But it was hopeless;
with her feet planted in the earth, and eyes dilated with
terror, she refused to move. A groan of misery escaped
me as this last hope was cut off; I tied the bridle to a low
branch, and sitting down upon the fallen tree, buried my
face in my hands, in hopeless, stupefied despair. The cold
night-air was chilling me to the heart; my habit was, at
best, but barely warm enough in the day, and when heated
with exercise; now, the wind seemed to strike through and

through me; and.I crouched down, hiding my eyes from the ghastly, fitful dancing of the moonbeams, and shook from head to foot.

Look in whatever way I might, there was nothing but terror staring me in the face. How many miles I was from any human habitation, I did not dare to think; but indeed it mattered little; I could not, benumbed and aching as I was, have walked half a mile, even with the certainty of help before me; and I doubted whether, if the horse could have been coaxed over the cruel obstacle that stopped her course, I could have mounted her again. I was bound, helpless, hopeless! My exaggerated fancy refused all hope, and seized all that was frightful, and held up before me the dread that, unless some unforeseen help should come, I should perish during the slow waning of the awful night that had but just begun. I saw life and youth,

> "And time and hope behind me cast,"

and one black shadow creeping toward me, slowly, but with unswerving tread; silently, but with intensest gaze, freezing me with horror. And with a sort of mockery, the words that had seemed so soothing and peaceful, when.life was sure and unthreatened, rang in my ears:

> "Death comes to set thee free—
> O meet him cheerily
> As thy true friend."

Starting to my feet, I cried aloud, as if stung with sudden pain: "No, no! not such death as this; I cannot! Oh, is there no help!" And calling passionately Mr. Rutledge's name, I listened as if it were impossible that I could call on him in vain. But no voice nor answer came; the swaying branches moaned loudly as the angry wind swept through them; the swollen stream rushed by with a mournful sound; the dead leaves fluttered in the fitful blast: this

was my answer—this was all the help my appeals would
gain. With a cry of anguish, I cast myself down upon the
earth, and sent to heaven such a prayer as only despair and
mortal terror can wring from the heart. Not as people
pray at home, morning and evening, with Death at worst a
distant enemy, and Terror and Temptation just so many
words; not as people pray from duty, or from habit, or out
of respect to religion, I prayed then. Not as I had often
asked for mercy, Sunday after Sunday, in the Litany, and
thought I was in earnest, did I ask for it now; but with
such agony of earnestness, such wild entreaty, as those ten
men in the Samaritan village put into their prayer for
mercy; a De Profundis that came from the lowest depths
of abasement and despair. It was a fearful struggle, but it
passed over, and left me calmer.

Whether it was that hope was dead, and the quiet that
crept over me was the quiet of despair, or that really faith
and resignation had come at last, I could not tell; but
exhausted, benumbed, half dead, I lay motionless upon the
ground, while the moments crept slowly on, and formed
themselves into hours; and still, with an ear that never lost
a note of all the dirge that sounded through the forest, I
lay, face downward, indifferent and apathetic. Consciousness never slept a single moment of the dreadful hours that
passed over me, but Fear and Excitement did; and these
terrible enemies only woke, when a sound that was not
brawl of stream or roar of wind, profaned the ghastly solitude. It was a sound far fainter and less appalling than
those I had been listening to, unmoved, so long, but it
roused the keenest terror. Far down the road, I first
caught it, so low that it might have been the falling of a
nut the high wind had shaken from its tree; again, this
time nearer, and the leaves rustle, and a chance bough
crackles. I do not stir a hair's breadth from where I lie—
the step approaches—I do not raise my head nor move a
muscle—I do not think, nor wonder what it is, but all facul

ties absorbed in one, all energies concentrated in that one effort, I listen for the approaching sound. Nearer and nearer; and the quick terror shoots through every chilled vein. In another moment—but with resistless power, horror sweeps over every sense, and in one wild surge, blots out reason, memory, and consciousness.

CHAPTER X.

" O, I have passed a miserable night,
So full of fearful dreams, of ugly sights,
That as I am a Christian faithful man,
I would not spend another such a night,
Though 'twere to buy a world of happy days ;
So full of dismal terror was the time."
                                   RICHARD III.

A SHAPELESS tissue of dreams follow this dark warp
upon the web of memory—how much the flashes of half-
received truth, how much the fabric of distorted fancy, I
cannot say. Into some such form as this, they have shaped
themselves: mixed up in a confused way with the sights
and sounds of that wild solitude, comes the recollection of
being clasped in arms whose familiar hold inspired no
terror ; of hurried words of endearment, and a kiss upon
my forehead that lulled the returning pulsations of fear
into repose again ; then a blank ; then shouting voices, and
the sound of footsteps, many and heavy, rouse me once
more into faint and fitful consciousness, and dim and spectral as a graveyard dance of witches, appear strange men
with lanterns, who cluster round me ; and as I close my
eyes in shuddering fear, Michael's face, in distorted ugliness, takes a hundred ghastly shapes, dances before my
eyes, and keeps out everything else, for a space of time
unspeakably frightful, as it is immeasurably long.

At last, dull stupor overpowers it ; and long, long, after
that, comes a woman's kind face and gentle touch ; then a
hand and voice that are unfamiliar and unwelcome ; cat-
like and soft, from which I shrink in aversion. Then, they
too vanish, and when next the uncertain mist of oblivion
rolls up, I am lying in a long low room, strange and new to

188

me, but not unpleasing, even by the dim light that burns
upon the table, shaded from me by a painted screen. My
eyes wander around inquiringly upon the simple furniture
of the room, the dark, low walls, the piles of books and
pamphlets that heap the shelves irregularly, till they rest
upon the two figures at the other end of the room. A fire
burns low on the hearth, and beside it sits a man, stooping
his head upon his hand. Another in an attitude that is
familiar to me, stands with his arm upon the mantelpiece
shading his eyes from the light. They talk low and
earnestly; sometimes the one standing by the mantelpiece
strides impatiently backward and forward, across the room,
and resumes his former attitude. He by the fire never
moves. I try to listen, but the effort confuses me; and it
is a long while before any of their words reach me, and
then only in a broken, uncertain way. The first I catch are
those of the voice that is familiar to me :

"It is the first time I ever rejected your counsel; the
first time I ever put aside your warning. Do you believe
me when I say it pains me to the heart, after so many years
of steadfast and close friendship, to rebel against the sacrifice it requires of me ? But you do not know what you
ask, indeed you do not !"

"Perhaps not, Arthur, perhaps not," answered his companion, in a low voice. "Do not think again of what I
said ; it was an over-anxiety for your happiness that
prompted me to speak ; and now forget the words, and
remember only the love that moved them."

"No, Shenstone, I will not forget them," the other says,
warmly ; "I know too well the value of your counsels. I
will remember what you have said, and keep the caution
by me, when there is need for caution. But you must not
blame me, if I cannot put aside at once a hope that has got
so strong a hold upon me. I promise you to do nothing
rashly, to let nothing blind my judgment, to put the test
of absence, change of scene, change of interest, upon us

both; years, if you will, shall pass before I dare attempt to realize my hope; years that shall prove its possibility, or show its folly; but do not ask me to give it up at once."

Mr. Shenstone shook his head. "Will it be easier to tear up the cherished hope of years, than to put down the fond fancy of a day, my friend, do you think?"

"I am not a man given to fancies, am I, Shenstone? A life as cold as the last twenty years of mine has been, does not look much like the pursuit of fancies. You have known—who better?—the bitterness that poisoned the very fountain-head of my youth; you have seen how it has tainted the current of my whole life; how that after years of suffering and self-denial, it only needs a word, a recollection of the past to bring the bitter flood back upon my heart. You know all this, and yet you deny me the only charm I see in life; the only light that gilds the dark future! Is this kind?"

He walked impatiently across the room, then came back to his place. The other did not look up nor speak.

"I know what you would say," continued his companion, after a moment; "I know you would remind me that the same blow that blighted my youth, struck deeper at your heart; that you have learned to live without what was life to you once; that I can learn the same hard lesson. I have tried, oh, my friend! I have tried to gain your heights of faith and hope; but still the unconquered flesh drags me down: the curse that generations of godless ancestors have laid upon me is unexpiated yet. You stand now where I cannot hope to stand till

"Death comes to set me free."

Death, that I shall have won! And hoped for, you know longingly, in the old days of wretchedness."

"That's past, Arthur, thank God's good grace; and life

*s no longer a penance to you; and that it never may be again, God in His mercy grant, and spare you what I dreaded for you. God bring you higher than I stand, but by a gentler way, if it be His will! Arthur, it was a fiercer struggle than even you can understand, in which my faith was born. It was a conflict that lasts through most men's lives, that I passed through at one dire struggle, and died unto the world forever. But, looking backward, oh, Arthur, I can look back now and see how

> ——" One dead joy appears
> The platform of some better hope."

Better, as heaven is than earth, as peace is than temptation, as the service of God is than the weary bondage of the world!"

He lifted his head a moment, as if in involuntary triumph, then bent it again, and was silent.

At that moment the door softly opened, and the woman I had seen before stole up to where I lay, and bending down, looked in my face with anxious inquiry, while the friends at the other end of the room hushed their earnest tones, and one (my head was throbbing too much to see which) started forward, and said anxiously:

" Has the doctor come back yet, Mrs. Arnold ?"

" He is in the hall at this moment, sir," she answered, with preciseness of manner, and a peculiar sweetness of voice.

Again the door opened, and again I heard the cat-like step, and felt the velvet touch that sent a shiver through me; and then succeeded a throbbing pain in my temples, dull aching in every limb, a high fever coursing through every vein, and I lived over again in delirium the scenes from which I had just escaped. Again I was lying beneath the roaring forest trees; again the sharp throes of mortal terror wrung from me the cry that I had uttered then, this

time to be soothed by a tender and familiar voice; then
restless with pain, and burning with fever, only pacified from
that dream to be hurried off into another, wilder and more
terrible. With glaring eyes and demoniac faces, the crowd
of men, with Michael at their head, were in mad pursuit of
a flying horse and rider; with hideous jeers and yells they
urge them on, and closing round the frantic steed, they tear
me, clinging round her, from Madge's neck, and holding
me down upon the ground, wrench from my arm the bracelet, that resists, at first, their strongest efforts, till the warm
blood flows, and the torn flesh quivers, as staggering back,
a ruffian lifts the bloody prize, and with a wild cry I wake,
only to drop into another broken slumber, and to dream
another hideous dream.

This time it is Mrs. Roberts, who, with rigid, cruel face,
holds me down, and binding my powerless hands, thrusts
me, struggling and frantic, into the dread, mysterious darkness of *that room.* And choking with terror, the agony is
dispelled by the low voice that says, " What is it now, poor
child?" and panting with fright, I cling to the hand that
soothes me, and only from its steady grasp gain anything
like peace. . And so the night wears on. How much of
these wild dreams revealed themselves in speech I know
not, and how much of the history of that night belongs to
fact, and how much to fancy, it is beyond me to decide.

CHAPTER XI.

"Oh! what a tangled web we weave,
When first we practise to deceive!"

SCOTT.

EMERGING from this sea of dreams tumultuous, I seemed, on a certain cold, grey morning, to be stranded on the shores of reality by an ebbing tide. of water gruel and weak tea. Having, from my extreme youth, entertained undisguised aversion to these articles of food, I had steadily refused to let a spoonful pass my lips; consequently, my nurse and doctor not having relinquished a hope that in time I would come to terms, many separate editions of these invigorating compounds stood upon the table by my bed, in bowls of larger growth, in teacups and saucers, and every variety of earthen and china vessels, all covered and ar.. ranged with consummate care and skill.

These observations I made with great interest, as after a long period of dreamy stupor, the " keen demands of appetite," or some indignant protest of nature against such indolent inactivity, roused me; and raising myself upon my elbow, I looked around with much curiosity and some be. wilderment. The room was entirely unfamiliar, long and old-fashioned looking. The bed and the one window were curtained with white dimity; the walls and ceiling were white-washed to a painful whiteness; the counterpane, the pillows, the sheets, were one drift of snow. Indeed, so forcible was this impression, that for a moment it was a question with me whether I had not just waked up from a nap in one of those snow-houses, so called, which it had been the delight of my childhood to construct, being excavations in some adjacent snow-bank, achieved with the help of a

friendly spade, in which I would lie and dream of icy pa-
laces, and frosty fairy fabrics. The idea that I had been
napping it in one of these juvenile architectural devices, was
favored by the lowness of the white ceiling, which seemed
almost within touch, and the long, narrow shape of the
room, terminating in a small, white-curtained window,
through which I caught a glimpse of cold grey sky, that
suggested snow and chill.

A tiny fire, however, in a tiny grate, and a woman sewing by what I had conceived to be the mouth of the cave,
but which, I was obliged to confess, was unmistakably a
window, quite dispelled the illusion, and I had nothing left
me but to come down to cold reality again, after a sojourn
in dream-land so long as to render me a little uncertain and
bewildered on all mundane matters. I looked quite attentively for some time at the woman by the window, then
startled her very considerably by saying suddenly:

" Are you the one they call Mrs. Arnold ?"

She dropped her work, started up, and approached the
bed, saying, in her precise manner and sweet voice:

"That is my name, Miss. Can I do anything for you ?"

" No," I said slowly, looking at her, " I don't think of
anything, thank you."

And while Mrs. Arnold, after arranging the pillows, and
in a neat, quick-handed way, straightening and tidying
everything on the table and around the bed, returned to
her work, I watched her very attentively, and I am afraid
very rudely, from the slight color that arose in her pale
cheek as she caught my eye again and again fixed on her
inquiringly. She was a middle-aged woman, about middle-
size, with nothing peculiar in dress or manner, except a
scrupulous precision and neatness. Her hair was very grey,
but her face was a younger one than you would have
expected to see, after looking at her slightly-stooping
figure and white hair. Her skin was unwrinkled and clear,
her eyes soft and brown, and the sweetest possible smile

sometimes stirred her lips. But it died very quickly always, and never seemed to come voluntarily; only "when called for," and then to cheer or comfort some one else— never because of any happy emotion within, that found that expression for itself. She conveyed the idea of a woman who had been a very high-spirited and impetuous one, but who was now a very broken and sad one; a soul

—"By nature pitched too high,
By sufferings plunged too low,"

but now past struggle and rebellion, subdued and desolated, waiting patiently for the end. This much I read, or thought I read, in her quiet face, as still leaning on my elbow, I watched her movements. I was irresistibly at-. tracted to her, and essayed to continue our brief conversation, by saying:

"Hasn't 'that Kitty,' as Mrs. Roberts calls her, been here since I have been sick?"

"She has been here, and went away only half an hour ago, to get some of your things. I expect her back every minute."

"I thought I'd seen her," I rejoined, meditatively. "And how about Mrs. Roberts, has she been here?"

"She has; she was here all yesterday afternoon."

I lay quite still for a little while, then said, rather abruptly:

"I can't exactly make it out—where am I, and whose house is this?"

Mrs. Arnold smiled kindly, and turning toward me, said:

"You have been too sick to know much about anything; you are at the Parsonage, and this is Mr. Shenstone's house, and I am Mr. Shenstone's housekeeper. And now do not puzzle your head with any more thinking; ask me any questions you want to know, and then try to lie quiet."

7

"I think I've been quiet long enough in all conscience!" I said, with energy. "I feel a great deal better, Mrs. Arnold."

"I am very glad to hear it, Miss. Will you have something to eat?"

"What can I have?"

"Some very nice gruel, Miss, or some "——

"Wait a minute, Mrs. Arnold," I said, rising up and speaking very impressively; "there is no use, indeed there is no use, in asking me to take such things; I never can, and you will only have to give it up at last. Miss Crowen had to; I stood it out till she thought I was going to die on her hands, I believe, and had to give me something decent at last. People are always trying to make me eat gruel, and farina, and arrowroot, and beef-tea, and such miseries, just as soon as I'm in the least bit sick, and begin to care what I eat. Now don't you be so' unkind, will you, dear Mrs. Arnold?"

Mrs. Arnold smiled; it was the doctor, she said, who had prescribed the gruel; if he was willing to give me something nicer, she should be very happy to prepare it for me.

"Do you know," I said, mysteriously, "that as a general thing, I don't think much of doctors? Country doctors least of all. One's common sense is the best guide in most cases. Why, it stands to reason, that I know better what I ought to have to eat, when I'm not well, than a great strong man does, who never lost his appetite in his life, and doesn't in the least care what he has to eat, as long as there's enough of it! I am the best judge, you must see plainly, Mrs. Arnold."

Mrs. Arnold shook her head; doctors mightn't know what we would like, she said, always, but it was just possible they might know what was best for us, being disinterested judges. Didn't I think so?

"By no means," I exclaimed, "unless they are pecu

liarly intelligent men, and not like that odious Dr. Sartain, who nearly frightened me to death, and nearly killed Mr. Rutledge, by setting his arm badly. Mr. Rutledge himself is ten times better a doctor. He can tell what's the matter with people by just looking at them; and," I continued, coming abruptly back to the point of interest, and hoping to carry it by the suddenness of the attack, "he would never make any one eat water-gruel if they hated it. I'm positive, if you asked him, he'd say, 'let her have what she wants, of course, it cannot do her any harm.'"

Mrs. Arnold shook her head again, and said:

"Ah, Miss, it's very hard to say 'no;' but it must be, till the doctor comes, whom I am expecting every minute."

"What's the doctor's name?"

"His name is Hugh, Miss; a very fine young man they say; he is just settled in the village, and every one is very much pleased with him; he is getting all the practice away from Dr. Sartain, who, though he lives so far away, has been for a long time the nearest physician. But here's his gig at the door now," continued she, coming up to the bed. "Are you ready to see him?"

"Yes, quite," I answered; and she hurried down to usher up the doctor.

Now I had my own views regarding this gentleman, and all Mrs. Arnold's commendation could not change the current of my feelings toward him; so when he approached my bedside, it was a very slight and stiff recognition that his arrival elicited from me. He did not seem a whit annoyed by it, however, and with unruffled blandness, laid down his hat and gloves, and seated himself, while Mrs. Arnold stood at the foot of the bed, unobtrusively attentive.

The new doctor was a good-sized, good-looking man, with reddish hair and whiskers, and very white teeth and very light eyes. That he "hailed" from New England no one could doubt after five minutes spent in his society; equality and fraternity, go-a-head-i-tiveness and go-to-the-deuce-if-you-get-in-my-way-itiveness were still visible to an impartial eye, under all the layers of suavity, professional decorum and good breeding, with which his educational residence in the metropolis had plastered over the native roughnesses of his rustic breeding. If the chill penury that usually represses the noble rage of the New England youth, had not been defeated of its cruel purpose by a "little annuity" from his maternal grandfather, elevating him from the plough to the practice of medicine, one could not help thinking how fine a specimen of the genuine Yankee he would have been. How he would have risen from a boyhood devoted to whittling, swapping, and carting lumber, to a youth engaged in itinerant mercantile transactions, and an early manhood consecrate to science and literature, in the onerous post of common-school teacher. The hero he would have been at quiltings and at singing-schools! The bargains he would have driven in tin and garden-seeds, exchanged for feathers and rags! The matchless cuteness, the inherent cunning, that would have marked his career!

"But whither would conjecture stray?"

The little annuity ($150) had intervened, and Dr. Hugh stood before the public a professional gentleman in the midst of a growing practice, a rising man in a country where, once started, it is easier to rise than to sit still. He was, at the moment when I was making these reflections on his character, suavely regarding me, and had softly laid two fingers upon my wrist, and, with head slightly inclined, was counting my pulse. The result gratified him; for looking up with a complacency that indicated very plainly the source to which he attributed the improvement, he said, addressing Mrs. Arnold:

"A marked change for the better, madam—a marked change."

It was an involuntary thing for me to pull my hand impatiently from his continued touch, and to turn my head away, so disagreeably did his manner impress me. No change of tone, however, indicated any resentment as he said, in apology for me, as it appeared:

"A little restless and feverish yet, I am afraid."

"On the contrary," I said, with great distinctness, turning toward him again, "on the contrary, I never felt quieter or less feverish in my life. I am quite well, except a little weakness, which will be remedied by allowing me suitable and nourishing food; and Mrs. Arnold is only waiting for your permission to get me some broiled chicken and roast oysters, which I have no doubt you are perfectly willing to allow."

The doctor looked astonished at this emphatic declaration and proposition, and for a space seemed inclined to resist such unheard of demands; but seeing, no doubt, the hopelessness of bringing me to reason, and the fear of alienating irretrievably so important a patient as the guest at the great house, he thought it best to yield as graciously as possible. The idea of losing the chance of the Rutledge patronage was not to be entertained for a moment, and it is my opinion that, with a view to averting such a blow to his success, he would have conceded me an unlimited grant of lobster-salad and turtle soup, if I had been pleased to fancy those viands. As it was, however, I bore my triumph very unexcitedly, merely giving Mrs. Arnold a significant look, which indicated as much hungry complacency as was consistent with my dignity; upon which she proposed descending to prepare my meal, and Kitty entering just then, she considered herself no longer necessary, and withdrew for that purpose. The doctor being engaged in writing a prescription, I had nothing to distract my attention from Kitty, who overwhelmed me with congratulations upon my improved condition; which congratulations, however, I could not with sincerity return, for having, in her eagerness,

run every step of the way to Rutledge and back, her condition was best described by the inelegant term, "blown."

"But oh, Miss," she exclaimed, in panting incoherency,
"it is so nice to see you opening your eyes and taking notice! Mr. Rutledge will be so glad!"

"How is he, and why didn't he come?" I asked.

"Well," said Kitty, candidly, "I wasn't to tell you, but
I don't see the harm. Mr. Rutledge's arm has been bad
again, and he can't go out of the house. But here's a note
for you from him."

And Kitty pulled from her apron-pocket a note, that I
seized eagerly. And forgetting doctor and maid, with flushed
cheeks and parted lips, I read and reread the brief note—
very brief, but very characteristic—kind, almost tender—
concise, pithy, and vigorous, with just a dash of humor and
raillery at the close, and "Always your friend, Arthur Rutledge." With a pleased smile, my eyes lingered over the
words, till raising them inadvertently, they encountered
the doctor's, fixed searchingly on my face. He averted
them in an instant, however, but not before he had caught
a sight of the quick blush that mounted to my temples.

"I was thinking," he said, apologetically, "I was thinking that the light was rather strong for your eyes. Shall
not the young woman darken the window a little?"

I rejected the proposal contemptuously, and the medical
gentleman, after an abortive attempt at a compliment,
and a bow that was a shade less complacent than usual,
took his leave.

"I hate that man!" I exclaimed, as the door closed behind him. "I never shall learn to treat him civilly."

Kitty shrugged her shoulders.

"The people in the village think there's nobody like him.
He's got a very taking way with all the common folks, putting his arm around the women's waists, and patting the
men on the shoulder, and talking to everybody alike. But
I don't like the look of him, for all his fair-and-softly ways.

And he's been watching you, Miss, for the last five minutes, as a cat watches a mouse."

I bit my lip, but merely said:

" No matter, Kitty; he may be a good doctor for all that, and he will not have a chance to watch me much longer, I hope. You may darken the window; I believe he was right about that matter, and I'll try to sleep a little till my breakfast, or whatever it is, comes up. In the meantime, perhaps you had better go and see if you cannot help Mrs. Arnold."

Kitty obeyed, and in a few minutes I was left alone, but unluckily with no very pleasant thoughts to keep me company, and no overtures from tired nature's sweet restorer either, to put them to flight. I was very much irritated at the doctor's manner, and a good deal annoyed at having expressed my irritation so warmly to Kitty; and compunctious visitings also troubled me about my self-will on the subject of the broiled chicken and oysters, to which was added a confused sort of penitential alarm about the purloined riding-skirt, and to crown all, a startling discovery, that made me absolutely weak with fright.

The miniature, which for some time past had been vacillating between my pocket and my trunk, as its safety demanded, had, on the afternoon of my ride, being lying on the table before me, while I was dressing, but on an alarm of Mrs. Roberts' approach, I had thrown the ribbon around my neck, and hid it in my bosom, whence, in my hurry and excitement, I had forgotten to take it, and it had remained there during my ride, for I remembered feeling it, with no pleasant association at the time either, while I was waiting for Michael on the common. This I distinctly remembered, and—now it was gone. That was all I knew; that was enough to make me sick with fright. I covered up my face, and lay quiet, but very miserable. What would I not have given if I had never touched that miniature, or worn that skirt. The business of deceit was new to me, and it

proportion it looked black. I had almost fretted myself
into a fever, when Mrs. Arnold reappeared with my *goûté*,
most temptingly arranged upon the cleanest of china and
whitest of napkins. She placed it by me, and announced
that it was ready.

I looked up in her face, my own rather flushed, no doubt,
and said :

"You see he let me have it, Mrs. Arnold."

"I see he did, Miss," she answered, quite gravely.

"I knew he would ; I was right after all."

"I hope so, Miss."

Her grave looks troubled me. I did not take the knife
and fork she offered me, but looking at her earnestly, I
said, abruptly :

"Mrs. Arnold, honestly, do you think that's bad for
me ?"

She looked somewhat startled by my question, but
answered quietly :

"Honestly, Miss, I think it is a risk; but the doctor has
consented, and I have nothing to say."

"Very well," I said, pushing the table back, "I am sorry
to have given you so much trouble for nothing. Will you
warm that gruel for me."

Mrs. Arnold paused in the act of raising the cover from
the oysters :

"Do you mean, Miss, that you do not intend to eat
this ?"

"Yes," I said, concisely, "I will take the gruel, if
you'll warm it, please. There's fire enough there."

She gave me rather a curious look; then quietly removed
the tray into the hall, and proceeded to warm the gruel. I
swallowed the tasteless compound without flinching, while
Mrs. Arnold watched me silently, and took away the
emptied bowl without a word of comment. I lay very
silent but very sleepless till Kitty came up ; then watched
anxiously till Mrs. Arnold should leave the room, which

she was very long in doing. When at last she did, I started up, exclaiming:

"Bolt that door, and come here, Kitty!"

She obeyed, but not very cheerfully, I fancied; indeed there had been a shade of anxiety on her face for some time.

"Kitty," I said, hurriedly and gravely, "I've lost the miniature; do you know anything about it?"

She did not look surprised, but very unhappy, as she answered:

"I know it's gone, Miss; but where, I know no more than the dead."

She then explained—that that night, just after she had been sent for, and arrived, as she came into the study where I was lying, she found Mr. Shenstone and the doctor both standing by me, Mrs. Arnold at the fire, preparing some medicine; Mr. Rutledge had just passed her in the hall. I seemed delirious, for I started up and exclaimed something incoherently, then fell back, and Mr. Shenstone stooping down, said something soothingly, but instantly started back, with an exclamation of dismay and astonishment, which of course did not escape either the doctor or Kitty. The latter hurried up, and stole a glance at me, and she could scarcely repress a similar cry when she saw the guilty miniature, which had slipped from my dress, lying in full view. Mr. Shenstone's face was pale, and he put his hand to his forehead, as if in pain. Her only hope was, that the light being dim, he had not seen it distinctly, and now the thing was to get it away before either he or the doctor had had a second look. Giving the table-cover a sudden jerk, she precipitated the lamp upon the floor, and involved the room in sudden darkness. Deprecating her awkwardness, she hurried to pick up the lamp. While the others were engaged in remedying the accident, and finding a light, about which there seemed much difficulty, she stole to where I lay, and attempted to rescue the minia

7*

ture; but, alas! in vain. Some one had been there before
her, and a cold hand on my breast touched hers, as she
groped for it, and was suddenly withdrawn. It was not
my hand, for mine were burning with fever; and when,
after a moment more of delay, a light was struck, Mrs.
Arnold and Mr. Shenstone stood in the middle of the room
by the table, and the doctor at the opposite end, by the
mantelpiece, looking for some matches that Mrs. Arnold
had said were kept there. She looked down at me; I lay
quietly, one hand under my head, the other at my side.
An end of blue ribbon hung from my dress; it had been cut
off hastily, for a glance told her the edge was too smooth
to have been torn.

Kitty was a keen observer, and her whole heart was in this
mystery; she watched, as if her life had depended on it,
to see who should betray the least sign of guilt, but she was
completely baffled. Certainly not Mr. Shenstone; he even
looked curiously at the ribbon, and then sternly at Kitty,
as if supposing she had taken it; not the doctor, for he was
at the other end of the room, and was more unconcerned
and indifferent than any one present; not Mrs. Arnold, for
not having been beside me when the miniature slipped
from my dress, she could not have seen it, and conse-
quently she could not have taken it in the dark, and so
readily too.

"Ah!" Kitty exclaimed, "I passed a dreadful night,
Miss; I didn't know what it was to close my eyes; such
awful thoughts as would come!"

"What do you mean?" I said hurriedly. "Which of
them do you think has it?"

"Ah, Miss!" she exclaimed, with a burst of tears, "I
wish I thought any of 'em had it! I've had enough of
meddling with dead people's things for the rest of my life,
that I have!"

"I wish you would speak intelligibly; what do you
mean?" I exclaimed, angrily.

Kitty answered by fresh tears, "Oh, don't make me ..k about it! Indeed, I cannot!"

"I shall be very much displeased if you act in this way any longer," I said, with emphasis, as Kitty still shook her head. I heard footsteps in the hall; catching her arm, I exclaimed:

"Tell me instantly what you mean!"

"Oh, Miss!" she whispered, white and trembling, "that hand, that awful hand! It was colder than any stone, and sent a chill through me when I touched it; I never, never can "——

"You foolish girl," I exclaimed, impatiently, "I didn't think you were so silly "——

But at that moment some one knocked at the door, and Kitty, wiping her eyes and smoothing her hair, ran to open it. It was only Mary, with some coal; but it interrupted our conversation, which could only after that be resumed by broken snatches, wherein I urgently impressed upon Kitty my certainty of the miniature's being in possession of one or other of the parties in the room at the time of its disappearance, and the entire contempt in which I held her superstitious theory in regard to it. Kitty's belief on that point, however, could not be shaken, and I grew weary of reiterating my arguments. At last I found an opportunity, when we were alone, to propound another question:

"What has been done about the riding-skirt?"

"Oh, Miss," exclaimed Kitty, uneasily, "why do you worry about those things now? It will make your head ache to talk; I know master wouldn't like it."

Kitty soon saw the futility of attempting to evade the matter; so she gave me a plain commonsensical statement of affairs, commencing from the moment I dashed down the avenue on Madge Wildfire's back; from which time it appeared, her difficulties began. Mrs. Roberts, after watching us out of the gate, the storm on her brow blacken-ing every instant, turned away with a determined step, and entering the house, called to Kitty, saying she was in a great hurry for the dress she had given her to press off; she had important business at the Parsonage, and there was no time to lose.

"I don't think you'll find Mr. Shenstone home, ma'am," Kitty had volunteered. "I saw him passing along the road toward Norbury, when I was down at the lodge half an hour ago."

This information had appeared to give great disquietude to Mrs. Roberts, and in consequence of it, she had given up her plan of going out, and had retired misanthropically to her room, while Kitty had danced down to the kitchen in great glee, to communicate to Sylvie her narrow escape. But in half an hour, Mrs. Roberts' bell rang hastily, and Kitty apprehensively went up to answer it.

"I have concluded, after all," said that lady, "to go to the Parsonage, and leave a note for Mr. Shenstone if he is not in; so get my dress for me as quickly as you can."

"Yes, ma'am," Kitty had answered; but in passing the window, she had cast a look out. "It's most five o'clock now, ma'am, you'll be caught out in the dark; hadn't Thomas better run down with the note for you? Or maybe I could go?"

But Mrs. Roberts was quite firm. "No, she did not care to trust to any one but herself in this case." And again she desired her to get the dress with all haste. Haste she certainly did make, in getting to the kitchen and calling Sylvie into consultation; which measure, however, did not tend to elucidate in any great degree the problem that at present perplexed her brain. Sylvie was one of the "raving distracted" kind, and invariably lost her wits on occasion of their being particularly required, and the only assistance she attempted to render, in this trying emergency, was ejaculatory and interjectional condolence on the apparent hopelessness of the case. Kitty, in disgust, slammed the

door in her face, put her hands to her head in a wild way
for a moment, then bounded upstairs again.

"Oh, dear Mrs. Roberts," she exclaimed, as she entered
the room, "it struck me on my way down, that perhaps
you'd rather wear your old black silk instead of that nice
bombazine, as it is getting so late, and the road is so dusty.
We haven't had rain, you know, for an age."

Mrs. Roberts drew herself up. Was she or was she not
capable of judging what clothes she was to put on? Would
it be necessary for her to go down and get the dress she
wanted herself?

"By *no* means," Kitty said; and starting forth again, sat
herself down on the third step of the stairs, in direst perplexity. But time pressed; there was no leisure for deliberation. She flew to a closet where some superannuated
garments of the housekeeper's hung, selected the most pre-
sentable of the series of black bombazine skirts suspended
in funereal rows upon the pegs; darted back, and with great
composure, laid it on the sofa, while, with officious zeal, she
proceeded to divest Mrs. Roberts of her house-costume, and
invest her with her walking-dress. By skillfully interposing
her person between the dress and the strong light, and
putting it on and arranging it entirely with her own hands,
she escaped detection. And arrayed in this ancient garment, the housekeeper sallied forth on her way to the
Parsonage.

Too anxious to be triumphant this time, Kitty stole out
after her, to see the effect of the sunlight upon the foxy,
faded black; but Mrs. Roberts was too much engrossed
with cankering cares of a sterner kind, to think of her
bombazine.

At the gate, however, to her great content, she encountered Mr. Shenstone on his way from Norbury, and stopping him, held a long and anxious consultation with him
(in which, said Kitty, *par parenthèse,* "I overheard her say
some pretty things about you; but no matter)." She then

parted from the clergyman, and returned slowly toward the house, Kitty following anxiously behind the hedge. The setting sun threw the most dazzling beams down the avenue. Kitty's heart beat, as she saw the housekeeper cast her eyes meditatively upon her dress; then, as the sunlight struck full upon it, she stooped a little down, and paused, and looked again, and again adjusted her glasses. She began, in truth, to "smell a rat," for passing her hand rapidly over the front breadth, she shook her head doubtingly, then lifted the suspicious garment to the sunlight, then holding it at arms' length, uttered an exclamation of surprise, turned it up, and examining the hem all around, dropped it; turned the pocket inside out—felt of the band around the waist—recognized its unfamiliarity—and with a low muttering of suppressed wrath, gathered herself up, and hastened toward the house.

"It's all up !" groaned poor Kitty, as, by the back way, she darted into the kitchen, and awaited with trembling the pull of Mrs. Roberts' bell.

"Kitty Carter," said Mrs. Roberts, in an awful voice, as she entered the room, "you have been practising upon me in an abominable manner. I have borne your saucy ways for a long time, but the end has now come. You can't deceive me; I'm too quick for you, and you shall be exposed. It's my intention to make Mr. Rutledge acquainted with your deceitful practices; and that, you are aware, is just the same as giving you warning ; for Mr. Rutledge has never been known to endure anything of the kind in his house."

Kitty quailed under this attack ; but, rallying in a moment, asked Mrs. Roberts if she'd please tell her what was the matter ? Her answer was a peremptory order to bring up the dress she had given her in the morning. For once in her life, Kitty had nothing to say ; while Mrs. Roberts exclaimed :

"It's my belief, Kitty Carter, that dress is lying where I put it this morning, and that you haven't touched it."

"I wish from my soul I hadn't," thought the unlucky girl.

"Now go down this moment and fetch it to me, finished or unfinished, or you forfeit your place."

The only way that opened for Kitty, was to assume a position, good or bad, and maintain it through thick and thin. Therefore, with staunch determination, she replied:

"I have not done the dress, ma'am; I didn't think you'd want it so soon; and I had rather not bring it up till it's finished."

"This minute, or you lose your place," said the exasperated housekeeper.

Kitty respectfully resisted the demand; it was contrary to her principles to give up work half finished. If Mrs. Roberts would give her time, she would do it; but before the dress was in order, she must decline bringing it up.

Then the storm burst in all its fury. Sylvie was called up; Mrs. Roberts made a descent in person upon the kitchen, which was placed under martial law, Thomas and two of the stable-boys guarding the different entrances, while Dorothy and one of the farm-hands accompanied Mrs. Roberts in her inquisitorial progress through the lower departments. Altogether, such a tragedy had not convulsed the basement of Rutledge for many a long year; not, indeed, since the pranks of Kitty's childhood had been the scandal of the place. Kitty remembered with comfort, that she had weathered more than one storm there; and remembering this, took heart again, though, it must be confessed, things looked black enough. The dress not being and appearing anywhere, "from garret to basement," Kitty Carter was formally pronounced suspended from her duties, until such time as Mr. Rutledge, being informed of her offences, should himself dismiss her from the house.

To that dark crisis had succeeded the alarm produced by the non-appearance of the equestrian party; then the consternation consequent upon the arrival of Michael, several

hours later, announcing that the young lady had been lost
hunted for, and found, by all the men in the village, and
was now lying, half dead, at the Parsonage; and, finally,
that by order of Mr. Rutledge, Kitty, her maid, was to
repair thither immediately to attend upon her. This materially changed the look of affairs; and it was hoped, by
the anti-administration party, that the storm. had blown
over, and, in the new excitement, would be forgotten. But
such hopes were futile indeed, and entertained by weak
minds, not capable of sounding the depths of a resentment
such as rankled in Mrs. Roberts' recollection. The very
next day, in a solemn interview in the library, Mr. Rutledge was informed of the nature of the complaint against
Kitty, and distinctly declared, that unless the matter was
very shortly cleared up, he should be under the necessity
of dismissing her from his service. And this sword was
now hanging over poor Kitty's head; and Kitty's stout
heart was sinking at the prospect of the only punishment
that could have had much terror for her; for Rutledge was
the only home she had ever known, and the only place she
loved.

"But it doesn't signify," she said bravely, dashing away a
furtive tear; "I can get another place, and I'll look out
that there's no Mrs. Roberts in the family."

"But, Kitty," I exclaimed, "why didn't you tell? Mr.
Rutledge would have overlooked it, I know."

"What, tell!" cried Kitty, scornfully, "and get you into
trouble, too? No, indeed, I know Mr. Rutledge well
enough to know he'd have been angry with you as well as
with me; and if you take my advice, Miss, you won't say a
word about it. One's enough to take the blow; it won't
make it any easier to have another getting it too. Just let
the matter stand as it is; it will be all right. There, don't
fret!" she exclaimed, cheerfully; "it worries me to death to
see you mind it so! Why, Miss, it's nothing; how need-
you care?"

"But, Kitty," I exclaimed, clinging to a last hope, "was the dress much spoiled?"

"Oh dear, yes! muddied, torn, stained, as if you'd been dragged through the streets in it." Our conversation was again abruptly brought to a close by the advent of Mary, this time with a message to Kitty from Mrs. Arnold, desiring her help downstairs.

And again, turning my face to the pillow, with a miserable sigh, I was left alone.

CHAPTER XII.

' The very gentlest of all human natures
He joined to courage strong,
And love outreaching unto all God's creatures,
With sturdy hate of wrong."

WHITTIER.

EVENING was closing in, and filling the little room where I lay with fitful shadows, which the tiny blaze of fire in the grate was incompetent to dispel. If it had been possible for me to be more miserable than I had been all day, I should indeed have "loathed the hour" when gloom and darkness so palpably and hopelessly descend, but the climax of misery and self-reproach had been reached by daylight, and outward dreariness could only increase, in a very slight degree, the inward gloom. The faults I had been guilty of, and the errors into which I had led, or allowed Kitty to go, seemed to me, and justly, the first steps in a most dangerous path. I fully realized the sins, and their effect upon my conscience, apart from their consequences and punishment. These last, I was aware, were hard enough. I knew I had done what must lower me in Mr. Rutledge's esteem; to be the accomplice in a deception, however slight, was to sink just that much in his regard, whose rigid truthfulness and honor were offended by the least prevarication. I knew I had given Mrs. Roberts grounds for all her former distrust and aversion, and placed myself lower than she could have estimated me. Above all, poor Kitty was the victim on whom it fell hardest, and how much of the blame of not checking her or guiding her right lay on my shoulders, I dared not think. I was really attached to the brave, quick-witted girl, and remembered, with humiliation, how igno.

162

rant, and untaught she was, and how naturally and unavoidably her faults were the results of her unguided impetuosity, while mine were committed in the light of an instructed conscience and educated intellect.

But with me to suffer pain, was to seek some cure for it. My repentances were not often fruitless; I could no more have lain there, and endured that self-reproach, without resolving on some way to allay it, than I could have submitted to a dagger in my breast without attempting to draw it out. The only remedy I could see, was painful enough, but there was no help for it.

"Mrs. Arnold," I implored, "do put down your work, and come and sit by me; I want to ask you something."

Mrs. Arnold left her seat by the window, and laying down the knitting that her rapid fingers plied alike through daylight and darkness, came to my bedside and sat down. She saw I was excited and feverish, and in her gentle way strove to soothe and amuse me. She talked of a great many things about the parish that she thought might interest me—of the school children, and the Christmas festivities that were preparing, and in some way Rutledge was spoken of, and its dullness and gloominess.

"But I don't think it's gloomy in the least," I said; "I think it's the most beautiful place I ever was in in my life. Don't you think it's delightful?"

"I used to think so," she said, sadly.

"Have you been there lately?" I demanded.

"Never since I left it first," she answered, musingly.

"Then you lived there once?"

She assented half unconsciously.

"What were you?" I asked, very suddenly; "were you kousekeeper?"

"No, I was governess, Miss," she answered; then started, as if she had said more than she had intended, and hastily turned the conversation to something else. But I could not so quickly turn my thoughts. This woman, then,

who tended me, with sad, soft eyes and voice, had been the
governess and companion of Alice—had known from the
beginning the storm that had burst over Rutledge, and was
herself, perhaps, involved in this dark story of the past, that
was meeting me at every turn. The miniature would have
startled her, perhaps, if she could have seen it. What if she,
in reality, had it now, and hers was the cold hand upon my
breast that had seized it ? But no ; Kitty was sure it was
not. And then my thoughts reverted to my own remorse
and trouble that had only been momentarily lulled by Mrs.
Arnold's conversation. There was a pause just then, and
raising myself on my elbow, I said, looking intently at my
companion :

" Mrs. Arnold, did you ever confess a sin to Mr. Shenstone, and ask counsel of him when you were very
miserable ?"

At my words, Mrs. Arnold gave a start ; but recovering
herself, she said, in a voice somewhat agitated :

" Why do you ask me such a question ?"

" Because," I said, too much absorbed in my own trouble
to heed her agitation, " because I am very miserable, and
don't know exactly what to do; I am sure he is the only one
who can help me, and I must tell him before I sleep to-night,
if only I can get the courage ! Oh, Mrs. Arnold! tell me,
is he very severe ? Or will he be kind—and would you
dare, if you were me ?"

" I cannot tell what trouble you have on your mind, but
I can answer for it, if human help can lighten it, Mr. Shenstone will give you all the help he can. And if it is but
between you and heaven, he will show you the way to get
at peace. Oh, my dear young lady! you need not be afraid
to open your heart to one who knows so much about God's
mercy and men's sins. You need not be afraid but that he
will be as tender as he is wise; indeed, you need not fear
him."

She spoke rapidly and earnestly; her whole manner of

precision and composure seemed to be broken down and melted before some recollection that my trouble seemed to recall. I laid my burning hand in hers, and said with a sigh :
" Oh, if I only dared !"
" But why should you fear ?" she continued, earnestly. " Why should you fear, when I tell you that he has only kindness and pity in his heart—that he has looked with forbearance and compassion on blacker sins than ever stained your young soul; and when I tell you—for I have reason to know—that he can bring light out of darkness, and can show a way of peace to even the most tortured and despairing. It may," she continued, " be but a very little sin that is weighing on you, and turning you out of the right way ; but from little sins grow heavy punishments, and better find now the best way of putting it out of your heart, and putting something good in its stead. You have all life before you," she said, with a weary sigh, " and repentance is easier and more hopeful work, than it is to come back, when one has spent one's inheritance of life in sin, having nothing to offer heaven but fruitless tears."

Her voice trembled with emotion ; she looked pityingly at me as, struggling to keep back my tears, I hid my face in the pillow, and caressing the hand that still lay in hers, she went on to persuade me to the only remedy she knew for my unhappiness. I still felt shudderingly afraid to make the dreadful effort, and faltered something about my fear of his goodness and superiority, and the contempt he would feel for me when he knew how weak and sinful I had been.

" Would it give you courage," she said, in a low tone, " to know how he once received the repentance of a very miserable woman—a woman who had not only sinned against heaven, but against him—who had done more than any one else to blight his happiness and make his life desolate, but who, having met the due reward of her deeds, came back to die in misery where she had failed to live in innocence ? Shall I tell you of this ?"

I whispered " Yes," and she went on in a low voice:

" It is no matter what the sins were that brought me to the misery I shall tell you of; it is no matter whether they were committed for myself, or for the love of one whom I would have died to serve ; it is no matter for me to tell you that they grew from little unchecked thoughts of pride and self-will, and little half-intended acts of deception, into the monster sins that overshadowed my life ; it is enough that I had come to the recompense of them—that in remorse, in utter consternation, I mourned as one without hope. What did I know of hope ? Six feet of foreign mound covered the remains of her I had served and sinned for. Shame and infamy covered her name ; hope was dead in my heart ; faith had never been lit there. Alone in a land of strangers, there was but one longing in my breast that exceeded the desire for death, and that was the craving to see home again. It makes me shudder even now to recall that journey—weary months of fatigue, and exposure and misery ; the only thought that kept me up, a dreary one at best, to see home once more, and die before a word of reproach could stab me, or a familiar voice recall the wretched past.

" It was a still, clear December night, when, footsore and weary, I saw, with a strange thrill, the lights of a little village, that my heart told me was the little village I had come thousands of miles to see, and that I had not seen nor heard from since my guilty flight, long years ago, on a December night, still and cold as this. I hurried on, my sinking strength nerved up for a last effort, till I should reach a woody knoll I knew overlooked the village, and there, I said, I will die. In my hand I held what I knew would free me ; I had carried it in my bosom for months and months, only waiting for this moment. At last I reached the spot, and sinking down on the hard ground, covered my face a moment with my hands, then looked down upon the scene before me. There lay the village, its white houses gleaming in the moonlight—there the familiar road wound round the foot of the hill—there was the broad street, the old mill, the placid lake in the distance, and beyond it, clear against the sky, the dark outlines of Rutledge; massive, and gloomy, and lifeless, it stood far off from the cheery village, with its animation and content. Not a window of the little hamlet but showed a kindly light, while the great house beyond was dark and silent—not a gleam of light from all its sombre front. A horror and remorse that you cannot understand came over me, such as I had thought my dead heart was incapable of harboring; then despair settled on it again, and I prepared for death. But as I was looking—and I was not dreaming—between the desolate house and me, distinct against the dark woods, there shone out a silver cross. I was not dreaming—I was terribly awake; but there it glittered, still and bright. Not a sound broke the stillness of the frosty air, not another feature in the landscape changed; I strained my eyes to catch the least wavering or fading of the distinct lines, but calm and clear the holy sign still lit the dark stretch of woodland between me and Rutledge, and never wavered or faded. I was not superstitious, but this came to me like a token from heaven, and I held the fatal vial unopened in my hand. What if this was meant to tell me there was forgiveness yet—that that there was a sanctifying calm even over the cold desolation of that dark house—that the sins were done away, and that mercy had shone out. With that sign before me, I did not dare to add that one sin more to those I had already committed; I did not dare to die by my own hand. And then a desire took possession of me to know something of what had passed in all these years, or if there was, indeed, none remaining to loathe and execrate me. And finally, hiding the vial in my bosom, I crept down, and keeping my eye still fixed on the shining cross, I turned into the broad street that led to the village. One after another of the cheerful lights I passed, not daring to go in, pausing before each gate, and then hurrying on, determined to try the next. By and by, the cross was lost among the trees, and my courage began to fail, when, on a sudden, I found myself at the gate of a church-yard, and looking up, saw, what was most unexpected and unfamiliar, the arches and spire of a little church, on the site of the neglected old graveyard I remembered ; and there, above it, gleamed the cross that had stayed my hand from suicide, which, catching the rays of the rising moon, had shone out with such a message of mercy.

"I opened the little gate, and stealing across the church-yard, bent down to read the names upon the graves that had been made since I had been away. I mournfully traced out one familiar name after another, till, with a groan, I turned away from the gloomy spot, and shutting the gate, struck off into the road again. I dragged on, till I reached the outskirts of the village, then sat down to rest. A single light, at a little distance, shone from a cottage on the edge of the woods, that I knew bordered Rutledge Park. A boy passed by me, and summoning courage, I stopped him, and asked him what house that was. 'The Parsonage,' he said. And there, I thought, is where I will go, and hear, perhaps, whether there is any hope for such as me in either world. When I reached the low gate of the garden in front of it, I did not allow myself time to think, but walked down the path, and stepping on the little porch, knocked faintly at the door. The blinds of the window where the light was, being open, I looked in, and saw the only occupant of it, who had been reading by the lamp on the table, rise to answer my knock.

"'Can I see the clergyman?' I asked, in a low voice.

"'Come in, this way,' he said, kindly, leading the way to the room he had left; 'I am the clergyman.'

"He told me to sit down by the fire, and then, in a tone that moved me strangely, asked if he could help or direct me in any way.

"I was too near the gate of death to see in him anything

but the minister of God; and, forgetting that he was a man and a stranger, began in a broken, husky voice, the recital of the doubts and the despair I had been fighting with. I do not know how much of my story I betrayed, or what, in this extremity of wretchedness, I said; but pausing at the end, and frightened by his silence, I raised my eyes, and faltered:

"'Would God have mercy after that, do you think?'

"The clergyman's face was white as mine: his voice shook as he said:

"'If He has let you live, He means to forgive you, you may be sure.'

"'He has let me live,' I said, eagerly, and I told him of the cross that had held me back from suicide. He pressed his hand before his eyes, then said, after a moment, in a broken voice:

"'Take it for a sign, then, that He is waiting to be gracious; that there is peace on earth, as well as mercy in heaven, for you.'

"'Never peace; I have no right to hope for that, only a chance of pardon before I die.'

"'A sure hope of pardon, if you verily repent, and a sure sense of peace, if you strive to put in deeds, the repentance that God has put in your heart.'

"'There is nothing left in life for me to do,' I said, with a bitter sigh.

"'So I thought once,' he said, 'but I have learned that God never leaves a soul on earth, without leaving some work for it to do, to keep it from despair, some sin to be atoned for, some duty to be fulfilled. Can you think of none?'

"'None,' I said; 'there is nothing left for me, my repentance comes too late; there is none left but my weary self, to profit by it.'

"'There is a work I know of waiting for you, Rachel Arnold,' he said, in a voice that thrilled through and

8

through me. It all came upon me then; with a low cry, I started up and sprang toward the door; but he interposed.

" ' Let me go,' I cried; ' I cannot face you in this world! Wait, before you bring your accusation, till we are at God's tribunal! Let me go, and I will never offend your sight again. Oh! why are you not dead, like all the rest? Why are you left to drive me back to despair again?' And in an agony I sank down at his feet.

" ' I am left,' he said, raising me up, ' to guide you back to peace and duty; to tell you of God's infinite loving kindness, and to show you how much of hope there is for you, in this world and in the next; and to assure you, if you need the assurance, that I as utterly forgive you, as I hope for God's forgiveness for myself.'

" ' You never would say so,' I murmured, ' if you knew all.'

" ' I know enough to understand your remorse; the rest you can tell to God; I say again, from my soul, I forgive you.'

" But I never raised my face, nor looked at him, till I had told him all, and he had said again:

" ' With all my heart I forgive you. The past is cancelled; stay here, and help me in the work that God has set us to do, and obliterate the sins that this place has seen, by faithful striving in the labor of restoring it to his service again.'

" My dear young lady," said Mrs. Arnold, in a trembling voice, " can you fear him after that?"

" No," I exclaimed, with tears; " let me see him now."

CHAPTER XIII.

"Make no enemies; he is insignificant indeed than can do thee no harm."
                                        LACON.

"WELL," says Mrs. Arnold, with an inquiring look, as she was preparing to leave me for the night, "was I right, or do you feel sorry you followed my advice?"

"Ah! no, indeed!" I exclaimed; "it's all right now! I can see all through it, and I am so much happier!" and I took her hand affectionately as she left me.

It was all right, or nearly so. I had found, after the first awkwardness, that it was very easy to tell Mr. Shenstone things that I had never supposed I could tell to any one; there was something in his manner that divested one of all fear and shyness, and suggested only the interest and earnestness of one whose highest desire it was, to set forward in the right way, all who were faltering and uncertain. He made my duty very clear, and gave me many simple suggestions that I wondered I had never thought of before. He then told me what it seemed to him I ought to do, in the matter of remedying the mischief I had caused. Acknowledging my fault to Mrs. Roberts in person, was a very humiliating, but a very wholesome mortification, and one which he unhesitatingly recommended. And the restoration to her of a dress equally as valuable as the one she had lost, was also his advice, and, if it shortened uncomfortably my already rather scanty supply of pocket-money, so much the better lesson it would be. He would himself undertake acquainting Mr. Rutledge with the circumstances, and representing them in the most favorable light. About the miniature I had just begun to tell him, intending

to say as much as I could without implicating Kitty, when
a knock at the door interrupted us, and " the doctor " was
announced. His visit was not quite as trying as it had
been in the morning, owing to the increased stock of
patience and good resolutions I had been laying in since
then ; and indeed, they continued to influence my endurance of him during the daily visits that he inflicted on me
while I remained at the Parsonage. I had had so much of
the effects of willfulness, that I determined never to be self-
willed again, and not so much as to ask him when I might
go back to Rutledge ; and he, fer his part, seemed determined not to volunteer the permission till I should ask
for it.

But the matter at last was settled by Mr. Shenstone, who
came up one morning while the doctor was with me, and
said he had just received a note from Mr. Rutledge, saying
that from the account the doctor had given him of me, he
should fancy I was well enough to come back, and if the
doctor's permission could be obtained, he would send the
carriage for me that afternoon at four o'clock. I looked at
the doctor with breathless interest ; the doctor looked at
me with searching curiosity, while he said, as slowly as the
occasion permitted, and with as long a preface, and as pro-
tracted an utterance as he could command :

" I should be most unwilling to be the cause of disap-
pointing Mr. Rutledge, or of occasioning any vexation to
the young lady, by denying the permission that Mr. Rutledge seems to expect and desire ; though I am certain, he
has no intention of influencing my decision against my better
judgment, or of inducing me to say anything, that in my
capacity of medical adviser, would involve any departure
from strict veracity and prudence. I am aware that it is
often difficult for a disinterested party to resist the reasonable and natural desires of those whose judgments are
warped by their wishes, and that the only reward the conscientious physician gets, in such cases, is the aversion and

coldness of those whose good he is most interested in. In this case, however, I am certain, that from the well-known good sense and sagacity of Mr. Rutledge, and the *unques-tioned amiability* of the young lady, I should have nothing to fear."

"Then," said Mr. Shenstone, kindly, evidently seeing my anxiety, and wishing to put an end to it, " then you do not consider it desirable to allow the change ?"

" I am not prepared to say so, entirely," he answered ; " I was going on to remark, that I should not have allowed any of the considerations I mentioned to influence me, had I really deemed it imprudent for the young lady to leave her present residence. But, considering her rapid convales-cence, and the mildness of the day, and the care I am cer-tain will be taken to make the drive an easy one, and the harm which a disappointment might occasion her, I think I am justified in according my consent to Mr. Rutledge's arrangement."

I don't think I could have endured a minute more of this kind of suspense, and probably the doctor knew this, and so brought his discourse to a termination, after having tried my nerves as long, and given me as many cuts, as he con-sidered me capable of enduring. I began to suspect, indeed, that he had perceived my aversion to him, and that in a quiet and unostentatious manner, he returned the senti-ment, and would lose no occasion of letting me benefit by it. This was mere conjecture, however, for the doctor's manner was as assiduously polite, as blandly gallant as ever. And indeed, his anxious interest would not suffer him to allow me to go unattended to Rutledge ; but at four o'clock, when I was bidding adieu to Mr. Shenstone, and being seated comfortably in the carriage by Mrs. Arnold and Kitty, the sorrel horse and shiny gig drew up beside us, and in an *empressé* manner, the doctor sprang out, and in his own person superintended the arrangements for my comfort, and declared that he should not feel quite easy till he had seen me safe at Rutledge; and for that purpose, as well as that of paying a professional visit to the master of it, he should drive on, and be there to receive us. An unconscious tinge of hauteur was all, in my manner, that escaped of the vexation I felt at the announcement.

His presence altered very much my conduct at leaving the Parsonage. If he had not been there, I am sure I should have managed to tell Mr. Shenstone something of the gratitude I felt for the unmerited interest in, and kindness toward me, that he had shown; as it was, I could only look down, and appear unspeakably awkward, at his kind expressions of affection and regret, as he said good bye. And, instead of throwing my arms around Mrs. Arnold's neck, as I wanted to do, and telling her I was fonder of her than of almost anybody else in the world, and that I should never forget her care and goodness, I could only, with that man looking on, give her my hand, and say something unintelligibly about coming to see her again before I went away. The carriage started, and the gig first followed, then passed it, and by the time we reached the gate, the sorrel horse was standing before the door, and the sorrel driver thereof waiting for us, in company with Mr. Rutledge on the steps.

"Now Kitty," I said, as we drove into the park, "now Kitty, keep your courage up. Mr. Shenstone says he has seen Mr. Rutledge, and he has promised to excuse you; all you have got to do is to make an apology to Mrs. Roberts, and that's nothing! Why, I've got to do the same thing, and you'll see how brave I'll be about it."

Kitty shook her head dejectedly. "I never hated to do anything more."

And here the carriage stopped, and Mr. Rutledge and the doctor came down to it. "Ah," said the former, kindly, "you have come back at last. I did not know whether the doctor and Mrs. Arnold ever meant to let you return to Rutledge."

His tone was kind—but—what more did I want? I did not dare to look up; I felt Dr. Hugh's eyes on my face, and murmuring some broken commonplace about being happy to be back again, hurried up the steps and into the house, Kitty following with my shawls and packages. At the head of the stairs, I stopped till she overtook me, and telling her hastily that I was going immediately to Mrs. Roberts, and she must give me the package that contained the dress, and be ready to go in, and make her apology as soon as I came out, I left her, and crossed over to the door of Mrs. Roberts' room.

It was a mean and cowardly thing to hope, no doubt, but I did, notwithstanding, most ardently desire that it might so happen that the housekeeper was not in her room, and that I might have a brief respite before the dreadful penance was undertaken, and in that hope I gave an undemonstrative knock, to which Mrs. Roberts' voice responded promptly, "Come in." Coming in was an easy part of it; walking up to her and saying, "How are you?" was easy too; and remarking, "I am better, thank you," was the easiest of all. But after that! Standing blankly before that rigid black bombazine figure, whose bluish lips were obstinately compressed, and whose unsympathetic eyes were regarding me inquiringly, it was anything but easy to say what I had come to say—it was anything but pleasant to remember I was to be humble. But there was no help for it. I gulped down my pride and aversion, and simply and honestly told my story, making every allowance truth would permit me for Kitty, putting all the blame that was possible on myself, making no cowardly excuses, and no submissive apologies, but telling a very straightforward and honest story, in a very downright and unequivocal manner, and winding up with a request that she would consider that I regretted my share in the business, and was desirous of making her every amend for the annoyance and inconvenience I had occasioned her. No other course could have been as well calculated to mollify Mrs Roberts; any undue humility would have aroused her suspicions—the least attempt to conciliate her would have settled her in her aversion—the smallest parade of penitence she would have stigmatized as hypocrisy; but as it was, she was met on her own ground, and could do nothing but yield, in an ungracious manner, an ungracious acknowledgment of my honesty and sincerity, and a promise to consider the offence atoned for. I put the package down on the table, telling her what it contained, and again recommending Kitty to her mercy, turned and left the room.

I found that young person awaiting me in an unenviable state of mind. I told her I should never have the least respect for her again, if she lost her courage now, and then I talked to her a little *à la* Shenstone, and then rallied her a little *à la* myself, and finally sent her off, quite staunch again, to meet her offended mistress, while I employed the time in taking off my bonnet and cloak, and arranging the different articles that I had brought back, in the drawers.

Despite my attempts at nonchalance, I felt a little unhappy. I did not yet know how far Mr. Rutledge had put me out of the place I had held in his regard, since he knew of my fault, and I could not feel quite at ease till I heard my pardon from his own lips.

At last Kitty returned, looking a little pale and agitated, but acknowledging that, on the whole, she was glad she had gone. The interview had been, it appeared, rather a stirring one, but Kitty had kept her temper, and Mrs. Roberts had, at last, after expending her wrath upon an unresisting subject, come to terms, and the curtain had dropped upon comparative tranquillity. Then I told Kitty we must have done with deceits, little and great, and related how near I had come to telling Mr. Shenstone about the miniature, and that I meant to tell him the very first chance, or else Mr. Rutledge. But Kitty fell into such an ecstasy of terror, and with such vehement tears and entreaties besought me never to expose her, and promised such eternal devotion to truth henceforth, if I would only spare her that insupportable mortification and disgrace, that at last I yielded, and, to my own sorrow, promised to hazard no attempt to clear up that mystery, and to make no confessions to any one in regard to it.

After dressing my hair and arranging the room, Kitty left me, and I sat down in my favorite seat in the bay window, with the double purpose of whiling away the time and watching for the doctor's departure. But that devoutly wished consummation did not crown my waiting ; moment after moment passed, and still the doctor tarried, and at last Thomas came out and led the sorrel horse away to the stable.

"That man's going to stay to tea, I know," I ejaculated, indignantly. "I've a great mind not to go downstairs."

The unremunerative policy, however, of spiting myself, had early been impressed on me, and I wisely abandoned all thought of pursuing it, and reconciled myself to the trial with all possible heroism. I should not go down till the last minute. That was all the indignation I should indulge in.

Twilight was descending fast ; the afternoon had not been a bright one, and contrary to the nature of such things, was particularly short-lived. There was a light streak around the horizon, that suggested to the weather-wise the idea of snow impending ; above, and all over the rest of the sky, there was nothing to relieve the dull grey hue. The line of light grew narrower and narrower, the cold grey shroud settled down lower and heavier, the lake and lawn grew more and more indistinct, the shadows thickened within, the darkness increased without, and imperceptibly night stole over us, and still I sat dreamily by the window, picturing to myself for the hundredth time, and as I did at all dreamy moments, Rutledge as it used to be—the halls filled with servants, the rooms with guests ; carriages rolling to the door ; music and laughter echoing through the house ; Alice

lovely and admired ; Richard, with his refined, aristocratic
face ; and the young Arthur, as the sketch he gave me, had
recorded him.   Then I joined to this links that I had caught
from Mrs. Arnold's broken story ; the flight, the dreary exile in a foreign land, and death finishing a career that
infamy and shame had branded.   But what had Mr. Shenstone to do with it all ?   Perhaps he had loved Alice ; perhaps it was the loss of her that was the terrible trial of
which he had spoken to Mr. Rutledge when I was lying
half unconscious in the study.   Then I tried to put together
more of what I had then heard ; but the more I pondered,
the more confused and indistinct it all grew, and ended by
bringing up, in all its perplexity, the tormenting mystery
of the lost miniature.   Why must I be so baffled about
that ?   Why had I put it out of my power, by my promise
to Kitty, to go to Mr. Rutledge honestly, and tell him the
story, and ask him to help me to discover who had taken
it, and so rid my fancy of the hateful idea that Kitty had
suggested, which, do what I would, had come, between
sleeping and waking, every time I had closed my eyes since
she had told me of it.   In the dead of night, the cold hand
upon my bosom would wake me with a start ; I would reason away the fright, and try to sleep again, but as soon as
unconsciousness would come, the chilling horror would come
too, and startle me into sleepless watching.

I despised myself for the folly ; but I had begun to hate the
darkness.   Even now, the dusky thickening twilight, with
its creeping shadows, made me nervous ; a chill seemed to
strike to my very heart, and I caught myself starting at every
sound, and trembling at every flicker of the dying firelight.

Under these circumstances, the hour that intervened between the closing in of twilight and the ringing of the tea-
bell, could not fail to be a very long and uncomfortable one,
and the promptness with which I hurried down at the sum
mons, attested my preference for social hours and habits
over solitude and contemplation.

CHAPTER XIV.

"What! old, and rich, and childless, too,
And yet believe my friends are true?
Truth might, perhaps, to those belong,
To those who loved me poor and young;
But, trust me, for the new I have,
They'll love me dearly—in my grave."

DR. HUGH was suavity and amiability itself; his host was courteous and attentive; I only, of the party, was abstracted and silent, and could not enter, with any interest, into the discussions, political, social, and educational, to which the medical guest led the way. He frequently appealed to me, but I answered mechanically and at random, and was soon involved in my own thoughts again, while the two gentlemen carried on the conversation learnedly enough between themselves. Though Dr. Hugh showed equal readiness in argument, and had, moreover, the advantage of choosing his topics in all cases, I could not help contrasting the brusque inelegance of his tone with the well-bred ease and quiet of Mr. Rutledge's. One was trying to please and to *appear*, the other was simply *being* what was innate and habitual.

Altogether the doctor was, on this occasion, the most animated and chatty of the trio at the tea-table, and though Mr. Rutledge did a proper share of the talking, still his manner was not unreserved, either to his guest or to me. Whether this was the effect of the change in his feelings toward me, or only the presence of a third party, I could not tell; but it was very tormenting, and made the doctor's stay unbearably tedious, and the termination of it an unspeakable relief. When the hall door closed behind him, however, I could have wished him back, for it was even worse to find myself alone with Mr. Rutledge, for the first

time since the strange night of which I had so many strange
recollections. Since then, was he alienated or altered, or
had he forgotten his interest in me during the days of absence that had intervened? His voice brought the perplexing reverie to an end, and dispelled the doubts forever

"Now that that tiresome doctor has taken himself off,"
he said, in a tone so changed and so divested of its reserve,
that it almost startled me, "perhaps you'll have the grace
to come to me, and tell me how glad you are to be home
again." He held out his hand, and I was by his side in a
moment. "'Home is not home without thee,'" he said.
"What, I should like to be informed, am I to do when
you're gone 'for good,' as this Yankee gentleman would
say?"

Surprise and pleasure brightened my face, and I had
some saucy words on my lips, when the door softly opened,
and *the doctor* stood hesitatingly on the threshold, apologizing for his abrupt return and entrance, on the ground
of having forgotten to impress upon the young lady the
importance of continuing the powders she had been taking
He had not thought of this neglect of his till he had actually got into his buggy at the door, and then remembered
it "on a sudden," and was so much alarmed at thinking
what the consequences might be, that he had sprung out,
and hurried in to give a parting charge on the subject.
Every three hours, he reiterated, and then apologized again
to Mr. Rutledge for the interruption.

Mr. Rutledge received his apologies rather stiffly, and
begged him to be easy on the matter of the powders; he
had no doubt the young lady would follow his advice im-
plicitly, and he trusted the result would be as gratifying as
Dr. Hugh himself could wish. And the gentlemen both
bowed, and Mr. Rutledge accompanied his guest to the
door with undiminished politeness, but with a slight contraction of the brow, that augured ill for the doctor's cause.

There was much expression in the doctor's parting saluta

tion to me; his glance had been rapid, but he had not omitted,
in his observation, the total change of attitude, expression
and voice, that had ensued upon his withdrawing from the
two people who had been so *distraits* and undemonstrative
all the evening; it was a significant fact, and he had not
been slow to seize upon it. And I liked him less than ever
after he left us for the second time that evening.

"Mr. Rutledge," I said, when he had returned from con-
voying the doctor to the door, "did you notice what a disagreeable impression Dr. Hugh seemed to make upon
Tigre? He keeps at a little distance from him, and barks
in the short, snappish way that he always does when the
tortoise-shell cat prowls into the barn."

Mr. Rutledge smiled at the analogy I seemed to trace.

"I don't altogether fancy the man myself, but one must
not be too readily influenced by fancies; no doubt he's very
good in his way, and seems to be much more of a physician
than old Sartain. It's a bad way to expect too much of
people, and I hope you'll never get as much in the habit of
it as I have always been."

With that he dismissed the subject, and presently point
ing to the seat beside him, told me I need not think of say
ing good night yet, as he had a great deal to say to me.
Without much reluctance, I sat down, and listened submissively.

"In the first place, you have not asked what your aunt
says to this new delay."

"Well, what does she say?" I asked, a little uneasily.

"She says, that unless you arrive very shortly at New
York, she shall feel herself obliged to leave all her pressing
household cares, sick children, undisciplined servants, and
come on for you in person."

"It's a new thing for her to be so anxious about me," I
exclaimed, impatiently. "I was sick a month last summer
at school, and she never suggested the idea of coming on to
see me."

" Be that as it may, her anxiety at present knows no
bounds, and I have in vain rendered the most elaborate accounts of your state, and in all ways endeavored to weaken
her fears. This very afternoon I received another letter,
more decided than the last in its request, that if you were
able to be moved, you might be brought on immediately;
if not, she would at once start for this place, and my
answer was to be instantly communicated to her by telegraph."

" You have sent it ?"

" Yes, three hours ago," he answered, looking at me attentively.

" Well, what did you tell her ?"

" That we should start to-morrow morning at eleven
o'clock."

I struggled hard to keep up, under the unexpected
blow, and answered, as I bit my lip and choked down the
tears :

" Very well, sir, I will try to be ready in time."

" The doctor says it will be perfectly safe," continued Mr.
Rutledge, quietly.

" And there is no appeal from his opinion," I interrupted,
tartly.

" I am so much better myself," he went one, as if he had
not heard me, " that there is no imprudence in my attempting it ; and I can see no objection to complying with your
aunt's request immediately. Indeed, I feel that I could not
do otherwise."

His indifferent way of speaking of what to me was such
a vital matter, roused my pride less than it wounded my
sensitiveness, and I had much ado to master myself enough
to say :

" If you had had the goodness to tell me before, I need
not have wasted this evening, but could have spent it in
packing."

" You cannot have much to do, I am sure. Kitty can

pack everything in the morning, and I thought it was best not to worry you by telling you of it before."

"I must go up immediately, however," I said, rising.

"I cannot let you go yet," he said, detaining me. "Do you remember this is the last evening you are to spend at Rutledge?"

"And what of that?"

"You ought to be sorry."

I shrugged my shoulders, and said, it was a pity I could not gratify his taste for the pathetic.

"Ah, nonsense, child!" he said, with a sudden change of manner, "we have so little time left, it's foolish to waste any of it in idle pretences. You may as well cry; I know you are sorry enough, I know you can hardly keep back your tears."

That broke down all my self-control; burying my face in my hands, I burst into a passion of tears. There was no use in attempting to command myself, and indeed I never thought of it. Mr. Rutledge took my hand, and attempted to draw it away from my face, then suddenly relinquishing it, walked rapidly once or twice across the room, returned, and sat down by me.

"You will make it harder than ever for me to let you go, if you cry so bitterly," he said, after a pause. "You will soon forget your grief, and be as happy in your new home as you have been here, while I shall, for a long while, miss you, and be lonely without you. Do you not see I have the most to regret?"

I shook my head, while the sobs came more chokingly than ever.

"Foolish child!" he said, "this is but a transitory feeling with you; it will vanish in the sunshine of to-morrow. In a week, you will have forgotten all about Rutledge."

Now my anger mastered my tears, and looking up, I exclaimed:

"You are always telling me I am a child! You are
always treating me as if I were a senseless plaything! I am
tired of it; I could almost hate you for it!"

He looked at my flashing eyes with a strange intentness,
as if he would read me through and through. "But you are
a child; it would be folly for me to treat you otherwise;
how can I know that your affections and sensibilities are
other than those of any ardent, impetuous child?"

With an impatient gesture, I interrupted him; and turn
ing away, hid my face on the sofa again.

"That is the way!" he exclaimed. "No child could
be more changeable; one moment, I have half a mind to
think you are a woman, and the next, you turn away, and
pout, and cry."

"You shan't have that to say of me again!" I exclaimed,
conquering my tears with a huge effort, and raising my
head. "I will be cold enough, if that's what you want. I
won't trouble you with my tears again, even if you try to
make me cry, as you did a little while ago. I can be as
indifferent and unkind as you are yourself, if that will be
any proof of my maturity and wisdom."

"Indifferent? Ah, there you show your childishness and
ignorance more plainly than you think! Culpably indifferent and unkind!" he said, with a short laugh. "But,"
with a softening of his voice, "whatever there may have
been of neglect or unkindness in my manner, remember,
when you think of it hereafter, that there was nothing that
answered to it, in my heart; remember that I shall never
cease to feel the strongest interest in you, the kindest affection for you; remember, whenever you need a friend, you
have promised to appeal to me. And remember, too," he
continued, in a lighter tone, "all the rest of the engage
ments that you entered into, of which that bracelet is to be
the souvenir. I have the greatest faith in it; I shall
never feel very far separated from you, with this little key
so near my heart," he said, touching the trinket on his chain.

"As for me," I exclaimed, bitterly, "I shall have to wear this bracelet as I've promised to; but I shall try my best to forget the giver and all about him! As for the promises, I don't care *that* for them!" And in emphatic contempt I snapped my fingers.

Mr. Rutledge smiled, as if he knew enough about my indignation to bear up under it, and said, coaxingly and low:

"Ah, surely you're not going to desert me already; my little friend is the one thing in the world I care for, just now; what would be the result, if she were to turn faithless?"

I averted my head. "You should have been prepared for that when you took a child into your friendship."

"Ah! that rankles still, I see. Well, now, turn your face toward me, and look up, while I assure you, solemnly you know, and most sincerely, that I do not think you are childish in most things, that I do believe you are honest and true, and altogether, excepting a few pardonable caprices, as good a friend as one need desire. Doesn't that satisfy you? What could I say more flattering?"

"Oh! as to saying, you are unrivalled at that; it's the doing that you are deficient in. It's all very fine for you to call me your friend, and say how lonely you shall be without me, and all that style of thing; and then, in the next breath, tell me to get ready to go away to-morrow, and remark that you cannot see the least objection to my aunt's plan—and look and laugh just as usual. That doesn't seem much like meaning what you say, surely!"

"But what," he said, "would you have me do? If it made me perfectly miserable to part with you, it is still my duty to do it. Tell me any way of getting out of it."

"Let me stay at Rutledge," I exclaimed, turning toward him with pleading eyes; "just let me stay here. I hate New York, I hate society, I don't even know my aunt; and here I am so happy, and I have just got used to it all, and am beginning to feel at home, and it is cruel to take me to another strange place! I will be so good and useful; I will study and improve myself, and help Mrs. Arnold with the school-children and the poor people, and keep Mrs. Roberts' accounts, and read to you, and write your letters, and be just as good and obedient as possible; not in the least self-willed, not a bit unlady-like. Just try," I went on, coaxingly; "you will not know me, I shall be so amiable!"

"But," he said, with a strange mixture of fondness and irony in his tone, "what would *Madame votre tante* say to such an arrangement?"

"She would say, of course, that if I wanted to, I was very welcome to stay; she has daughters enough already, and not having seen me, she can't be expected to know whether she wants me or not."

"Very well; supposing for a moment, that your aunt had given her consent, and that there was no obstacle in the way of your remaining here, how many weeks do you suppose it would be before you would begin to think regretfully of the gay life you had given up, and the pleasures you had put out of your power, before you would begin to sigh for companions of your own age, and excitements greater than your life here could offer? Believe me, it would not be long before you would be thoroughly 'aweary' of the quiet routine of Rutledge, and thoroughly tired of your bargain."

I protested against this injustice, and exhausted every argument to prove my superiority to such fickleness, but Mr. Rutledge remained unconvinced.

"I do not say you are more fickle than are all other untamed young things of seventeen; it isn't your fault that you are not older and wiser; it is my misfortune. In the nature of things, you cannot stay forever ignorant and innocent, and indifferent to the world—

" ' Let the wild falcon soar her swing,
She'll stoop when she has tired her wing.' "

"It's very strange," I said, "that you should tell me I must put myself in the way of the very temptations that you were so earnest in cautioning me against not long ago. Why must I go into society, when I don't want it? Why must I try the snares of the world, when, in reality, I am best content away from it?"

"You must first know what it is you renounce, my pretty child; you must first see what other places are like, before you can judge whether Rutledge will content you, and what other friends are like, before you can tell how worthy of your affection this first one is. Wait till you are a little older; wait a year or two, and then if you still turn to Rutledge, it is your home forever."

Wait a year or two! If he had said, "Wait till the early part of the twentieth century," it could hardly have seemed a more insupportable term of banishment.

"Ah!" he said, with a sigh, "a year or two seems an age to you now; when you have passed through as many as I have, you'll begin to realize how short they are, how very small a part of a life they form, and how very quickly they pass."

I shook my head. "They would go soon enough if there was anything pleasant to mark them; but if they are to be passed in longing for their end, they will be ages indeed."

"No fear that the next two or three years of your life will be passed in that way, my friend. It would be a heavy blow, indeed, that would take the elasticity out of your spirit, and daunt the courage that I know will make your life a worthy one. Be true to yourself; keep your heart pure, and the world will not hurt you; you will only see how far it is from satisfying you."

"Oh!" I exclaimed, "if I might never have to go in it!

If I could *only* stay here. You can't understand how
miserable it makes me to go among strangers again. And
I am so fond of this place! You need not be afraid that I
shall get tired of it; I don't get tired of people and places
when once I like them. Do you suppose I ever was tired
of my own dear home, or ever would have been, if I had
not been taken away from it?"

And at that recollection the tears came blindingly into
my eyes.

"You have never told me about your home. Were you
happy there?" he asked, kindly. "Tell me about it."

It seemed strange when I remembered it, but it did not
seem so at the time, that I should tell him what I had never
told to the dearest of my confidants, had never before put
into words; but there was a sympathy in his tone that was
irresistible; for the time, my grief seemed his; I did not
wonder why his interest was so strong in my recollections;
I did not think it strange that tears shone in his eyes when
they filled mine, nor that his voice trembled as he told me
of his sympathy; he was my friend; he was kinder and
better than any one else in the world; that was enough.

"Poor little homesick child, you must have been miserable enough, among so many strange faces, with such an
aching heart. It was a cruel thing to send you off so far,
without a single familiar face to comfort you, and so soon
after such a shock."

"Aunt Edith thought it was best for me, I suppose.
Perhaps it was; that is, if it is best for anything living to
be wholly miserable, it was very good for me. And now,"
I went on, turning to him, beseechingly, "how can you
know whether it's best for me to be sent away from here?
I shall be dreadfully homesick there, I know; I shall be so
strange and forlorn among all those gay people; I know
you will be sorry if you don't let me stay. I know you
will say, when it is too late, 'she was right after all; I
should not have made her go.' You will miss me, I know

you will. Think how dreary the long evenings will be, and how lonely!"

" Ah! Don't appeal to my selfishness; let that slumber if it can; don't make my duty any harder than it is already. Be a good, self-denying child, as you have always been, and go because I think it is best for you, and because it is your duty to go, and mine to send you. Will you try?"

"Yes," I said, sadly, "if there's no help, I will try to make the best of it, and think as little as possible about what might have been, and as much as possible about what I ought to do."

" That's my brave little friend again! You haven't been with Mr. Shenstone without profit. He has made you already as philosophical as himself."

" If I could be near Mr. Shenstone," I said, with a sigh, " there would be some chance of my learning to control myself and be good. One can hardly help doing right, with his teaching."

"It may seem so to you," he answered, " and I acknowledge it is a great assistance; but, alas! good counsel cannot accomplish the warfare. If it could, those who have the benefit of Mr. Shenstone's would be fortunate indeed; but we have to struggle and conquer for ourselves; no one can do it for us."

" But you do not mean to say that it isn't the greatest advantage and comfort to have the advice and guidance of such a wise and holy man? You do not mean that you do not think Mr. Shenstone the best and the most devout of men?"

Mr. Rutledge smiled at my enthusiasm.

" Do not be afraid that Mr. Shenstone will suffer at my hands. He has been my guide and counsellor ever since I was younger than you; and so, you see, I have reason to know, experimentally, the value of his counsels, and the possibility of not doing right in spite of them. He is the noblest of men, the most clear-sighted and wise of counsellors, and my nearest and truest friend, and yet, for all that,

I have often gone contrary to his rules, and, no doubt, often grieved his kind heart. But, so it goes! The human heart, you are aware, my young friend, is the very perversest of all created things. Now, at this very moment, would you believe it, I am doing what that same good and wise Mr. Shenstone has warned me not to do; and, moreover, mean to continue doing it."

I looked in astonishment.

"I wonder at you, sir. You will be sorry in the end. Mr. Shenstone, I am certain, knows better than you do."

"How can you possibly know? You cannot tell anything about the right of the case."

"No, of course I don't know anything about it; but from the nature of things, Mr. Shenstone is the most likely to be right. He's older than you, he's a clergyman, and—well—you will not be angry, but I think he is much less likely to be governed by his wishes than you, much more likely to see the right, and give up everything else for it, and to look at things clear of the mists that other people see them through. You know what I mean," I continued, " even though I don't express it very well; and oh! Mr. Rutledge, I am sure you must see, if you think about it at all, that it is very unwise in you to reject Mr. Shenstone's advice. The time may come when you'll regret it."

"Nevertheless, I shall do it."

From perversity, perhaps, as much as anything else, I continued to urge what I thought right. There was quite a fascination in contradicting and opposing Mr. Rutledge; it gave me a giddy sense of elation to think I dared do it, and though I did not gain my point, it diverted me from the thoughts of to-morrow's pain, till the clock struck, and I started up in alarm.

"It's only eleven, Cinderella; there's no need for such a frightened look. There is an hour left of your last evening at Rutledge."

"No, indeed; Kitty is waiting for me, and there is so

much to be done before to-morrow at ten o'clock. Good night, sir."

"Ah, I see you are in a hurry; you are tired. Why didn't you go before? Ten is your usual hour."

The clock had struck another half hour before my last evening at Rutledge was ended—before the last good night was spoken at the library door, and, with a sad enough heart, I ascended the stairs, and traversed the dreary hall, where not even ghostly terrors would have had power to startle me from the heavy grief that was lying at my heart.

My room was cheerless; the candle died flickeringly as I opened the door; the fire was dead long since; poor Kitty, tired with waiting, had fallen asleep on the rug, with one of the sofa pillows under her head. I covered her softly with some shawls, wrapped one about myself, stole to the bay window, and leaning my forehead against the pane, cried as if my heart would break.

CHAPTER XV.

" What is this passing scene ?
A peevish April day !
A little sun, a little rain,
And then night sweeps along the plain,
And all things fade away."

KIRKE WHITE.

THE grey dawn was just breaking when I woke Kitty.
She started up bewildered, and her bewilderment did not
decrease when I told her the object of this réveillé. I never
had any cause to doubt the sincerity of the grief she showed
on this occasion. I had added as much to the pleasure of
her life since I had been at Rutledge, as she had increased
the comfort of mine ; and it was with no very light hearts that
we went about the business of packing. There was too much
to be done, however, to admit of much sentiment, and we
both bestirred ourselves so diligently, that before the breakfast bell rung my trunk was strapped and labelled, my bag
filled with everything necessary for the journey, and my
bonnet, cloak and shawl lying ready on the bed. There
was not another article now about the room that belonged
to me. What a dreary and forsaken look it had already ;
the toilet-table dismantled of its recent ornaments ; the
books and work that had given so bright and familiar a
look to the pretty room, now all removed, and a bit of card,
a ball of cord, and some withered flowers, were all that
graced the étagère and the table.

I did not dare trust myself to enter into particulars, even
in thought, and with a very resolute voice, telling Kitty I
would come up immediately after breakfast, and see if there
was anything more for her to do, I went downstairs.

192

The first floor presented signs of an exciting stir; there was a very unusual bustle and movement in the quiet hall—a trunk and a valise stood at the front door, a pile of cloaks and wrappers lay beside them; Thomas' long limbs were animated with unwonted energy, Mrs. Roberts bustled in and out of pantries, and to and fro through side-doors and entries, in a very startling manner; Sylvie was more raving distracted than ever—flew unmeaningly up and down stairs—took the wrong thing to the wrong place—irritated everybody, and was in the way generally. Mr. Rutledge, in the library, gave audience to farmer, gardener, groom, and carpenter—delivered orders—paid bills—settled accounts—the one undisturbed member of the commonwealth. It was evident that the sudden marching orders had taken them all by surprise, and unsettled most of their brains. Stephen, alone, I was happy to notice, seemed to preserve in some degree the possession of his reasoning faculties, and did not "haze" to the same extent as the others. Kitty, I thought, comes honestly by her *sang froid*.

I stood some minutes by the hall window gazing out upon the dreary winter landscape, the dull sky, the brown bare trees, the hard grey earth, ashes of roses in hue, the nether millstone in hardness. It had been the coldest night of the season, the water that stood in the narrow carriage-tracks and in the little crescents that the horses' hoofs had made, was frozen hard; the trees, the hedges, looked as if they were, too—so still and stiff they stood. Not a bit of wind was stirring, but the temperature was evidently moderating.

"Softening down for snow," Stephen remarked, as he passed out; "you'll not have it so cold for your journey, Miss. It's too bad that you're going, such fine sleighing as we have at Rutledge a little later in the season. You should stay and enjoy it, Miss."

"I wish, indeed I could, Stephen," I said, with great

9

sincerity. "It's a long while since I've had a good sleigh-ride. The roads must be splendid for it here, so broad and clear."

"Beautiful, Miss; packed smooth, and hard as the house floor, and as dry as sand. You might walk over 'em in your thin slippers, and never wet your feet. And the snow lays sometimes better than a month without a rain or a thaw, the weather as clear as a bell and as cold as Christmas—thermometer down to nobody knows where, and nobody minds, after they're used to it. But maybe you're afraid of the cold?"

"Not I! It's the very thing I like. I'd give anything for a ride behind those bays, wrapped up to the eyes in furs, on the coldest day Rutledge ever saw. I know they must go like the very wind when there's snow on the ground; don't they?"

"Aye, Miss, that they do!" exclaimed Stephen, warming up at the mention of his favorites; for though the garden was his particular province, as the oldest man in the service, he took a fatherly interest in everything animate and inanimate on the place. "That they do! There's nothing in this part of the country has ever begun to come up to 'em. I'd like you to see 'em go, when their spirit's up! 'Taint many young ladies," he continued, with a "gentleman of the old school" bow, "'taint many young ladies as can tell a horse when they see him; but everybody says that you sit like a born horsewoman, and Michael, stupid rascal as he is, swears you ride like a cavalry officer. Nobody but the master ever managed that Madge so before."

I acknowledged the compliment with a laugh and a blush, and encouraged Stephen to continue his bulletin of the stable, in which he well knew my interest. Indeed, the worthy gardener was not to blame for his loquacity, as this was by no means the beginning of our acquaintance; many a chat I had had with him over the garden-gate, while he leaned on his spade, and discoursed willingly of the ancient glories of the house of Rutledge, and the manifold virtues of the present master of it. I knew he was a faithful, honest old fellow, shrewd and intelligent beyond his class, and altogether, inestimably superior to many old fogies in the higher walks of life, and being certain that he was very much delighted to be talked to, I very much enjoyed talking to him.

He was just saying, with great appearance of sincerity, that he did not know what they should all do, now I was going. I had waked up the old place "amazing;" it was a long while since there had been anybody so cheerful-like and bright in it; and as for his Kitty, he really did not know how she could content herself after me—when we were both startled by finding that Mr. Rutledge had been an undemonstrative auditor of the whole conversation, and ostensibly engaged in putting some books into the valise behind us, was quietly listening, and no doubt criticising, all that had been said.

Stephen looked a little confused, only a very little though, and with dogged dignity gave me many good wishes for the journey, bowed and withdrew. I turned around and faced the intruder with a determination not to be ashamed of myself, and not to acknowledge that I had been unduly familiar with an inferior, and to submit to no lecture; but his face was so different from anything that I had expected, that I blushed, and looked very foolish, instead of very defiant. He laughed outright.

"Upon my word," he exclaimed, "I never saw old Stephen so nearly embarrassed in my life; during an acquaintance of some forty years, I never saw him approach so near a blush! And you, young lady, certainly have an extraordinary taste for low life! You have no greater passion, that I can see, than the one you have just been acknowledging to Stephen, for horseflesh generally; and as for dogs, your mind runs on them continually; Kitty shares your confidence—Stephen is hail-fellow-well-met—Michael swears by you, and "——

"That's enough for the present, if you please," I said, hurrying into the dining-room.

"You will have coffee, sir?" I continued, very blandly, sitting down at the table.

"Are you sure you know enough of such things to make me a palatable cup? I know you could saddle my horse for me in extremity, and groom the bays to perfection, but whether you're to be trusted with anything so feminine as making coffee, really you must excuse me for being a little skeptical."

"Ah! please, Mr. Rutledge!"

But it did not please Mr. Rutledge to do anything but tease me just at that time. After breakfast was over, he told me, looking at his watch in his precise manner, that there was just an hour and a quarter before it would be time to start, and if I had nothing better to do, I might come down to the stables with him, and give my parting orders about the care of the horses and dogs. I did not know whether this invitation was given sarcastically or sincerely, but I preferred accepting it in the latter sense; so I ran upstairs and put on my bonnet and cloak and joined him in the hall in a very short time. He evidently did not mean to give me opportunity for any sentimental regrets, for he never before had been half so teasing. I could not do anything right, though I was a baa-lamb, as far as submissiveness went. I walked either too slow or too fast, was too chatty with the groom, or too taciturn with him; there was not a fault or indiscretion in all our previous acquaintance that I did not then and there have to bear the penalty of. It was only when I came to say good-bye to Madge that my courage gave way completely, and I leaned my forehead on her glossy neck to conceal the silly tears that filled my eyes.

"I verily believe," said Mr. Rutledge, "that she knows

you. She does not submit to such familiarity from strangers."

Finding that I did not answer, he continued, in a kinder tone:

"I think, as you broke her in, to feminine usage at least, you are entitled to her; so I make her over to you, body and soul, if soul she has, to have and to hold, from this day forward; and a tender mistress may she find you."

"Thank you," I said, without raising my head; "a very useful gift; of about as much service to me as if you should make over to me your right and title in the fastest pair of reindeer in the employ of the Hudson's Bay Company."

"Why, don't you mean ever to come here again? If you don't, you had better take her with you. Any way, she is mine no longer. What shall be done with her? Shall Michael blanket and prepare her to accompany us to New York? or will you leave her here till you come back?"

"Ah! Do you fancy I am child enough to believe in such a conveyance as that? It wouldn't stand in any court of law."

"What would you have? There isn't a magistrate within four miles, and we haven't the time to draw up a document properly. I will tell you what can be done as next best. I will record the transaction here, above her manger, and there it shall remain to remotest ages, 'to witness if I lie.'"

Mr. Rutledge took out his penknife, and with considerable ingenuity carved in the sturdy old oak beam, the transfer of Madge Wildfire from himself to me, using, for brevity, only initials, and then the date. I climbed up to the fourth round of the ladder when it was completed, and did my best to achieve a signature, but the result was so unsatisfactory that Mr. Rutledge put beneath it, "her mark," and so it stands to this day, I suppose. This transaction having consumed a good deal of the hour and a quarter that we had before starting, Mr. Rutledge rather hurried up my adieux with my new favorite, and it was very ungraciously that he submitted to wait till I had cut a lock from her black mane, and embraced her tenderly for the twentieth time.

"Nobody is to ride her, remember," I said, as we went out; "only, of course, the man who takes care of her, when it is necessary for exercise."

"Your orders shall be obeyed. Any further instructions that may occur to you in the course of the winter you had better commit to paper and send to me, and I will observe them faithfully."

"Oh, I depend entirely on your integrity; I am confident you will be careful of her. Anyway," I continued, "it's a comfort to know I own anything at Rutledge, and have a sort of claim upon its hospitality still. Ah! how long it will be before I walk up this road with you again, Mr. Rutledge!"

"Maybe not," he answered. "You shall, if you will, come back and make me a visit before many months are over; you shall come back and see how Rutledge looks in her June dress,

"'When all this leafless and uncolored scene,
　Shall flush into variety again;'

when this dull November sky shall have given place to the warmest summer sunshine, and this hard, frozen earth shall be soft and brown, and roses shall be blooming about this dreary porch, and the garden shall be one wilderness of sweets, and the trees and the lawn shall be all of the richest green. Will you come then, if I send for you?"

I checked my look of delight with a sigh: "you'll forget before that time, I'm afraid. And I don't believe my aunt would let me come."

"You may trust that to me. Haven't you seen that I make people do as I wish them to? Do you not believe that I can induce your aunt to let you come, if I continue to want you, and you continue to want to come?"

"Perhaps so," I said, half incredulously; "but if I remember right, my Aunt Edith is fond of her own way too, is she not?"

"She has that reputation," he answered, with a short laugh. "But *cela ne fait rien*. You shall come if you wish to. Leave it to me, and say nothing about it."

✔ June is a long way off yet, but it is better than two or three years, the term of my 'honorable banishment,' that you first decreed."

Before we reached the house, the snow-flakes began to descend, large, and soft, and white, floating down in fast-increasing thickness,

> "As though life's only call or care
> Were graceful motion."

"How pretty it makes the landscape!" I said, pausing on the steps. "In among the bare trees there, it makes such a charming variety and lightness, and in a few minutes every twig will be feathered with it, and fences, and roofs, and all. Why can't we wait till we have had one sleigh-ride?"

"This snow will not amount to anything; we should have to wait a long while for a sleigh-ride. It is too early yet for that entertainment; a fortnight hence will be time enough to expect it."

"I think you are mistaken," I said, looking wisely at the clouds, "there's plenty of snow up there, and we shall have enough of it before night, depend upon it. Hadn't we better wait till to-morrow? It would be dreadful to be caught in a heavy snow-storm on the way."

"Have you forgotten your good resolutions of last night?" he said, in a low tone. "There's the carriage."

And without answering a word I ran upstairs. Kitty wrapped me tenderly in my soft shawl, and fastened my fur tippet carefully round my neck.

"Oh, Kitty! you'll smother me!" I cried. But it was something less tangible than tippet or shawl that was smothering me just then, and choking my breath. I gave one glance around the room, thrust a *douceur* into Kitty's hand, and telling her to bring down my travelling-bag, hurried out without a second look, and downstairs without a second thought, sustained by the determination not to make a baby of myself and cry.

The library was empty; I passed on through the hall. Mr. Rutledge was already at the carriage, superintending the packing in it of numerous valises, books, shawls, and packages. Mrs. Roberts, bluer than ever with the cold, stood by him, busy with all the arrangements for his comfort, and looking a shade more cheerless than usual, at the prospect of separation from the master who stood to her lonely old age in the place of son and friend. "I believe she does love him," I thought, and warming toward her at the idea of one redeeming weakness, I walked up to her and said, extending my hand:

"Good bye, Mrs. Roberts. I am afraid you will be glad to get rid of such a troublesome guest; but I assure you I am very sorry to have given you trouble, and very much obliged to you for the attention you have shown me."

Mrs. Roberts gave me her hand, and answered, without any undignified haste:

"All attentions you have received from me you are very welcome to. I hope never to be wanting in my duty to any guest of Mr. Rutledge's."

"Then you can't regard me with favor for any other cause? Ah, Mrs. Roberts, I don't know why it is you would never like me, even before I gave you any reason to dislike me."

"Mrs. Roberts will learn to think differently some day,

hope," said Mr. Rutledge, without looking up from his occupation. " Is there anything more to go here?"

There was nothing, the last package was bestowed in its place, the last strap secured. Thomas, who was to accompany his master to New York, stood waiting for us to enter the carriage. Michael was on the box.

" We are all ready, then," and he motioned me to enter. " Good bye, Mrs. Roberts," he continued. " I believe there is nothing further that I wanted to say to you. Make yourself as comfortable as you can this winter, and let me hear from you occasionally. I shall be back by the latter part of January, however, and I hope everything will go on well till then."

Mrs. Roberts looked very much as if she thought nothing more improbable than his being back in January, but only said:

"Good bye, sir. I shall write."

Mr. Rutledge followed me into the carriage, and shut the door. I bowed again to Mrs. Roberts, and looked out anxiously for Kitty, who had not appeared since she brought down my bag; but at that moment Kitty, in person, was discovered at the other window of the carriage, bringing me a glove she said she had found, which, however, I guessed was only a ruse to get another good bye.

" Ah, Kitty, that's the glove Tigre gnawed, and I never have found the mate to it since that day; of course it's useless, so you'd better keep it to 'remember me by,' as they say. Good bye, again."

Kitty said, " Good bye, Miss," but with so tearful and woebegone a look, withal, that even Mr. Rutledge was touched, and leaning forward, he said:

" Don't take it so very much to heart, my good girl. Your young mistress will be back again, sometime, I hope. And be as obliging and submissive as you can to Mrs. Roberts, Kitty; remember it was my last charge."

And dropping some coins into her hand, he told Michael

to drive on. At this moment Tigre rushed whining to the carriage, and I begged he might be allowed to drive to the station, and come back in the carriage. Mr. Rutledge consenting, Kitty placed the tawny favorite in my arms, and,

> "Smack went the whip,
> Round went the wheels,"

but I have known gladder folks. From the back of the carriage I watched the lessening figures on the piazza, as we drove rapidly down the avenue, and an involuntary sigh escaped me as a winding of the road hid the dark house, with its snow-capped roofs and porticoes, from my sight.

"Good bye till June," I said, regretfully.

"Till June," repeated Mr. Rutledge, pulling Tigre's ears, and making him yelp. "Do you understand, Tigre? This young lady means to come back in June, if she doesn't change her mind. Understand the condition, Tigre. What do you think of our chance?"

The cur, by way of answer, began gnawing at my tippet.

"Don't destroy that too, sir," I exclaimed. "You've ruined one pair of gloves for me already. Isn't it singular, what could have become of that other one," I continued. "I've searched high and low for it—everywhere, in fact."

"Where did you see it last?" he inquired.

"I cannot remember anything about it, after—after—Tigre and I started on our race. Don't scold," I said, coaxingly, "you know I am going to reform."

"Careless girl," he said, gloomily, "what will you lose next?"

"It wasn't my fault; I've looked everywhere for it. Isn't it strange what has become of it?"

"Very strange," said Mr. Rutledge, gravely. "Indeed, I may say, in a high degree mysterious."

CHAPTER XVI.

"Get thee back, Sorrow, get thee back!
My brow is smooth, mine eyes are bright,
My limbs are full of health and strength,
My cheeks are fresh, my heart is light."

MACKAY.

"Why, which way are we going?" I exclaimed, as we turned off, on an opposite road, about quarter of a mile before reaching the well-remembered depot and gloomy suburbs which had been, I supposed, our destination.

"To tell you the truth," said my *compagnon de voyage*, "I have begun to look upon railroads as an invention of the enemy, and to prefer any other mode of travel. So that, considering we are both invalids (a fact you are constantly overlooking), and cannot bear fatigue or excitement, I have arranged our route after this manner: we drive, to-day, by easy stages as far as W.; then a night's rest there; and to-morrow morning go on to C., where we part with the carriage, and take the day-boat down the river, which will bring us to the haven of our desires to-morrow evening about seven o'clock. This seemed a more agreeable plan than going by cars, and I thought would be less fatiguing."

"*A la bonne heure!*" I cried, remembering it was three times as long as the railroad route.

It proved a most delightful journey; the further we went, the thinner the snow-clouds grew, and as the day wore on, they disappeared altogether, and the sun came out, faint and pale, and the air grew soft and mild. The carriage was the easiest imaginable, the roads were in good condition, the horses disdained their burden, and the occasional

respites which their master decreed, the scenery was as
varied and charming as inland scenery at that season of the
year could possibly be; every change and amusement that
the limits of the carriage admitted of, Mr. Rutledge's care
had provided; and we were two companions who had at
least the charm of freshness for each other, and were not as
yet bored with one another's society, whatever we might
be in the course of time. We tried to read, but the pages
of my new novel did not turn very fast; I gave it up before
the heroine (the records of whose nursery reminiscences
occupied two thirds of the volume) had entered her tenth
year. Mr. Rutledge's review had, I afterward found, but
two of the leaves cut, though he read it assiduously for an
hour and a half.

So we tacitly agreed to resign literature, and devote our
attention to the scenery, which, as we approached the Hudson, certainly did grow worthy of attention. The purple-
headed mountains already were discernible against the pale
sky; the hills grew steeper, the roads wilder. There was an
anecdote or a legend attached to every dark wood or anti-
quated farmhouse we passed. Mr. Rutledge seemed to
know every inch of the way, and to be familiar with its
history since its settlement by the pale-faced gentry; though
it is my belief, that where he did not know of any entertaining tradition "to cheat the toil, and cheer the way," he
waived all conscientious regard to veracity, and improvised
one on the spot. Very engrossing they were, however,
whether manufactured from "whole cloth" or founded on
fact, and it was quite three o'clock before any of the party
(inside passengers at least) began to revolve seriously the
question of dinner. Then, however, it appeared that Mrs.
Roberts' care had provided us with the most delicate and
tempting of collations, and we stopped to enjoy it at the
outskirts of a little village, by the side of a fresh, clear
brook that was on its way, I suppose, "to join the brim-
ming river," that was our destination also. We went by

different routes, however, and I never have seen the pretty little eddying streamlet since that pleasant lunch upon its banks, when Mr. Rutledge filled my cup from its clear waters, and Thomas cooled the wine in its bosom. Rather a superfluous service, I couldn't help thinking, in consideration of the season and state of the thermometer; but it brought out in strong relief the methodic precision of Thomas' mind. He was an invaluable machine; once wound up correctly, he ran for any given time, but as to any exercise of his reasoning faculties in the discharge of his duties, that was as totally wanting as in other machines. Any display of it from him, would have been as startling to his master, as it would have been, had the watch in his pocket suddenly addressed him in good English. Thomas, however, was just the servant for Mr. Rutledge; he would have been worse than useless to a lazy man who wanted a valet to take care of him; but Mr. Rutledge chose to do his own thinking in most cases, and only wanted his orders promptly executed, which Thomas certainly was capable of doing, and did to admiration.

A very nice lunch Mrs. Roberts had prepared for us, and we drank her health gratefully in some very superior Burgundy. We did not hurry ourselves at all; and as I treated Tigre to some of the remaining delicacies, and Thomas packed up the baskets again, Mr. Rutledge lazily sketched the group from the carriage window, on a blank leaf in my book; making rather a spirited drawing of it, only caricaturing grotesquely the length of Thomas' legs, and my eyelashes. Then we got *en route* again, and with occasional stoppings to sketch, which I insisted on, and occasional pauses at village inns to water the horses, or rather to wash their faces, the afternoon wore on.

"Tired?" Of course not, never fresher in my life. What a nuisance railcars are, with their distracting racket and bustle and jar. Why do not people always travel in carriages?

Mr. Rutledge agreed with me that it was very pleasant; indeed, he seemed to enjoy it, just as he did that ride I had such good cause to remember. He left all care and sadness behind at Rutledge, and gave himself up to the present. In that little travelling-cap, too, I was sure he didn't look a day over thirty.

"Mr. Rutledge, you look to-day so like that crayon sketch of your young relative, that you gave me. It is really wonderful."

Mr. Rutledge laughed, and asked me if I continued to admire it.

"Oh, as much as ever," I answered, laughing, and blushing, too, under cover of the twilight, for the short November day had faded. He evidently thought I was still deceived about the picture, and I did not enlighten him.

"I mean to hang it in the very best light in my room in New York, where I can look at it from 'morn to dewy eve,' if I choose."

"I advise you not; Josephine will ferret out the mystery, and expose your romantic devotion. She isn't given that way herself, and will not spare you. Your ideas of hero-worship and hers might not agree."

"Well, if they do not, it may prove fortunate in the end. We shall not be so likely to interfere with each other."

"If you do, 'may I be there to see!'"

"Which would you bet on?"

Mr. Rutledge, after a protest against such language from such lips, deliberated somewhat upon my question, and then favored me with his opinion. We were, he thought, in point of will, about equally matched; but my French-bred cousin, he was afraid, had a little the advantage of me in coolness, and had enjoyed the benefit of a training and experience which might tell heavily against me. And much more to the same effect, which I only laughed at then, but remembered afterward with less amusement.

All this while it was growing darker and darker, and we did not arrive at W——, as it was proper we should have done some time since. This seemed at length to strike Mr. Rutledge, and he called to Michael to know if he was sure of the road. Michael was sure, and again we went on. At the end of another half hour, however, Mr. Rutledge again stopped him, and as it was too dark to see anything of the road, he directed him to drive toward the only light we could discover, which proved to emanate from the dingy window of a low farmhouse about a quarter of a mile off. At Thomas' thundering knock, appeared a bony rustic in his shirt-sleeves, who came wonderingly to the carriage, shading a candle with his hand, which threw fantastic shadows on his rough, open-mouthed visage, followed by an untidy-looking woman, and a whole troop of shaggy, uncombed children, evidently just roused from their first nap. Mr. Rutledge, after long perseverance, elicited the information that he sought, which proved anything but agreeable, being a confirmation of his fears. We had come five miles out of our way, W—— lying just ten miles to the south, while we had been, under Michael's guidance, pursuing a course due north.

Michael was a miserable and a scared man, when the thunders of his master's wrath fell upon him. Mr. Rutledge was not very demonstrative or vehement, but he conveyed the idea of an angry man as alarmingly as I should care to see it represented. No wonder Michael was scared; even I felt a little awe-struck till after he had shut the carriage door, and we had turned to retrace our course.

"Are you very tired?" he said. "I would not have had this happen upon any consideration. You will be utterly worn out, and unable to travel to-morrow. I thought I had arranged it admirably for you, but this Hibernian numbskull has upset it all."

I assured him that, on my account, he need not anathematize the luckless Michael further, for I was not in the least tired, and did not mind the detention at all. Owing to this little contretemps, it was ten o'clock when we arrived at W——, and halted at the door of its most promising hotel, which was at best but a shabby affair. I would not have acknowledged it on any account, but I was dreadfully tired and sleepy, and could hardly conceal these humiliating frailties, while the landlord and a drowsy waiter or two bustled about to get us some " tea;" which meal, arranged upon a remote end of a dreary, long table, in a dingy, long room, was utterly unpalatable, and I was but too grateful to Mr. Rutledge for excusing me when a chambermaid appeared to say my room was ready, and conduct me to it.

It seemed direfully early next morning when the same functionary appeared to awake me, with the intelligence that breakfast would shortly be on the table, and the gentleman had sent her to call me, and to see if there was any way in which she could help me. "The gentleman" had evidently backed his suggestion with some specimens of the United States currency, for she was overwhelmingly attentive, and helped me to dress in "no time." Breakfast, arranged again as a little colony, at the end of the long table, was considerably more inviting than last night's meal, Thomas having had orders to beat up the town for spring chickens and fresh butter, and, being a veteran in the recruiting service, had of course succeeded. Mr. Rutledge looked a little anxiously at me, and said I was wretchedly pale, and he did not know about going on. I laughed at the idea, and we were soon *en route* again, driving briskly along in the eye of a strong wind, and with the bluest of skies overhead.

Arrived at C——, we had an hour to spare, before the arrival of the boat, which I spent in the parlor of the very pretending steamboat hotel, in writing a few lines of adieu and apology to Mrs. Arnold, accounting, as satisfactorily as

I could, for my unceremonious and abrupt departure, and desiring a renewal of my acknowledgments to Mr. Shenstone. Of this, Mr. Rutledge approved, and wrote a few lines to Mr. Shenstone to accompany it. Then came the parting from Tigre, and the sending back of the carriage, which seemed like severing the last tie to Rutledge. Tigre was much affected, poor beast, and looked wistfully back, out of the carriage window, as far as we could see.

A bell rings, a rush occurs, Thomas devotes himself to the baggage, Mr. Rutledge gives his arm to me, we thread the crowded wharf, the blue Hudson dances in the sunlight, the fine steamer holds her breath, and tries to lie still while we get on board.

> "O Tiber! Father Tiber! To whom the Romans pray,
> A Roman's life, a Roman's arms, take thou in charge this day."

I am luxuriously established in the saloon, with every imaginable wish attended to, and easy-chairs, books, papers, and cushions enough to satisfy five invalids, but they do not satisfy me. I am bored with the heat, and the whimpering of the pale children, whom a lean, sallow-looking mother feeds unremittingly with "bolivars" and "taffy;" I am tired with the swinging of those lamps overhead, and the everlasting rocking of a stout lady in a red plush rocking-chair, and with looking at the gaudy colors in the carpet, and I rush out for a brisk walk on the deck with Mr. Rutledge. What a day it is! How impossible to be otherwise than happy and hopeful; how inevitably the dark phantoms of doubt and dread take themselves off in the light of such a sun as this, and in the sight of such a scene! The waves dance bright and gay in the sunshine ; the mountains rise, on either hand, into the blue and cloudless sky ; in a word, the loveliest river in all this lovely river-braided New World lays before me, the heart of seventeen beats in my bosom, the glow of health and exercise tingles in my veins; what wonder that I forget the tears of yesterday, the separation, the homesickness, the loneliness that I so dreaded.

Neither can my companion altogether resist the influences of the hour. If the sharp air and the quick walk have, as he says, made the tardy roses bloom again on my cheeks, they have also brought a glow to his face, and a sparkle to his eye, and untamed wit and sarcasm to his lips. He quizzes our fellow voyagers, tells me odd stories of former travel, droll sketches of western journeyings, and California "experiences." Then the laugh dies, as some winding of the river brings suddenly before us a picture too grand to be looked at with trifling words and laughter on our lips. And Mr. Rutledge has the "right thing" to say then, in his rich manly voice, and the right words to embody the voiceless thoughts that crowd to my own lips —words that do not jar or desecrate, but make the beauty tangible and the grandeur more ennobling.

By and by, most of our fellow travellers give up to the cold and go below; and at last we are left with only a persevering artist, who holds his hat on with one hand, and sketches with the other, and a couple of ladies, whose ruddy cheeks, thick shoes, grey dresses, plaid shawls, "boas" and big bonnets, proclaim indisputably to be H. B. M.'s loyal and unalienated subjects. It has always been a question with me, as yet unanswered, whether by any act of Parliament these "proud islanders," out on their travels, are prohibited from appearing in anything but the invariable grey dress, plaid shawl, boa, and big bonnet, in which they invariably do appear. After a while, even they go down, and a solitary cadaverous-looking man, in the dress of a Romish priest, is our only companion. He paces up and down one corner of the deck, never raising his heavy eyes, but reading prayers diligently out of a little book, his thin lips moving rapidly. It is no doubt a good and pious thing to read prayers out of a little book; but it seems to me, that with that grand and glorious lesson spread upon the mountains there before us, it would be a very pardonable thing to look up at it, and to give God thanks.

It is rather a bore to go down to dinner, and after that, to be sentenced to a term of imprisonment in the saloon, because, forsooth, it is too cold outside, and I must rest. But late in the afternoon, I plead that the wind has fallen, that there is no possible chance of my taking cold, and I must see the sun set among the Highlands, and I gain reluctant permission; and now for another walk!

The sunset is beyond my hopes; the twilight steals down after it, soft and dusky, and broods about the rocky Palisades, and dulls to dimness the dancing waves, and settles, grey and thick, around the pretty villas and white cottages that dot the banks, and deepens slowly, till all is one sombre hue in earth and sky, and one fair star comes out to establish the reign of night.

We are late this evening in arriving at New York; we should have been there some time ago; in less than half an hour we shall be at the wharf, Mr. Rutledge says. All my gaiety and spirits have fled; I wonder that I could have forgotten. Still we pace the deck; there is no talk of cold or fatigue now; indeed, not much talk of any kind.

"We are in sight of your new home now," says my companion, pointing

> "Where the lamps quiver
> So far in the river."

And I cannot reply, to save my life. A mist of tears dim the glare of those lights, at first sight. We near the wharf; the bell rings; the busy hum of the city reaches our ears less and less faintly; the dim figures that crowd the wharf grow more distinct.

"We had better go below," I say, with a shiver, "I have to find my books and shawls, and it is growing so cold."

Perhaps if I had known more about that " untold, untried
to-morrow," which I so vaguely dreaded, I should have
shrunk more even than I did, from ending this short hour
before its dawning.   But,

" It is well we cannot see
What the end will be."

CHAPTER XVII.

‡ "And all that fills the heart of friends
When first they feel, with secret pain,
Their lives henceforth have separate ends,
And never can be one again."
                                    LONGFELLOW.

THOMAS being at once the most determined and the most imposing of attendants, he speedily succeeded in clearing a way for us through the crowd of hackmen, carmen, and newsboys, and in selecting the most promising of the array of vehicles offered for our accommodation; installing us and our luggage therein and thereon; and bestowing his own long limbs *à côté du cocher*, we were soon rattling over pavements, rough and jarring to a miserable degree. Mr. Rutledge perceived how frightened and nervous I was, and first tried to laugh away, then to coax away, my foolish dread of meeting my aunt. It was in vain; for once, his kindness and eloquence were lost upon me. I could think of nothing but the approaching interview; and looking out of the window, counted eagerly the blocks we passed.

" How much further is it ?" I asked, despairingly, as we rumbled through bewildering labyrinths of dark and narrow streets. " Aren't we nearly there ?"

" My dear little rustic, we are not quarter of the way. We have a long drive before us yet, and if you will renounce the pleasure of looking out at those crazy lamp-posts, and turn your face this way, I will promise to tell you long enough before we reach Gramercy Square, for you to get up a very pretty speech to rush into you

213

aunt's arms withal. In the meantime, think about me, and not about her."

I tried to obey, while my companion amused and humored me like the spoilt child I was fast becoming under his indulgence. It was impossible not to feel reassured by his manner, and soothed by it, half teasing and half tender; but all the terror returned, when, looking at his watch, and then out into the street, he said:

"I promised to tell you; we are now in Fourth Avenue; in about three minutes and a quarter, we shall turn into Gramercy Square, and in about one minute and three quarters from that time, we shall stop at the door of your new home. You have just five minutes to smooth your hair, pinch some color into your white cheeks, say good bye, and tell me how good and faithful a friend you are going to be."

"Oh," I cried, in great alarm, "surely you will go in! I shall *die* if I have to go alone. Dear Mr. Rutledge! You would not be so unkind. Just think how little I know my aunt, and how I shall feel to be all alone without one soul I know. You surely will not leave me."

Mr. Rutledge laughed and yielded; before I was aware, the carriage had stopped, and Thomas had mounted the steps and rung the bell. In a moment, a stream of light from the hall showed the bell was answered. Thomas returned to open the door of the carriage, and with Mr. Rutledge's kind words in my ear, and the kind touch of his hand on mine, I crossed the dreaded threshold. The servant, who recognized Mr. Rutledge deferentially, showed us into a parlor, where the soft light, the rich curtains, and the pleasant warmth, gave one an instant feeling of luxury and comfort. The next room was only dimly lighted; but beyond that, through lace hangings, was visible a brighter room, and glimpses of glass and silver, made it apparent that dinner was but just over.

From this room, pushing aside the drapery with graceful

haste, issued a lady, who I knew at once to be my aunt Edith. There never was a firmer and more elastic tread than hers, nor a better turned and more graceful figure; the modish little cap upon her head, with its floating ribbons, was all that at that distance looked matronly enough to designate her as the mother of the demoiselle who followed her. Mr. Rutledge advanced to meet her, thus shielding me a moment longer. Her greeting to him was as gracious and cordial as possible, but she looked eagerly forward, saying quickly:

"*Mais où est l'enfant ?*"

Mr. Rutledge laughed, and turned to me, "*La voici,*" he said, appreciating her look of amazement.

"Impossible!" she exclaimed, starting back. "My child I never should have known you," she continued, taking me by both hands, and kissing me as affectionately as she could for her bewilderment. She held me off, and looked at me again; then gave Mr. Rutledge a quick, searching look, and said rapidly in French, in a tone that was not altogether as light and jesting as it was meant to appear, "And this is the 'little girl' you have been writing to me about for the last three weeks; this is 'the child' you have had the care of. Upon my word, monsieur, your notions of infancy and mine differ !"

Mr. Rutledge answered lightly, but very indifferently; really he begged Mrs. Churchill would forgive his misrepresentation of facts, if he had been guilty of any; he was, he acknowledged, culpably unenlightened on the different stages of rosebud-opening; it had struck him that the rosebud under discussion was in the unopened and undeveloped state, and so he had spoken of it; but he begged Mrs. Churchill would excuse his ignorance and inattention.

Mrs. Churchill said, recovering an easy tone :

"Ah, we all know your sad willfulness and coldness!" This in French; then in English, "Josephine, my child, here is your new cousin."

Josephine came forward, and with pretty *empressement*, kissed me on both cheeks, and held my hand affectionately as she exclaimed :

"Why, mamma! she is taller than I am, and so much older than I expected!"

"And you are so different!" I said, gazing admiringly at her slight, elegant figure, and pleasing brunette face.

"Do not forget your old friend for your new one, though, Miss Josephine," said Mr. Rutledge, extending his hand.

Josephine looked very coquettish and pretty, dropped her eyes, and gave him her hand, saying :

"You were so long in coming, we began to doubt whether you cared for that title."

"Put my long-delayed return, Miss Josephine, down to a combination of the most adverse and unconquerable circumstances. What with runaway cars, and runaway horses, broken arms, and brain fevers, the wonder is, not that we did not arrive before, but that we arrived at all."

"Do not keep that poor child standing any longer," exclaimed my aunt, drawing me gently to a sofa, while Mr. Rutledge and Josephine seated themselves opposite, and talked as if they were, indeed, "friends of old," while Josephine's laugh, which, gay as it was, hadn't altogether a true ring to it, conveyed the idea of more familiarity and intimacy than I was quite prepared for. Meanwhile my aunt untied my bonnet-strings, smoothed my hair, and said I was growing so like my poor dear mother. No doubt it was kindly meant, but I had never yet learned to bear calmly the least allusion to my grief, and the tears rushed into my eyes, and the dawning confidence and self-possession were miserably dashed back again, and I had to struggle hard to make any reply at all. My aunt soothingly praised my pretty sensibility, and only made matters worse. Then she told me to wipe away my tears, and come into the dining-room with her. I followed gladly, and she rang and ordered coffee, and made me sit beside her and tell her all about my journey, and whether I still felt any ill effects from my accident, and how I liked Rutledge, and whether I was glad to leave school. It was strange, that with all this kindness my reserve did not melt faster; but it was a miserable fact, that I felt more awe and admiration for, than ease and sympathy with, my new-found relative. I longed to appear well in her eyes, and win her affection, but I never was more awkward and ill at ease. She had a way of looking at me that showed me she was making up an estimate of me, and I felt as if I were sitting for my picture all the time, and was as easy and natural as persons generally are under those circumstances.

I asked, at last, where my other cousins were. Grace was at her lessons, but would be down presently; Esther was sent to bed. Indeed, a violent scuffling and roars of "Let me see her, too," smothered by a voluble French reprimand, had announced to me, upon first entrance, that *la petite* was about making her exit. I took off my cloak, and accepted my aunt's suggestion, that I should not go to my room till I had had a cup of coffee. Mr. Rutledge and my cousin were presently summoned from the other room, and coffee was served. Josephine was very bright and piquant, talking well and amusingly; Mr. Rutledge was more sarcastic and man-of-the-world-ly than he had been at home; my aunt was graceful, winning, and polished, only making my wretched awkwardness and silence more conspicuous and striking. I longed to redeem myself, but there was a spell upon me; monosyllables and unfinished sentences were all the contributions toward the conversation that I could command, till Josephine exclaimed:

"Why, how quiet you are! You do not say a word. Is she always so silent, Mr. Rutledge?"

Mr. Rutledge smiled, and turned toward me.

"How is it, mademoiselle?" he said. "I have had but a short experience of your cousin's conversational powers," he continued, to Josephine; "I must confess that I have

10

sometimes fancied that she held those powers somewhat in reserve ; but I have no doubt that among companions of her own age, and in the congenial society of her young cousins, she will become as charmingly loquacious."

Josephine patted me patronizingly on the shoulder ; my aunt looked at me thoughtfully ; Mr. Rutledge turned to me for confirmation of his words, with a bow and a smile that staggered me completely. I began to wonder whether he had ever been anything more to me than the polite stranger he now appeared. Whether, in truth, the last three weeks had not been all a dream, and that railroad accident had not in some way affected my brain.

Just then the door opened, and enter my second cousin. If I may be pardoned for applying so unadmiring an epithet to so near a relative, I should describe this young person as very insipid-looking ; very undeveloped for her age, with an unmistakable flavor of bread-and-butter and pertness ; with rather a drawl in her tone, and rather a pout on her lips ; fair-skinned and fair-haired, rather pretty, perhaps, but far from lovable. On the whole, I was not attracted toward my cousin Grace, but I kissed her dutifully, and held her limp, inexpressive hand a minute or so in mine, while she said, "How d'ye do, Mr. Rutledge," in a drawling voice, that formed a striking contrast to her sister's vivacious tones.

Before very long, Mr. Rutledge turned to my aunt, and apologized for intruding so long on a family reunion, and promising himself the pleasure of waiting on her very soon again, said a cordial good night. There had been some commenting on a new picture, and we were all standing in a group before it, at the other end of the dining-room, when Mr. Rutledge took his leave. There were many jesting and pleasant words exchanged with the others as he withdrew, having shaken hands with them. I had shrunk into the background, and waited, my heart in my throat, to know whether I was forgotten, when he suddenly turned back, before he reached the door, and said :

"*Pardon!* Have I said good night to my young travelling companion? Ah! there you are. I am afraid you are very tired; I am not sure that we have not travelled too fast for such an inexperienced tourist."

"She couldn't have done Switzerland at our pace, last summer, I am afraid, could she?" said Josephine, complacently.

Mr. Rutledge made some rejoinder complimentary to Miss Josephine's powers of endurance, then concluded his brief adieux to me, and with "more last words" to the others, withdrew. Josephine leaned rather listlessly against the mantelpiece, said, "Mamma, how very well Mr. Rutledge is looking!" then going to the piano, asked me if I played, and sitting down, ran her fingers lightly over the keys, while I approached, and standing by her, listened admiringly to her delicate and masterly touch. I felt stranger and forlorner than ever, though, as she played on, talking to me idly as she played, till her mother called to her, rather sharply:

"Josephine, you are very thoughtless; don't you know she is tired? Come, my dear, you had better go upstairs immediately."

Josephine leaned over her shoulder, touched my cheek lightly with her lips, and said, "Good-night; you'll feel brighter by to-morrow."

My aunt called Grace to take me up to my room, kissed me good-night, and said she hoped I would be comfortable. Grace, who had just established herself at her embroidery, pouted slightly, and said in French (a language with which, it seemed taken for granted, I was unacquainted), "Why can't Josephine?" rising slowly to obey, nevertheless. A few sharp words silenced her speedily; another silvery good-night to me, and I followed my cousin upstairs. A more cat-in-a-strange-garrety, uncomfortable, bewildered feeling I never before had experienced; from Mr. Rutledge down, they all seemed to treat me as if I were somebody else. "If I be I, as I do hope I be," I ejaculated, with a miserable attempt at a laugh, as the old nursery rhyme came into my head, "perhaps I shall know myself when I am left alone and have time to think." But Grace did not seem inclined to allow me that luxury; for, having conducted me to my room, she came in, and did the honors rather more graciously than I had expected, lit the gas, pulled down the shades, put my bonnet and cloak away in the wardrobe, and then sat down on the foot of the bed, and looked at me with great appearance of interest. The fact was, Grace possessed, in no ordinary degree, that truly womanly trait, curiosity ; and justly considered, that as she had been made to come upstairs against her will, it was but fair that she should compensate herself in any lawful way that presented, and now that she was up here, to see as much as she could of the manners and habits of the new comer.

With a view to this harmless little entertainment, she began her investigations by saying :

"Where's the rest of your baggage ?   In the closet ?"

(She was leaning over the balusters when my trunk was brought up, and knew, as well as I did, that there was only one.)

"No," I said, blushing, "I didn't have but that trunk."

Grace squeezed up her mouth a little, but didn't make any rejoinder.

"Do you like your room ?" she asked, after a minute.

As I had just been contrasting it mentally with the blue room at Rutledge, I could not help another blush, and a little confusion, as I replied that it did very well.

"Mamma seemed to have an idea that you were quite a little girl," she continued, "and that this was very nice for you.   It opens out of the nursery, you see, and if you don't mind Esther's squalling, it *is* very nice."

She laughed a little, and I tried to smile as I answered

that I liked children, and should not mind being near my little cousin.

"I hope you'll like Esther," said Grace, with a shrug of her shoulders. "When she isn't kicking Félicie, or howling to be taken out, or squalling after mamma, she's sitting on the floor in the sulks, and as that's the least troublesome of her moods, nobody interferes with her. Oh, she's a sweet child!"

And Grace's laugh sounded more like thirty than fifteen. I was ashamed of myself for being so embarrassed and abashed by a girl so much my junior, but there was something about Grace that I was not used to; a sort of gutta-percha insensibility, a lazy coolness that I had not expected from her drawling, listless way. Nothing of the woman. seemed developed in her but the sharpness; and with that she was born, I suppose. She was still a little girl in her tastes and pursuits; loved to play with Esther, whom I afterward found she bullied and teased shamefully; did not aspire to beaux and young-ladyhood, but contented herself with keeping the sharpest imaginable lookout upon the concerns of every one in the house, and having a finger in every possible pie; being at once the pertest and most persevering of meddlers.

She kept up a desultory talk while I was unbraiding my hair and preparing for bed; asked questions that galled me, told facts that discouraged me, till I was fairly heart-sick, and would have been willing to have bought her off at any price; and looked upon the advent of Félicie with a summons from madame for her, as the most blessed release that could have been.

I locked the door after her with a bursting heart, and threw myself upon the bed in an agony of crying. What would have been merely a fit of homesickness, and a loneliness soon to be conquered and forgotten with girls of a different temperament, was a longer and more lasting struggle with me. It was wholesome discipline, no doubt but now, disheartened, I recognized no hope in all the dark horizon; saw nothing in the future that was worth living through the present for; disappointment, pain, and loneliness had taken the color out of every hope, and made what should have been morning, a night, and that of the blackest.

"Would it last?" was a question I asked myself even then, the dawning reason of the woman within me combating the passion of the child. "No, no," reason whispered; "'to mortals no sorrow is immortal;' the storm will spend itself, and calm of some kind will come."

But the child's heart refused to be comforted, and passionately rejected reason; there was no truth in friendship, there was no kindness in any one; there was nothing but loneliness, and coldness, and cruelty in all the world.

CHAPTER XVIII.

"A month ago, and I was happy! No,
Not happy—yet encircled by deep joy,
Which, though 'twas all around, I could not touch.
But it was ever thus with Happiness:
It is the gay to-morrow of the mind,
That never comes."

BARRY CORNWALL.

SLEEP, which proverbially forsakes the wretched, paid but little court to me that first night in my new home; my swollen eyelids were sullied with too many tears, in truth, to win his favorable regard; but toward morning, exhaustion and unconsciousness came compassionately to relieve the misery and wakefulness that had guarded my pillow all night; and the dull light of a winter morning, struggling in through the half-drawn curtains, was the next summons that I had to consciousness again. I started up, aroused more fully by a sharp pain in my arm, that had momentarily been growing harder, till it had succeeded, with the aid of the advancing daylight, in waking me thoroughly. It was some seconds before I knew what it was caused by; the bracelet on the arm that had been under my head had been pushed up from the wrist, and in that way, had grown tighter and tighter, till, indeed, the pain had been unendurable. It brought Mr. Rutledge's words to my mind strangely enough; with a blush of shame and pleasure, I bent over the souvenir; "I will never doubt again," I whispered, sincerely repentant. Heaviness had endured, bitterly, for the night, but joy, or a faint and tiny promise of it, had as surely come in the morning; and with energy and something like happiness, I set myself to make the best of my little room, and my new position. No Kitty to braid

my hair, no Kitty to unpack my trunk; so the sooner I got
used to performing those little offices for myself, the better,
decidedly.

"Something to do" was the kindest boon that could
have been given me, and as such, I received it, and before
the house was astir at all, I had unpacked my trunk,
arranged my books upon the table, my dresses in the wardrobe, and the little knick-knacks that were regarded as
decorative, on the mantelpiece and under the dressing-glass.
The crayon-sketch never saw the daylight in Gramercy
Square. A stolen look at it, now and then, under the half-
raised lid of my trunk, was all I ever ventured on.

Mine was not a very cheerful or attractive room, certainly; but I should soon be used to it, I reflected, and it
would seem nice enough. Then I drew up the shades, and
looked out with much interest upon my first daylight-view
of the great metropolis. Certainly, the wrong side of city
houses is no more advantageous a view of them than is the
wrong side of other fabrics; and in proportion as the velvet
is rich and gorgeous, so is the reverse dull and plain. My
room being in the rear of the house, I of course had the
benefit of the wrong side of the neighboring houses; which,
I will do them the justice to say, were as dismal and unpre-
tending as houses need be. They had all of them, with one
consent, put their best foot foremost; the gorgeous foot
presented to the street, was of brown stone, plate glass, and
carving; the slip-shod foot left in the background, was
dingy for want of paint, unsightly with clothes-lines and
ash-barrels, neglected and forlorn. However, I thought
cheerfully, some strange comfort attends even so exalted a
state as "two pair back;" there was an unlimited view of
the sky, much greater than the lower rooms could command. Indeed, when there was anything but lead-color
overhead, I concluded that these windows must be very
cheerful. The spire of a church, however, not far off
(which, I was happy to observe, had no wrong side), was

the one grace of the prospect. It would not do to think of the way in which the mists were rolling up from the lake, this grey, hazy morning, nor how the pines on its bank were reflected in its still surface; nor, indeed, at all of the scene, bold and picturesque even in its wintry desolation, that had met my waking vision for the last few happy weeks.

Late breakfasts were apparently the order of the day in this establishment; the hands of my watch were creeping around toward nine o'clock, and still no indication of the approach of that meal. Beyond the occasional smothered sound of a broom or duster in the hall, there had been nothing to suggest that any one was awake throughout the house, except a fretful little voice that I had heard at intervals since dawn, in the room next mine. Listening very attentively, I found that it proceeded from the young troublesome, whose picture had been so feelingly drawn for me last night by Grace. She was evidently importuning Félicie to get up and dress her; and the tone, peevish and whining as it was, had a sort of pathos for me, remembering, as I too distinctly did, the cruel punishment that it is to a child to lie in bed after being once thoroughly awake. For two hours, little Esther had been tossing about, and crying to get up, and the only response she had received from her nurse, had been now and then a sleepy growl or an impatient threat. Injustice always irritated me; besides, I had a curiosity to see this child, who evidently met with so little favor, and time was hanging rather heavy on my hands just then, so I went to the door that communicated with the nursery, and opening it softly, looked in. The shutters being darkened, it was still not many removes from dawn, and I could but dimly make out the dimensions of the large, scantily furnished room; but there was light enough for me to see the figure of the child, sitting up in her little bed, crying piteously, " *Lève-toi, Félicie, j'ai si froid.*"

She stopped suddenly on seeing me, and looked up in my face as I approached her.

"Is this my little cousin Essie?" I said, sitting down on the bed and taking one of her icy little hands in mine. Cold she certainly was; the fire had gone out entirely, and she had been sitting up undressed so long, that her teeth were chattering and her lips fairly blue. I kissed her wet cheeks, and giving her to understand that this was her new cousin, asked if she was not going to be very fond of me? She looked more amazed than before, but beyond a cessation of her tears, she made no attempt at a rejoinder. I rubbed her hands, and tried to warm her cold little feet, talking to her kindly all the time.

"Is this your dressing-gown, Essie?" I asked, taking up a little blue flannel garment from the foot of the bed. She nodded an assent, and I put it around her

"Now," I continued, taking her up in my arms, "will you go into my room and get warm by my fire?"

"Yes," said Esther, laconically. So picking up her shoes and stockings, I raised her in my arms and carried her into the other room. She was between five and six years old, but so slight and childish that her weight was nothing. I sat down by the fire and held her in my lap, while I put on her shoes and stockings, and warmed her into something like animation.

"So Félicie wouldn't wake up," I said, at length.

I had touched the right chord; the vehement childish sense of wrong was stirred, and with eager, blundering earnestness, she detailed her grievances. Félicie never would wake up; Félicie wouldn't give her a drink of water some nights when she was *so* thirsty; Félicie left her alone sometimes when it was *so* dark; and Félicie was cross, and Félicie was wicked, and, in fine, she hated her.

I shook my head at this, and gave her a little moral lecture upon the wickedness of hating nurses, further illustrating and embellishing my subject by the story of a little girl who had once indulged in that dreadful passion, and had come to a very sad end in consequence. The moral lecture, I am afraid, was overlooked; but the story was most greedily received, and I was obliged to succeed it with another and another, before I could induce her to go and get her clothes, and let me put them on for her. When she was nearly dressed, Félicie woke up, and not finding her young charge in bed, was somewhat startled and unmistakably angry, and in no dulcet tones was calling her name, when she looked into my room, and, on seeing me, sank suddenly into a softer strain, and apologized for oversleeping: she had had such a wakeful night, was not well, etc., and would Mademoiselle Esther come and have her hair brushed now?

Mademoiselle Esther, a moment before the quietest, gentlest child alive, had, at the sound of that voice, flushed up into angry defiance, and planting herself at my side, met her nurse's advance with a very ugly scowl. She wouldn't go and have her hair brushed; she didn't want a nice clean apron on; she didn't care if she was late for breakfast; and Félicie, though she never lost the bland tone she had assumed, looked malignant enough to have "shaken her out of her shoes and stockings." At length I persuaded her to submit to Félicie's proposals, and be made ready to go down to breakfast with me, and she held very firm possession of my hand, as, after the bell had rung, we descended the stairs.

My aunt was already below; Grace and Josephine straggled in after long intervals; indeed, we were half through breakfast before they came down. My aunt looked charmingly in her fresh morning dress and pretty cap, was very kind, gave Esther and me her cheek to kiss, and, after reading the paper, talked to me somewhat. Esther seemed not to have much appetite; but having set her heart upon a roll and some cold chicken, her mamma had graciously allowed her to be gratified, and she was very tranquilly eating her breakfast, when the entrance of Grace, who made some teasing little gesture as she passed, made her pout and whine, and disturbed her serenity considerably. It was not, however, till Grace, calling to the servant for some marmalade, suggested a forbidden dainty to her mind, and she exclaimed, "I want marmalade, too," that the worst came.

Grace interposes pertly, "You can't have any—mamma says you can't;" Essie passionately protests, "I will;" mamma sharply interposes, "You shall not;" a burst of tears from Essie, and a smothered titter from Grace, then Essie passionately pushes back her plate, and refuses to touch another mouthful; whereon mamma asserts her authority, and sternly orders her to resume her biscuit and chicken under pain of banishment. The sobbing child does not, cannot, *I* think, obey, and, at the end of an ominous silence, mamma motions John to remove her from the table, which is effected after violent resistance and struggling, and amid a tempest of screams and protestations, exit Essie in the arms of John.

It was well that my aunt did not order me to resume my breakfast. After that little episode, I am afraid I should have been unable to obey, and I should not have liked to have been carried out in the arms of John. Josephine exclaimed upon the nuisance of crying children; Grace laughed slily, as if she thought it capital fun; mamma sighed over the strange perverseness and dreadful temper of that child; but my heart ached for the wretched little exile. How Félicie would gloat over her disgrace, I knew, how indigestion, injustice, and mortification, would bring on a fit of the sulks that would last half the day, and pave the way for the repetition of a similar scene at lunch. Perhaps because I had been a willful, sensitive, and passionate child myself, I knew how to appreciate the disadvantages under which poor little Essie labored. I knew what exquisite tenderness and gentleness were necessary to guard

that sensitiveness from turning into the very gall of bitterness, and that quick temper from becoming the uncontrollable and damning passion that would blight her whole life.
More watchful care, more prayerful earnestness, does such
a child's rearing require, than if she had been laid upon her
mother's love, a moaning cripple, or a blind and helpless
sufferer. Just as soul is more precious than body, so is the
esponsibility heavier, the task more awful, of training and
molding such a sensitive nature, to whose morbid fancy a
cold repulse is a cruel blow, and an impatient word a rank-
ling wound. The tenderest and most yearning love should
surround and guard such a child's career, putting aside with
careful hand the snares and trials that beset the way of life,
till the maturing judgment shall have learned to control the
exaggerated fancy. The winds of heaven should not be
suffered to visit too roughly such a restless and unquiet
heart, till the uncertain mists of dawn and early morning
have melted before the clear and certain day. Between
the rough and torturing world and the scared and shrinking soul, the mother's love should interpose, shielding,
soothing, reassuring. God meant it to be so; may His pity
be the guard of the little ones, whom death, the world, the
flesh, or the devil, have defrauded of their right!

No one could look at my hollow-eyed and puny little
cousin, with that unhappy and unchild-like contraction of the
brow, and that troubled expression of the eyes, without
knowing that she was of a nervous temperament the most
excitable and keen, and of a will and temper the strongest.
To Josephine's spirit and Grace's acuteness, she added an
almost morbid sensitiveness and delicacy of organization,
of which they were entirely innocent, and which they could
in no way comprehend. That she did not inherit it from
her mother, was pretty evident; Grace was the nearest
copy of the maternal model; "la petite" was altogether a
stranger and an alien, not understood and not attractive.
Her mother had never forgiven her sex; a boy had been

the darling wish of both parents, and this third disappointment had not been graciously received, at least by the
mother; for I believe "the baby" had held a tender part
in her father's heart during the two years of her life which
he lived to see. Perhaps my uncle would have understood
the wayward child better than his wife did, had he lived to
see her develop; there must have been, I was sure, depths
of gentleness and tenderness in his heart; for though he
was almost a stranger to me, living as we had done, so far
from the world in which he had held a busy part, still he
was my mother's only brother, and they had never forgotten their early affection. The recollection of it helped me
to bear with patience the caprices and willfulness of his little
daughter; for, pity her as I might, there was no denying
that Esther was a very vexatious and trying child, and
there certainly was a very fair excuse for the disaffection
of the household. How far the household had to thank
themselves for it, however, was another matter, and one
which I thought would have repaid investigation.

The scene consequent upon the Marmalade Act, must
have been no novelty in the Churchill breakfast, for the
waves closed over poor Essie's banishment in an instant,
and things resumed their smooth and unruffled appearance
almost immediately. The next disturbance they received,
was in the form of a sharp ring at the bell, which caused
Josephine, without raising her eyes from the paper she was
reading, to adjust with better grace the sweep of her dress
upon the carpet, and to present to view an eighth of an inch
more of the rosette on her slipper; while Grace, looking
up from her plate, said saucily:

"What's the use, Joseph? It's too early for anybody
but Phil; and you know you don't care for Phil."

Josephine gave her a snapping look out of her black
eyes, and if there had been time, no doubt would have
made good their promise of a tart rejoinder, but the opening of the door, and the entrance of the six feet two inches

of manliness, known and described as "Phil," prevented its consummation. I did not know at the time, but I soon did know, who and what this privileged Phil was, who was so much at home at my aunt's house, and so well received and constant a guest.

Philip Arbuthnot was, it appeared, my Aunt Edith's only nephew, and the most invaluable and untiring of escorts; supplying the place, in short, only too willingly, of son and brother to his aunt and her unprotected daughters. In the matter of securing opera boxes and concert tickets, cashing drafts, looking after the family interest in Wall street, having a general supervision of the stable, keeping coachman, footman, and waiter in wholesome awe, and in a thousand other ways, he was of inestimable service. What the family would have come to without him, is too painful a speculation to be entered upon unnecessarily. Figaro-ci, Figaro-là, and Figaro liking nothing better than his occupation. He bent his whole mind to it; I never could discover that he had any other interest or employment in life; lounging around to Gramercy Square after breakfast, embellishing the library sofa with his listless length till lunch, while Josephine practised, or my aunt talked business with him. Then, at one o'clock, after putting them in the carriage (he was not a ladies' man, and hated morning visits), Phil would lounge back to the Clarendon, and by dint of a series of smokes in the reading-room, an hour or so at billiards, and a drive on the road, would manage to get rid of the day, and, at or about five o'clock, would lounge back again to Gramercy Square for dinner and the engagements of the evening. He had been educated at West Point, and though he had not, strictly speaking, covered himself with glory, at the rather searching examination of that rigorous old institution, just passing and that was all, they said, escaping emphatically by the skin of his teeth, still he had been in a very fair way of promotion, when, just before the departure of his aunt's family for Europe,

he had unexpectedly and abruptly resigned, and accompanied them. Having inherited a fortune just large enough
to serve as a narcotic to ambition and energy, and just
moderate enough to prevent his playing any prominent
part in Vanity Fair, Phil seemed in the enjoyment of an
existence very much to his taste, and entirely satisfying to
him. If, in my crude and enthusiastic view of life, it struck
me as an existence at once debasing to his nature, and dis-
honest to his manliness, it was because I had not yet
learned that what one-third of the men, and two-thirds of
the women in society look upon as the proper business of
their lives, must, in the nature of things, be the correct
view of the subject. "The night cometh when no man
can work," I thought, in my simplicity; the day, at best, is
but a short and uncertain one; for every soul sent on earth
there is a work allotted; what less than madness is it for
the strong man to lie down in his strength and sleep away
this day of grace? Seeing that the undone work does not
fade with the fading daylight, but an evergrowing and thickening shadow, will horribly increase the blackness of that
night; will be a treasure of wrath against that time of wrath,
and the perdition of such men as have chosen to be ungodly.

Such naïve and unpracticable ideas as these, would, no
doubt, have brought an avalanche of ridicule on my head,
had I been unwise enough to impart any of them to my new
friends; but a protective instinct kept me from such a
blunder; and as I hourly saw with clearer eyes the dissimi-
larity between them and me, so I hourly grew more
reserved and silent.

"Don't she ever say anything?" I could not help over-
hearing Phil ask, as I left the breakfast-room. I longed to
hear Josephine's reply; but an inconvenient sentiment of
honor prevented my stopping to listen for it. I could not,
however, avoid being auditor to the lazy laugh that it
elicited from Phil, and the blood mounted to my temples at
the sound.

"I wonder if they think me stupid or sulky," I said to myself. "I wonder if they ever thought how it must feel to be a stranger in the midst of people who know and understand each other. I wonder if I ever shall be one of them."

There was another, however, of the household that I felt pretty sure was as much a stranger and an alien as I was, though she had spent nearly six years in it, and I turned my steps naturally to the nursery. Poor little Essie had, as I expected, fretted and cried herself into a sick headache, and was sitting sulkily in a remote corner of the room, her doll untouched beside her, and her hands in her lap. Félicie, sitting by the window with a sardonic smile on her lips, employed herself about ripping up an evening dress of Josephine's. I called to Essie to come into my room; she pouted and averted her head. I made a coaxing promise of "something pretty," when Félicie interposed "that she was in disgrace, and perhaps mademoiselle had better not speak to her, as her mamma had sent her up for a punishment."

"Her mamma did not mean that she should be made unhappy for all the morning, however," I said, advancing boldly.

"As mademoiselle pleases," answered Félicie, with a very wicked look, and a very sweet voice.

Esther at length accepted my overtures, and consented to heal her bosom's woe with a picture-book and a bon-bon out of my trunk. I shut the door between my room and the nursery very tight, and gradually Essie's fretful unhappiness relaxed into something like childish enjoyment, in the comparative cheerfulness of my room, and the exertions I made for her entertainment. She possessed the characteristic, very rare and invaluable among children, of being easily amused, and also of continuing amused for a long while, with the same thing. So it happened, that the picture-book did not pall upon her taste, nor the bon-bon lose its charm, for two full hours, and she was still sitting demure as a kitten beside me, while I worked and occasion-ally explained to her the pictures, when Aunt Edith entered. She had evidently forgotten the occurrence of the morning, and seemed very well pleased to find us both so well pro-vided for. After looking about the room, and ascertaining that I had everything that I needed, she sat down by the fire, and resumed the estimate she had been interrupted in making up last night. The conscious blood dyed my cheeks, the faltering words found only awkward and constrained utterance; the more my aunt tried to read me, the more blurred and unreadable did I become. She tried me upon all possible questions—school, and its studies and routine; Rutledge, and my visit there; the journey, and my escort. Upon all points, I was equally unsatisfactory, and the inter-view had but one decisive result, which I attained only by great effort. I had determined that whenever I should have a chance, I would ask a favor of my aunt; and this appearing a fitting opportunity, with many misgivings and much trepidation, I propounded it to her; and was unspeak-ably relieved and surprised to find that she not only acqui-esced in, but most cordially approved of the motion. It was to the effect, that for this winter, I should be excused from going at all into society, and might be allowed to study and improve myself.

The proposal, I saw, relieved my aunt's mind from some weight that had encumbered it. She agreed with me most heartily in considering it much the most judicious course. I was really too young to go into society; she had never ceased to regret having brought out Josephine so early; next winter I should be so much better fitted to enjoy it, etc. The plans for the employment of my time were very soon arranged. I was to share Grace's French and German lessons, and to read history and philosophy with her, under the guidance of one Mr. Olman, a young and inexpensive professor of literature and the belles-lettres, who came

three times a week. My hours of study and recitation
were all distinctly marked out, and it was agreed I
should begin that very day. Grace was sent to bring me
her French grammar and show me the lesson, and after
lunch, we were summoned to the study (a small front
room on the second story), to meet Mr. Olman, our literary
professor.

Certainly, if I had looked upon Grace as a marvel of
sharpness last night, my respect for her in that regard,
suffered no diminution after seeing the manner in which she
slipped through Mr. Olman's literary fingers, and came out
triumphant at the end of the two hours, without the vaguest
idea of what he had been laboring at. She hated history,
philosophy, and the belles-lettres, and never thought of
preparing the abstracts and reviews that he requested; and
as he was unspeakably afraid of her himself, she found no
difficulty in eluding the detested tasks. He was a slim
young man, dressing in black and wearing spectacles—very
nervous and very much given to blushing. Indeed, his face,
at the end of the lesson, was ordinarily of a violent *rose de
chine* color, and his hands so trembling and cold, that it was
a great relief to me when he succeeded in collecting his
books and papers and getting on his overcoat. I never saw
so merciless a persecution; the slyest, "cutest," and the most
naïve way of tripping him up in the full tide of his discourse,
and then bewailing her mistake; never by any chance
omitting an opportunity of making him blush and putting
him in an agony of nervousness. I am certain, so acutely
did he suffer at her hands, that if in an unguarded moment
he had been brought to acknowledge who of all others he
most detested and dreaded, he would have answered,
unhesitatingly, "my pupil, from two to four, on Monday,
Wednesday and Friday."

Indignant as I felt at Grace, it was no easy matter to
keep from laughing at the results of her pertness and
aplomb; and notwithstanding Mr. Olman was evidently a

well-read and cultivated scholar, I anticipated in these lessons more of pain than of pleasure; and although I determined to apply myself thoroughly to all he directed, still, four o'clock was, and would, I feared, continue to be, a release.

At dinner, that evening, Grace gave the bulletin of "Mr. Olman's latest," and though her mother reproved her, no one thought it necessary to discourage her by not laughing. Phil's "Ha! ha!" was honest and unequivocal; he meant, he declared, some day to secrete himself under the piano, and see Grace put the professor to rout and confusion. He hated professors, for his part, and he'd like to see 'em all put to rout and confusion.

"Professors arn't in your line, are they, Phil?" said Grace, with a laugh.

"I beg, Phil," exclaimed Josephine, "that you'll never present yourself unexpectedly to that wretched man. I am sure he'd swoon at the sight of your breadth of shoulder and length of limb. You'd make at least three of him."

"Say four," put in Grace. "The professor doesn't weigh an ounce over thirty-five pounds. I asked him, the other day, apropos of ancient weights and measures, if he'd ever been weighed, and what the result was."

"You saucy child," said Phil, "I wonder he didn't box your ears."

"No danger of that," responded Grace, complacently. "The professor knows better than to quarrel with his bread and butter; he knows that pupils don't grow on every bush, and it would take a great deal more than that to provoke him into a retort. He only bites his lips, and grows red in the face, and says, "This is irrelevant, Miss Churchill."

"Upon my word," said Josephine, with a sneer, "by the time the poor man finishes your education, I think he'll be fit to be translated to his reward, without any further sojourn in the church militant. No honest council would deny him canonization after such a fiery trial."

"Poor old Mabire must have a high place by this time, if his reward is at all proportioned to his sufferings," said Grace, slily. "You remember, Josephine, how sweet you used to be to that old man? I liked to listen at the study door, and hear him walk up and down the floor, and grind his teeth and gasp, 'C'est trop, c'est trop!' I suppose the bread-and-butter question prevented his speaking to mamma; but, really, you must confess, he was a victim! Now *I* never go the lengths of biting and scratching, but always confine myself to "——

"Grace, *mon ange*," cried Josephine, flushing up angrily, "if you don't want to be sent to take your meals in the nursery, you had better learn to be less pert and "——

"Truthful's the word you want, dear," drawled Grace, unconcernedly.

"It's the last word I should think of applying to you," retorted her sister.

"*Tout doucement, chérie!*" ejaculated Grace, squeezing up her mouth.

But at this juncture, mamma, who had been engaged in opening some notes and cards of invitation that John had brought in, now becoming aroused to a sense of the impending storm, came to the rescue, and in a few cutting words used up everybody present, Phil and myself included, and restored a forced peace; and during the remainder of the meal, Josephine sulked, Phil looked heartily distressed, and I felt miserably uncomfortable, Grace alone preserving an unmoved and complacent demeanor. It was just as we had finished dessert, that there came a ring at the bell that made me start. Foolish as it was, I had been listening to the bell all day, with a vague kind of hope that it would prove of interest to me; and when John presented a card to my aunt, which contained the only familiar name to me in this strange place, and, in fact, the only name I cared to see, I really feared that Grace's quick ear would catch the loud throbbing of my heart, as she surely did catch the quick blush on my cheeks.

"It is Mr. Rutledge," said my aunt. "Josephine, will you go into the parlor, and I will join you in a moment? Phil, may I ask you to look over that deed we were speaking of this morning? The library is vacant; I suppose you do not want to be interrupted. And you,.young ladies (to Grace and me), will find a good fire in the study, and an excellent chance for preparing your German for to-morrow. Mr. Waschlager, you know, comes at ten on Thursdays."

Josephine, with a coquettish look in the glass, hurried off to the parlor; Phil accepted his lot with a resigned sigh; Grace grumblingly obeyed, and I followed her, biting my lips, and struggling to keep back the tears of disappointment, as I heard, through the half open door, a familiar voice and laugh, that my homesick ear had been longing for all day.

CHAPTER XIX.

———" Sweet heaven, she takes me up
As if she had fingered me, and dog-eared me,
And spelled me by the fire-side, half a life !
She knows my turns, my feeble points."

E. B. BROWNING.

CHRISTMAS came and passed ; my birthday came and
passed ; the holidays were " over and done," and we were
busily at work again with our various professors ; and, in my
heart, I acknowledged that I liked work better than play
in my new home. Sundays and holidays were the times
that tried my soul. I do not mean in church ; Christmas
anthems, Christmas hopes and aspirations had never before
touched me so deeply as now, when there was so much of
dullness and coldness in the world outside. In church I
did not feel my loneliness so much, but it was the coming
back to the frivolity and uncongeniality of home that left
the greatest blank. I do not mean to suggest, that during
all these weeks I had been· as pining and heartsick as I had
been on the first day of my initiation. That day, it is true,
had been a fair index of the rest, but the acute disappointment and pain had worn off, and I had learned to make the
best of it, and to go through my daily routine with a less
heavy, but perhaps an emptier and less hoping heart. " The
ox, when he is weary, treads surest." I was weary and
unhopeful, and so, perhaps, trod more safely the somewhat
devious and perplexing path that lay before me. If the
subduing effect of a keenly felt and unkind disappointment,
and a miserable loneliness and want of sympathy, had not
kept my impetuosity and self-will in check, I perhaps should
not have passed with so little injury through scenes that

were quite new and bewildering to me. As it was, I was sad enough to think, sober enough to choose, and yet young and elastic enough not to be crushed by the weight of my trial, but to bow and fit myself to the yoke. I reasoned in a way that was childish in its simplicity, and yet wise in its unworldliness.

"I have been very presumptuous and vain," I thought. " I have fancied myself the companion and friend of one who, by forgetting me, has shown me my mistake, while there was yet time to correct it. I have been indulging in a very foolish, though a very happy, dream; but as long as he knows nothing of it, I am certain I can conquer it in time, and be more humble for the rest of my life. I have not found much sympathy or love in the only home I shall probably ever have; I don't suppose I shall ever be particularly happy again, but there is something higher than mere happiness that I can try to gain, and make myself worthy of that communion of saints in which I have been taught to believe; stretching through earth and heaven, of all kindreds and peoples and tongues, among whom I have no present comrade, it is true, but there is one saint at rest, who has no other care than her child's peace—who loved me better than all the world beside, when she was here— who will not forget her love and tenderness in the rest that she has entered into."

And so, with a humbled heart, I set myself to the "trivial round, the common task," that gave me, indeed, much room for self-denial and patience, but gave me, too, the peace that impatience and resistance never would have brought.   Much there was, indeed, of error and folly, many mistaken steps and struggles of conscience, much sinning and repenting, but, on the whole, it was a straighter and a safer path than a pleasanter one would have been. There was, in truth, little danger of being in love with the world, seen from the stand-point I had been placed in.

Home continued pretty much as usual. Of my aunt and Josephine, we of the study and the nursery saw comparatively little. As the season advanced, and the gaiety increased, there was not much time, of course, at my aunt's command for any but the most imperative home duties; this being Josephine's first winter in New York, it was a thing of the highest moment to bring her out properly, and no sacrifice was considered too great. Not that she neglected her household, or regular duties; at whatever hour she may have returned home the night before, my Aunt Edith never failed to appear at breakfast punctually; never failed to hear Esther repeat her Collect, and glance over Grace's theme; never failed to overlook the grocer's, baker's, and butcher's accounts; to visit in person daily, kitchen, laundry, butler's pantry, nursery, and study; to keep, in short, that eye over her entire establishment that it required to preserve its matchless order and regularity. No wonder that my aunt looked haggard and worn; no wonder that unwelcome wrinkles were writing themselves on her brow, and that her rounded figure was fast losing its roundness. To serve one master is as much as one human being is capable of. In the miserable attempt to serve two, how many wrecks of soul and body are daily wrought.

I said we saw very little of my aunt; it seemed very little, for her daily visits to us, though regular, were of necessity hurried, and at meals she was generally either preoccupied and thoughtful, or busy with Phil in arrangements and plans for the pressing demands of society. Josephine, now-a-days, had her breakfast sent to her room, and was not ordinarily visible before twelve o'clock. Then came visiting hours; and at dinner, though, when they did not dine out, we enjoyed the society of my aunt, and Josephine, and Phil, still it seemed to me, they were all rather listless and stupid; but perhaps they were only reserving their energies for the evening. After study hours, sometimes, and just before my bed-time, I would go down to Josephine's room by particular request, and assist her at her toilette ; her new maid, Frances, being, she declared, the clumsiest, stupidest thing that ever breathed, and having a most unbearable trick of bursting into tears whenever she was scolded, which, I suppose, deprived Josephine of all plea-sure in her attendance. My services suited her better, and I often had the honor of superseding Frances. Not that I minded it at all ; it was the only glimpse I had into the gay world that I was as yet so ignorant of. I liked to array Josephine in her elegant Parisian dresses, to arrange the drooping flowers in her glossy black hair, and to clasp the rich bracelets on her arms. Grace, on these occasions, was strictly forbidden the room ; late hours, dissipation and fatigue had not materially improved Josephine's temper ; and her pert young sister's allusions to bones, necks à la gridiron, etc., tried her beyond endurance ; and mamma interposing, Grace, for once, was kept at bay. I will not deny a vague feeling of regret and longing, as I watched my cousin's floating drapery downstairs, and thought of the gay scene she was starting for ; and as Phil wrapped her light cloak around her, and whispered his honest praises in her ear, as she followed her mother to the door, and I turned back to my lonely little .room, it did seem to me that there was great need of faith to believe that her lot and mine were ordered by the same unerring and impartial Wisdom.

Our lessons went on pretty much as at first. With Mr. Ohnan, I was rather a check upon Grace, and the poor man began to regard me with something like gratitude. He was a good teacher, and gave me plenty of work, for which I, in my turn, was grateful. Our French lessons, it appeared to me, were rather a hollow mockery, Mdlle. Berteau, our preceptress, being a chatty little woman, who spent one-half her time in gossiping with Grace about Paris and pretty things, and the other half in helping her write the exercises she had been too lazy to prepare the night before. I also found later, that mademoiselle had been in the habit of supplying her young pupil surreptitiously with some rather questionable French literature. Upon a threat of disclosing this circumstance to mamma, Grace made me a solemn promise to renounce it; but I must confess I never felt any great security about its fulfillment.

Our German proved rather more satisfactory. Mr. Waschlager, a strapping, burly, bearded fellow, with a loud voice and considerable energy of manner, inspired Miss Grace with much greater respect than delicate Mr. Olman, with his nervousness and tremor. His imperfect knowledge of our mother-tongue, also, rendered any sly innuendoes quite powerless to annoy him, and Grace's very strikingly imperfect knowledge of *his* maternal mode of speech, put it quite out of her ability to insult him, if she had dared. So that, with the exception of having ordinarily to write her exercises for her, and give her the benefit of my researches in the dictionary at the last moment, I enjoyed my German lesson very much, and made quite rapid advances in that language.

A week or two before my arrival, Esther's daily governess (from all accounts a miserably weak and injudicious person) had been dismissed, having been found entirely incompetent to manage her young charge; and, till another should be procured, I had asked my aunt if I should not teach her for an hour or two every day. The offer had been very gladly accepted, and, somehow, after a week or two, all question of obtaining a new governess had died out, and Essie and her lessons had quietly devolved on me. I did not mind it very much; the child was good enough, and, with a little coaxing, got on tolerably well; but it was rather hard always to be tied down to that duty for the hours that I invariably felt most like reading or sewing, both of which occupations I found entirely incompatible with the due direction of Miss Esther's early mathematical efforts, and the proper supervision of her attempts at pen

manship. I had the benefit of her society at other hours
also ; she kept pretty closely at my side during my leisure
moments, favored by my vicinity to the nursery, and was
my invariable companion in my walks : Grace never walked,
except when ordered out under pain of her mother's dis-
pleasure, and Félicie was, of course, only too glad to shift
the duty of exercising Miss Esther upon me. And as my
aunt had a prejudice against full carriages, she and Josephine were generally considered a sufficient burden for the
horses on Sunday, and Grace being commonly threatened
with headache on that day, Esther and I were left to ourselves in the matter of church ; and finding one not far
distant, that had some free seats within its ample limits, we
profited by the discovery, and pretty constantly filled two
of them ; Esther holding fast to my dress, never for a
moment letting go of it through service or sermon ; at
times it seemed to me, as I caught her strange troubled
eyes fixed on the rich colors of the chancel window, or the
misty blue of the vaulted roof, that " her heart was envious
of her eye," and she clung to me, uncertain and hesitating,
as her one tie to earth. I never could quite make out the
child ; with all her pettishness, and very willful and trying
naughtiness, there were moods and fancies about her that
thoroughly puzzled me. The only way, I found, was to be
as patient as possible with the one, and humor the other as
far as was practicable.

I introduced her to her Prayer-book frequently at church,
but to little effect ; she would obey for the moment, then
the book would drop unheeded from her hand, and she
would presently be gazing dreamily before her again.
Never letting go my dress, she would slip down on her
knees when the others did, but when I glanced at her, it
was always to find that strange wistful look on her upturned
face, that always gave me a vague feeling of uneasiness.
She was by no means a precocious child—rather a backward
and undeveloped one ; but sometimes she startled me with

questions that were as much beyond what I had expected of her, as they were beyond me to answer lucidly.

Besides our dislike of Félicie and our liking for Trinity Chapel, there was another bond of sympathy between my little cousin and me, and that was, our cordial antipathy to "company" days and times. Not that we ever had much personal interest in them, but the moral atmosphere of the house, for the whole of the day on which one of my aunt's elaborate dinner-parties occurred, was extremely grating to our nerves. My aunt was always a little more decided and hurried, Josephine a shade more imperious, Grace perter, Félicie more hateful, John more given to short answers—in fact, no member of the household but felt oppressed by the coming event. Grace and I dined with Esther at "the little dinner." at one, on such occasions, and all we saw of the contents of the carriages that, about six, began to roll up to the door, was seen from over the balusters of the third-story staircase. My aunt, it is true, had at first proposed to me to put on my new silk, and come downstairs, but it seemed to me that the invitation was rather luke-warm, and she agreed with me very readily in thinking that for this winter, it was better for me to stay altogether out of society.

"You will be all the fresher when you do appear, my love," said my aunt Edith.

So, *par conséquent*, I saw but little of the visitors at the house, though, through Grace, and the general table talk and accidental meetings in the parlor, I kept the run of the most intimate and familiar ones. Among the gentlemen, there was a Captain McGuffy, an army friend of Phil's, who was a good deal at the house, principally noticeable for his appetite and his moustache. Also, a stale old beau named Reese, who was a kind of heir-loom in fashionable families, handed down from mother to daughter along with other antique and valued relics, to grace their entrée into society. He had been an admirer of my aunt Edith's in her opening

bloom, but was now made over to Josephine, by that
unselfish parent, to swell the list of the younger one's
retainers. Besides these, there was a Mr. Wynkar, very
young and very insignificant, endured principally, I fancied,
for his utility; and a young Frenchman, who was quite new
on the tapis, and much the rage.

But it was a fact patent even to my simplicity, that Mr.
Rutledge was, *par excellence*, the most courted and desired
guest in Gramercy Square. For him, Josephine's smiles
came thickest and sweetest, and the daring freedom of
speech and wit that characterized her bearing with Phil and
his military *confrère*, were, in his presence, toned down into
a spirited, but most taking coquetry, and the anxious frown
on Aunt Edith's brow was smoothed away whenever John
announced, "Mr. Rutledge, madam." That those announce-
ments were very frequent, could never cease to be a matter
of interest to me, though there seemed little excuse for my
feeling any deeper personal concern in them than John himself. Being always expected to retire directly from dinner
to the study, we of course lost all evening visitors, and in
the daytime, it was even less likely that we should encounter
any one from the parlor. More than once, on dinner-party
nights, I had stood so near him, that I could have whispered
and he would have heard; shrinking down in the shadow
of the landing-place, I had watched him leave the dressing-
room slowly, always walking through the upper hall very
leisurely, and looking attentively around. But the darkness
of that upper landing-place would baffle even his keen eye;
my very heart would stand still—the breath would not pass
my parted lips, and there would be no danger that his quick
ear should discover that which I would have died rather
than he should have known. I would watch him down the
stairs, see him pause a moment before the parlor-door, then,
as he opened it, there would come, for an instant, the gay
clamor of many voices, the rustling of silks, the ringing of
laughter, then in an instant shut again, and I would creep

back to my dark and cheerless little room with a heart that, had I been older and less humble, would have been bitter and resentful, but as it was, was only aching and sad. I often wondered whether, if that bracelet had not been fastened irrevocably on my arm, I should have taken it off? Whether, if I could, I would have put far out of sight, all souvenirs of that happy visit, that nobody seemed to remember now but me. Whether it would have been any easier to forget, if I could have broken my promise as he most assuredly had broken his. Of course he had broken it; the only folly had been in my ever expecting him to remember such a jest an hour after it was spoken. A one-sided friendship, indeed it was, upon reflection, a very absurd friendship, between an ignorant school-girl and an elegant, high-bred, cultivated gentleman, and one who, as Grace said one day at the table, if he wasn't the coolest and most indifferent of men, would be a perfect lion in society.

"He's too *jeuced* stiff and haughty to be tolerated," said Mr. Wynkar, who, with Capt. McGuffy and Phil, was dining with us in such *petit comité*, that it was not considered necessary to exclude the juniors from the board.

"You and he arn't intimate, then," said Grace, with a sly laugh, which Josephine rather encouraged in a quiet way.

"I never could see," said Capt. McGuffy, from under his moustache, "what everybody finds in that man so remarkable. He has a tolerably correct idea of a horse, and rides pretty well; but beyond that, I think he's rather a stick."

Grace elevated her eyebrows, and Mr. Wynkar went on to say, "that for his part, he thought there was nothing about him but his money and his family. Rutledge was a good name, and he was, without doubt, the best match in society."

"Match!" exclaimed the captain. "He's no more idea of marrying than a monk. I pity the girl that sets her affections on his establishment. *Ma foi!* She'd about as well make *beaux yeux* at the bronze general in Union Square. Her chance of making an impression would be about as good."

"McGuffy's right," said Phil, warmly. "If everybody knew as much as he does, they'd let Mr. Rutledge alone, and turn their attention to subjects that would pay better."

"Army men upon a thousand a year, for instance," said Josephine, under her breath, and with an irritated contraction of the brow.

"Yes," said Mrs. Churchill, quite blandly, "it is peculiar that any one can see in him a marrying man. At his age, it is very seldom that one of his disposition feels any inclination to form new ties and interests, and enter upon so different a life. Nothing could surprise me more than to hear that Mr. Rutledge was going to be married."

Grace squeezed up her mouth in a significant way, and gave a funny look at her mother as she said this, evidently exercising great self-denial in not answering.

Mr. Ellerton Wynkar took upon himself that office, and agreed entirely with Mrs. Churchill, adding, however, that there were some stories about the early life of the gentleman, that he didn't know whether to believe or not. Was it true that he had been so dissipated when he was a young man?

Mrs. Churchill smiled, and shrugged her shoulders. She knew nothing about that; he had spent most of his early life abroad, she said, and sowed his wild oats, if he had any to sow, on another continent, and it was but fair for us to be content to take him as he wished to appear at home, and ignore the other continent.

"You may bet your head," exclaimed the captain, emphatically, "that no man with a fortuné like his, ever settled down into morality and farming, without having a good time or so, to begin with. Trust him for that! The ladies wouldn't like him so well, if there wasn't a touch of the sinner about him."

Aunt Edith shook her head, and said that was a shocking doctrine; while Josephine declared, with a laugh, they had to like sinners—there was nothing else in society; and Mr. Wynkar taking it as a personal tribute, pulled his pale moustache and smiled, while the captain concentrated his herculean powers on an appropriate rejoinder, and Grace drew the attention of the table to me, by exclaiming:

"Why, what's the matter? You look as if you had been shot."

"Rather, as if she'd like to shoot us," said Josephine, laughing. "What *have* we done to excite such horror? I hope you're not making yourself unhappy on Mr. Rutledge's account. I think he's able to take care of himself."

"If I had known," said Mr. Wynkar, with an apologetic wave of the hand, and a smile that was meant to be ironical, "if I had known that Mr. Rutledge had so enthusiastic a friend present, I should have been more careful; and I most humbly beg, that what I have said may be forgiven."

The captain laughed a great laugh, and said he might have known that wherever there was a pretty face, there was a friend to Mr. Rutledge; and Grace asked, artlessly, what made me blush so; while only good-natured Phil came to the rescue, and in his blunt, honest way, exclaimed:

"It's my opinion she's much in the right of it. I shouldn't think much of her, if she wasn't angry at hearing anybody used up so, all on suspicion, too. If there's anything against him, why, hang it, come out and say so; but this making a man out a rascal, because people like him and because he's got a fortune, upon my soul, I think it's a scurvy sort of trick, that I do."

"Don't hit him any more—he's got friends," whined Grace.

"Phil quite mistakes us if he thinks we are not all Mr. Rutledge's friends," said Mrs. Churchill. "No one dreamed of saying anything that could possibly be considered uncomplimentary."

"I don't know, Aunt Edith," said Phil, rather warmly; "but I hope you don't pay me that sort of compliment when I'm not by."

"Indeed we don't," exclaimed Josephine, laughing. "When you're absent, Phil (which isn't often, you know), we all say you're the best fellow in the world, and count the hours till you come back."

"Then I think the best thing I can do is to stay away," he answered, with a sort of sigh.

"Ah, Phil, I know you wouldn't have the heart!" said Josephine, in a low tone, with a bright flash of her coquettish eye; which had the effect of subduing her cousin for the rest of the evening, and keeping him obedient to her slightest whim.

Though the rest of the family seemed to forget very soon the little episode that had been so excruciating to me, and so amusing to them, I do not think it was lost upon my aunt. I always found her looking at me very narrowly whenever Mr. Rutledge was mentioned, and she on more than one occasion, in my presence, took pains to speak of him in a way that seemed to put a greater distance than ever between us, of his age, his eccentricities, his reserve. My aunt might have saved herself the trouble. I "knew my place" by this time, and shrunk as naturally from meeting him now, as I had before been eager and forward. On the one or two occasions when I could not avoid encountering him, it had been in her presence, and I had been shy and cold to a degree that must have been unaccountable to him, if he had given the matter a thought, which I very much doubted. I had excused myself as hurriedly as possible, and slipped back to the study, glad to be by myself again, yet bitterly sorry, as soon as it was too late, that I had not staid where only I wished to be—where only I found any pleasure, if such a doubtful emotion indeed could be called pleasure. It was the nearest approach to it, however, that my life presented; it was what I looked forward to, spite of my good resolves from day to day; yet, when the wished-for pleasure came, with strange shyness and perverseness, I thrust it away out of my own reach, then cried passionately at the disappointment, and began to hope again. The most inexplicable and contradictory thing in all this world of contradictions, is a woman's heart, before experience has tutored it. The woman herself does not understand it. What wonder if its strange willfulness and sudden impulses hopelessly bewilder and mislead the one of all others whom she most desires to please, and for whom alone, if the truth were known, the foolish heart throbs and flutters and pines.

CHAPTER XX.

"Doth not the world show men a very Judas' part, and betray them unto Satan, saying, whom I kiss with a feigned sign of love, take them—torture them?" SUTTON.

"MAMMA says," drawled out Grace, sauntering into the study one snowy morning, as I sat busy at my German, "mamma says, that as you write a good hand, you may direct these cards for her, and she will excuse you to Mr. Waschlager, if you don't have time to finish your German before he comes."

I could not help a slight exclamation of impatience as I relinquished my books, and took the long list of names and the basketful of blank envelopes that Grace handed me.

"How glad I am that I don't write a nice hand!" she ejaculated, as she threw herself lazily into a chair by the window, and leaning on her elbow, gazed out into the streets, now "dumb with snow," but where, before an hour was over, the jingling of an occasional sleigh-bell would be but a prelude to the merry music with which, till the snow vanished, they were to resound.

"I should think you'd be glad to get rid of your German; though, I suppose, it's only 'out of the frying-pan,' for you have a good morning's work before you in those precious cards."

I didn't trust myself to answer, and, after a pause, Grace went on:

"I should think mamma might have set Josephine to write those things herself, don't you? The party's all on her account, and she and Phil are doing nothing down in the library this morning."

Grace looked a little longer at the lessening snow-flakes, then continued, pleasantly :

"What shall you wear? For we've got to come down, mamma said so; and she said, too, that she didn't believe you had anything fit to wear."

"I haven't given a thought to the subject. Pray, don't talk, Grace, you confuse me."

"But you'll have to give it a thought," she exclaimed. "Josephine's going to wear her new pink silk, and I should think you'd want to look nicely the first time you go into company. Ella Wynkar was saying the other day, she thought it was the queerest thing you never went any-where."

"Grace, really if you can't be quiet, I must go into my own room. I won't waste any more time misdirecting these cards, which I cannot help doing if you talk all the while."

She subsided for a few minutes, but pretty soon began again.

"It's going to be splendid sleighing; it's stopped snow-ing altogether, and I believe the sun is actually coming out; don't you wish there was any chance of your having a sleigh-ride?"

"No," I exclaimed, impatiently; "I don't wish for anything but quiet, and if you must be lazy yourself, I don't see what need there is of making other people so."

"You're shockingly out of temper this morning," said Grace, shrugging her shoulders and getting up to go. "I think I shall have to 'leave you to your own reflections,' as mamma always says after giving any of us a lecture. I must go and see what mischief Esther is in. She has been too quiet this morning."

I saw, by the sly gleam in Grace's eye, that Esther's peace was over; I knew the futility of argument, and attempted none; ten minutes after, a distressed little voice outside, crying, "Won't you speak to Grace? She's got the brushes out of my paint-box, and she won't give em to me," showed me how Grace was killing time. I opened the door for the little *malheureuse*, told her not to mind about the paint-brushes, but if she'd be a quiet child, she might sit down here and look at the big "Pilgrim's Progress;" so I installed her in Grace's vacated seat, by the window, and she dried her tears, and looked the book through twice; then, kneeling in the chair, gazed out into the street, so quietly that I almost forgot her existence. My task was a distasteful one, insomuch as it interfered with pleasanter occupations, and I had great difficulty in keeping my patience to its completion; but at last it was ended, and the last name on the list copied on the envelope of the last card, and replaced in the basket, and, fagged and dispirited, I pushed them away, and, crossing over to the window, sat down by it, and took the child on my knee.

No wonder the scene had fascinated her so long; it certainly was bright and picturesque. Snow is as magical a beautifier as moonlight; it freshens up, gilds over, and brightens the worn-out surface of every-day, and makes a pretty picture of a common reality. I had never suspected Gramercy Park of beauty before, but under the light mantle of this snow it became lovely. The trees bent with its light weight; it capped and decorated the iron railings, and crested the roofs and window-casings of the houses on the square. It lay white and unsullied on the ground, and in the courtyards; only a few children had as yet burst nursery bounds, and, wild with delight, rushed into the new element; and but a few shovels and brooms were at work. The sky had come out gorgeously blue, the sunshine was glittering gaily on the white snow; it was altogether a brilliant picture, done in high colors, but possessing the advantage that nature's pictures always enjoy, of not having an inharmonious or jarring tinge. Even the sleigh-loads of gaily-dressed people that began to dash past, seemed to nave got themselves up to match and not mar the scene. The bright colors of the sleigh-robes, the flashing of the silver bells, the red cheeks of the girls, the gay clothes of the pretty children, were quite harmonious and quite effective. Esther looked at it for a long while in perfect content, as she would have looked at a nice picture-book; by and by, it began to assume a more personal character on her eyes.

"I should like to go out and ride myself," she said, at length.

"So should I, but there doesn't seem much chance of it," I answered; "therefore, it's best not to think about it."

"Other children go," she said. "I don't see why I can't. I think mamma might have a sleigh."

"That's mamma's business, and not yours," I said; "and there are more little children who don't ride than there are little children who do. There is one, for instance, coming out of the area, who has been poking about, in all the ash-barrels in the square, for a few cinders to keep him warm at home. Poor little fellow! Don't you feel sorry for him, Essie? His ears and nose are so red, and his lips are almost purple. I don't believe *he's* had a sleigh-ride, do you?"

Essie looked down thoughtfully at him, but didn't answer; no more repinings occurring, however, I inferred that she had profited by the train of thought the shivering little object below us had suggested. I still sat by the window, with Essie in my lap and a book in my hand, when, with a cry of pleasure, she started up, exclaiming, as a sleigh drew up at the door:

"There's Mr. Rutledge, and I know he's come for us to ride! Hurrah!"

I bent forward, just in time to meet his eye, as he sprang from the sleigh, and to return awkwardly his salutation. Esther waited for no permission, but bounded from my lap,

flew across the room, and downstairs before I could recall
her, and opened the door for him before he had rung the
bell.   There was a very enthusiastic meeting between them,
and an excited "That's good!" from the child, and in a
moment she was back again at my side, breathless and
eager, exclaiming :

"Mr. Rutledge has come for us all, to drive out to High
Bridge. Put on your things quick—quick as ever you can."

"Who's going? Who did he ask?" I said, breathless
as the child herself.

"You, me, mamma, Josephine, all of us! Be quick."

"But listen, Essie," I exclaimed, following her to the
hall, as she bounded off up to the nursery. "Stop a
minute. What did he say?—did he say *me?*"

"Yes, yes, he said, 'run up and ask your cousin if she'll
take that ride this morning that we talked about at Rutledge, and I'll go into the parlor and ask your mamma and
Miss Josephine;' and now let me run for Félicie to get me
ready;" and the child was off again, but came back obe-
diently when I called her. I held her tight by the hand,
as, with a beating heart, I leaned over the balusters, and
heard the merry voices in the hall below. I could not distinguish what Mr. Rutledge said, but I heard Josephine's
laughing rejoinder:

"I assure you, I didn't mean to hint, last night, when I
said I longed for a sleigh-ride again; but it was just like
you, to remember it. It's a charming day. How we shall
enjoy it!"

I led Essie to the stairs, and leaning down, said:

"Go down and tell Mr. Rutledge, that he's very kind,
but I beg he will excuse me to-day."

The child looked bewildered, and exclaimed : "But,
aren't you going?"

"No; go down and say just what I have told you,
remember; and then come back, and I'll help you get
ready."

Esther wonderingly obeyed, and slid down the stairs like a spirit. I scorned to listen any longer, though I would have given anything and everything I possessed to have unravelled the tangled maze of voices in the hall, and known how my refusal was received. Pride to the rescue! however, and I was bending over my German, when my aunt looked in a moment at the door, to inquire if I didn't care to go.

I said, " No, thank you ; I have my translation to finish, and, if you are willing, I will stay at home."

Just then, Josephine and Grace came up, and Essie burst into the room, exclaiming:

" Mamma, mamma, what shall I wear ? What frock had I better put on ?"

" Why, you're not going," cried Josephine, pettishly. " Surely, mamma, you do not mean to let that child go. There's no room for her if Phil goes, and she'll be whimpering with the cold in ten minutes."

" Mr. Rutledge only asked her for politeness," said Grace. " He never thought of such a snip really going."

" She'll spoil everything," said Josephine, decidedly. "I don't care to go if she does."

"I think, on the whole, my dear Essie," said Mrs. Churchill, " that it is best for you not to go. You must amuse yourself at home, and be a good child; we shall not be gone very long."

The little girl's lips moved, as if she would speak, but no words came, and, as the others left the room, I looked at her with some anxiety. I never saw a face so changed. The brief radiance that had lighted it had passed away, and in its place was a livid look of passion that fairly frightened me.

" Why, Essie, child, don't take it so to heart," I said, soothingly, attempting to touch her cold, clenched hand, but with a fierce gesture she released herself and turned away. I tried to pacify and divert her, but received no

word in answer, till, from the window, we saw the party
enter the sleigh, and after a moment of adjusting sleigh-
robes and furs, the fine horses started spiritedly forward, to
the music of their own merry bells; then, with a violent
scream, the child threw herself upon the floor, and shook from
head to foot with a passion that many men and women pass
through life without experiencing. Such tempests cannot
fail to blight the souls they sweep over; they bow the
cracking forest, and strip it of its leaves; the tender sap-
ling, alone and unprotected in its flexile youth, can hardly
escape undesolated. Swayed and whipped about with the
fierce blast, all that is tender and delicate about it must be
blighted; the stem that should have been fair and straight,
must, if it survive the trial, be twisted, and rough, and
gnarled; it may strike a deeper root; it will never cast as
fine a shade, nor be as fair a tree. If, unable to sustain the
storm, the frail stem snap, and the life-blood ooze away, is
it a questionable providence, or an utter mercy?

"Essie, my dear little girl," I continued, as the child still
lay sobbing on the floor, long after the first burst of temper
had expended itself, "Essie, you will surely make yourself
sick; you are chilled through already, and the room is getting cold; come upstairs with me."

But no, the headstrong child would not go upstairs, but
would lie there, and only there, and sob, and cry, and
refuse all comfort. It was not till the shaking of sleigh-
bells at the door announced the return of the party, that
my arguments had the least effect.

"Don't let them see you lying there, Esther. Come up,
and let me wash the tears off your face and smooth your
hair," I said; and she allowed me to lift her up, and lead
her upstairs, before her sisters came in. Félicie was busy
with a skirt of Josephine's, so I shut the nursery door and
kept the child with me. But this time there was no soothing her; she was fretful and trying beyond anything I
had ever seen; perhaps if I had not been so miserable

myself then, I could not have been as patient with her, as I remember I was. I was wretched enough to have lain down and sobbed myself, but the office of comforter is incompatible with that of mourner, and so is an office twice blessed; for tempting as is the luxury of tears, the reward of self-control is always greater and more lasting.

"The dinner-bell will soon ring, Essie, and you will not be ready to come down to dessert; come and let me brush your hair."

"I don't want to go down; I don't want any dessert," she whined.

Her hands were now hot and feverish, her teeth chattering with nervousness, and I recognized the approach of one of her sick headaches. I did not much wonder that she did not want to go down, so I coaxed her to let me undress her, and put her to bed, "and if you'll be a good child, you may sleep with me to-night."

"Very well," she said, laconically, with a weary sigh; and before the dinner-bell rang, I had laid her, quieted, in my bed, with, however, a very wide-awake and nervous stare about her eyes, but no tears and not much fretting.

For the next few days, the absorbing cares of the approaching party must have prevented my Aunt Edith from seeing the real indisposition of Esther. That her increasing irritability was the result of illness, I could not doubt, as I had ascertained for myself, that she could be as quiet as other children, when she was well. Josephine declared, I spoiled the teasing little object. Grace said, with a laugh:

"You can't reproach yourself with anything of the kind, can you, Joseph?"

And Phil, taking "the teasing little object" on his knee, said:

"Aunt Edith, upon my word, the child grows lighter every time I take her up. Is she well?"

"I mean to have the doctor this morning," she answered,

looking up from her writing. "I am rather worried about her; she is a little feverish. Esther, don't stay by the window; it is too cold for you. Go up to the nursery, and tell Félicie to put a little sacque on you."

So Esther was remanded to the nursery, and it being the day before the party, there was plenty to be done and thought of for all hands. And though the doctor came, he did not seem much impressed with her state of health—left a very innocent prescription that was not sent for till the next day, and eased everybody's mind exceedingly. What a very comfortable thing it is to be able to pin one's faith to a medical coatsleeve, and according as it is elevated or depressed, be soothed or terrified.

Any disinterested observer, ⅃ think, would have agreed with Esther and me, that party-giving was not in any way conducive to home comfort. That wretched day, lessons of course were given up; the study being turned into a dressing-room, and the nursery sharing the same fate—my room was the sanctuary where Grace and Esther sought refuge from the bustle and confusion of the first and second floors, and no paradise it proved, Essie being unbearably peevish and Grace unbearably provoking. Aunt Edith tore herself away from the claims of upholsterer, florist, and waiter for a moment, to look in upon us—gave the final directions about our dresses, and pronounced Esther's sentence, which she had been dreading for days, to wit, that she must not go downstairs. It was a most proper sentence, but it was a cruel disappointment, and the child of course cried herself into another headache. I induced her to go to bed about seven o'clock, but she sat bolt upright, watching eagerly the operations of the hairdresser, who had come to Grace and me, before arranging Josephine's hair.

"Esther, do go to sleep, and stop bothering!" cried Grace. "You've done nothing but worry this whole day."

A fresh burst of tears was the answer to this, and Grace was more incensed than ever.

"I think this is a pursuit of pleasure under difficulties, indeed," I exclaimed, despairing. "I hope all parties are not as much trouble! Will it pay, do you suppose?"

"*Cela dépend*," said Grace; "if you get attended to, it may; if you have to talk to the old ladies, and look over books of engravings in the corner, it wont."

I inly wondered which would be my fate, as I glanced at the pretty muslin on the foot of the bed. "Not the old ladies and the engravings I hope." It was my first party, and though everything seemed to conspire to make it a punishment, still I would have been more than human if I had felt no excitement when I first dressed myself in party-dress. White muslin and coral ornaments were not very elaborate certainly, but they were a great contrast to the plain clothes I had seen myself in since I could remember. When Grace was dressed, she went down, but Essie clung to me and begged me to stay so piteously, that I could not resist; and turning out the gas, I sat down on the bed by her, and told her stories by the dozen, and sung her hymns, in the vain hope of getting her to sleep; but she seemed to grow wider awake every minute. Ten o'clock chimed; the music began; the carriages were rolling to the door, and still she held my hand firmly, and said, "go on," in a hopelessly-clear voice, every time I paused in my recital. I was beginning to be in dire perplexity about leaving her, when the door opened, and Grace put her head in, saying, hurriedly:

"Mamma sent me up to say you must come down directly; half the people are here, and they are beginning to dance. Come as quick as you can," and Grace disappeared.

There was another burst of grief from Esther to be soothed and subdued, and at last, taking my gloves and fan, and kissing her good night, I stole out of the room, thinking her quite reconciled; but when half way down the stairs, I looked back, and saw the child, in her long white nightgown, standing at the head of the staircase, and heard her heart-broken voice begging me to come back, it was so lonesome, she was so sick. At the foot stood Grace.

"Mamma is displeased that you do not come."

What should I do? I ran upstairs again. Essie stood shivering at the door, a bright spot on each cheek, and an excited glitter in her eye.

"Essie!" I exclaimed, "why will you be so naughty? Don't you know mamma has sent for me twice? Do you want me to be scolded?"

"No, but I don't want to be left; it is so lonesome up here."

"But don't you know I promised to send Félicie up; and do I ever break my promises?"

"I don't want Félicie to come; she's cross," said the child.

"Well, then, Frances shall come; will she do?"

"Frances is busy, and you'll forget all about me when you get down there among the people."

"No, I won't, my darling," I said, stooping down, as she put her arms around my neck. "I will send Frances, and come up and see you in a little while myself. Be a good child, and go get in bed. Good night."

She laid her burning little cheek against mine for a moment; then submissively went in, and I turned to go downstairs. As I rose from my stooping attitude, I looked in at the nursery door, which, in my hurry, I had forgotten was the gentlemen's dressing-room; and that, as well as the hall, was strongly lighted. Two gentlemen, just within the door, had been witnesses of the scene of distress just enacted, and apparently not inattentive ones either. They were evidently strangers to each other, and one was so to me; I never remembered to have seen him before. The other was Mr. Rutledge.

He held out his hand with a smile, as I started back in confusion on seeing them. I gave him mine with a despe-

rate blush, and saying, hurriedly, that I must go down for
Frances, without giving him time for another word, I ran
down the stairs, and into the second hall, whence, picking
my way as daintily as I could, I threaded the narrowness
and darkness of the private staircase, that led to the
butler's pantry. There I found, as I had expected, an
eager group of domestics gazing in through the windows
into the parlors, watching the dancing with an interest only
second to that of the dancers themselves. I singled out
Frances from the group, and calling her to me, told her
my errand, and she, with a submissive sigh for the lost
festivities, followed me upstairs. I saw her safely at the
door of Essie's room, then, turning, began to descend, this
time more slowly, and to think seriously of the alarming
matter of my entrée. As I neared the parlors, the music,
the odor of the flowers, the brilliant lights, the gay dresses,
all crowded intoxicatingly upon my brain.

> "I only knew 'twas fair and sweet,
> 'Twas wandering on enchanted ground,
> With dizzy brow and tottering feet."

It was not a ball-room, it was the fairy-land, the magic,
the romance, of which I had dreamed; what adventures
lay within it for me; what untold delirious joy should I
experience when I had crossed the threshold. And how
should I cross it? Alone and timid, how could I stem that
flashing, glittering crowd? And, among them all, whose
protection should I seek, to whose side should I make my
way? There was no time for hesitation; I was at the
door; the gentleman whom I had seen upstairs, stood aside
to let me pass; two or three ladies made way for me, and
in a moment more I found myself at my aunt's side.

"You are very late," she said, in a low tone.

"I could not help it, Aunt Edith," I began; but a new
arrival took up her attention, and I was left to make my

own reflections upon the scene before me. It took a few minutes for me to come to my senses sufficiently to look about, and see things reasonably. It was some time before I recognized Josephine among the many strange faces. She was not dancing, but, with an admiring crowd around her, stood at the other end of the room, dispensing her coquettish smiles with tact and judgment. Grace was dancing with a lazy sort of grace that became her. Her partner was a painfully shy, undeveloped college youth, of whom, I could see, she was making all manner of ridicule, judging from the contortions of merriment visible on the face of her *vis-à-vis*, Captain McGuffy, with whom she exchanged a whispered witticism every time they met. Phil, with a self-denying heroism I had not given him credit for, was doing the agreeable to every one, dancing with all the girls who didn't seem to be having a nice time, and doing the honors of the house to the gentlemen without a groan. An occasional smile from Josephine, and a few words of approval from Mrs. Churchill, seemed to be all the reward he asked.

Many of the faces about me were familiar. Grace had pointed them out to me in the street, and I had occasion ally met them in the hall; but, of all the crowd, only one was an acquaintance, and that very far from a familiar one. Josephine's most intimate and particular confidante, Miss Ella Wynkar, gave me a look in passing, that was not striking for its graciousness, and a little nod. I had seen her at dinner more than once, when she had dined with us, and gone to the opera under my aunt's chaperonage. I never could understand her intimacy with Josephine; I knew they were dying of jealousy of each other, and Josephine, for one, never omitted an opportunity of saying an ill-natured thing about her friend behind her friend's back; and her friend, I felt certain, was not any more scrupulous; notwithstanding, they were the most loving and tender of companions, and continually seeking each other's society.

Josephine made visits with Ella, and Ella shopped with Josephine. Mrs. Churchill took Ella to the opera, and Mrs. Wynkar chaperoned Josephine to matinées and weddings. Ella was the whitest of blondes, and neither intellectually nor physically at all in Josephine's style; she had not a pretty or expressive feature in her face; a general look of whiteness and sweetness about her, being her sole attraction. She was very much below Josephine in intelligence, but was not destitute of a certain shrewdness of her own, which, with some little exertion, kept her up to her friend's level. She lacked Josephine's nice French tact and polish, and was very American and very New York in her rather "loud" style, and very high-colored mode of expressing herself. Josephine must have an intimate friend, however, and so, I suppose, the most advantageous and proper one was selected. Such coalitions are recognized in society, whereunto, of course, people must conform.

Ella, as I have said, was not at the pains to recognize me very affably on the evening of the party. I bit my lip and didn't mind, but somehow the glamor of romance was beginning to recede from the scene, and I was beginning only to see a roomful of people, strange to me, and none too affectionate to each other, flirting, dancing, quizzing each other; dowagers in velvet watching daughters in tarletan, young beaux elbowing old beaux, and every man showing himself unmistakably for himself. At first, it amused me to watch the people and their ways, but soon, like Essie and her sleigh-ride, I began to feel as if it would be very pleasant to have somebody to talk to, and be entertained by, as the other young ladies had. I felt hopelessly frightened, and shrunk as far as possible into the corner behind my aunt, whenever I caught any one's eye; which wasn't often, however, for every one seemed too busy with themselves and their partners, or companions, to notice me. Grace, passing near me with a young collegian or two, whispered, "Are you having a stupid time?" and the truth that I was

having just such a time, made the blood rush to my cheeks.
My aunt turned to me and said :

"Why are you so quiet? Go and amuse yourself; you
are at home, you know—talk to some one," and she turned
away.

I was at home, yes, I knew that. As one of the young
ladies of the house, I was of course entitled to be freed from
some of the trammels that society imposes upon those of my
age and sex. I might with propriety go and talk to any
young ladies who were disengaged and silent ; but I really
felt no inclination to avail myself of this privilege. Every
one seemed engaged but me ; no one noticed me, and I
retreated further into the corner than before. It was very
kind in my aunt to tell me to go and amuse myself. I
wondered if she had contented herself with giving such a
kind permission to Josephine on the night of her first
party, when she was new to society, and strange and
partner-less in it ?

"This is society, then," I said to myself. "Mr. Rutledge
needn't have warned me so against it. I do not see much
danger of my loving it too well. It isn't any too pleasant
to be alone and unattended to ; it is rather bitter to feel
that every one who looks at me must think, 'what a dull
time that girl is having!' and wonder why I know no one."

It *was* bitter enough, and for a while I longed to get out
of it all, and steal upstairs, and be by myself, but I knew
for the present that was hopeless, so I did the wisest thing
I could have done, viz., set to work to reason myself out of
my discontent and folly, and tried the "dodge" recommended in the old Greek comedy, that is, "being revenged
on fortune by becoming a philosopher." And a philosopher,
in white muslin and coral, then and there I became ; and in
ten minutes, the pettishness had all vanished from my
heart, and, *par conséquent*, from my face, and I was myself
again.

This was a strange termination of all my day-dreams ; a

strange entrée into the world; but no doubt it was the best
thing that could have happened to me. Had I not promised
to renounce it, and had it not been very wrong for me to
have gone on hoping to reap some pleasure from it, notwithstanding? Was not this the kindest way to bring to my
remembrance the vow and promise that I had so nearly forgotten. Was it not better for me to remember at the out-
set, that it and I were never to be in league, never to be
other than enemies? ·That if "there was no way but this,"
this was not so very hard and cruel a way? Poor Frances
upstairs, with her swollen eyes and wan face, had doubtless
a harder yoke to bear in her youth than I had, and so, with
a hundred other swollen-eyed and wan-faced girls whom
I daily met in the streets. "Let's think on our marcies," I
mentally ejaculated, quoting with a half smile, the words
of old "Aunt Chloe" to her husband on their cruel parting. Which, by the way, is the finest passage in all that
strange story of "Uncle Tom;" a passage unalloyed by
affectation, exaggeration or false sentiment—simple, great,
and heroic—worth twenty little Eva's dying speeches, and
unnatural angelhood.

After the lapse of an hour, I thought I might be allowed
to keep my promise to Essie, so I stole quietly out of the
gay crowd, and went up to my room. Esther had gone to
sleep, and Frances, startled from an attitude of weeping,
obeyed my permission to go down and watch the dancing
for half an hour, while I should relieve guard and take care
of the child, whose burning temples and restless moaning
made me certain that it was not right to leave her alone.
She did not wake up, however, during my vigil, and Frances
came back very punctually. I kissed the little sleeper again,
and with a very much sobered fancy, descended to the
parlors. Mr. Rutledge stood at the foot of the stairs, and
joined me as I reached the hall.

"Hasn't *la petite* gone to sleep yet?" he asked, offering
me his arm.

"Oh yes! some time ago."

"Then you prefer upstairs to downstairs, even on gala nights?" he inquired, with a smile.

"I don't know exactly," I answered; but at this moment, Phil made his appearance with the gentleman who had been at the dressing-room door when Essie had made her unexpected *début*.

"Ah, here you are!" he exclaimed; "we have been hunting you high and low for a good half hour."

And he presented, "Mr. Viennet."

The name, and his very slight foreign accent, assured me that this was the young Frenchman of whom I had heard so much from Grace and Josephine. He was at once "the best dancer," "the handsomest fellow," and "the cleverest man" in society, so when he bowed very low and asked me to dance, it was as if the planet Mercury had slid down the starry floor of heaven and demanded the honor of my hand. All I could do was to drop my eyes, blush very much, and assent.

Mr. Rutledge released me instantly, bowed and drew back. Mr. Viennet gave me his arm, and in a moment we were on the floor.

Nobody that dances well but loves it. I danced well, and I loved it. Mr. Viennet told me he knew *that*, the moment he looked at me, and as he seemed to take a wicked pleasure in saying such things, and making me blush, I soon regained my self-possession, and a certain degree of sauciness wherewith to parry these remarks. The captain was my vis-à-vis, and he whispered as we met:

"Upon my soul, Miss Josephine 'll have to look to her laurels; my friend Victor seems mightily *épris*."

"Is the captain asking you to dance?" demanded Mr. Viennet.

"Remember, mademoiselle, you are engaged to me for the next."

The next dance proved a polka. I had half resolved never

to dance anything but quadrilles; I had not thought much about the matter, but I had an indefinite sort of idea that some people condemned polkas and waltzes, and that it would be better not to indulge in them. But I had made no resolution strong enough to resist my partner's persuasions, and that fine floor, and the magic of the music. Before I knew it, I was flying down the room with Mr. Viennet, and having once tasted of that delirious pleasure, there was no putting the cup from my lips. One dance merged into another, polka, redowa, waltz, succeeded each other in intoxicating rapidity; a turn in the hall, or an ice in the library, being the only rest between. It did not take one whit from my pleasure, rather added extremely thereunto, that a face I knew too well, but sterner and colder than I had ever seen it, was watching me with marked disapproval. I avoided meeting his eye as I floated past him; I never laughed so gaily or danced so well as when I knew we were near him; my handsome partner owed half the smiles I gave him, to the fact of that stern face. I had been unnaturally depressed too long not to be unnaturally excited now. I was all my school-days' self again, with an under-current of something stronger and deeper, and more dangerous.

"You don't look like the same girl. How you do love to dance!" said Phil, in a low tone, as he brought up some one else to introduce. "Victor, my fine fellow, you must come and talk with somebody else. Mrs. Churchill says you shall not dance with her niece again. Go and make your peace with her."

"*De tout mon cœur*," he returned. "And I will release mademoiselle for this dance; but of course she remembers that she has promised me the next."

I laughed at this bold invention, as I went off with my new partner; but Mr. Viennet claimed me resolutely at the end of the quadrille, and though there was no lack of partners now, still he continued to be the prominent one, *malgrè*

Josephine's black looks, and Aunt Edith's distant coldness.
Not all the king's horses, nor all the king's men, could bring
me back to where I had stood before I knew my power. I
was dizzy with my triumph yet; it was no time to talk to
me of moderation. I had just begun to feel that there was
no reason why I should not enjoy myself as other girls enjoyed themselves. I did not feel submissive toward those
who had kept me down so long. I answered Josephine's
sarcasm with a sarcasm as biting. I returned Grace's compliment with interest. To Ellerton Wynkar, who asked me
to dance, I regretted, but was engaged for the rest of the .
evening, and sent him away with a hauteur that paid off all
old scores. At supper, I held a miniature court at one end
of the room, and not Josephine's self ever swayed a more
despotic rule. And when "the German" began, no one
ever led the German but Victor Viennet, and with no one
else would he dance, so I was then and there initiated into
the intricacies of that genteel game of romps.

As we paused in the first figure, I glanced at my silent
mentor. He was just bidding my aunt good night, and left
the room without a look toward the dancers. My interest
in the game began to flag somewhat after that, but still it
was dancing, and I loved that well enough never to tire.

The dance was ended, and the room nearly deserted, before my partner left me. As the door closed on the last
guest, Josephine threw herself into an easy-chair, exclaiming:

"I'm tired to death! I thought they would never go."

"Tired! I could dance till noon," I cried. "It's a
positive punishment to go to bed. Good night," and I ran
upstairs.

It was one thing to go to bed, and another thing to go
to sleep—one thing to shut my eyes, but quite another thing
to shut out the pageantry of fancy that the darkness did not
quench. Conjecture, hope, anticipation, longing, made wild
work in my brain that night. Everything was too new,

and strange, and dazzling, to yield at once to the control of reason. The curtain had risen upon too brilliant a scene to fade from my imagination, even after it had fallen. New faces, snatches of music, conversations, danced through my mind; but above all other sensations, a new sense of injustice and resentment made itself felt, and defiance took the place of the unquestioning submission I had rendered before. This was the thorn in my new crown of roses that took away from it its simplicity, its unalloyed beauty, and, perhaps, its innocence.

CHAPTER XXI.

" Who pleasure follows pleasure slays ;
God's wrath upon himself he wreaks ;
But all delights rejoice his days
Who takes with thanks, yet never seeks."

COVENTRY PATMORE.

Two days after this, I was surprised by the appearance on my plate, at breakfast, of two notes. The first proved to be an invitation for a party from a Mrs. Humphrey, cards for which Mrs. and Miss Churchill had received a week ago.

"Well!" exclaimed Josephine, unceremoniously, "I wonder what inspired Mrs. Humphrey to send you an invitation."

"It would be difficult to say," I returned, taking up the second. "Certainly no suggestion from you."

"Alps on Alps!" exclaimed Grace, looking over my shoulder. "Tickets for the Charity Ball! What next?"

"What, indeed," I said. "John, some more sugar in my coffee, if you please."

"Really, you don't seem much excited by your invitations. I suppose you don't intend to accept them?"

"Accept them!" echoed Josephine. "What an idea! It would be perfectly absurd to think of it, when it's understood that she's not out yet."

"I think I'll risk that," I answered, decidedly. "If Aunt Edith has no objection, I will avail myself of any invitations that I may receive for the next ten days. After that, Lent, you know, will decide the matter for us all."

"You must follow the dictates of your own judgment,"

returned my aunt, coldly. "Staying at home was your own choice, going out is at your own option."

"I know, dear aunt," I replied, with unaltered *sang froid*, "that you would do anything to indulge me in anything reasonable, and as I have quite set my heart upon this, I am sure you will not make any objection to it. You are the last person to put anything in the way of my pleasure and advantage."

"Pleasure and advantage are not always synonymous terms, my dear. What you might be pleased to consider pleasure, I might look upon as anything but advantageous, you know."

"Oh! we shall not differ as to that, I fancy. You cannot be more careful of me than of Josephine, and she has certainly tested pretty thoroughly the merits of the question. I should not think of going out as she does, to two or three parties of an evening, and spending the intervening hours of daylight in bed; but just three or four balls before the season closes, to see what it's all like, I really must enjoy, with your permission."

"Or without it," muttered Josephine. "You have enough *aplomb* to sustain you in that or any other impertinence you might undertake."

"Josephine," said her mother, sternly, "you forget yourself. My dear," to me, "you know I shall put no obstacle in the way of your enjoyment. You have my full permission to do as you think best."

"Thank you," I answered; "and I have the greatest desire to go to one of these mammoth charity balls. How lucky that it comes to-night, and that Mrs. Humphrey's is to-morrow, so that I can go to both."

"In what, if I may ask," said Grace, "do you propose appearing?"

"That's a question, I fancy, that has not occurred to our young friend," remarked Josephine.

"It's easily enough settled," I answered. "White mus

lin, 'with variations,' will be a sufficient toilette for *me*, you know."

"You'll excuse me for saying, that I think it is a matter of very little moment to any one but yourself," said she, with a laugh, as she rose from the table.

"Don't be spiteful, Joseph," said Grace, the only error of whose tactics was, that she could not confine herself to any one side in an encounter, and could not resist administering a blow on any exposed cranium, indiscriminately of friend or foe—"don't be spiteful, Joseph. She couldn't help taking off Victor, you know. It was trying, to be sure, but then it left you more time for 'the substantials.'"

Josephine, pressing her lips together, darted a threatening look at her sister, who, with a pleasant little nod, slipped through the folding doors and vanished.

"May I speak to you a moment?" I said, following Mrs. Churchill into the butler's pantry.

"Certainly," she answered, in a tone that did not invite confidence.

I had followed my aunt to say two things to her: the first was about myself, the second was about Esther. I had meant to say that if she really thought I was doing an unwise thing in going to these balls, I was willing to give them up. Conscience had made a suggestion or two that morning, and I was not yet careless about its admonitions. A kind word of advice, a look of motherly reluctance to deny me pleasure, and yet of motherly solicitude for my good, would have settled the doubt, and put me in the right way. But the tone in which she said "certainly," and proceeded to fit the key into the wine-closet, without so much as a look toward me, roused all the evil in my heart.

"You will never be troubled with any of my repentances," I thought, angrily; and then, in a tone that I suppose took its color from my thoughts, I said:

"I came to say, Aunt Edith, that perhaps you are not aware how much it irritates Essie to have Félicie take care of her. Félicie doesn't seem to have a pleasant way with her, and now she is confined to the nursery, she is continually fretted and unhappy. I find her more feverish every time I go upstairs, and I thought perhaps if you were willing to let Frances sit up there instead, she would amuse and keep her quiet better. She seems to like Frances."

Mrs. Churchill turned around and regarded me attentively for a moment, then said:

"I am sorry that your own good sense did not teach you the impropriety of such an interference as this, and that I am obliged to remind you of our relative positions, before you can understand how much such a thing as this offends me. The management of the household is my province, and any interference or advice concerning it I reject decidedly. If Esther is peevish and ill-tempered, I certainly hope Félicie will be strict with her. I have no intention of humoring her caprices, or disarranging the family to suit her whims. You may dismiss the subject from your mind entirely."

I bowed and left the room, with what bitter and resentful feelings it is easy to imagine. When Essie came crying to the door of my room, half an hour after, I sent her away; I was busy, she must not come in, and though her miserable face haunted me, I stubbornly put back the counsel that it gave me. I had been told not to interfere, and I would obey. All day I did not interfere—all day the evil spirit ruled, and I heard, without a remonstrance, the storm from the nursery, which, however, gradually subsided as the day advanced. I had enough employment, meantime, to keep down conscience; there was a flounce of my white dress to be repaired, and the blue bows to be made before evening. Mr. Waschlager did not come; Mr. Olman, poor man, had been ill for a week, and to-morrow was Miss Berteau's day, so there was nothing of duty to fill up the hours that would have hung heavily if it had not been for the anticipations of, and preparations for, the evening.

I turned the key of my door on Grace, and the key of my
heart on poor little Essie, and toward evening threw myself
into a chair by the fire, and read the latest number of "The
Newcomes." And who ever read Thackeray without feeling the greatest longing to see the world which he de-
cries? Who ever laid down a volume of his without a
more eager thirst for the pomps and vanities than they had
ever felt before? Who wouldn't have been Ethel, "with
all swelldom at her feet," even if she did cheat herself of
her happiness, and stored up sorrow for the heavy years to
come? Who could have the heart to say that Pen, in his
zenith, wasn't to be envied? or that George Osborne wasn't
a good fellow? I, for one, never felt any less attracted toward them because Mr. Thackeray, after spending on them
the finest colors on his pallet, tells us they are not to be
approved after all, and that they are not in the right way,
and that they have any amount of discipline to go through
before they are perfected. I always felt inclined to "skip"
the discipline; the natural man was the genuine one—the
improvement wasn't spicy. So, on this occasion, I read on,
fascinated, till twilight's gradual fingers stole between me
and the page, and I reluctantly gave it up, and dreamed on
about the story till the dinner bell rang.

Then I started up, struck with a feeling of remorse that
Essie had missed her accustomed twilight story for the first
time this winter. I smoothed my hair and hurried into the
nursery. Silence reigned there; Félicie sat by the dim
light, quietly pursuing her work. I asked for Essie, and
she rather sullenly pointed to the bed. It was unusual for
her to sleep at this hour; indeed at all hours she was a
light sleeper, and I had never before known her to be
willing to lie down even in the daytime, so it was with
some surprise that, on stooping down, I saw she was sleeping, and sleeping heavily.

"Why does she sleep so soundly, Félicie?" I said,
looking up.

"Because she's sleepy, I suppose, mademoiselle," she answered, rather shortly.

It was not worth while being angry with the woman, and indeed I did not feel like resenting any impertinence to myself, as I looked down at the quiet face of the little girl. Asleep, and free from the haggard, restless expression that her features ordinarily wore, she was almost pretty, almost child-like, but even in sleep there was a weary look about her that was pitiful. "Poor little mite," I murmured, "I've been unkind to you all day. Why won't you wake up and kiss me?"

But she did not wake; and when, in the selfishness of my self-reproach, I lifted her up and kissed her, in the hope that it would rouse her, the little arms fell down, limp and lifeless, and the little head sunk heavily back on the pillow, and she slept on unmoved. My interference in the morning had not been without its effect; as I left by one door, my aunt entered by another. She had been up twice since morning, and I could see she was uneasy; but, looking down at the child, I heard her say, in a tone of relief:

"Ah! she's sleeping nicely now!" and the voice of Félicie responded blandly. I think it was a load off her mind, for at dinner she was unusually affable.

Phil and Captain McGuffy were dining with us, and were to accompany us in the evening. The captain was extremely gracious to me; and as on former occasions he had appeared as nearly unconscious of my presence as was possible, I simply concluded that the sagacious captain was like the rest of the world, and was better satisfied to trust looking through his neighbors' glasses than through his own.

"Ever so many people," he said to me, as the soup was being removed (the captain rarely conversed much while there was anything engrossing on the table), "ever so many people have asked me about sending you invitations, and I've told 'em by all means; for you certainly were going out."

"Why didn't you remind them of Grace and Esther, and let them have the whole of the nursery, while they were about it?" asked Josephine, scornfully.

"Grace can speak for herself," said that young person, tartly. "You may tell them, if they ask anything about *me*," she continued, turning to the captain, "that they needn't look for my *début* till Josephine is disposed of, and I am, *par excellence*, Miss Churchill."

"Then," said the captain, gallantly, "you will not have a long time to wait, if what they say is true. I hear it hinted, Miss Josephine, that since Mr. Rutledge came from abroad this last time, he is quite changed, softened, you know, and made rather a society man; and they *do* say that his friends in Gramercy Square have something to do with it."

"I can't imagine how," said Josephine, all smiles and blushes.

"If Joseph knew when she was well off," interposed Grace, who loved to damp her sister's triumphs, "she wouldn't blush; she doesn't look well; she grows mahogany color, doesn't she Phil. Why, you're blushing too! What's the matter with everybody?"

"Everybody is blushing at your rudeness," said Mrs. Churchill, gravely. "I am sorry to be obliged to reprove you at the table; but I assure you, if you are not more careful"——

"Oh, mamma! you've always said it wasn't polite to deliver a reprimand in company; don't break through your rule. I won't say another word about blushing. Let's talk of something pleasanter. So," she continued, turning to the captain, "they really say Mr. Rutledge wants to marry Josephine?"

"Grace, leave the table," said her mother, concisely, but in a tone there was no mistaking, and which fell on the ears of the startled company with uncomfortable clearness, and on none more unexpectedly than on those of the young delinquent herself, who had never been so unequivocally disgraced before. She had trusted greatly to her mother's partiality and her own acuteness in warding off reproof, and this took her quite by surprise. She had not calculated the dangerous nature of the ground she was treading on, nor the decision of her mother's character when once roused, and so this edict came upon her like a clap of thunder. She was constitutionally incapable of blushing, or of looking confused, but she approached on this occasion more nearly to a state of embarrassment than I had ever supposed she could; but recovering herself in a moment, she deliberately folded her napkin and put it on the table, pushed back her chair, made a low courtesy, and saying, "Bon soir, mesdames; bon soir, messieurs," retreated in good order.

Rather an awkward pause ensued upon her exit; but it was soon broken by Mrs. Churchill's half laughing apology for her pertness, and Josephine was too much delighted with her adversary's discomfiture to be long silent. And she almost forgot to be spiteful to me, too, in the triumph of her acknowledged conquest. Even the dreaded task of dressing and preparing for the ball was accomplished without half of its accustomed drawbacks. Grace wisely kept out of sight, and Frances was less fluttering and timid than usual, so that at nine o'clock we all mustered in the parlor with comparatively undisturbed tempers.

I had left Esther still asleep when I came down. Félicie had undressed her and put her back in bed without arousing her. "You'd hardly let me go so quietly if you were awake, I think," I said to myself, as I bent down to kiss her.

I found myself much more excited than I meant to be, as the carriage drew near the Academy of Music. My excitement, however, had time enough to cool, for carriages

choked the streets on every hand, and it was the work of
half an hour to effect an entrance. The steps were crowded,
the lobbies were crowded, the cloak-room was a hopeless
crush, but the full sense of bewilderment did not overcome
me, till following the captain and Mrs. Churchill, we
ascended another pair of stairs, and passing through a side
door, stood looking down upon the magnificent scene
below. The captain said he had never seen anything finer
in this country, so I felt at liberty to be enchanted with it.
The decorations and lights were brilliant, the music delightful, and the sight of so many thousands of gaily-dressed
people crowding the boxes, the passages, the floor, could
not fail to excite the enthusiasm of one so new to such scenes
as I was. To Josephine, on the other hand, the ball seemed
by no means a wholly rapturous affair. A ruthless foot had
trodden on her dress, and torn the lowest flounce; Phil was
out of humor, and refused to be devoted; the captain had
his hands full with mamma, and Josephine searched in vain
among the crowd for the one or ones she wanted. We were
in a private box, and too far from the floor to recognize the
dancers easily, and by some neglect, the opera-glasses had
been left in the carriage. Josephine was unspeakably
annoyed. They might as well be looking out of the third-
story window at home, she declared. For me, the scene
was enough for the present, without any nearer interest in
it. If I could have been further forward, it would have
been pleasure enough to me to have looked on, but my aunt
and cousin occupying the front of the box, left me no view
of the house, but over their heads.

By and by, however, the door of the box opened, and
Mr. Rutledge entered. He had exchanged a few words
with me before Josephine saw him; her face lighted up
instantly, and after a cordial welcome from mamma, a place
was made for him in front. This, however, he declined to
occupy, as the captain had been on the ground before him,
and was better entitled to the position. He had an opera-

glass, which he handed to Josephine, and good humor was partially restored. The captain availed himself of the front seat, and criticised the dancers for madame's benefit; Phil stood behind his cousin's chair, and Mr. Rutledge was left to me. I knew this arrangement did not suit; I knew my aunt was hearing very little of the captain's commentary; I knew that Josephine, but for Phil's jealous watchfulness, would have paid much more heed to Mr. Rutledge's low conversation with me, than to her desired opera-glass. I remembered, but too vividly, the conversation at dinner; and though I struggled hard with my pride and my timidity, the words died on my lips, my answers were hesitating and reserved, and for the most part, insincere; I said the very things that, the next moment, I would have given worlds to have unsaid; I felt that every word was estranging us more hopelessly, and yet there seemed a spell upon us—I could not be myself. The questions I had meant to ask him, if I should ever have a chance, the sentences of which I had said to myself a hundred times, I could now no more have uttered than if they had been in an unknown tongue.

When he spoke of Rutledge, the blood that always flashed into my face at the name, now rushed to my heart, and left me paler and more listless than before. If my manner wore any change while he talked of his return there in a few days, and of my friends, Kitty and Stephen, Madge and Tigre, it was an increased indifference and coldness. I said no more than "yes" when he asked me if I still remembered them with interest, and "I don't know exactly," when he asked what message he should take to them from me. Then he changed the subject, and with his accustomed way of reading my face while he talked, he asked me about my impressions of society. Which was most to my taste now, city or country?

"I don't know exactly," I said, hesitatingly.

"I think I know," he said, with a laugh that nettled me, low and pleasant as it was. "I think there is small doubt

about your preferences just now. You acknowledge my
wisdom at last, do you not? You see it was best for you
to come to the city?"

"Yes," I said, lifting my eyes for a moment. "You
were very right. I ought to thank you very much for your
advice."

"My dear," said my aunt, leaning toward us, "you cannot see at all there. You must take my place for a little
while, I insist upon it."

The captain rose with great *empressement*, and insisted
upon my accepting his seat, and in the midst of the confusion consequent upon this change, the door of the box
opened again, and Mr. Viennet entered. Mr. Rutledge was
placing a chair for me as I looked up and recognized the
new comer. The chilled and frightened blood that had
crept fluttering round my heart, at this moment rushed into
my face, and burned guiltily in my cheeks, as I caught Mr.
Rutledge's eye. Mr. Viennet, after a moment devoted to
salutation, inquiry and compliment, entered a protest against
our remaining any longer in such a detestable corner, pro-
nouncing it *detestable*, in his charming little French way.
No one could get at us; he had only found us by the
merest chance. We must come downstairs—everybody
was on the floor—everybody was dancing. He assured
madame it was perfectly *convenable;* it was spoiling the
pleasure of too many to hide ourselves any longer.

This met Josephine's views exactly, and she importuned
"mamma" very prettily to yield. "Mamma" looked
doubtingly for a moment at Mr. Rutledge, who responded
to the look by saying that he really thought her strict ideas
of propriety might allow this liberty without suffering any
outrage. It was something new for New York, but these
balls had taken very well, and the best people attended
them, not only as spectators, but as participators. As for
dancing, he said, with a slight shrug, he rather wondered at
any lady's liking such an exhibition; but a promenade

on the floor for half an hour or so, he really should think we would find more entertaining than remaining in our box.

This partly settled the wavering in Mrs. Churchill's mind, and with a dainty sort of reluctance, she gave her consent to our going on the floor for a little while.

"Cheek by jowl with Tom, Dick and Harry," muttered Phil, giving his arm to Josephine, who took it with but indifferent grace, and bit her lip in annoyance, as, standing nearest the door, Mr. Rutledge and Mr. Viennet at the same moment offered me an arm. Can any girl understand the impulse that made me accept Mr. Viennet's? No man possibly can; my only hope of comprehension is from my own incomprehensible, perverse, self-torturing sex.

Once on the floor, it was hardly to be expected that we could obey my aunt's injunction to keep together, and within sight of her. In five minutes her ermine and diamonds, and the captain's moustache and epaulettes, were, though very dear, of course, to memory, utterly lost to sight, and Paul and Virginia were not more romantically alone than were we, in that vast human wilderness. It was a very amusing and nice thing to be lost. For half an hour we searched for our party, though not, it must be confessed, as if our whole happiness in life depended on our success, but no trace of them could be discovered.

"We must amuse ourselves. alors, mademoiselle, and let them look for us," said my companion. "Was there ever such a waltz before? You cannot resist it any longer, I know you cannot."

Perhaps I might have resisted it, as well as his eloquent pleading, if, raising my eyes at this moment to the boxes we had occupied, I had not caught sight of Josephine and Mr. Rutledge, who had returned there, evidently much more interested in each other than in anything below them.

"I'll dance once," I said, and in a moment his arm was on my waist, and we were floating along the elastic floor to such music as the fairies dance to, on soft summer nights, with the blue vault of heaven above their heads, and the green sward beneath their feet, and all wild ecstatic and untamed rapture thrilling in their elfin bosoms.

Conscience was drugged that night; self-will and pride, self-appointed regents, were holding sway as only usurpers can; and the glowing hours fled away without record or remorse.

"*N'importe*," murmured my companion, when I suggested a doubt, and *n'importe* I allowed it to be, as, whirling giddily from end to end of the vast area, or sauntering slowly through the gradually lessening crowd, we let the minutes slip away into hours. It was rather a startling recall to stern reality, when, at one end of the hall, suddenly encountering Phil, he laid a heavy hand on my partner's arm, exclaiming:

"Victor, my boy, if you've any mercy on that unlucky girl, come this way. There is such a scolding in store for her as she never had before. The carriage has been waiting an hour, and the captain and I, being detailed for the detective service, have pursued you faithfully, but you have eluded us most skillfully, I'll do you the justice to say! And Mr. Rutledge and the ladies have watched you from upstairs, and said—well, we won't say what pretty things."

"Extraordinary!" exclaimed Victor. "Why, we have been hunting for *you* till we were entirely discouraged disheartened, in despair!"

"Ah, well!" exclaimed Phil, with a laugh, leading the way. "I only hope you'll be able to make Mrs. Churchill believe it. It's my duty to prepare you for the worst, however."

"And our duty to be brave," said my comrade. "And fortune favors such, they tell us, mademoiselle."

Certainly I could not feel otherwise than grateful to my protector for his ingenious and powerful defence, as we appeared before the offended group at the door of the cloak-room. Though my aunt received it politely, I well knew the wrath that her knit brow portended, and Josephine's look of contempt was unmistakable. Mr. Rutledge had his visor down; no earthly intelligence could discover any-thing of his emotions through that impassive exterior. Even the captain was irritated; Phil was neutral, but Vic-tor was my only friend.

"Good night," he whispered, as he put me into the car-riage. "We'll finish that redowa at Mrs. Humphrey's to-morrow night."

I wished, with all my heart, it was to-morrow night, and all that I foresaw must intervene, safely past. The scolding was not to come before morning, I saw at once, and when my aunt, on our arrival at home, dismissed me to my room, it was with a cold, "I wish to have a few minutes' conver-sation with you after breakfast to-morrow."

With that dread before me—with a guilty sense of wrong-doing, and a bitter sense of shame, a humbled condemna tion of myself, and an angry resentment toward others, the restless hours of that night offered anything but repose, any-thing but pleasant retrospect or anticipation.

CHAPTER XXII.

"And if some tones be false or low,
What are all prayers beneath
But cries of babes, that cannot know
Half the deep thought they breathe?"
                                        KEBLE.

MRS. CHURCHILL understood, if ever any did, the art of reprimand. Without the least appearance of agitation herself, with a perfectly unmoved and stony composure, she managed to overawe and disarm the prisoner at the bar, whatever might be his or her offence, or shade or degree of guilt. Defence died on my lips at the dreaded interview, and I bore my sentence in silence, which was, a total seclusion from society after to-night—a return to the oblivion of the nursery and study. This ball at Mrs. Humphrey's was to be my last appearance in public till I should have learned how to behave myself. As I had accepted, it was proper I should go to-night, otherwise she would by no means have allowed it.

"Nous verrons," I said to myself, as I went upstairs. "If I continue to want to go to parties, no doubt she will have to let me go. I am a fraction too old to be put in a dark closet, or sent to bed for being naughty, and Aunt Edith knows it."

That Wednesday was a very busy day to Mrs. Churchill and Josephine. A wedding reception took up the morning, from which they returned but to dress for a dinner at the Wynkars, and thence returning, made a hurried toilette for the ball. It seemed making rather a toil of pleasure, if one might judge from my aunt's haggard looks, and Josephine's impatient complaints.

There was an anxious contraction on Mrs. Churchill's brow as she came down from the nursery after breakfast, and apparently a struggle in her mind between home duties and social duties, when it became necessary for her to decide about going out. That she sincerely believed in the stringent nature of both, no one could doubt who watched her closely. It was not pleasure that took her away from little Essie that morning ; it was a mistaken sense of duty. She had set up for her worship an idol, in whose hard service she had unconsciously come to sacrifice time, ease, and affection, as stoically as many have suffered in a cause whose reward is not altogether seen and ended in this world.

So it was, that, trying to make up for her absence by many injunctions and cautions to those left in charge, she turned her back upon the child for the greater part of the day.

"I hoped," said she, as she paused at the nursery door, in her rustling silk and heavy India shawl, "I hoped that the doctor would have come before I went out, but I really do not see but what you can do as well as I can, Félicie. Pay particular attention to his directions, and send John out immediately for any prescription he may leave for her. And be sure you tell him just how she was yesterday, and how well she slept last night. I don't like," she continued, taking off one glove to feel again of the child's hot forehead, "her having fever again this morning. I thought yesterday she was so much better."

"Oh, madam is too anxious. It is nothing but a little excitement that has brought it on again," said the nurse. "If madam would tell Mademoiselle Esther how very naughty it is for her to cry to go into her cousin's room, and fret and strike me when I try to keep her quiet, perhaps she might mind better. It is that that brings her fever on, madam, I am afraid."

"Now, Esther," said her mother, with authority, "I

shall have to punish you if you do so any more. I shall be
very angry if you do not mind Félicie to-day, and if you
hurt or strike her, remember I shall punish you when I
come back—do you hear?"

Esther heard, yes. She sat bolt upright in her little bed,
and looked at the speaker with her parched lips parted, and
a strange, bewildered expression in her eyes, and a restless
movement of her tiny hands. Before the interview was
over, however, the startled look had settled into a vacant,
listless stare; and a peevish moan, after her mother left the
room, was all the evidence she gave of being impressed or
alarmed by the injunctions laid upon her. I heard the
miserable little complainer unmoved as long as I could;
after a while, putting down my book, I went into the
nursery. She stretched out her arms, and cried:

"Take me to your room."

"If you will stop crying," I said, taking her up in my
arms, and wrapping her dressing-gown about her.

Félicie looked up quickly, and said, "*Madame a dit
que non.*"

Félicie always lied in her native tongue, and this was
but an additional proof to me that madame had said no
such thing, and I told her so, rather strongly. Grace
came in just then, and Félicie appealed to her for confirmation.

"Certainly," said Grace, promptly, "mamma's last
charge was that Esther should not go out of the nursery;
so, missy, you may just make yourself easy where you are.
Don't suppose everybody is going to spoil you like your
precious cousin there."

Essie still clung tightly round my neck; much, however,
as my pride rebelled, there was no way but to submit to
the orders they promulged. So, carrying her back to the
bed, and loosening her arms from my neck, I put her down
with,

"No matter, sweetheart; if Mahomet brings his work,

and sits down by the mountain, that will do as well, will it not?"

"I don't know what you mean," said the child, uneasily.

"She means to plague you, Esther; she's been scolded this morning, and she's in bad humor," said Grace.

"Don't throw stones, Miss Grace," I retorted. "I wasn't sent away from the table, if I was scolded."

"Mamma'll never forget your performance last night, the longest day she lives," continued Grace. "I never saw her half so angry before. In fact, from all accounts, you must have got it from all quarters, but what Mr. Rutledge said was the worst."

"What did he say, pray?"

"*Wouldn't* you like to know!" she cried, in her teasing, school-girl fashion.

"I don't believe you could tell me, if I did."

"I could if I wanted to," she exclaimed. "I heard mamma and Josephine talking it over this morning. The door of the dressing-room was open a crack, and I heard every word. Now, honey, *don't* you wish I'd tell you?"

"I don't want to hear half as much as you want to tell me," I returned, trying to be unmoved.

"Oh! don't be uneasy on my account," she said. "I haven't the least idea of telling you. Only, I didn't suppose Mr. Rutledge could be so severe, and on 'his little friend,' too!"

"That—for Mr. Rutledge!" I exclaimed, with a disdainful snap of my fingers. "I don't care the fraction of a pin for his opinion!"

"I'll tell him," cried Grace, with delighted eyes.

"Do," I answered; and hiding my burning face on the pillow with Esther, I said:

"What shall we do to amuse ourselves this morning, Essie? Shall I tell you a story?"

"Yes," said Esther, looking pleased.

"Ask her to tell you about the ball last night, and Mr. Victor Viennet," said Grace, as she went out of the door.

"No," said the little girl, "I'd rather have her tell me about the little dog Tigre at Rutledge, and how he used to stand outside of her door, and whine to come in. Won't you now?"

"Oh, that's tiresome, Essie," I said, "I'll tell you something else."

"Then tell me about the boys that stole the chestnuts, and about the lake, and the great trees, and the artemisias and the grapevines in the garden. Tell me, won't·you now?" she went on, coaxingly.

"You'd rather hear a fairy story, Esther," I said; "or something out of your pretty Christmas book, I am sure."

"No," said Esther, "I want to hear about the country, I wish they'd take me to the country," she continued, wearily; then, raising herself on her elbow, and looking at me earnestly, she said, "do you believe they ever will? Do you believe I'll be made to always stay in this nursery, without any flowers or birds, or anything I like? If I should die in it, would I stay in it always, or would they take me out? Tell me, would they?"

"Of course, Essie," I said, half impatiently, uncomfortable under her earnest eyes. "I do not like to hear you talk so. You know, I've told you often, that there's a home for us where we shall go after we die, better than any home here, where good children are, and holy men and women; and it's all a great deal brighter and happier than anything we can imagine; so don't trouble yourself to think about it; only be good."

"But I am not good," she said, with a sort of agony in her voice; "you know I am not."

"Essie," I said, soothingly, drawing her toward me,

"nobody is good. I am not, and you are not, and nobody is; but if we are sorry when we're wrong, and ask God to forgive us, and help us, He will, you may be sure. Why, Essie, He loves you, little foolish girl as you are, more than you can possibly tell. He loves you, and he would not let you perish for anything."

"Are you sure of that?" she said, eagerly.

"Perfectly sure," I answered.

"Madame ordered," said Félicie, "that Miss Esther should be kept perfectly quiet. She's talking too much, and exciting herself. It would be better to have the room darkened, and let her go to sleep."

"I can't go to sleep, and she shan't go away," exclaimed the child.

"I haven't the least idea of going, Essie; so lie down, and I'll tell you about the country."

And, till my own heart ached as hers did, in its narrow city bounds, I told her of the country, and how soon the first warm spring days would loose the ice-bound brooks, and let the pines see themselves once more in the lake. And in the lots, the violets would be springing up thickly in the moist sod, and the faint green would be coloring the meadows and lawns, and the skies would be soft and blue, and the slow, warm wind would waft along the fleecy clouds, and stir the budding trees, and linger over the soft, wet earth, and creep into cold and wintry houses, and into cold and wintry hearts, and stir all things with a sense of warmth and ecstasy.

Throughout the day I hardly left my little cousin; she was feverish and restless, and never closed her eyes or rested a moment. About four o'clock, however, I went down to practise for an hour, and when I came upstairs again, she had fallen asleep. Her mother, coming up at the same time, was much relieved to find her sleeping, and Félicie gave a very satisfactory account of her; so that she dressed for the dinner in comparative comfort. The doctor's visit had occurred while I was downstairs, and had been a very hurried one. Grace and I dined alone, very sociably and cheerfully, Grace reading a French novel, and I "the New-comes," in all the pauses of the meal.

I went upstairs as soon as it was over, and found Esther still asleep. It was a wet, miserable evening. The rain was dripping slowly and heavily from the roof to the window-sill, and from the window-sill to the piazza below. A thick, suffocating fog, possessed the earth, through which the distant lights blinked drearily; even the noises of the streets sounded muffled and subdued. It was so warm, that the low soft-coal fire in the grate seemed oppressive; yet, when I opened the window, there was a damp, choking heaviness in the air that was worse, even, than the dry heat of the room. It seemed as if the spirit of the fog was sitting a night-mare on my breast, and pressing down with a hand like lead the beating of my heart, and stopping my very breath. There was no shaking off the weight, nor driving away the gloomy fancies that the hour bred. It was in vain that I lit the gas, and closed the blinds, and laying my ball-dress on the bed, tried to interest myself in my preparations for the evening. Between me and all plea-sant anticipation, there hung a black pall of presentiment, and no effort of my will could put it aside. The very struggle to free myself from it, seemed to make the gloom close thicker around me. The house was so still; the ser-vants were all downstairs; the ticking of the clock on the nursery mantelpiece was all the sound that broke the still-ness, and that, so regular, so monotonous, was worse than silence. It was a time

"For thought to do her part,"

for conscience and reason to be heard. Should I go into the world and try to forget it? Should I leave the little helpless child asleep there, in charge of a woman I distrusted

and disliked, and go where music and pleasure would drown
the dread for her that was gnawing at my heart? What,
that was good for hours of trial, had I learned in my short
experience of pleasure? What, that I could remember
with satisfaction, had occurred in the two nights of gaiety
that I had just passed through? What, in the flatteries of
Victor Viennet, in the admiring eyes of strangers, in the
envy of my cousin, that I could dare to remember in
church—on Sunday—under a quiet evening sky—or on a
fresh, pure early summer morning? Alas! it was out of
tune with all of these; there was utterly a fault about it—it
turned to ashes as I grasped it. It was not true pleasure.
It was not a worthy pursuit. As far as I had followed it
already, it had led me into sin, into pride, insincerity and
anger. It had done me no good. I felt that. Had I the
courage to put it away from me now? Could I say, without an effort, I will keep myself out of the way of seeing
Victor Viennet again? I will never remember but to condemn the hours that I have spent with him? Could I
return to the dull routine I had formerly marked out for
myself, without an effort that would cost me many tears?
But if I could not do this, what was my religion worth?
If this self-denial was so hard, did it not prove that
the world had got a very tight hold of my heart, and
that the sooner I wrenched myself from its grasp the
better?

On the other hand, there was no definite reason why I
should not go, there was only this vague feeling of uneasiness about Essie that tormented me and kept me back, and
this unsettled question about the profitableness of going into
the world. How should I decide? My affection for my
little cousin tugged strongly at my heart. Pride and inclination pulled as fiercely the other way. A feeling that I did
not give a name to, but which was stronger than either,
prompted me to follow my own desires, and leave Essie to
her fate. What business was it of mine? If other people

neglected their children, and left their duties for their pleasures, why need I concern myself? Why need I take upon
myself their discarded responsibilities?

At last I stole on tiptoe to the bed again, to see if she
still slept. Not much sleep in those frightened eyes.

"Why! Essie, my pet, when did you wake up?"

With a sigh of relief, and a little relaxing of the look of
terror, she raised herself up, and saying hurriedly, "how
still it is! I thought you had gone away," she twined both
small hands tightly round my wrist.

"Oh, no!" I said, sitting down by her, "it isn't time yet.
I shall not go for an hour or two."

"Don't go at all, please don't go," whispered the child,
panting for breath, and clinging to me in an agony. "If
you knew how awful it was to be alone, and how still the
room was, you wouldn't leave me, indeed you wouldn't.
Besides," she went on hurriedly, "how can you tell what'll
become of me while you're gone? Nobody else loves
me, nobody else is good to me. I am troublesome and
wicked—only God and you care anything about me."

It was useless to soothe or reason with her now. I knew
little of illness, but I saw in a moment that the wild delirium
of fever was burning in my little companion's veins, and
raging in her brain. I was frightened at the strength of
the little hands that fastened themselves on mine, and the
hurry and wildness of the broken sentences she uttered.
All I could do, was to promise that I would not go, and
assure her that there were no "ugly shadows" on the
wall—that nobody was coming to take her away—that it
was all because her head ached so. But when Félicie
appeared, it was a less easy matter to control her. She
screamed, and hid her face, and cried to me to send her
away—she hated her—she gave her horrid stuff—she made
her angry, and a thousand other vehement exclamations in
alternate French and English. The nurse, with a subdued
glare of anger in her eyes, would fain have soothed her, for

her voice, shrill with the strength of fever, could easily have been heard downstairs, and Mrs. Churchill had come home and was now in her dressing-room. My alarm had overcome my pride by this time, and loosing my hands from the child's grasp, I gave her into Félicie's charge, and ran downstairs.

The door of the dressing-room was locked, and it was some minutes before I was admitted, and during those minutes, my alarm had time to cool, and when at last I entered the room, it was with a full recollection of the last rebuff I had received when I pleaded Esther's cause, and a cold determination to do my duty and no more.

"Why are you not dressed, if you intend accompanying us?" she said.

"I do not intend going this evening," I answered; "and I came, Aunt Edith, to say that I think you had better see Esther before you go out; she has a great deal of fever, and is very much excited."

I never before had realized how dangerous a thing it was to touch with even the daintiest hand, the festering wound that both pride and remorse conspire to hide from the sight even of the sufferer's self. I could not have done anything worse for poor Essie's cause, than just what I did do, and she shared with me in the feeling of vexation and resentment that my words awakened in her mother's breast.

I soon forgot the severity of the rebuff I had received, however, when coming into the nursery, I took the struggling child from Félicie, and watched with anxiety the gradual subsiding of the fit of passion that had convulsed her. From whatever cause it might be, she was evidently growing quieter, and in less than half an hour, the little head on my arm had relaxed its tossings, and sunk into repose, while a dreamy languor dulled the wildness of her eyes, and save when the slightest movement woke an alarm that I would leave her, she lay quite motionless.

"She is better now," said Félicie, in a low tone, who was watching her with her basilisk eyes as she lay apparently sleeping. A nervous tightening of the slight fingers on my wrist at the sound of her voice, showed me that it was only apparently.

When Mrs. Churchill had completed her toilette, she came upstairs. Esther, with her long eyelashes sweeping her crimsoned cheeks, lay so quiet that there seemed some reason in her mother's cutting rebuke for the unnecessary alarm I had given her. I began to feel heartily ashamed of it myself, and wondered that I had been so easily frightened. Félicie, with a wicked look of exultation, said, that if Miss Esther hadn't been in a passion, she wouldn't have brought the fever on again. She had been better all day, the doctor had said she had scarcely any fever, when he was here.

Mrs. Churchill hoped, with a withering look, that I would get used to ill temper in time, and not think it necessary to disturb the household whenever Esther had a fit of crying. Then feeling the child's pulse, and giving many and minute directions for the care of her during the night, she went away. As, a moment after, the hall door closed with a heavy sound, a momentary tremor passed over the child's frame, and opening her eyes, a strange light fluttered for an instant in them, as she murmured, "you will not go away?" then closed them again, and she seemed to sleep. I watched beside her for an hour; then releasing myself from her unresisting hands, and kissing her lightly, I went into my own room.

I returned several times to look at her again, before I put the light out and lay down to sleep. How many times the monotonous nursery-clock struck the half hour before I slept, I cannot tell; the heavy air was broken by no other sound; there was nothing in the silent house, shrouded by the close fog without and the dead silence within, to keep me awake, yet it was long before I slept. But sleep, when it came, was heavy and dreamless—a sort of dull stifling of consciousness, in keeping with the night.

Hours of this sleep had passed over me, when a fierce grasp upon my arm, and a hissing voice in my ear, woke me with a terrified start, and chilled me with horror, as struggling to collect my senses, I tried to comprehend Félicie's frantic words. In a moment, they made their way to my brain, and burned themselves there.

"I've given her too much—I cannot wake her! O mon Dieu! *Je l'ai tuée! Je l'ai tuée!*"

A horrible sickening faintness for an instant rushed over me, then a keen sense of agony like an electric flash thrilled through me, and without a look, a thought, a word, I was kneeling at the little bed in the nursery. But, as my eager eyes searched the whitened face on the pillow there, and as my aching ears listened for the almost inaudible breathing, and my hand touched the cold arms that lay outside the covers, such a cry burst from my lips as might have waked the dead, if dead were indeed before me. But there was no voice nor answer; there was an awful stillness when I listened for response; when I raised my eyes in wild appeal from the white face of the child, there was but a horrible face above me, whereon was all the pallor of death, without its calm repose; such a face as the lost and damned may wear when their sentence is new in their ears—when endless perdition is but just begun, and life and hope but just cut off.

Another moment, and all the house was roused. Putting back, with one strong effort, the agony and hopelessness that welled up from my heart, I mastered myself enough to direct the terrified and helpless servants. Dispatching different ones to the nearest doctors I could think of, another for my aunt, another for all the restoratives that occurred to me, the next few minutes of suspense passed.

But before the doctor could arrive, I knew there was no need of his coming. There had been a little flutter of the

drooping eyelid, ever so slight a quiver of the parted lip,
and bending down, I had listened, with agonized suspense,
for the low breathing, and called her name with the tenderness that never finds perfect expression till death warns us
it shall be the last. Then a little arm crept round my neck,
the soft eye opened for a moment, a sigh stirred the bosom
that my forehead touched, and, as the arm relaxed its faint
clasp, I knew that Essie was a stranger and an alien no
longer, but was where it were better for us all to be—where
there is peace, eternal, unbroken, beyond the reach of sin
forever.

For those first moments, when I knelt alone beside the
little bed, with the soft arm still round my neck, and the
breath of that sigh still on the air, there was no feeling that
I had suffered a bereavement, that death and sorrow had
entered the house; but holy thoughts of God and heaven—
strange longings for the rest that she had entered into—a
sort of hushed and hallowed awe, as if the new angel still
lingered, with a half regret at leaving me alone—as if the
parting, if parting there were to be, were but for a "little
while"—as if the communion of saints were so divine and
comfortable a thing, that there was no need for tears and
sorrow.

But when there came a sudden tumult below, hurried
steps upon the stairs, a sound beside me, a pause, and then
a cry that made my blood freeze in my veins, I knew that
there was more than joy in heaven—that there was bitter
agony on earth: that there was more than an angel won
above—that there was a child dead below—a household in
mourning—a mother's heart writhing in torture—a judgment fallen—a punishment following close upon a sin—a
remorse begun that no time could heal, that no other life
could quench, no other love allay.

' back, then, complainer; loathe thy life no more,
Nor deem thyself upon a desert shore,
Because the rocks the nearer prospect close."

KEBLE.

FÉLICIE had fled. When, in the agonized confusion of
that dreadful night, she was at last remembered and
searched for, there was no trace of her to be found, and all
future inquiry was equally unavailing. The wretched woman need not have concealed herself with such desperate
fear; no one felt any heart to search her out, or revenge on
her the death of her little charge. No one of that sad
household but knew, in their hearts, that there was a sin at
more than her door—a sin that lay heavy in proportion to
its unnaturalness and strangeness.

Those were wretched nights and days that followed little
Esther's death. The vehement grief that, in the first hours
of amazement and remorse, had burst from the miserable
mother, was succeeded by a calm more unnatural and more
alarming. My heart ached for the misery that showed
itself but too plainly in her haggard face and restless eyes;
but, shutting herself up in her cold and speechless wretchedness, from all sympathy, I longed, but did not dare, to
offer any. And I, perhaps more than any other, involuntarily recalled the phantom she was trying to fly, the remorse that she was struggling to subdue. Though her
self-control, even then, was almost perfect, I could see that
she never looked at me unmoved—that she winced at any
attention from me, as if a newly bleeding wound had been
roughly handled, and shrunk more than ever into herself.
She refused all visitors, even the most intimate. Josephine

was the only one of the family whose presence did not seem to pain her, and at times even she was sent away. She was too strong and proud a woman not to bear her sorrow, as she bore all other emotions, alone. Not even Josephine saw any further into her heart than strangers did.

With the resumption of the ordinary household ways, came the cold insincerity that custom sanctions, of banishing from familiar mention the name that, a month ago, had been a household word, now recurring hourly to the lips, but hourly to be hushed and sent back to deal another pang to the aching heart. No more allusion was made to Essie than if, a few short weeks ago, she had not been one of this small circle, the youngest, and "the child," who, welcome or unwelcome, had necessarily, and by virtue of her position, claimed some part of the time and notice of those around her.

It was impossible to define how much of the subdued apathy of Grace's manner was owing to the grief she felt at her sister's loss, and how much to a sort of cowardly nervousness and shrinking from the idea of death. For days after the shock, she was like my shadow, dreading, evidently more than anything else, to be left alone, shunning her mother and everything that brought the hateful subject to her thoughts, trying, with all ingenuity, to divert herself and think of other things. It was useless to attempt to lead her higher, to make her see in her little sister's death anything but dread and horror. She shrunk from all mention of it with aversion, and turned eagerly to any diverting subject, and before any other member of the family, she shook off the depression it had caused. With Josephine it had been different. At first she was awe-struck and stunned, and for a while there seemed a danger of her falling into a morbid state of feeling; but as the freshness of the shock wore away, her elasticity returned, and with it the old impatience and imperiousness, that the absence of amusement and excitement only heightened.

A storm indeed had passed over our house, but a storm that had not purified and cleared the atmosphere, only left it more close and sultry than before; the black sky, indeed, had brightened again, leaving comparative sunshine overhead, but threatening clouds still lingered around the horizon, and distant rumbling still warned of danger.

I missed more than I had fancied possible, my little companion and pupil. No hour in the day but brought some fresh souvenir of the tortured young life that had ended its penance so early, the shrinking little soul that had been released so soon. It was not seldom, in those dark days, that I thought, with something like envy, of the peace she had inherited, and with something like repining of my lonely lot. How many years of warfare might stretch between me and the end; how many chances that I might fail or faint, grow weary, or yield to sin; while the little child I had so long looked upon with pity, so long tried to help and guide, now redeemed and safe, and everlastingly at peace, had passed "the golden portals of the City of the Blest." Good angels had pitied her, struggling and bewildered on her way, and lifting her in their arms, had carried her home; floating through the blue ether, in a moment of time she had passed the rough and weary road that would have taken a lifetime to have traversed alone. But no angels, it seemed to me, looked on my weary path; no sympathy, from heaven or of men, came to help me as I pressed on alone. Parting and death, repentance and self-accusation made that Lent a time of heartfelt sorrow; and before Easter-week was over, the low fever that had been hanging about me since the spring began, accomplished its errand, and laid me on a tedious bed of sickness.

Is there any one who has ever been sick "away from home," among strangers, courteous and attentive, perhaps, but whose courtesy and attention were of duty, not love, that cannot understand what it was to be lying, day after day, in a "home" like mine, knowing it was the only one

I had a right to, or a hope of, this side heaven, and know-ing, through all the exaggerating excitement of fever, and the languid hopelessness of slow convalescence, that in it there was no one to whom the care of me was not a penance, that no hour was so grudged as that spent by my bedside? Cold faces met me when I waked from my fever-ish, troubled sleep, commonplace, unsympathetic voices fell upon my ear, when, unnerved and childish, I longed for nothing so much as for a kind word or a caressing touch.

They were very attentive; I had every care; my reco-very was as rapid as the doctor wished; it had not been a very alarming illness; nobody was particularly excited about it. They said it was a " light case," and I could not be doing better. They had a right to know, certainly; but oh! the weariness of that dark room, the length of those spring days, the stillness of those warm nights, the loathing of those city sounds, the longing for the country!

June was now not many weeks off; and hour after hour, the question, " would Mr. Rutledge remember his pro-mise?" perplexed my brain. I knew I had done enough to have forfeited it; I knew it had been made hastily; that, indescribably and unaccountably, he was changed since then, and we had ceased to be anything like friends. Still, I was nearly certain he would keep his word; what-ever else he might forget, he would not forget that. No matter if it bored him, as I almost knew it would, I was sure he would do it just the same. Though I had a thou-sand fears that I should not be allowed to go, I knew I should be sent for, and I was not disappointed.

It was the first morning that I had breakfasted down-stairs; I had been well enough for a week, but a languor and indifference possessed me that made me averse to all thought of change or exertion. Now, however, that I was actually in the cool dining-room, where white curtains

replaced the heavy winter drapery of the windows, and
white matting the thick carpet, I wondered that I had not
made the effort before.   It was vastly more attractive than
my own room, certainly; and the parlors, as I glanced into
them, looked in comparison, almost imposing in their vastness.   The world, I saw, had been creeping in again.
There were notes and cards on the table, and a lovely
basket of violets; the piano was open, and some new music
lay on it.   Josephine, too, at breakfast, talked of drives
and engagements that showed the days of mourning were
over.   There was little difference in my aunt's manner
from formerly, but she looked ten years older, and was
somewhat colder and more precise.

"Who on earth can that be from?" Grace exclaimed,
as John brought in the letters, and Mrs. Churchill took up
the only one that did not look like an invitation or a mil-
liner's circular.   "It's from out of town," she continued,
reaching out her hand for the envelope, as her mother laid
it down.   "It's postmarked Rutledge!   What can Mr.
Rutledge have to say to mamma?   Joseph, doesn't your
heart beat?"

If Joseph's didn't, mine did, and so quickly, too, that I
felt sick and faint, and dreaded lest Grace's prying eyes
should inquire the cause of my alternating color.   But the
letter absorbed the attention of all, and I could only wait
till Mrs. Churchill should divulge its contents.   Josephine
tried to look undisturbed, but there was an accent of impatience in her tone, as she said:

"Well, dear mamma, may I see it, if ever you should
finish it?   I suppose there is nothing that I may not know
about."

"It is a very kind letter," said Mrs. Churchill, as she
glanced back to the beginning; "very kind, indeed, and
you are all interested in it.   Mr. Rutledge says that he has
been detained at his place several weeks longer than he had
anticipated, and there is now a prospect of his being obliged

to remain till possibly the middle of summer; in which
event, he thinks that we could not do a kinder thing than
come and pay him a visit. He describes the country as
looking very delightfully, and promises all sorts of rural
amusements if we will come; and, by way of insuring the
enjoyment of the young ladies, he begs we will make up a
party to accompany us, and suggests the Wynkars, Mr.
Reese, Captain McGuffy, Phil, of course, and any one else
we may choose to ask. He is really very urgent, and begs
we will not refuse to enliven the gloomy old mansion with
our presence for awhile. He puts it entirely into my hands,
and begs I will invite whom I choose."

"Delightful!" exclaimed Josephine. "Mamma, could
anything be nicer?"

"Mr. Rutledge is 'a gentleman and a scholar,'" said
Grace; "he ought to be encouraged. You'll accept, of
course?"

"*Cela dépend*," said her mother, thoughtfully.

"Oh, mamma!" cried Josephine, "you cannot dream of
refusing. What possible objection can there be? We do
not want to go to Newport before the middle of July, and
of course we can't stay in town all through June. This is
the very thing; and you know I'd rather go to Rutledge
than any other place in the world. Surely, mamma, you
cannot think of refusing."

"There are a great many things to be considered, my dear."

"Ah," cried Grace, with unusual animation, "there'll be
no peace till you say, yes. I long to get out of this dusty
city. What else does he say, mamma?"

"Not much," answered her mother, glancing down the
second page. "He says he only heard a few days ago of
my niece's illness, which he hopes will not prove serious,
and that a change of air, and return to the scene of her
last year's convalescence will be of benefit to her."

"How do you imagine he heard she had been sick?"
asked Grace.

"I haven't the least idea, I am sure," said Josephine. "It's of no great consequence, any way. But, mamma, who shall we ask? The captain, of course, and Phil, and, I suppose, the Wynkars; Ella will be delighted, no doubt, and think it's all on her account! And about Mr. Reese— he's such a tiresome old fogie, let's get somebody in his place."

"Ask Victor Viennet," said Grace, "just to spite Ella Wynkar. You know she hates him. He's as nice as anybody."

"I haven't quite made up my mind," said Josephine, with dignity.

"Wait till I have made up mine," said her mother, quietly.

So this was the way which Mr. Rutledge had found to keep his promise to me, and gratify his own wishes at the same time. It took away all the pleasure of my anticipations, however, to have it fulfilled in this way. It seemed to me a sort of desecration of the grand, quiet stateliness of the old place to have all these gay people invading it. I could hardly fancy it full of careless, noisy, chattering guests, resounding with the captain's loud laugh, and Ella Wynkar's unmeaning cackle. What would Mrs. Roberts say? How would Kitty like it?

CHAPTER XXIV.

"In all his humors, whether grave or mellow,
 He's such a testy, touchy, pleasant fellow,
 Has so much mirth, and wit, and spleen about him,
 There is no living with him, or without him."

"The next station will be Rutledge," said Phil, leaning back to announce the fact to the detachment of our party in the rear.

"I am not sorry to hear it, for one," said Ella Wynkar, with a yawn. "Josephine, chère, are you not tired to death?"

But Josephine, chère, was too busy with collecting books, shawls, and bags, and loading the captain therewith, in anticipation of our arrival at the station, to vouchsafe an answer.

"Travelling all day is rather exhausting," said Phil, looking at his watch. "It's half-past six—a little behind time, but it won't hurt Mr. Rutledge to wait for us awhile. Ah! there's the whistle. We shall be at the station in another minute. Now, Aunt Edith, if you and Miss Wynkar will trust yourselves to me, I think the rest are provided for. Victor! what are you about? Don't you see we're here, man?"

Victor started up, and taking my parasol and shawl, offered me his arm as the train stopped, and the conductor, bursting open the car door, shouted "Rutledge!" as if we were to escape for our lives.

I heard Mr. Rutledge's voice before I saw him. We were the last of the party, and there being a little crowd at the car-door, we were obliged to stand for a moment inside, while the others stepped on the platform. It was a lovely June evening; the air was fresh and soft, and the sunset had left a rich glow on the sky, and lighted up with new verdure the green earth. It was so delicious to be out of the city; it was so bewildering to feel I was at Rutledge again. And with a beating heart, I followed my escort, as he forced a way for me through the crowd, and stepped down on the platform.

Mr. Rutledge was waiting to receive us. I was not quite self-possessed enough myself to be certain that I saw a slight change in his manner as he recognized my companion; if it did occur, however, it was overcome as quickly, and he welcomed Mr. Viennet courteously. With a few words of welcome and congratulation upon my recovery, he led the way toward the carriage. My aunt and Miss Wynkar were already in it. Josephine and Captain McGuffy were established in a light wagon by themselves, while the open carriage and the bays stood as yet unappropriated.

"I think, Mrs. Churchill," said Mr. Rutledge, standing at the open door of the carriage, "that perhaps you had better make a place for this young lady inside. She is not very strong as yet, I fancy, and the evening air"——

"Oh! pray," I exclaimed, shrinking back, "let me go in the open carriage. I hate a close carriage—it always makes my head ache."

"There's not the least dampness in the air to-night," urged Mr. Viennet, and meeting with no further opposition, I turned to the open carriage, and at a whispered suggestion from him, mounted up upon the front seat. He sprang up beside me, and taking the reins from Michael, who, bowing delightedly, had been saying, "Welcome back, Miss," ever since the train stopped, we only waited for Grace and Ellerton Wynkar to get in, before we started off at a round pace, leaving the carriage and the captain, and Mr. Rutledge, who was on horseback, far behind.

It was a lovely evening. The fields and woods were in their freshest green ; everything, from the grass by the roadside to the waving forest trees, looked as they never can look after June. The dust of summer, and its parching heat, had not yet soiled and shrivelled the smallest leaf or blade ; but fresh from the warm spring rains, and the pleasant spring sunshine, they budded and shone as if there were no such thing as scorching summer heats, and choking dust, and parching thirst, to come. The sky—fit sky to bend over such an earth—was of the clearest blue, and the few clouds that hung around the setting sun were light and fleecy, tinged with rose and tipped with gold. The soft breeze, coming out of the west over fields of clover and acacias in bloom, and lilac hedges, and cottage gardens full of early flowers, and cottage porches covered with blowing roses and climbing honeysuckles, steeped the listening senses with a sort of silent ecstasy, that made commonplace conversation a profanation of the hour. Why *would* Grace and her companion keep up such a constant chattering. It was unbearable; and when Ellerton, leaning forward, offered Victor his cigar-case, the latter, with a quick gesture of impatience, exclaimed :

"Ah ! *merci*, not to-night. It's too nice an evening, my good friend, to be spoiled with such perfumes. The young ladies like roses better than cigars, I fancy."

And Ellerton, who reverenced Victor as a high authority on all social questions, quietly put away his cigar-case, and said no more about it.

It was a long drive from the station to the house, and our hopes of being the first of the party to arrive, were dashed by the occurrence of a little accident just as we entered the village. The off horse, shying violently at a loaded wagon, as we passed it rapidly, reared and fell back, breaking the pole in two, and throwing himself and his fellow into ecstasies of fear, plunging and struggling with the want of presence of mind, and the reckless disregard of consequences always manifested by terrified horseflesh under circumstances of sudden alarm.

Victor, however, was a good horseman, and after a short battle, brought them to terms, Grace, meantime, shrieking violently, and Ellerton imploring him to let him get the ladies out at once, which looked rather like one word for the ladies and two for himself. Victor requested him simply to hold his tongue and sit still, and Ellerton, without a remonstrance, acquiesced, as the horses, now subdued, stood quite unresisting, while Victor, giving the reins to me, sprang down, followed by Michael from behind, and the countryman, whose load of brush had caused the accident. We were, fortunately, just by a blacksmith's shed, and in a few minutes that official himself, in his leathern apron and bare arms, was busily employed in remedying the mishap.

The horses were still a little restive, and Victor was standing by the head of one and Michael by the other, when the rest of the party came up. Quite an excitement was created, of course, at seeing us in this disabled condition, and our host, springing from his horse, hurried up in some alarm to ascertain for himself the extent of the accident, which Ellerton Wynkar, standing up in the carriage, explained at large to the rest of the party, adding that, "it might have been something serious if we had not been very prompt."

Victor bit his lip to keep from laughing, and Grace turned away her head; nothing but the consciousness of not having distinguished herself during the action, restrained her from bringing down Mr. Wynkar "a peg or two" by a statement of facts.

Mr. Rutledge, finding that the repairing of the pole was likely to occupy some little time longer, said that the young ladies had better get in the carriage; he had no doubt Mr. Arbuthnot would willingly give up his seat.

Phil, of course, most urgently begged we would do so,

but for me, the idea of being cooped up in the carriage with Mrs. Churchill, and Ella, and Grace, was insupportable, and I expressed my resolution of staying by the ship. Mr. Viennet and the smithy said it would only be a few minutes more, and I declared I didn't in the least mind waiting, it was such a lovely evening, and I couldn't think of crowding the carriage.

Grace, partly from perversity, and partly from a little lingering fear of the bays, said she should accept Phil's invitation, and without more ado, gave her hand to Mr. Rutledge and sprang out.

"May I advise you?" said he, coming back to me after he had put Grace in the carriage.

"Not against my will, if you please. Indeed, I had rather wait."

"That settles it," he answered, bowing. "I'm sorry, gentlemen," he continued, to Victor and Ellerton, "to leave you in this fashion, but my duties, as host, require me to ride forward with the ladies, and I hope you will soon follow us."

Victor assured him of his perfect confidence, that we would be at home almost as soon as they would; and then, with a polite commendation of his fortitude under misfortune, Mr. Rutledge threw himself upon his horse, and galloped after the carriage. I could not help feeling a little awkwardly; it is never pleasant to be the only lady among a number of gentlemen. Besides those of our own party, several men of the village had collected around us, and with their hands in their pockets, and in a very easy, sauntering way, were offering their comments on the accident.

Victor walked angrily up to one, who, with a short pipe between his lips, had ventured rather too near, and was leaning nonchalantly against the fore-wheel; and knocking the pipe out of his mouth, took him by the shoulder and ordered him to take himself off. Didn't he see there was a lady in the carriage?

The man moved sulkily away, but I saw him more than once look back with an ugly expression in his eyes toward Victor, as he crossed the road and disappeared in the woods that skirted the highway.

Just at that moment, a sorrel horse drew up beside us, and an inquiring face was thrust out from the gig behind it.

"What's the matter, Michael? Anybody hurt? An accident, did you say?" inquired a voice that gave me a cold chill.

"That detestable doctor already!" And returning stiffly his salutations as he recognized me, and hurried up to the carriage, I said there had been no accident to anything but the pole of the carriage, and that was nearly remedied, and we had plenty of assistance.

The doctor bowed, but did not seem in the least discomposed by my too obvious rudeness, and leaning comfortably on the wheel, as the dismissed clown had done before him, continued to address me in a tone of easy familiarity that was too annoying to me to be concealed, and my face must have told the story; for Victor, calling to one of the men to hold the horses a moment, walked quickly up behind the doctor, and laying his hand heavily on his shoulder, said, in a tone by no means equivocal:

"I say, my good fellow, you are annoying this lady, and I must ask you to step back!"

The doctor did step back, and turning quickly, faced him.

"Victor Viennet, as I am a sinner!"

I looked on in wonder, as I saw Victor give a violent start, and change color; then recovering himself after a moment, he said, in altered voice:

"I ask your pardon, Dr. Hugh, I didn't see your face. How, under heaven, did you happen to turn up here?"

There was an expression on Victor's face, as he said this, which seemed involuntarily to indicate that the fact of

Dr. Hugh's turning up here, was just the most disagreeable fact that could possibly have transpired, and so essentially " cute " a man as the doctor, could not have failed to see it, but it did not seem in the least to interfere with his complacency.

" How did I happen to turn up here ? Why, my good fellow (as you said just now), by the most natural process in the world. You see, after we parted, a year ago, in the city "——

" Yes, yes," said Victor, hurriedly, and in a low tone, " I've got to look after the smith now. You can tell me there."

And making some apology to me for the continued detention, he turned to retrace his steps. The doctor followed, and passed his arm familiarly through Victor's, at which I saw he winced, but did not attempt to resent; and the doctor continued to talk to him in a low and confidential tone. Twilight had already descended before the smith pronounced the job completed, and Michael, backing up the horses, put them to the carriage. While this was being accomplished, Victor and Dr. Hugh, standing a few paces apart from the others, talked together, or rather, the doctor talked and Victor listened with ill-concealed impatience.

I could not hear a word that passed, but I could see that Victor was suffering torture at the hands of the bland doctor, and his face, for several minutes after he had parted from him and resumed his seat in the carriage, wore an expression of pain and anger. We had started and driven on for some distance before either spoke, and the first to break the silence, I said, with more curiosity than courtesy :

" How in the world did you happen to know that detestable doctor ? I didn't suppose anybody had ever seen him before he came here."

" Detestable you may well call him," said Victor, below

his breath, and with a sort of groan. " I'd rather have met the arch-fiend himself!"

Then hastily remembering himself, he apologized, exclaiming, with a laugh, that the fellow always put him out of temper, and bored him to death, and he hoped he should never see him again, and he didn't mean to trouble himself any further about him. With that last resolution, his spirits rose, and in a few minutes he was as gay as ever. We were dashing along at such an inspiriting pace, that no one could help throwing dull care, and all things sad and gloomy, to the winds, and being pro tem. in the highest spirits.

" I am sure you drive as well as you dance," said Victor, putting the reins into my hands. "Let me see whether you know how to handle the ribbons."

Put upon my mettle in that way, nothing could have induced me to have declined the undertaking, though I happened to know a thing or two in the early history of the bays that Mr. Viennet was evidently ignorant of, and the recollection of which put a nervous intensity into the grasp I had upon the reins.

" Admirable!" said Victor, with enthusiasm; " I see you understand what you are about. You manage those beasts as well as I could, and there's no denying it, they do pull."

" *Pull* isn't the word," I thought; " but no matter."

" What a good road!" exclaimed Victor. "We're going like the wind. Ellerton, this is fine, is it not ?"

" Charming," said Ellerton, feebly, from the back seat; " charming; I never saw a lady drive so well; but don't you think, it's getting so dark, it would be better for you to take the reins? You can see better, you know."

" On the contrary," said Victor, with great glee, " on the contrary; the female vision, you know, is proverbially the sharpest. Shall I touch up that near horse? He rather lags," he continued, wickedly, to me.

14

"Oh no, thank you!" I said, breathlessly, but **trying to** laugh.

"I'm sure you're tired," said Mr. Wynkar, with **great** feeling. "You speak as if you were. Victor, you lazy dog, take the reins, if you have any politeness left."

"I haven't," said Victor, leaning back with composure. "I haven't a vestige left. I used up the last I had about me on that boor with the short pipe, who gave me such a gracious look as he walked off."

"Yes," I exclaimed, "I think you'll hear from him again."

"Not improbable," said Victor, coolly. "I have a knack at getting into scrapes that's only exceeded by my knack at getting out of them. Now I think of it, he didn't look like a pleasant sort of fellow to meet in a dark piece of woods like this."

We had just driven into the woods that stretched about half a mile this side of the gate of Rutledge Park, and the faint young moon that had been lighting us since we left the village, had no power to penetrate the dense foliage that met over our heads, and shut out moon and sky. It did not make me any more comfortable to remember that there was a short path from the village across these woods, and that any one on foot could reach this point almost as soon as in a carriage by the road. I did not feel like laughing at Ellerton Wynkar's little gasp of fear, and Victor's gay laugh and easy tone of assurance, far from inspiring me with confidence, made me doubly nervous and apprehensive. I only wished that I dared ask him to be quiet till we were out into the open road again. But he seemed possessed with mischief—he quizzed Ellerton, told droll stories, and laughed till the woods rang again. But through it all, I strained my ear to catch the faintest noise by the roadside; and when the horses, more intent than I, shied violently to one side and dashed forward, with a quivering, desperate pull upon the reins, I was quite prepared for what succeeded.

A large stone whirred swiftly through the air, just grazed my cheek, and fell with a crashing sound on the other side of the road.

"Good heavens!" cried Victor, starting forward, "are you hurt?"

"No, no," I exclaimed; "for heaven's sake, be quiet."

"Give me the reins," he cried, snatching them.

"No, no!" I answered, keeping them by a desperate exertion of strength. "I shall never forgive you if you stop the horses."

"I shall never forgive myself for the danger I have brought you in," he said, in a low tone. "You will never trust yourself to my protection again, I fear," he continued earnestly, as we drove into the park gate.

"Oh, I'm not afraid as long as I hold the ribbons," I answered, trying to laugh, but drawing a freer breath as we cleared the woods and came into the moonlight again.

"You are cruel," he said, in a lower tone still.

"There's the house at last!" exclaimed Ellerton, with a sigh of relief so profound that we both started.

"How are you getting on, behind there?" asked Victor. "I'd forgotten all about you, Ellerton. That was a neat little compliment from our friend in the woods, now wasn't it? But the least said about those little attentions the better, I've always found; you understand 'Oh no, we never mentions him,' under any circumstances."

"Of course not," said Ellerton, acquiescently. "I should not speak of it on any account."

"And, Michael, my man," continued Victor, putting his hand in his pocket, "whist's the word about this little adventure, you know."

Michael touched his hat, and, pocketing the coin that Victor tossed him, promised absolute silence on the subject.

The horses, as we came up the avenue, slackened their pace, and gave us time to look around. Sunset, starlight

moonlight, had neither of them abdicated the bright Juno
sky, but all combined to light up the picture for us, and
make the lake a sheet of silver, and the dark, old house as
fair as it could be made.

"A fine old place, indeed," said Victor, with a temporary
shade of seriousness on his face. "It must be pleasant to
have such an ancestral home as that. These Rutledges are
a high family, are they not?"

"One of the very best in the State;" answered Ellerton,
feeling that "family" was always a toast to which he was
called upon to respond. "There are very few in the country
who can go back so far. The Rutledges have always been
very exclusive, and held themselves very high, and so have
never lost their position."

"Ha!" said Victor, with a little darkening of the brow.
"That's the style, is it? Our host, then, is a proud man, I
am to understand—one who values birth, and that sort of
thing, and plumes himself upon it, and regards with a proper scorn all who have come into the world under less
favorable auspices than himself."

"Exactly," said Ellerton. "I think that's Rutledge
exactly. He's what you'd call a regular aristocrat, and
proud as Lucifer himself."

"I kiss his hand!" cried Victor, with a dash of bitterness
in his tone. "Commend me to such a man as that! I
reverence his largeness of soul, his nobility of nature! I
long to show him in what esteem I hold him."

"I think you mistake Mr. Rutledge," I began eagerly;
but before I had time to say another word we were at the
door, and Mr. Rutledge himself, descending the steps
quickly, and speaking with some anxiety, exclaimed:

"We have been very uneasy about you. I have just
sent orders to the stable for horses to start to meet you.
Has anything happened?"

"The pole required just three times as long to repair as
Mr. Smithy said it would," answered Victor, "and we, very

foolishly depending upon his word in the matter, were much disappointed in not reaching the house three-quarters of an hour ago. I am sorry to have caused you any uneasiness."

"It is dissipated now," said Mr. Rutledge, courteously. "I only regret that your arrival should have been marked by such a misadventure."

"What would he say if he knew of misadventure number two?" said Victor, *sotto voce*, as he assisted me to alight. "I feel positively superstitious. No good is coming of this visit, depend upon it!"

As we were half-way up the steps, I found I had forgotten my parasol, and Victor went back to look for it. Mr. Rutledge, seizing the opportunity of his absence, said to me quickly:

"I see you drove those horses; you must promise me you will never do it again."

"Why not?" I asked, haughtily.

"No matter why; you must promise me you will never touch the reins again behind them."

"I am sure I drove them up in style; Michael himself could not have done it better. I don't think I can bind myself never to do it again. You'll have to excuse me from promising."

"I remember; you have a prejudice against promising."

There was something in his tone, and in the short laugh that followed these words, that brought back so much of what I had been trying to forget, and revived so much of what I had half forgiven, that I made no effort to keep back the hasty words that rushed to my lips.

"Can you wonder at it? My experience has been so unfortunate; why, less than a year ago, I made a promise that, I suppose, was as binding as most other promises, and meant about as much; and I have found it a chain at once the lightest and most galling—empty as air, and yet the hatefullest restraint—the veriest mockery, and yet a thing

I cant't get rid of! That's briefly what I think of promises, and why you must excuse me from making one."

" I will excuse you," he said, looking at me with eyes that never faltered; " I will excuse you, with all my heart, from making or keeping any promise to me."

This upon the threshold! Under the very shadow of the doorway! I felt faint and giddy as I passed on into the hall. Kitty, with a low cry of delight, sprung forward to meet me.

" Kitty, I am so glad !" I said, laying my hand upon her arm. " Isn't it a long time since I went away? But I am so tired; do take me to my room."

Kitty flew up the stairs in delight, only stopping occasionally to ask me if I didn't feel well, and if she couldn't help me. All the others had gone to their rooms; not even Mrs. Roberts was to be seen.

" She's got her hands too full to prowl around now," said Kitty, with a wicked shake of the head. She led the way to my old room, and, to my surprise, putting her hand in her pocket, drew out the key, and fitted it in the lock.

" What's the reason of its being locked up ?" I said in surprise.

" Reason enough, Miss," said Kitty, with a profound look. Then, admitting me and shutting the door carefully, continued, in a less guarded tone: " The idea of your coming back here and having any but your own room! And it's been just as much as I could do to keep Mrs. Roberts from putting Miss Churchill in it. Such a time as I had about it when the baggage came! None of the ladies had come upstairs yet; they were all walking about the piazza and hall with master, and Thomas was seeing to the trunks being carried up, and I overheard Mrs. Roberts say: ' Thomas, Miss Churchill's baggage is to be put in the blue room, and her mamma's and Miss Grace's in the oak-chamber opposite, and Miss Wynkar's goes in the south room.' ' No, I beg your pardon, ma'am,' I says, coming forward, *my* young lady's trunk goes to the blue room, if you please. I've master's own orders for it, and I'll go ask him again if you choose.' '*Your* young lady, indeed!' says Mrs. Roberts, throwing me such an awful look. 'Thomas, you will attend to my orders.' I flew upstairs and put the key in my pocket, and Thomas tipped me a wink, and left your trunk outside the door. And now," said Kitty, stopping a moment to recover breath, "don't you think it looks pleasant, Miss?"

"Indeed it does, Kitty," I said, gratefully, sinking down in an easy-chair, and looking about me admiringly. It looked whiter and cooler than ever. There were new book-shelves in the recesses, and new curtains at the windows; roses, mignonette and heliotrope, filled the slender vases, and the wax candles on the dressing-table shed the softest light around the room. Kitty, busying herself about putting away my bonnet and shawls, chatted on eagerly.

"Gay times, these, for Rutledge," she went on, after having answered my inquiries for Stephen and the others. "Gay times, and busy times. Who'd ever have thought to see this house full of company again?"

"Yes," I said, "so busy, I am afraid, I shall not have much of your attendance, Kitty. It will not be like last fall, when you had nothing to do but wait on me. What nice times those were! I wish all the rest of the people were miles away, Kitty, and there was no one in the house that wasn't here last November."

"Oh!" exclaimed Kitty, deprecatingly, "I'm sure you'll enjoy it, Miss, with so many young gentlemen and ladies. I'm certain master thought you would, or he wouldn't have asked them. And as for my waiting on you, why that's all settled, and Mrs. Roberts knows it too. Mr. Rutledge told me this very morning that he supposed it would please me to be allowed to attend upon you, and that I was to consider that my duty as long as you were here. Mrs. Roberts had come in for some directions, and she heard it all. She jerked her head, and flounced a little, but didn't dare to say a word. But," continued Kitty, anxiously, "I'm afraid you are not well. Can I get you anything? Won't you lie down? Oh! I am afraid you are crying."

Kitty's fears were not unfounded. The tears rushed to my eyes, and hiding my face in my hands, I tried, but vainly, to suppress the hysterical sobs that choked me, as I essayed to answer her anxious questions. She was so disappointed and alarmed at my unexpected mood that she hardly knew what to do, and I tried, as soon as I could speak, to assure her that I was really very glad to get back, that there was nothing the matter, only I was very nervous and tired.

"And there's the tea-bell!" exclaimed Kitty, in dismay, "and everybody else is dressed! What's to be done?"

"There's nothing for it, Kitty, but to let me go to bed. I can't go downstairs to-night—it would kill me. Undress me, and then don't let a soul come in—not even my aunt. That's a good Kitty: it isn't the first time you've taken care of me."

"Ah!" said Kitty, with tears in her kind eyes, "if I only knew what to do to make you better! It isn't the head-ache that I mean—a cup of tea and a good night's rest will make that all right; but you ain't the same young lady that you were last fall. I saw that the minute you stepped into the hall. There's something on your mind; I knew it the instant you spoke. When you used to talk, it was as if there was a laugh in your voice all the time, and now you talk as if you were tired, and hated to open your lips."

"So I am, Kitty," I said, with a fresh burst of crying. "I am tired and heart-sick, and when I talk it's no wonder there are 'tears in my voice.' There are a great many things to make me unhappy; you mustn't ask me anything about them; but it's so long since I've had anybody to care for me, and nurse me, that it makes me babyish, I believe.

There!" I exclaimed, after a minute, conquering my tears, "don't think anything more about it, Kitty, but help me to undress."

There could have been no better medicine for my aching head and heart, than that Kitty administered. It was a perfect luxury to resign myself into her hands, to feel that I needn't think again to-night if I didn't choose, that I was sure of being watched over and cared for, come what might. I had not realized, till I came into its sunshine again, how perfectly necessary to anything like happiness an atmosphere of love is. I had known that, in my home, I had felt chilled and forlorn. I had given no pleasure to others, and received none myself; but, child-like, I had only known it was, and had not asked why. But now, that kind and tender hands rendered the services that I had long wearily performed for myself, and a watchful care provided for my comfort and remembered my tastes, I realized how unnatural and unkind a thing it is for anything of human mold to be denied human love and sympathy; I realized how necessary to the fair growth and goodly proportions of a nature, is the sunshine of kindness and affection. Since I had left Rutledge, I had never known what it was to be caressed and favored; misconstrued, slighted, and put aside by those around me, the natural result had been reserve, distrust, and aversion on my part. I was, as Kitty said, not the same girl I had been. I knew better than Kitty did how deep the change had gone—how far below the surface the blight had struck. The brave, gay heart of the child was dead in my bosom forever. Whatever there might be to hope for, in the future, it must be the life-and-death struggle and victory of the woman, not the careless happiness of the child.

CHAPTER XXV.

'Love is hurt with jar and fret,
Love is made a vague regret,
Eyes with idle tears are wet,
Idle habit links us yet—
What is love? for we forget;
Ah! no, no!"

TENNYSON.

My bright eyed maid had something evidently on her mind the next morning, as stealing early to my bedside, she found me awake and quite ready for her services. I caught sight of her perplexed face in the glass, as she dressed my hair, and said at last, "What are you thinking about, Kitty, has anything happened?"

"Happened? Oh, no, Miss," she said, blushing, and a little confused. "I was only thinking—I was only wondering"——

"Well, Kitty?"

"I mean that—that is—are you very fond of Miss Churchill?"

I laughed and blushed a little in my turn, and said:

"Why no, not particularly, I think."

"Because *I* think she's a very haughty lady, for my part; and if I am any judge, her maid, Frances, is a much-put-upon young woman, that's all."

"What has led you to that conclusion so soon?" I asked, with a smile.

"Oh! nothing particular, ma'am, only some of Miss Churchill's ruffled morning dresses got crushed in the packing, and Frances was in the laundry till after twelve o'clock last night, fluting 'em over; and I've noticed, Frances starts and flusters when her lady's bell rings, as if there were a scolding for her at the other end of the wire, that's all."

"Oh, that's a trifle! Frances is nervous," I said, apologetically. "What did my aunt say when you told her my message last night?"

"Nothing but 'very well,' and 'I am sorry to hear it.' There wasn't time for any more, for the gentleman they call Captain, with the big moustache, came up for her to play whist, and she went away with him. But," said Kitty, hesitatingly, and looking at me very sharply, "I don't know whether I ought to tell you, but there was a gentleman who didn't seem to take it quite so coolly as Mrs. Churchill did."

"Who, pray?" I asked, as the blood started to my cheeks.

"The young French gentleman, Miss; I think they call him Mr."——

"Oh, Mr. Viennet!"

"I wonder, Miss, why you say 'Oh, Mr. Viennet!' as if you were disappointed," said Kitty, quite nettled. "I'm sure he's the handsomest gentleman among 'em; and if you could have seen him, when he followed me up the stairs, and asked about you, I am sure you'd think better of it; and he's got the handsomest eyes! I can't think why you don't like him."

"I have not said I did not; and besides, Kitty," I continued, gravely, "it's not right for you to talk to the gentlemen; you must be careful."

"I know, Miss; but who could help talking to such a nice gentleman, just answering his questions? I'm sure he could get round Mrs. Roberts herself, if he tried! let alone people that ain't made of stone or leather. And," continued Kitty, "isn't it odd, Miss, but all the time he was talking to me, I couldn't help wondering where I'd seen him before? I know for a certainty, that he's never been within forty miles of Rutledge till now, and I've never been twenty

miles away from it; and yet, for my life, I couldn't get it
out of my head, that some where or other I'd seen him
before!"

"It's a very foolish idea to have in your head, Kitty, and
a very improbable one at the best; so I wouldn't trouble
myself any further about it, if I were you."

I did not mention it to Kitty, but I could not help being
struck with the similarity of my own impressions on first
meeting Victor Viennet. It was the vaguest, mistiest chain
of reminiscence that his face seemed to stir, but till I had
seen him several times, it continued to perplex me. I could
not account for it in any way; but the association or recollection, or whatever it was, had faded before a closer
acquaintance; and now Victor Viennet's handsome face
suggested Victor Viennet, and nobody or nothing more.

"These will match your lilac muslin exactly, Miss," said
Kitty, offering me a handful of purple "morning glories."
"I ran out to get you some flowers before I came in to
wake you, but I was in such a hurry, that I couldn't go as
far as the garden, and so just picked these out of the
hedge."

I thanked her as I fastened them in my dress; they
looked lovely with the dew still shining on them. It
was yet a good while to breakfast, but I turned to go
downstairs, accepting, with a smile at the newness of such
services, the dainty handkerchief that Kitty shook out
for me.

The fresh morning breeze swept softly through the wide
hall as I descended the stairs. Summer had come in and
taken the gloomy old place by storm. A pyramid of flowers
stood on the dark oak table in the centre, a mocking-bird in
its gay cage hung at one end, and over the cold marble
pavement the sunshine was creeping fast. The house was so
quiet, that I could almost fancy I was alone in it, and crossing the hall, I went up to the library door; but a cowardly
irresolution made me turn away, and pass on to the north

door of the hall, which, as well as the front one, stood wide open. The broad fields stretched far away June-like and lovely in the sunshine; the hedges and trees were in such luxuriant leaf, that they quite hid the stables and outhouses on the left that last fall had been so prominent in the landscape. Looking from the parlor windows, there was the same view of the lake that I had from my room. The mists were rolling up from its fair bosom, and the foliage that crowned its banks was of the freshest and glossiest green. The dew was glittering on the lawn, early birds twittered and sang in the branches overhead, and on the breeze came the rich perfume of the roses that climbed from pillar to pillar of the piazza. Rutledge had fulfilled my anticipations; in my weary, longing day-dreams, I had never pictured anything fairer than this.

It was with a half-defined feeling of curiosity that I wandered through the large parlors, furnished in an odd mixture of old-fashioned splendor and modern elegance. It was *terra incognita* to me; I had never entered these rooms before. I could hardly understand how the sunshine and fresh air came to be so much at home in them, as it seemed they now were. It was difficult to believe that these finely furnished, habitable looking apartments, had been closed and unused for twenty years and more. They had been thoroughly revised, no doubt, and the past put to the rout; but they were strange and unattractive to me, and I turned again to the library. Listening at the door before I pushed it open, I entered noiselessly. There was no need of so much caution; this room was as untenanted as its neighbors, save by thronging memories and torturing regrets, and they entered with me.

Here at least there was no change; the wide casements were open to the morning, but the white north light seemed subdued and cold after the sunshine of the other rooms, and the dark panelling and frowning moldings looked a defiance at the intruding summer. I liked it better so · there had been change enough without this last stronghold of memory being invaded.

Every article of furniture in the room—the table, with its pile of papers at one end and books at the other, the familiar paper-cutter lying by the unopened review, the heavy bronze inkstand, the graceful lamp, the chair, pushed back half a yard from the table—minded me of the happy hours that it would have been wiser to forget. One of the book-cases stood open, and a book lay on the table as if recently read, and a card marked the reader's place. I took it up involuntarily. It was Sintram, and the words swam before me as I bent over its familiar pages. On the card that had served for a mark, were written a few lines in a well known hand; and as I raised my eyes from them to the window, I saw Mr. Rutledge himself approaching the house from the direction of the stables. With a hurried movement I slipped the card in my pocket, and finding nothing else to replace it with, pulled one of the flowers from my bosom, and hastily shutting it between the leaves, threw the book on the table, and ran into the hall. If I had been a fugitive from justice, I could not have had a more guilty feeling than that which now impelled me to escape from meeting Mr. Rutledge. But there was no time to get upstairs; he would see me from the piazza if I went into the parlor; and while I stood in the hall, trembling with eagerness, and alarm, and irresolution, my retreat was cut off by the sudden appearance of Victor descending the stairs, who with an exclamation of pleasure, hurried toward me, and taking my hand was bowing over it in most devout fashion, when Mr. Rutledge entered the hall. Victor looked a little confused, and paused in the midst of an elegant French speech, while the quick crimson dyed my cheeks, all of which Mr. Rutledge appeared to ignore, as, approaching us, he said good morning with his usual courtesy of manner, expressed his pleasure in the improvement apparent in my looks, and then to Victor his astonishment at finding him a person of such early habits.

"Pray do not give me any credit for getting up this morning," said Victor with a hasty wave of the hand. "I assure you I detest early rising with my whole French soul, and haven't seen a sun younger than three hours old since I can remember; but, my dear sir, with all homage to the most comfortable of beds, and the pleasantest room I ever occupied in my life, I never passed such a night! When at last I slept, my dreams were so frightful that I was thankful to wake, and would have resorted to any means to have kept myself awake, if there had been the slightest danger of my closing my eyes again."

"What room did you occupy?" I asked.

"The corner room at the north end of the hall, it is, I think."

"It is most unfortunate," said Mr. Rutledge, looking a little annoyed. "Are you subject to wakeful nights?"

"Never remember such an occurrence before," he returned. "I have enjoyed the plebeian luxury of sound sleep all my life, and so am more at a loss to account for my experience of last night."

"Were you disturbed by any noise—conscious of any one moving in the house?"

"No, the house was silent, silent as death! *Ma foi!* I believe that was the worst of it. If I were superstitious, I should tell you of the only thing that interrupted it; but I know how credulous and absurd it would sound to dispassionate judges, and how I should ridicule anything of the kind in another person; but this strange nightmare has taken such possession of me, I cannot shake it off."

His face expressed intense feeling as he spoke, and the usual levity of his manner was quite gone.

"What was it?" I said earnestly, and Mr. Rutledge looked indeed so far from ridiculing his emotion, that Victor went on rapidly:

"You will think me a person of imaginative and excitable temperament, but I must assure you to the contrary, and that I never before yielded to a superstitious fancy, and have always held in great contempt all who were influenced by such follies. Will you believe me then, when I tell you that. last night I was startled violently from my sleep, by a voice that sounded, from its hollowness and ghastliness, as if it came from the fleshless jaws of a skeleton, calling again and again, in tones that made my blood curdle, a familiar name, and one that at any time, I cannot hear without emotion. Sleep had nothing to do with it! I was as wide awake as I am now. But pshaw !" he exclaimed, suddenly turning, "I shall forget all about it in an hour, and I beg you'll do the same," and not giving either of us time to answer, he went on in an altered tone : " Mr. Rutledge, what a fine place you have ! I have been admiring the view from my window. Have you purchased it recently ? I don't remember to have seen a finer estate in America."

" It is a valuable and well located farm," answered Mr. Rutledge, rather indifferently ; " but farming is not my specialty, and I never should have encumbered myself voluntarily with such a care, if it had not devolved upon me by inheritance."

" Ah !" said Victor with a slight accent of irony, that from last night's conversation I was prepared for ; " It was then a case of greatness thrust, etc. But sir, it must add a great charm to this already charming home, to think that it has been the birth-place and family altar, as it were, of generations of your ancestors ? Surely you are not insensible to such sentiments of pride and affection."

" Associations of that kind, of course, invest a place with a certain kind of interest ; but I cannot lay claim to as much feeling on the subject as perhaps would be becoming. Like you, sir," he said, with a bow, " I have a dread of claiming credit for habits and feelings that I do not possess and entertain."

Victor looked a little annoyed that he had not succeeded in drawing out Mr. Rutledge's aristocratic and overbearing sentiments, and he would not have given up the subject, had not Mr. Rutledge, with a firm and quiet hand, put it aside, and led the way to other topics.

"How is it," he said to me, "that you have not noticed your small friend Tigre? He has been at your feet for the last five minutes, looking most wistfully for a kind word."

I started in confusion and surprise, and stooping down, covered the dog with caresses. The poor little rascal was frantic with delight, springing up to my face, and ejaculating his welcome in short barks and low whines, tearing around me, and then running off a little distance and looking back enthusiastically.

"He is evidently inviting you to another steeple-chase," said Mr. Rutledge.

I blushed violently at the recollection, and wished Tigre anywhere but where he was.

"Have you lost your interest in the turf, since your season in town, or have other interests and tastes developed themselves while it has lain dormant?"

"Other tastes have developed themselves, I believe," I answered.

"Break it gently to Tigre, I beg you then, for I am sure he has been living all winter on the hope of another romp. He does not appreciate the lapse of time, and the changes involved, so readily as his betters, you know."

"He has, at least, the grace to receive them more kindly," I returned, stooping to pat him. "Tigre, if I am too old to run races, I am not debarred as yet from taking walks, I believe, and I would propose that we indulge in one. Mr. Viennet, are you too old to be of the party?"

Mr. Rutledge turned shortly toward the library, Victor and I passed out on the piazza, and, with Tigre in close attendance, descended the broad steps to the terrace.

Breakfast was nearly completed when we returned, and the party at the table looked up in amazement as we entered the room.

"I should admire to know," exclaimed Ella Wynkar, who affected Boston manners, and "admired" a good deal, "I should admire to know where you two have been! Mr. Arbuthnot declares that Mr. Viennet has been up since daybreak; and as for *you*," she said, turning to me, "I heard your door shut hours ago."

"Restrain your admiration, Miss Wynkar," said Victor, as he placed a chair for me. "We have been taking a short turn on the terrace for the fresh air. I wonder you did not emulate our example."

"Terrace, indeed!" exclaimed Phil. "I've been on the piazza for half an hour, and I'll take my oath you weren't within gunshot of the terrace all that time."

"Don't perjure yourself, my good fellow," said Victor, coolly, "but assist us to some breakfast. The terrace has given us an appetite."

"How is your headache, my dear?" said my aunt, from across the table.

"My headache, ma'am? Oh, I forgot—I beg your pardon; it's better, thank you."

"How serious it must have been!" said Josephine. "Oh! by the way, Mr. Rutledge, it isn't worth while to ask them to join us in *our* party this morning, is it? They didn't ask us to go with them."

Mr. Rutledge shrugged his shoulders. "I think, Miss Josephine, we are safe in asking them; they wouldn't accept, of course, and we should save our credit, you know."

"I would not trust them, sir. It's my advice that they're not asked."

"Then," returned Mr. Rutledge, with a low bow and his finest smile, "as with me to hear is to obey, I resign all thought of remonstrance, and acquiesce in the decree."

Josephine accepted the homage very graciously, and the jest was kept up around the table till I, for one, was heartily sick of it. No one supposed, however, that I would be fool enough to take it in earnest; but I was just such a fool; and when, an hour or two later, the horses were brought to the door, and the scattered party summoned from library, parlor, billiard-room, and garden, to prepare for the drive, I was struggling with a fit of ill-temper in my own room, which resulted in my "begging to be excused," when Thomas came to the door to announce the carriage.

My refusal didn't seem to damp the spirits of the party much. I looked through the half closed blinds to see them start. Victor at the last minute pleaded a headache, and "begged to be excused," on which occasion the captain made one of the jokes for which he was justly famous, and led off the laugh after it.

"The pretty darling's in the sulks, I suppose," I heard Grace say; but no one was at the pains to resent or applaud the remark, and I listened to the departing carriage-wheels and the lessening sound of merry voices with anything but a merry heart.

One never feels very complacent after spiting oneself; the inelegant describe the state of feeling by the adjective "small;" and I was not rendered any more comfortable by finding that I had made a prisoner of myself for the morning. If Victor had only gone, as I had anticipated, I should have consoled myself for the loss of the drive by a nice ramble around the grounds, and down to the stables; but as it was, I would not, for any consideration, have run the risk of encountering him. I heartily repented my walk before breakfast, and the relative position it seemed to place us in, made worse by our both remaining at home. Everybody and everything seemed to conspire to place us together, and my pride and my honesty both rebelled against such an arrangement. So, after listening to the sound of his steps pacing the terrace, the hall, and the piazza for a full hour, I began to find my captivity intolerable, and determined to make a visit to the housekeeper's room, and pay my devoirs to that functionary. Looking stealthily over the balusters, I ascertained that Victor was still smoking in the hall, so I ran across to the door of Mrs. Roberts' room, which was standing partly open, and asked if I might come in. Receiving permission, I entered, and did my best to appear amiable in Mrs. Roberts' eyes. She was, of course, as stiff as anything human could well be, but she was too busy to be very ungracious. This sudden influx of visitors had startled her out of the slow and steady routine of the last twenty years, and though, on the whole, she acquitted herself well, it was a very trying and bewildering position for the old woman. I longed for something to do to appease the self-reproach I felt for my bad temper, and it struck me that I couldn't do a more praiseworthy and disagreeable thing than to help Mrs. Roberts in some of the duties that seemed to press so heavily upon her. So, sitting down by her, I said:

"Mrs. Roberts, you'd better let me help you with those raisins; I haven't a thing to do this morning."

"That's a pity," said Mrs. Roberts, briefly. "In my day, young ladies always thought it most becoming to have some occupation."

"That's just my view of the case, Mrs. Roberts, and if you'll allow me, I'll have an occupation immediately."

Sylvie set the huge bowl of raisins on the table, and I drew them toward me, saying she must allow me to help her with them. Mrs. Roberts thought not; it would spoil my dress.

"Then I'll put an apron on."

She was afraid I did not know how.

"You can teach me, Mrs. Roberts;" and I began without further permission. To say that Mrs. Roberts melted before all this amiability would be to say that Mrs. Roberts had ceased to be Mrs. Roberts. She was a degree or two less gruff, I believe, at the end of the long hour I spent in her service, in the seeding of those wretched raisins; but that was all, and fortunately I had not expected more. I undertook it as a penance, and it did not lose that character from any excess of kindness on her part.

After the raisins were dispatched, Mrs. Roberts applied herself to the copying of a recipe from an old cookery-book, for which she seemed in something of a hurry. Dorothy was waiting for it, Sylvie said. "You'd better let me do it for you, Mrs. Roberts," I said, leaning over her shoulder. Mrs. Roberts declined, with dignity, for some time, but at last thoughtfully slid the spectacles off her nose, and seemed to deliberate about granting my request. She was not a very ready scribe, and she had a dozen other things to do, all of which weighed with my urgency, and in two minutes I was at the desk, copying out of a venerable cookery-book, the receipt that Mrs. Roberts indicated. I was in pretty engrossing business, I found one duty succeeded another very regularly; Mrs. Roberts, I saw, had determined to get as much out of me now as she could.

A dread of draughts was one of her peculiarities, so the door and the front windows were closed against the pleasant breeze, and to this I attribute it that we were unconscious of the return of the riding party till the door opened suddenly and Mr. Rutledge entered.

"Mrs. Roberts," he said, "you are wanted below. Miss Churchill has hurt her ankle in getting out of the carriage, and I have come to you for some arnica."

Mrs. Roberts bustled over to the medicine chest, and, taking the bottle of arnica and a roll of linen in her hand, hurried out of the room; while Mr. Rutledge, crossing over to the table where I sat, stood looking down at me without speaking, while I nervously went on with my writing without raising my eyes.

"Why did you not go with us this morning?" he said at last, sitting down by the table.

"I didn't want to."

"That is a very good reason; but I think you would have done better to have thwarted your inclination for once. There are two reasons why it would have been wiser to have gone."

"What is one?" I demanded.

"One is that your staying looked unamiable, and as if you could not take a joke."

"Well, it only looked as I felt. I was unamiable, and I didn't like the joke. What is the other?"

"The other, I am pretty sure to make you angry by giving, but I must risk that. Your refusing to go looked very much as if you preferred another tête-à-tête, to the society of us all."

"I cannot see that," I said, looking up flushed and angry. "When I supposed that I was the only member of the party who intended to stay at home, I cannot see how it could be inferred that I remained from any such motive."

"I, for one, had no doubt of it."

"You are kind!" I cried. "It is pleasant to feel I am always sure of one, at least, to put the kindest construction on what I do."

"Is my niece accounting for her willfulness in staying at home this morning?" said the slow, soft voice of Mrs. Churchill, that crept into my senses like a subtle poison, and silenced the angry words on my lips. "Are you not penitent, *ma chère*," she said, approaching me, and laying her cold hand lightly on my hair. "Do you not begin to see how unwise such tempers are? How often must I entreat you, my love, to be less hasty and suspicious and self-willed? Though I am not discouraged with these childish faults, Mr. Rutledge," turning to him apologetically, "I own they are somewhat trying. Ever since that unlucky night at the Academy of Music, I have felt "——

"Aunt Edith!" I exclaimed, with flashing eyes, averting my head from her touch and springing up. "Aunt Edith, that time has never been mentioned between us since you gave me my reprimand. I cannot understand why you bring it up now, and before a stranger!"

"Mr. Rutledge can hardly be called a stranger," she began.

"If not so to you, remember he is to me," I interrupted.

"However that may be," she went on, "he was unluckily the witness of that evening's errors. He saw the self-will and temper that you took no pains to conceal, and the love of admiration that led you to a most unaccountable act of imprudence."

"I should think," I returned, trembling with passion, "that that time would have no more pleasant memories for you than me. I should think we might agree not to stir among its ashes. There may be some smoldering remorse alive in them yet!"

For a moment, my aunt's face grew white, and her eye faltered and sunk; angry as I was, I bitterly repented the stab I had given her. Then she raised her eyes and fixed them on my face with a stern and freezing look. I don't know what she said; it was too cruel to listen to. I don't know what I answered; would that it had no record anywhere!

From that date, there was no disguise between aunt and niece of the sentiments they had mutually inspired. The flimsy gauze that reserve and decorum had raised between them was torn to fragments before that storm, and henceforth there was no pretence of an affection that had never existed. Two natures more utterly discordant and unsympathetic could not well be imagined. There was nothing but some frail bands of duty and convenience, that had kept up the mask of sympathy so far, and then and there they were snapped irrevocably; and the mask fell prone upon the ground and was trampled under foot.

They had better have turned me houseless into the street than have turned me out of their hearts in this way; in one case, I could have sought another shelter, and won myself another home. In this, I was driven out, burning with anger and stung with injustice, from every heart I had had a right to seek a home in, and before me lay a cold and inhospitable world. Was the outcast or the world to blame for the inevitable result? The outcast, no doubt; outcasts always are.

"Look—look, Josephine!" cried Grace, bursting into the library, where most of the party were assembled that evening. Josephine, with her foot on the sofa, being the nucleus. "Ella, and Phil, and I have just come from rowing on the lake, and see what we found, up by the pine trees at the other end of the lake, floating on the water."

"What is it?" said Josephine, languidly; "a water-lily?"

"Water-lilies used to be white when I studied botany, Joseph, and this, you may observe, is purple."

"And morning-glories, when I studied botany," said Phil, "did not grow on lakes, but in gardens. Now, as this was discovered on the water, the question naturally arises, how, by whom, and under what circumstances, did it get there?"

"And putting this and that together," said Ella Wynkar, "we think that the young lady who had morning-glories in her dress this morning, must have taken a row on the lake, instead of a walk on the terrace."

"That doesn't follow," said Victor, "any more than it would follow that Miss Wynkar had visited the desert of Sahara, if a straw hat similar to the one she has in her hand, should be found there."

"Mr. Viennet, you are not sufficiently calm for such difficult reasoning. The fact is established; don't attempt to controvert it," said Josephine.

"In any case, I am entitled to the flower, I think," he returned, taking it from the table, and fastening it in his button-hole.

"No one will dispute it with you, I fancy," said Josephine, with a laugh.

"You seem to have marked your way with morning-glories," said Mr. Rutledge, who, sitting by the table, was turning over the leaves of a book. There was another, crushed and faded, and staining the leaves with its purple blood.

"One can hardly believe they are contemporaries," said Victor, "mine is so much fresher."

"They are the frailest and shortest-lived of flowers," said Mr. Rutledge, tossing the flower away. "Hardly worth the passing admiration that their beauty excites."

CHAPTER XXVI.

" If hope but deferred causeth sickness of heart,
What sorrow, to see it forever depart."

"This rain knocks the pic-nic all in the head," said Phil,
lounging into the breakfast-room, "and everybody's sure
of being in a bad humor on account of the disappointment.
What shall we all do with ourselves?"

"Play billiards, can't we?" said the captain.

"I hate billiards, for my part," said Grace, looking dismally out of the window. "And Josephine's ankle's too
bad to play, and Ellerton isn't well enough, and my pretty
cousin there never did anything she was asked to yet; and
Mr. Viennet consequently will refuse, and Phil's too lazy,
and mamma won't take the trouble, and Mr. Rutledge has
letters to write; so I think you'll be at a loss for anybody
to play with you, Captain McGuffy."

"So it would seem," said the captain, consoling himself
with some breakfast. "I can't see anything better to be
done than this, then."

"It is rather your vocation, I think," returned Grace.
"But with the rest of us, it is an enjoyment that at best
cannot last over an hour, and there are twelve to be got rid
of before bed-time."

"It *is* trying," said Josephine. "And I've no more
crimson for my sofa-cushion, and no chance of matching it
nearer than Norbury. I really don't know what I shall do
all day."

"If one only had a good novel!" yawned Ella Wynkar.
"But there isn't anything worth reading in the library. I
wonder Mr. Rutledge doesn't get some interesting books."

"There he comes; ask him," said Grace, maliciously.

"No, I don't like to. Mr. Rutledge is so odd, there's no knowing how he might take it."

Mr. Rutledge entered at this moment, followed by Tigre, and Miss Wynkar, partly because she was glad of anything to amuse herself with, and partly for the sake of a pretty attitude, sprung forward and caught the dog in her arms.

"Take care! he's just been out in the rain," exclaimed Mr. Rutledge, but not in time to save the pretty morning dress from Tigre's muddy paws; and with an exclamation of disgust she threw down the dog, who, whining piteously from a blow against the table, came limping over to me.

"Poor fellow! that was a sudden reverse," said Victor, stooping to pat him. "Give me your paw, my friend, and accept my sympathy."

Ella darted an angry look toward us, and, I am certain, never forgave the laugh that escaped me.

"This is a dull day, young ladies," exclaimed Mr. Rutledge, throwing himself into a chair. "How shall we dispose of it?"

"Philosophy to the rescue!" said Josephine, with a charming smile. "It is only dull compared with what you had promised us."

"The pic-nic will hold good for another day, we'll trust. In the meantime, what shall we do to-day?"

"Who ever heard of doing anything but growl on such a day as this?" said Phil, leaning over Josephine's chair.

"Ladies wern't made for anything but sunshine, I'm certain," said the captain, thoughtfully, over his last cup of coffee.

Miss Wynkar and the Misses Churchill made the expected outcry at this speech, and Mr. Rutledge, after the excitement had subsided, went on with a proposal that quite brought down the house. It was to the effect that, as the gay people of the neighborhood, the Masons of Windy Hill, and the Emersons of Beech Grove, had each

proposed something for the general benefit, it seemed expedient that some entertainment should be got up at Rutledge. What should it be? The Masons were to have
tableaux, and the Emersons' invitations were out for a *fête
champêtre.* What was left for them to do?"

"Oh! a thousand things," exclaimed Josephine, with
sparkling eyes. "A ball, or private theatricals, or a
masquerade—anything, in fact, would be delightful."

"A plain ball would never do after the fête and tableaux,"
said Ella Wynkar, decidedly.

"Whatever you do, I beg, don't let those simpering
Mason girls get ahead of you," suggested Grace. "They've
been rehearsing their tableaux for a fortnight, and they
mean to have them perfect."

"What do you think of theatricals, then?" said Mr. Rutledge. "We can send for dresses, etc., from town, and we
have plenty of time to rehearse. And, Arbuthnot, I know
you have all the requisites for a manager, and could bring
out a play in excellent style."

"You will be astonished to find the amount of dramatic
talent undeveloped in this company," exclaimed Victor.
"All the improvement I can suggest is, that the play represented should be written for the occasion. Now, if I might
be allowed, I should propose that Miss Wynkar and Captain McGuffy be named to write the play, and Ellerton, as
the man of the most cultivated literary taste, and soundest
judgment, be appointed to révise and correct it. The éclat
of producing such an entirely original play, you must see,
would be immense."

The irony of his speech was too broad for even the Wynkars to miss, and Ella colored angrily, while Ellerton, who
was not a proficient at repartee, moved uneasily on his
chair, and looked very wretched, till Mr. Rutledge came to
the rescue with a few words, that, administering the keenest, quietest, politest possible reprimand to Victor for his
impertinence, reinstated the objects of his ridicule in com-

placency again, and quite changed the face of the day.
Victor bit his lip; these two liked each other less and less
every day, it was but too evident. Victor's overbearing
and tyrannical disposition found an incessant obstacle to its
gratification in the iron will and better disciplined, but
equally unyielding character of Mr. Rutledge. I tried in
vain to remove Victor's prejudices against his host; but
there was an angry flash of his eye whenever the subject
was mentioned, that did not encourage me to continue it.
And it was equally impossible not to resent Mr. Rutledge's
misapprehension of Victor's character. In everything he
misjudged him, and, it was evident, put down to the worst
motive much that was only hasty and ill-judged. While
my reason told me that he was often to blame, the injustice
and harshness of Mr. Rutledge's judgment often roused my
sympathy in his behalf, and that dangerous sentiment, pity,
was creeping insensibly into my heart. He was, it was
true, a man of no religious principle, but I had come to regard that as the inevitable result of his foreign education,
and in no way his own fault. Then there was a light,
careless tone in his conversation, a disregard of others, an
almost imperceptible sneer, that a month ago I should have
looked upon with alarm and distrust. But the subtle flattery of his devotion, the contrast between his manner and
that of Mr. Rutledge, and, indeed, of all the others, had
melted away these prejudices, and now I hardly saw, and
only half blamed, the self-willed impetuosity and impatient
sneering of the young foreigner, who, there could be no
doubt, was daily becoming more unpopular among the party
at Rutledge.

Our host had never liked him; Miss Churchill could not
be expected to continue her favor, now that he took no
pains to conceal what was the attraction for him at Rutledge; Grace had never cordially liked any one in her life,
but Victor had been rather a favorite, till he had put down
her sauciness, on one or two occasions, in such a manner as

to make her as vehement in her dislike as her lazy nature
rendered her capable of being; Ella Wynkar hated him—
he laughed at her French, and never omitted an opportunity
of turning her pretensions into ridicule; Ellerton had formerly been very much infatuated with the young Frenchman, who had carried all before him in society, and been so
general a favorite, but Ellerton was too tempting a subject
for Victor's humor, and he was very careless of his popu-
larity; even with Phil and the captain he was growing
indifferent and distant.   Mrs. Churchill alone showed no
change in her feeling toward him; he was only acting the
part she meant him to act, and fulfilling the design she had
in inviting him to accompany us.   These feelings, and their
causes, so apparent on a retrospective study of them, were,
of course, by the restraints of good breeding, and the relative positions of all parties, studiously concealed, and only
to be guessed at in unguarded moments.

"You are not going to follow the dramatic corps, I hope,"
said Victor, with a curl of his lip, as the party moved off to
the library, to look over some plays and consult about the
proposed entertainment.

"They would have asked me if they had wanted me, I
suppose," I answered, reddening a little.

"Then, is there any law to prevent our staying where
we are?" he asked, throwing himself back in the deep window seat opposite me.   And there we passed the live-long
morning, Victor idly twisting the worsteds of my work, and
idly gazing out upon the storm, or in upon my face, and
idly talking in his low, rich voice, and holding me, against
my will, enthralled.

The portraits on the walls looked down upon us with a
dumb intelligence, almost a warning sternness; the rain
tried to weary us out; the old clock struck the passing hours
distinctly; the sound of voices in the library, after a long
while, died away, and then the party passed through the
hall and into the parlor, and Josephine's voice, at the piano

succeeded, and then a dance, but still we did not move. What was the spell that kept me there, I could not have told. Whatever it was, it was tightening the toils around me, and shutting me off more hopelessly than ever from all paths but the one I had almost involuntarily taken.

It appeared at dinner, that the theatricals were given up, owing, principally, I could not but suspect, to the want of harmony that has characterized all the attempts at private theatricals that I have ever witnessed, no one, under any circumstances, having been known to be pleased with the rôle assigned to him or her, and all manner of discontent prevailing on all sides. But Mr. Rutledge, with great discretion, put it upon other grounds—the short time that intervened for preparing them, etc. It was agreed that patriotism and propriety both pointed to the Fourth of July as the appropriate day, and a *bal masqué* was determined on instead of the theatricals. It was to be the most delightful affair. Mr. Rutledge had promised to ask everybody, to send to town for dresses, and to have the house so beautifully decorated.

"Ah!" said Josephine with a ravishing smile, "Mr. Rutledge is the best, the kindest of men."

Mr. Rutledge, starting from a fit of abstraction at that moment, certainly did not convey the idea of any very excessive kindness or goodness. The sternest frown contracted his brow, and in the cold rigidity of his face, one would never have looked for anything gentle or tender, and the expression that succeeded it under the influence of Josephine's smile, was bitter and cynical, even to the most indifferent observer.

Rain-storms in June have a way of abating their violence toward evening, and breaking away enough to let the declining sun look for half an hour over the wet and shining earth, and make of the desolate place the freshest and most beautiful of Edens, cheering the silenced birds into song, and the wet flowers into perfume, and the breaking clouds into

yellow lustre. A whole fair sunshiny day is nothing to it.
The sudden brilliancy and freshness are worth all the gloom
that have made them so dazzling.   There was not a tree in
the park that afternoon, not a flower on the lawn, that did
not shine and sparkle with a brightness it had never worn
before.   There was a fine coolness too, in the fresh wind,
soft and June-like as it was.

"Is it too late for a ride?" asked Josephine, stepping out
on the piazza where we were all sitting.   "A ride on horseback would be delightful, would it not?"

"Delightful!" echoed Ella Wynkar.

"It would be a capital thing," said Phil, rising.   "I wonder how it is about saddle-horses—are there any fit for ladies in the stable, do you know?"

"There are only two that would do for us ladies, Mr.
Rutledge said," answered Josephine, "but several that you
gentlemen could ride, and I think it would be the nicest
thing in the world to have a brisk canter this fine afternoon.   What do you say, Captain McGuffy?"

"By all means," responded the captain.   "I wonder where
Mr. Rutledge is."

"In the library," said Grace.

"Then, Miss Josephine, you are the proper person to go
and ask his permission.   We know for whose sweet sake all
obstacles are overcome, and if you ask, we are sure of our
ride."

"Yes," said Ellerton, who was excellent in chorus.   "Yes,
there is no doubt he'll have the stables emptied in five minutes, if you want a ride."

Phil bit his lip, as Josephine, with a very conscious look,
sprang up, saying, "Absurd!   It's only because you are
afraid to ask yourselves that you want me to go."   And
with a coquettish shrug of the shoulders, and a very arch
laugh, she ran through the hall and disappeared at the library door.

In a few moments she reappeared, and accompanied by

Mr. Rutledge, joined us on the piazza. There was a subdued tone of triumph in her voice as she said,

"The horses will be at the door in five minutes, good people, not a moment to be lost. Who is going?"

"I am sorry," said Mr. Rutledge, "that there are but two horses fit for the ladies' use. There are enough, however, for all the gentlemen. Mr. Viennet, you will find that chestnut mare you were admiring yesterday, very good under the saddle."

Victor bowed, and, looking at me, said, "What do you ride?"

"I do not mean to ride this afternoon," I said quickly.

"Come, Ella!" exclaimed Josephine, "it will take us some minutes to put on our habits," and the two friends flew upstairs.

Mr. Rutledge approaching me, said in a low tone, "Will you lend Madge to your cousin or Miss Wynkar if you do not ride yourself?"

"It is a matter of very small moment to me who rides Madge," I returned haughtily. "You cannot imagine that I attach any serious meaning to the jest of last fall."

"That's as you will," he said, carelessly turning away.

I had no desire to see the equestrians set off, so going into the hall for my garden hat and a light shawl, I was stealing quietly out at the north door, when on the threshold I met Mr. Rutledge and Grace, who had come around the piazza and were just entering.

"Where are you going?" said that young person inquisitively.

"I have not quite made up my mind," I answered, trying to pass her.

"You're going to walk, and I have a great mind to go with you," she said, intercepting my exit.

"You will excuse me for saying I had rather not have you," I returned shortly.

"Sweet pet! Its temper don't improve," she said provokingly.

"You are an insufferable child," I exclaimed, vexed beyond endurance, and, pushing her aside, I hurried through the doorway. But the fringe of her shawl caught in the bracelet on my arm, and, much against my will, I had to turn back to release it. Grace enjoyed my vexation unspeakably, and did not assist very materially in unfastening the fringe, which, if the truth must be told, was a very difficult task for my trembling and impatient fingers. The touch of Mr. Rutledge's cold, steady hand on my arm, as he stooped to help me, added tenfold to my impatience.

"Break it," I exclaimed, "you'll never be able to untangle it."

"Oh that mysterious bracelet!" cried Grace. "You'd never tell me where it came from."

"It is a perfect torment," I exclaimed, trying to wrench the long silk fringe from the links in which it had become hopelessly twisted. "It catches in everything."

"Then why do you wear it, may I ask?" said Mr. Rutledge, coolly.

"Only because I cannot help myself."

"Can't I assist you?" asked Victor, who had followed me.

"Very possibly," said Mr. Rutledge. "It is rather a delicate affair and requires patience, more, I confess, than I have at command."

"And some strength. Can't you break this thing, Mr. Viennet? I cannot unclasp it, and it annoys me beyond endurance."

"I have no doubt that Mr. Viennet can," said Mr. Rutledge, laying the arm, bracelet, and entangled fringe in Victor's hand.

He tried in vain for a moment to disengage the fringe or unclasp the bracelet, while Grace drawled,

"I advise you to hurry, Mr. Viennet; my cousin bites her lip as if she were desperately angry."

"I cannot break it," said Victor, "without hurting you, of course."

"No matter for that! I am so anxious to have it off, that I should not mind a little pain."

Victor shook his head. "Do not ask me to do it."

"Perhaps I should be less tender," said Mr. Rutledge, bending over it again, and the frail links yielded instantly to the vice-like grasp of his strong hand. A cry escaped me as the bracelet snapped, and fell on the ground at my feet.

"You are hurt!" exclaimed Victor, starting forward and catching my hand over which the blood from the wrist was trickling.

"It is nothing," I said, pulling it away, and wrapping my shawl around it. "It is only scratched a little."

"Not very deep, I fancy," said Mr. Rutledge; while Grace, shrugging her shoulders, exclaimed, as she entered the house:

"Well! you are the oddest set of people! All three of you as pale as ashes, and as much in earnest as if it were a matter of life and death! Mr. Rutledge, I shall coax you to tell me all about it."

"About what?" asked Mr. Rutledge, following her. And as I caught Grace's saucy voice, and Mr. Rutledge's quick, sarcastic laugh, as they passed down the hall, my very breath came quick and short, under the maddening pressure of a pain I had never felt before. Pique, jealousy, vexation, I had known enough of, but this, that dashed all other passions to the dust, and held me gasping in such terrible subjection, was nearer to a deadly sin. It shot so keen through every vein, it burned so madly in my brain, that for a moment, pride and reason were stunned; and, regardless of Victor's eyes fixed on my face, with a low cry of pain, I pressed my hand to my forehead, then flew down

the steps, and vanished from his sight in the shrubbery.
He could hardly have followed me if he had chosen; I was
out of sight of the house before he could have realized that
I had left him. The cool, fresh wind in my face only
allayed the pain enough to give me fresh strength to fly
from what, alas! could not be left behind. The still,
unruffled expanse of the lake, as I reached its banks, gave
me that sort of a pang that it gives one to wake up from a
short troubled sleep, when death and trouble have come in
the night, and find the sunshine flooding the room. It was
so utterly out of tune, so calmly impassive while such
hot passion was raging in my heart—so smiling and indifferent while I was throbbing with such acute pain, that I
sprang away from the sight of it, and hurried on into the
woods, never pausing till I had reached the pine grove at
the head of the lake.

It was better there; the pine-trees moan when there is
no breath to stir them—sunshine and singing-birds pene
trate their solemn depths but rarely; and at last I stopped,
panting and trembling, on a knoll that rose abruptly in the
midst of this forest sanctuary. I sunk down on the slippery
ground at the foot of a tall pine, and leaning my throbbing
temples on my hands, tried to think and reason.

Do the wild flowers and mountain herbage raise their
heads and meet the sunshine and shake off the blight, an
hour after the burning lava has swept over their frail
beauty? Thought, reason, faith, were as impossible at that
moment to me, as growth, and feeling, and verdure are to
them. I did not think—I could not reason; some hateful
words rang in my ears, and a wild, confused purpose
mingled with the chaos that passion had made in my mind;
but beyond that I was incapable of thought.

An hour, perhaps, passed so; the sunset was fast fading
out of the sky, when the sound of voices through the woods
struck my ear, and listening, I recognized the tones of the
returning riding-party. There was a bridle-path, I knew,

just below this knoll, through which they were returning from Norbury, and springing up, I gathered my light muslin dress about me, and pressing through the thicket that lay between it and me, waited for them to pass. A low fence ran across the ravine, and half-kneeling behind this, I watched for them with eager eyes. At last they came, defiling past me one by one, through the narrow path, the gentlemen first, then Ella Wynkar, and in a moment after, Madge Wildfire's glossy head appeared through the opening, so near that I might have patted her arched neck, or felt the breath from her dilated nostrils, and touched the gloved hand that held the reins so tightly in her impatient mouth. Josephine's dark cheek glowed with exercise and excitement, and as she sat, with her head half-turned, in attention to the low tones of the horseman who followed her closely, I could not help acknowledging, with a sharp pang, the beauty that I had never before appreciated. And her companion saw it too ; his stern face softened as he watched the radiant smiles chase each other over her varying mouth ; his eye, restless with an impatient fire, fell with pleasure on her eager, attentive face.

He was thinking—how well I knew it ! A thousand devils whispered it in my ear—he was thinking, " this face is gentle and womanly—it turns to me for pleasure—it is bright and gay—no storms sweep over it ; it has never repulsed and disappointed me. Shall I end the doubt, and say, it is the face that shall be the loadstar of my future, the sunshine and pleasure of my life ?"

The horses threaded their way daintily down the narrow ravine—the pleasant voices died away in the distance ; I raised myself from my bending attitude, and with blanched cheeks and parted lips, strained my gaze to catch the last trace of them. If the assembled tribes of earth and air had been there to see, I could not have brought one tinge of color to my pallid face, nor taken the deadly stare out of my eyes, I could only have done as I did now, when suddenly I found I was not alone, utter a faint exclamation, and turning sick and giddy, lean against the fence for support. The stealthy, cat-like tread of the intruder brought him to my side in a moment. I knew, from the instant I met the glance of his basilisk eyes, that he had been reading my face to some purpose—that he knew the miserable story written on it.

"You look agitated," said Dr. Hugh, bending toward me obsequiously. "May I ask if anything has happened to distress you?"

His tones were so hateful that I cried quickly:

"No, nothing so much as seeing you;" and, springing across the low barrier, I hurried down the path. I knew he was following me stealthily; nothing but that fear would have driven me back to the house again. The path was narrow and irregular; other paths branched off from it, and before I got within sight of the lake again, I was thoroughly bewildered, and in the gathering twilight, the huge trees took weird forms, the "paths grew dim," and no familiar landmark appeared to guide me. Pausing in fright and bewilderment, I crouched for a moment behind a clump of trees, and listened. I had eluded my pursuer; in a second's time, I heard his soft step treading cautiously and swiftly down the path that I had inadvertently left. With a sigh of relief, I looked about me, and finding that the lake was just visible through an opening in the trees, knew my whereabouts immediately, and only waited for Dr. Hugh to be well out of the way to start across the park toward the house.

Several minutes elapsed before I ventured to rise from my hiding-place; listening again intently, I was about to spring from the thicket, and effect my escape across the park, when, with a start of fear, I heard a heavy step crashing among the underbrush in the direction from which we had come; a heavy step, and then a pause. My heart seemed to stand still as I waited to hear more. The next sound was a low whistle; a long pause, and then the signal was repeated. No answer came; and with a low and surly oath, the new-comer advanced nearer to where I crouched. Through a gap in the thicket, I could see him as he approached, and even by this dusky light, I recognized the thickset figure and slouching gait of the man whom Victor had so wantonly insulted on the evening of our arrival—of whose enmity there could be no reasonable doubt. It was not a comfortable thought, but certainly some evil purpose must have brought him here; and for whom, too, was that signal given? It seemed almost incredible that such a spirit of revenge should possess itself of such a sluggish, low-born nature; yet I could not doubt that it was some design of revenge that kept him lurking about the neighborhood. I knew that Victor would be in peril if he were abroad to-night. And it was not comfortable, either, to remember that it was my fault that he had given the insult; for my protection that he had incurred this malice. How should I ever forgive myself if any evil came of it? Victor was my only friend at Rutledge; I could not but be grateful; the recollection of a thousand kindnesses started up at the thought of the danger I had involved him in, and I almost forgot that now I shared it.

Motionless and breathless, I saw him pass within two feet of me, stop, whistle again, and then, after a pause, throwing himself at full length on the ground, with his face toward the park, within a few yards of where I was, lie waiting for I did not dare to think what. Victor, I was certain, would be somewhere about the grounds, watching for my return; this direction, sooner or later, he would inevitably take. Moment after moment crept on; every movement of the stranger—even his heavy breathing—were as distinct as if he had been within reach of my hand, and the least motion on my part—the faintest rustle of my dress, or of the branches of the thicket—would, of course, be as audible to him, and most dangerous to me; indeed, if he were to turn

this way, I could hardly hope·to escape detection, for m
light drapery, only half hid behind the dark thicket, would
inevitably betray me. How long this would last—how determined he could be in his vigil—I dreaded to conjecture.
None but Victor was likely to come to my assistance, and
that was just the very worst of all.

There was still enough light left in the west to distinguish,
as I looked eagerly that way, that a figure, from the direction of the house, was crossing the lawn toward us. I
turned sick with fear as I recognized, bounding before the
rapidly-approaching walker, Victor's constant companion,
little Tigre; and this, no doubt, was Victor. I alone could
warn him of the danger that awaited him; but, faint and
almost paralyzed with fear, I had not strength nor courage
to stir. The villain beside me, less quick-sighted, had not
yet discovered his advance.

He was not yet half-way across the park; there might be
time. I made a desperate resolve, and, clearing the copse
at one bound, flew, as only terror and desperation can
fly. I heard the startled oath the man uttered, and the
cracking of the birch boughs as he regained his feet; I
heard him spring forward in pursuit, but by that time I was
out of the wood and on the lawn, and in another instant I
had reached my goal.

Catching his arm, I exclaimed vehemently, forgetting
everything in my terror:

"Don't go near that horrid wood, *Victor!* Come back,
as you value your life!"

I was too much terrified to await his reply; but, calling
to him to follow me, I ran on at the top of my speed, and
never paused till I had reached the terrace, and, sinking
down on the stone steps, I covered my face with my hands,
panting and exhausted. Raising my head as I heard his
step beside me, I began:

"You don't know how narrow an escape you have had!
That"——

"You have made a mistake," interrupted my companion. "It is not *Victor*."

With an exclamation of amazement and chagrin; I sprung from him up the steps. I had made a miserable mistake, indeed; it was Mr. Rutledge.

CHAPTER XXVII.

"But 'mid his mirth, 'twas often strange
How suddenly his cheer would change,
His look o'ercast and lower—

Even so 'twas strange how, evermore,
Soon as the passing pang was o'er,
Forward he rushed, with double glee,
Into the stream of revelry."

SCOTT.

THE *fête champêtre* proved a success; it was a perfect day; the house, a very fine modern one, and the grounds, had appeared to the best advantage; the dancing tent had been just full enough, the toilettes lovely, and the whole thing so well got up and successful, that Josephine began half to repent not having decided upon such an enter-tainment for the Fourth instead of the proposed masque-rade.

"This is just the place for a fête," she said, as we were all sitting in the parlor next morning ".talking it over." "This lawn is twice the size of the Emersons', and this piazza, inclosed and decorated, would be the prettiest thing in the world. Indeed, there is no doubt in my mind but that it would have been an infinitely handsomer affair than theirs, if we had decided upon a *fête*."

"It would not have been dignified, Miss Josephine," said Mr. Rutledge, with a smile, "to have followed so closely in their steps, and I do not think we need have any fears for the masquerade."

"Not the smallest," said Mrs. Churchill. "With Mr. Rutledge as leader, and Josephine as aid-de-camp, I am certain there is no such word as fail. This absurd child," she continued, bending gracefully over her pretty daughter, "this absurd child,. Mr. Rutledge, enters so with all her heart into whatever she undertakes, that I have to laugh at her continually. She can think of nothing now, but this masquerade, and only this morning"——

"Now, mamma!" remonstrated Josephine.

"Only this morning," her mother went on, "she said to me, 'I was so worried, mamma, I couldn't sleep last night, for Mr. Rutledge has trusted to my taste about the decorations, and if he should be disappointed, I should be perfectly miserable.' Did you ever hear of anything so silly?" she continued, with a light caress.

"Never," said Mr. Rutledge, looking admiringly at Josephine's averted conscious face. "Am I so very terrible, then?"

"No," said Josephine with a pretty shyness, "oh no! but then, you know—you see—I should be so sorry to dis_appoint or displease you. I know you wouldn't say a word, but I should be perfectly miserable if you were not pleased."

"Where are you going, Phil?" asked Grace, as her cousin strode out into the hall.

"Anywhere, Gracie," I heard him say, under his breath. "It doesn't make much difference where."

Poor Phil! There was a sharp pain at his honest heart, I knew. I watched him from the window, as with hasty strides he crossed the lawn, and disappeared into the woods. But Josephine didn't see; Mr. Rutledge was sketching a plan for the decorations, and she was leaning over the paper with fixed attention.

"If those people are coming to lunch," said Ella Wynkar, getting up from a tête-à-tête chat with the captain, "it is time we were dressed to receive them. Come, Josephine, it would never be forgiven, if we should not be ready."

"Yes," exclaimed Mr. Rutledge, starting up and looking

at his watch, "I had forgotten about that. They will be here in half an hour. Miss Josephine, did you ever effect your toilet in half an hour, in your life?"

"You shall see!" cried Josephine, dancing out of the room. Mrs. Churchill followed, with a laughing apology for her daughter's wild spirits; since she had been at this delightful place, she had, she declared, been like a bird let loose.

> "The linnet born within the cage,
> That never knew the summer woods,"

I longed to say to my aunt, would hardly know how to enjoy them. The miserable prisoner that had spent all its life, in narrow cramped limits, on the sill of a city window, hopped on a smooth perch, and eaten canary-seed and loaf-sugar since its nativity, would hardly be at home in wide, sunny fields, or "groves deep and high," would shudder to clasp with its tender claws the rough bark of the forest twigs, and would be doubtful of the flavor of a wild straw-berry, and think twice before it would stoop to drink of the roaring mountain-stream. It would, I fancy, before nightfall, creep miserably back to its cage, as the fittest, safest, most comfortable place for its narrowed and timid nature.

"So!" said Victor, looking at me with a curl on his handsome lip, as the drawing-room was vacated by all but ourselves. "Are you going to spend an hour of this splen-did fresh morning in making yourself fine?"

"Not if I know myself intimately!" I exclaimed, cram-ming my work, thimble, and scissors into my workbox, and springing up. "I do not fancy devoting three hours to those tiresome Mason girls nor their horse-and-dog brothers. I shall never be missed, and I am going to the village for a walk."

"Why to the village?" said Victor, following me, and reaching down my flat hat from the deer's horns tLat it had been decorating in the hall. " "Why will you not come to the lake and let me row you up to the pines?"

"I ought to have paid my devoirs to the housekeeper at the Parsonage the very day I arrived," I answered, as we descended the steps. "She is a great friend of mine, and she will be hurt if I neglect her any longer. Indeed, it's a very pleasant walk, and you'll be repaid for taking it, if we should find Mr. Shenstone at home. He is so kind, and the very best man in the world."

"That's the clergyman?" said Victor, making a grimace. "I don't affect clergymen, as a general thing, but for your sake I will try to be favorably impressed; your friends I always try to admire; our host, for instance, who just passed down the terrace, without so much as a look toward us, though he could not possibly have avoided seeing us. Why do you bite your lip?" continued he, watching me narrowly. "I cannot learn the signs of your face. Pale and red, smiling and frowning, like any April day. There! what chord have I touched now? The thought gave you actual pain."

"Nothing!" I exclaimed, hurriedly. "There's Stephen on the lawn. I want to talk to him," and I ran across to where he stood, leaning on his rake, watching us. While I talked to him, Victor threw himself upon the heap of new-cut hay at a little distance from us, and played with Tigre. I saw that Stephen's eyes often wandered to where he lay, his hat off, the wind lifting the dark hair from his handsome face.

"If I might make so bold," said Stephen, in a low tone, as I was turning away, "has that young gentleman lived long in this country?"

"I do not know, really," I said, with a laugh. "Shall I ask him, Stephen?"

"No, Miss, I shouldn't like you to ask him; but I should like to know."

"I'll find out for you sometime," I said, as I nodded a good bye and rejoined Victor.

It was, as he said, a splendid day—all sultriness dissipated by the strong wind. We had a beautiful walk through the woods, though I couldn't quite forget "our rustic friend," as Victor called his unknown enemy; but he made such a joke of it that it was impossible to have much feeling of alarm connected with it. The village, however, he seemed not to care to visit.

"Had I not better wait for you here?" he said, lingering as we passed out of the woods into the lane that led to the village.

"No, indeed," I said, perversely; "if you stay here I shall go home another way."

He laughed, but rather uneasily, and followed me.

I bent my head so that my hat hid my face as we entered the low gate of the Parsonage, for I dreaded Victor's inquiring eyes just then. I preceded him down the little path bordered with flowers, and, stepping on the porch, raised the knocker. We waited for several minutes, and still no answer; so, telling my companion to follow me, I passed on into the study.

"What a cool, shady, pleasant room!" said Victor, as he gave me a seat and threw himself into another. "I am sure I could write a sermon myself against the pomps and vanities if I had such a sweet, calm retreat to repose in meantime."

"Pshaw!" he exclaimed impatiently, "what do these men know of temptation, who have never felt a passion stronger than this summer wind, nor seen a rood beyond their own study windows! These calm, slow natures, bred in the retirement and quiet of the country, can preach, perhaps with profit, to their humble flocks; but to men who have been in the thick of the fight, never."

I shook my head. "You will not say that after you have seen Mr. Shenstone; but here he comes."

The clergyman stood for a moment in the doorway before he entered, his tall, stooping figure nearly filling it. I advanced to meet him, and Victor rose. The room was so dark that at first he did not recognize me, and, of course, saw but indistinctly my companion. But as I spoke, he extended his hand cordially, and gave us both a kind reception.

"I have been expecting a visit from you," he said, sitting down beside me, and speaking in the quiet tone that was habitual with him, and looking at me with his kind smile. "You have been here some days, have you not?"

"Yes, sir, and I've meant to come; but there has been something going on every day that has interfered, and I have supposed every day, sir, that you would be there."

"Ah!" he said, with the slightest perceptible fading of the smile, "I have been so long out of gay company that I should not be at home there now. The quiet of my little village suits me best."

I knew this would be a confirmation of Victor's judgment, so I hurried on to say, "But, sir, you sometimes go among gay people. I am sure you are often at Windy Hill, and at the Emersons, are you not?"

"Sometimes—oh! yes; but it seems different with Rutledge. It would be to me," he went on in a lower tone, "unspeakably grating and painful to see that place throw off the gloom and silence that it has worn for twenty years —twenty years and more. But you cannot be expected to understand this. I had forgotten you were nearly a child as yet. You only know regret and sorrow by name, I suppose."

There must have been an involuntary denial of this on my face, for he looked at me attentively for a moment; then, in a tone that had a little sadness in it, he said:

"But you are older than you were last fall, my child, I see; one takes quick strides sometimes toward maturity after one has crossed the threshold. This little girl and I, Mr. Viennet, were very good friends last year and I hope that the world has not separated us quite, though it has changed one of us a little, I fear."

I could not keep back the sudden tears that rushed into my eyes; the tone of sympathy so strange to my ears exorcised the evil tempers that had swayed me so long. If it had not been for Victor's presence, I should have thrown off the reserve and silence that I had so long maintained toward all around me, and have saved myself perhaps from years of misery.

Only Mr. Shenstone's compassionate eyes saw the emotion that flashed through mine; murmuring some excuse about finding Mrs. Arnold, I quitted the room. I found her in the apartment that had been my sick-room, busy as ever with her silent, rapid needle. Throwing my arms around her neck, I kissed her affectionately.

"Why have you not been before ?" she said, quietly.

"Because I haven't done anything right or pleasant since I came," I returned, with a little bitterness.

Mrs. Arnold shook her head. "Mr. Shenstone would tell you not to let that go on."

"Don't !" I exclaimed, with an impatient gesture; "don't tell me what I ought to do—don't talk to me about my duty. I am sick and tired of it all. I want to forget all about everything that makes me miserable, and only be petted and made much of," and, throwing myself down on a low stool at her feet, I drew her hand around my neck.

"You were always willful," she said, sadly; "but you used to like to hear about your duty."

"I don't now; I've got over that. I shall never come to the Parsonage if you talk to me about it. We don't have time for duty at Rutledge now-a-days. Oh! Mrs. Arnold, it seems like a different place. Why don't you come and see how fine the house looks. There's to be a masquerade on the Fourth. You should come and see how beautifully it will be decorated, and how pretty all our dresses will be."

The hand around my neck was quickly withdrawn; with a sudden start, she rose and walked nervously about the room, the color fluttering in her cheeks, and her hand passing rapidly over her smooth, grey hair.

"Yes, yes," she said at last, sitting down and trying to command herself. "I know it is all right; you are young and you ought to enjoy yourself. I hope you are happy there."

"You need not imagine that I am!" I exclaimed bitterly. "You may be sure I have enough to keep me down, and make me wretched, gay as they all are. But I'm not going to talk about it," I said, interrupting myself, "for you'll begin to tell me how I ought to bear it, and that I can't listen to now. Tell me how the school goes on. Does the new teacher work well, and do the children like her?"

"Very much," said Mrs. Arnold, relapsing slowly into her ordinary manner. "I should like you to go with me some day to see them."

The archives of the Parish School, and many minor matters of interest, served to occupy our tongues, if not our minds, for the next half hour, and it was only the sudden recollection of having left Mr. Shenstone and Victor, two entire strangers, at each other's mercy, that brought an end to the interview. Starting up, I said:

"It is time for me to go. Come down, Mrs. Arnold, and see whether you think Mr. Viennet as handsome as Kitty does."

She very reluctantly followed me downstairs, and waited in the porch to see us, and say good bye as we should pass out.

I found Victor and Mr. Shenstone talking. Victor, it seemed to me, treated his entertainer with several degrees more of reverence than I had imagined he could either feel or affect toward any one. Mr. Shenstone's manner was rather less tranquil than ordinary, though, it struck me. He accompanied us to the door, and looked very earnestly at Victor as we came into the stronger light.

"I shall hope for the pleasure of another visit before you leave the country, Mr. Viennet," he said slowly, as we parted at the threshold.

"I shall not fail to do myself the honor," returned Victor, in a manner less French, and more sincere than usual, bowing very low.

"Isn't he handsome?" I whispered, in a careless aside to Mrs. Arnold, as we passed her on the porch. But to my surprise, she had started back, with the same dilated, agitated look in her eyes, that she had worn upstairs, and the fluttering color coming and going on her face as she watched Victor, while her pale lips opened, but no sound passed them. I stared in wonder, but she drew back hastily, and disappeared in the house.

"You will have a pleasant walk," said Mr. Shenstone, thoughtfully, as he watched us down the path.

"I'm afraid not," muttered Victor, between his teeth, as at the gate Dr. Hugh joined us with a most affable bow. He proposed to accompany us on our way, he said, if agreeable to us. He was going as far as the Park, to see that delicate-looking young Mr. Wynkar, to whom he had just been summoned.

"Over-eaten himself, no doubt," said Victor, impatiently.

"Ah?" said the doctor, nodding intelligently, "is that his trouble? I fancied as much. Your pale, cadaverous-looking people generally are the very mischief among the provisions."

Victor's lip curled; I could see he chafed under this familiarity. Why does he endure it, I thought. His imperious temper brooks no annoyance from those around him; daily there is some new evidence of his self-will and determination; why does he so tamely submit to what, there wants no penetration to see, is galling him to distraction.

It was almost impossible to realize that this was my gay, sparkling companion of an hour ago. Pale and abstracted he walked beside me, answering, at random, the doctor's many questions—gnawing his lip at the occasional familiarities of his manner, but offering no affront or slight.

Our constrained and uncomfortable walk brought us to the house just as the Masons were getting into their carriage. The whole party stood on the piazza, and the approach for us was anything but a pleasant thing.

"Courage," whispered Victor, seeing me falter as every eye turned toward us. "Be as queenly as you can. You had a right to go; there was no intimation given you that there was to be company at lunch. It would be cowardly indeed to mind *their* slights."

Victor had touched the right chord; the color flashed back into my cheeks, and with as queenly a step as he could have desired, I advanced to meet the strangers.

"You must excuse my cousin," cried Grace, interrupting our rather formal greetings. "She never allows anything to interfere with her rural tastes, and as she is addicted to tête-à-tête rows and lonely rambles, we are quite cut off from her society."

The Misses Mason looked at me as if they were afraid of me, the Messrs. Mason as if they would have been, if they had not been such brave men. I do not know exactly what I said, it was all a kind of dream, I was so intensely worked up; but whatever my answer was, it must have been clever, and a good retort, for Victor's clear laugh rang in the air, and the young ladies tittered, and looked at Grace to see how she bore it, and the least ponderous of the two young gentlemen slapped the captain on the back with a low:

"By George! She's not to be put down! I like her spirit."

A month ago, perhaps, the interview that I had to go

through with my aunt after the departure of the guests, would have made me quite miserable; but now, it was utterly powerless. We were openly at war, and no hostile message could alter the state of affairs. I could have laughed in her face, for all the impression that it made on me, but of course I preserved the external respect I owed her, and neither by look nor word betrayed how indifferent a matter it was to me whether she approved or dissented.

"A word with you, my friend," I heard the doctor say to Victor, passing his arm through his and leading him off toward the terrace. Victor set his lips firmly together, and his face darkened; there was a storm brewing; the wily doctor was going too far, if he did not wish to feel the wrath of it. For half an hour, I watched them from my window; they had gone to a retired walk in the shrubbery, where only at a certain turn I could catch sight of them. Victor's face, whenever I could see it, was white and passionate, and his gestures showed that he had dashed aside the restraint he had set upon himself. His was not an impotent and childish anger either; it was the strong wrath of a strong man, snared and trapped, exasperated and tor-tured by an enemy wily and powerful, with some secret hold upon his victim, that gave his weakness and meanness the strength of a giant. I watched, fascinated and terrified, for every glimpse of the two faces, as the two men strode up and down the alley. If Victor's tormentor had seen his face as I did, surely he would have paused. How could confidence and pride so blind a man as to make him insensible to the danger of rousing to such a pitch, such a fierce southern nature? They had blinded him, however, for Dr. Hugh's face expressed nothing but cunning and triumph, guarded and subdued by habitual self-control.

That night, as we were separating for our rooms, Victor announced carelessly that his pleasant visit was nearly at an end. He had that day received letters that made it neces-

sary for him to sail in next week's steamer, and he should
have to tear himself away from Rutledge in a day or two.
The color went and came in my face as I met Mr. Rutledge's eye; Victor studiously avoided looking at me, and
the others were too much absorbed in the announcement to
heed me.

"Why, Victor!" exclaimed Phil, heartily, stung perhaps
with some slight self-reproach for his recent neglect; "why,
old fellow, we shan't know what to do without you! It's
a shame to break up a pleasant party like this. Make it the
next steamer, and stay over another week, and we'll all go
together."

"Do, I beg of you, Victor," echoed Ellerton.

"And you couldn't go without that day's woodcock
shooting we've been talking of," said the captain. "The
law's up next week, you know."

"And you've forgotten the masquerade!" exclaimed
Josephine.

"And the Masons' tableaux!" cried Ella.

"And my cousin's feelings," added Grace, slily.

"And what of your own, my pretty Miss Grace?" said
Victor, carrying the war so abruptly over into her territory
that she had no time to collect her wits for a retort. "My
own heart is broken at the idea of leaving you. Are you
perfectly unmoved at the sight of my sorrow? I shall
never believe in woman again."

"I do not know," said Mr. Rutledge, "what other in-
ducements we can hold out of sufficient power to detain
Mr. Viennet longer. If there is anything so imperative as
he suggests, however, I imagine that our persuasions will
be thrown away."

"Quite thrown away, sir, I regret to admit," said Victor,
with a low and significant bow. "I can enjoy your hospitality no longer than Wednesday morning."

CHAPTER XXVIII

"An 1 as the dove, to far Palmyra flying
 From where her native founts of Antioch beam,
 Weary, exhausted, longing, panting, sighing,
 Lights sadly at the desert's bitter stream,

"So many a soul, o'er life's drear desert faring,
 Love's pure, congenial spring unfound, unquaffed,
 Suffers—recoils—then, thirsty and despairing
 Of what it would, descends, and sips the nearest draught."

"You are cruel," said Victor, in a low tone, as I followed the rest of the party into the library after dinner. "This is my last day, and you will not give me a moment."

"Who's for a ride? Mr. Rutledge wants to know," said Grace, coming in from the piazza.

"Not I, for one," exclaimed Ella, throwing herself back on the sofa. "I'm going to save myself for this evening."

"And you, too, Josephine, dear," said her mother, "had better not tire yourself any more. You will be perfectly fagged if you go to drive, and you want to keep yourself fresh for the Masons."

"Aren't you made of sterner stuff?" whispered Victor. "Aren't you equal to a drive and a party in the same twenty-four hours? It is heavy work, I know, but your constitution seems a good one."

"I think I'll venture," I said, following Grace into the hall. "There's Kitty on the stairs. Mr, Viennet, tell her to bring me my bonnet, please."

Kitty was only too glad to obey Mr. Viennet's orders at any time, and she flew to get my things.

"Get mine at the same time, young woman," drawled Grace.

Before Kitty had returned from her double errand, the horses were at the door.

"Our friends, the bays," said Victor. "But I think our host means to drive them himself. He has the reins in his hands."

"Are these all your recruits, Miss Grace?" said Mr. Rutledge.

"Yes. Josephine and Ella are afraid of their complexions, or their tempers, or something, and won't come, and I can't find Captain McGuffy or Phil."

Victor stood ready to hand me into the carriage; I immediately took possession of the back seat.

"This is a very selfish arrangement," said Victor, discontentedly, as Grace was about to follow me. "Miss Grace, you'd have a much better view of the country up there beside Mr. Rutledge."

"And Grace might drive," I added; "she's so fond of horses."

"As you please," she said, with a shrug. "I only go for ballast yet awhile, I know, and it's evident I'm not wanted here. Mr. Rutledge, do *you* want me?"

"Miss Grace, my happiness will not be complete till you comply with Mr. Viennet's disinterested suggestion;" and Grace mounted up beside him.

I had undertaken, in that drive, more than I was quite equal to. I had brought myself into the position that I had been avoiding all day, a tête-à-tête of the most unequivocal kind with a man whose devotion it was impossible to ignore, and I had gone too far to retract entirely. It was cruel to treat him with coldness, now that we were on the eve of a long separation, and to repel with indifference the tenderness that shone in his eloquent eyes and faltered in his low tones. Our companions left us entirely to ourselves; my awkward attempts to draw them into a general conversation were all frustrated by Mr. Rutledge's cool indiffe-rence, and Grace's cool impertinence.

The only time that Mr. Rutledge addressed a single remark voluntarily to me, was on our way home. We had driven around by Norbury, and were returning by way of the post-office. Suddenly drawing the reins, Mr. Rutledge stopped for an instant on the brow of the hill.

"Do you remember this?" he said, abruptly, turning to me, and fixing his eyes on my face.

Remember it? My cheek was crimson with the recollection then; the scene would never fade but with life and memory. It was just here, that, in the glow of the autumn sunset, he and I had parted on that ever-to-be-remembered evening, when my willfulness had led me into such danger. Hemlock Hollow lay dark and dense below us. Far off at the left, the mill and bridge that had served as a landmark then, gleamed in the setting sun. The forest foliage was greener and thicker now, but the picture was the same; I could never have got it out of my memory if I had tried; and yet, when Mr. Rutledge asked me that sudden question, a wicked lie, or as wicked a prevarication, rose to my lips.

"Yes, I think I remember it. Didn't we go this way to the Emersons' the day of the fête?"

"I think we did—yes," said Mr. Rutledge, with an almost imperceptible compression of the lips, as, bending forward, he startled the eager horses with a galling lash of the whip.

Grace was quite white with alarm as we reached the village.

"Mr. Rutledge, why *do* you drive so frightfully fast? I am terrified to death."

He drew the horses in a little, and, looking down at her, said:

"Were we going fast? I am sorry I frightened you; for my part, I thought we crept."

He paused a moment at the Parsonage gate. Mrs. Arnold was in the garden; Mr. Rutledge called out to her that he had brought Mr. Shenstone's letters and papers, but had not time to stop to see him. She approached the carriage, looking so lady-like and attractive, with her soft, white hair smoothed plain under her neat cap, and her clinging dark dress, that Victor said, involuntarily to me:

"What an attractive-looking person! I never saw a gentler face."

She was quite absorbed in attending to the message Mr. Rutledge left for Mr. Shenstone, and in her retiring modesty I do not think she ventured a look at us, till Victor, who had been watching her with interest, addressed some remark to her. She raised her eyes at the sound of his voice in a startled way, the same fluttering, frightened look transformed her quiet features, and trying in vain to command herself, she stammered some excuse, and turned away.

"Strange!" exclaimed Victor, as we drove on. "Did you notice the odd way in which that person looked at me, both now and the other day?"

"It *is* strange," said Mr. Rutledge, thoughtfully. "Can you account for it in any way?"

"In no way, sir. I do not think I ever enjoyed the happiness of meeting her before I visited this neighborhood; and since my residence in it, I cannot remember having done anything to have rendered myself at all an object of interest to her."

"Who's that bowing so graciously to you?" interrupted Grace.

"Oh! Ellerton's medical adviser."

"By the way, Mr. Viennet," said Mr. Rutledge, turning rather abruptly to him, "the doctor tells me he is an old friend of yours."

"Hardly a friend, if I understand the term aright," returned Victor, changing color slightly. "I knew him when he was studying medicine in the city two or three years ago. I lost sight of him entirely after that, and the renewal of our acquaintance has been attended with more zest on his part than on mine."

" I believe he is rather apt to presume," said Mr. Rutledge, briefly, and there the conversation dropped.

We were rather a taciturn party for the remainder of the way. Tea was waiting for us on our return, and after it, Grace and I had to make quite a hurried toilet for the party, the others being already dressed.

"Aunt Edith, be kind enough to let me accompany you," I said, hurriedly, following her into the carriage, as we all stood, ready to start, on the stone walk below the piazza. Victor, with a look of disappointment, closed the door upon Mrs. Churchill, Grace, Ella, and myself.

" Miss Josephine," I had heard Mr. Rutledge say, "'it is such a lovely night, you will surely not refuse to let me drive you. It will be infinitely pleasanter than going in the carriage, I assure you."

It was a very long and a very silent drive for the inmates of the carriage, to Windy Hill; and when we arrived there, we found the gentlemen of our party awaiting our coming with some impatience. The curtain would be raised in a moment, Phil said ; the tableaux had been retarded as long as possible on our account. Where were Josephine and Mr. Rutledge ?

" Echo answers where," said Grace. " Taking the longest way, you may be sure, and making the most of this lovely moonlight."

Mrs. Churchill did not seem very uneasy, and after a little consultation in the dressing-room, it was decided that we should not wait for them, but should all go down to the parlor. Accordingly we descended the stairs and entered the room *en masse*. It was quite full, and as they had only been waiting for our arrival, in a few moments the curtain rose.

The tableaux were very fine, no doubt; there were murmurs of applause and exclamations of admiration from all the company. All were enthusiastically received, and some were encored. I tried to attend, but my recollection of them is only a confused jumble of convent and harem scenes, trials of queenly personages, and signings of death warrants and marriage contracts; Effie Deans, and Rebekah at the well, the eve of St. Bartholomew, and the landing of the Pilgrims. I tried to attend, both to the tableaux and to Victor's whispered conversation, but there was " something on my mind " as Kitty would have said, too engrossing to allow me to succeed. Do what I might, I still found myself listening eagerly for the sound of carriage wheels outside. Victor noticed my abstracted and nervous manner, and turned away at last with a half sigh.

The curtain rose and fell many times, the audience admired, applauded and encored, with untiring enthusiasm, the little French clock above me on the mantelpiece, marked the departing minutes faithfully, and still they did not come. This was as unlike Josephine as it was unlike Mr. Rutledge. Something dreadful had happened, I was sure; something that would make the memory of this night forever terrible, and what a miserable mockery it was for us all to be laughing and talking so thoughtlessly. Mrs. Churchill was anxious, I could see, but she tried very faithfully to conceal it, and laughed and turned off all conjectures about them with her usual skillful nonchalance. Phil had walked the piazza as long as he could endure it, then throwing himself upon his horse, had galloped off in the direction of Rutledge.

At last the parlors were cleared of all the appurtenances of the tableaux, and the dancing began. I was standing by a window listening—oh, how eagerly!—for the sound of wheels, when Victor approached me, and asked for the next dance.

" Indeed you must excuse me, I cannot dance," I said almost impatiently, " ask somebody else."

The look with which he turned away would have cut me to the heart, if my heart had not been too selfishly misera

ble to mind the pain of others. He did not dance, but leaning against the window opposite gazed abstractedly out.
The gay music and merry voices grated perhaps as cruelly
on his mood as on mine.

I never had had less the command of myself; the persons
who came up to talk to me, could make nothing of me ; I
could not talk, could not find a word of answer to their questions. At length a gentleman who had been standing near
me for some minutes, said kindly :

"These rooms are too warm for you, will you come on
the piazza for a little while ?"

I gave him a grateful look, and taking his arm, followed
him out into the fresh air. Several others were there before
us, and accepting my cicerone's offer of a seat, I leaned
against the vine-covered pillar, and looked intently down
the road that led winding up from the lodge. My companion evidently understood and pitied my anxiety and did not
attempt to make me talk.

At last! there came a distant sound of wheels, and as they
rapidly neared the house, I involuntarily covered my face
with my hands. What might they bring? What news
might I hear in another moment ?

"They are safe," said my companion, kindly. "Look,
they are at the door."

I looked up. Josephine, with a light laugh, was springing
up the steps. Mr. Rutledge, who had thrown the reins to a
servant, was following her. Mrs. Churchill and a group of
others hurried out to meet them.

"My dear," she exclaimed hurriedly, "what has detained
you? We have been excessively worried about you."

"Why, mamma," laughed the daughter, lightly kissing
her mother's cheek, "I knew you would scold, and I didn't
mean to have been so naughty, but you know it was such a
sweet evening, and Mr. Rutledge said that wild Hemlock
Hollow looked so picturesque by moonlight, that we couldn't
resist the temptation of going that way, and after we had

driven—oh! I can't tell you how far—we suddenly came upon a huge old tree that had fallen across the road, and over it of course we could not get, and the woods were so dense on either side that it was impossible to get around it, so the only thing left for us to do, was to turn, and make the best of our way back."

"I assure you, Mrs. Churchill," said Mr. Rutledge, "I am very much annoyed at having caused you this anxiety. You will fancy me very careless, but it was a contretemps I had never dreamed of."

The whole party passed out of sight into the hall. A group who stood near us and had been watching the scene, also moved on toward the door, but as they turned away I caught the words from one of them:

"It looks very much like it, and it will be an excellent thing on both sides; but I never thought till lately, that he would marry."

"Will you go in," said my companion.

"Yes, if you please," and we followed the crowd.

"Ah! you look like a different person," he said, smiling as we went into the light. I saw as we passed a mirror that a bright spot was burning on each cheek, and my eyes were shining unnaturally. "I could see you were dreadfully anxious about your cousin, and indeed I could not wonder at it."

"For the last time," said Victor in a low tone at my side, "will you dance with me?"

I yielded, and in a moment we were on the floor. Not an instant after that did I stop to think. If I had, my cheek would have paled to have found at the mercy of what fierce hatred, resentment and jealousy, my unguided soul then was, and whither they were hurrying me. To others, I was only a gay young girl, revelling in her first flush of triumph, thoughtless, innocent and happy. God help all such innocence and happiness!

It was the last dance; the carriage was already at the door. Mrs. Churchill had limited us to five minutes more two or three were contending for my hand. Victor had hung around me all the evening, and I caught a gleam of his sad, expressive eyes. Josephine, on Mr. Rutledge's arm, passed us at the moment. Turning toward Victor, I said to the others with a smile, "Mr. Viennet says this will be his last dance in America. I think I must give it to him."

A flash of hope lighted up his handsome face. I trembled at what I had done as I took my place among the dancers. The words that I knew I must hear before we parted, I heard now. There was but a moment for the recital, but it sufficed. Was it that such homage soothed my wounded pride; or that, bewildered by this tempest of emotions, I had mistaken gratitude for tenderness, kind regard for love? Whatever may have been my motive or excuse, the fact remained the same. Before I parted with Victor Viennet at the carriage door, I had accepted his love, and promised myself to him irrevocably.

How hot and still the night had grown! I leaned my forehead on the carriage window to cool its burning. The horses seemed to creep over the smooth road; I clenched my hands together to quiet their impatience. My companions, leaning back on the cushions, slept or rested. This very tranquillity maddened me, and, holding my breath lest they should know how gaspingly it came, I wished and longed to be alone once more. I could not, did not dare to think till there were bolts and bars between me and the world. At last I caught sight of the welcome lights of Rutledge, and almost before the deliberate horses had stopped in front of the house, I burst open the carriage door, and flew up the steps.

"Have the others got home yet?" I asked of Kitty eagerly.

"No, Miss; but they'll be here in a minute. I see the lights of the barouche just by the park gate."

The other ladies paused in the parlor till the rest of the

party should arrive; for me, I never stopped till I was with-in the sanctuary of my own room.

"No matter for undressing me to-night," I said to Kitty, who had followed me. "I can do all that is necessary for myself, and don't come till I ring for you in the morning; I am so tired I shall want to rest."

With a look of some disappointment she turned away, and I slid the bolt, with a trembling hand, between me and the outer world. But not between me and conscience, not between me and memory, not between me and remorse. I had thought, when once I am alone, this misery will vent itself in tears—this insufferable pain will yield to the relief of solitude and quiet. But I did not know with what I had to deal. I did not estimate what foes I had invoked—what remorse and regret were to be my comrades through the slow hours of that night.

With suicidal hand, it seemed to me, I had shut myself out forever from peace, forever from all chance of happiness. Nothing now but misery: the past, a sin and guilt to recall; the future, weariness but to imagine. The promise I had given was to me as irrevocable and sacred as the marriage vow itself; and self-reproach only riveted the fetters more hopelessly, as I remembered the manly love of which I was so unworthy. To draw back now, would but add perjury to my sins, and deal undeserved misery to the man I had deceived. No, hypocrisy became a duty now; he should never know the agony that I had wrestled with when I had first looked my engagement in the face. He should never know how the first hours of it had been black-ened. But oh! plead repentance, I will bury this hateful secret in my heart; I will only live to serve him; I will make him happy; I will be a true and faithful wife.

True? questioned a voice within me; and with a misera-ble groan I hid my face, and owned that I must leave truth at the threshold of this new relation. I must enter it with a dead love in my heart, a false vow on my lips.

CHAPTER XXIX.

"Alas! I have nor hope nor health,
Nor peace within nor calm around—
* * * * * *
I could lie down like a tired child,
And weep away the life of care
Which I have borne, and yet must bear
Till death, like sleep, might steal on me."
                                        SHELLEY.

"How late you have slept, Miss!" said Kitty, as she hurried up in answer to my bell. "I have been expecting you
would ring for the last hour. Did you know, Miss, they are
all at breakfast?"

"It will not take me many minutes," I said, sitting down
for her to braid my hair. Kitty was in a desperate hurry
this morning; her fingers trembled so she could hardly
manage the heavy braids.

"The other young ladies are down some time ago," she
said, with a sharp look at me in the glass. "I suppose if
they were tired, they would get up this morning out of politeness to Mr. Viennet, as he goes away at ten, and he might
think rather hard of it if they didn't take the trouble to
come down in time to say good bye to him."

Encouraged, perhaps, by the color that suffused my face,
she went on: "As for him, he's been up since daybreak,
walking up and down the hall, and on the piazza, and starting and changing color every time a door opened or any
one came on the stairs. I don't believe he wants to go
away very much."

"Kitty, you are getting my hair too low; you're not
thinking of what you are about."

Kitty blushed in her turn, and said nothing more, but

hurried on my toilet. It was soon completed. I would
thankfully have delayed it, but there was no longer anything to wait for, no longer the least excuse, and, to Kitty's
inexpressible relief, I turned to leave the room. Kitty did
not suspect with what a beating heart it was, though, and
with what a blur before my eyes. I hardly saw the familiar
objects in the hall, hardly distinguished a word in the hum
of voices in the breakfast-room, as I paused an instant at
the threshold. But there was no time for wavering now.
I pushed open the door and entered.

There was a momentary hush on my entrance; Phil made
a place for me beside him, saying:

"It is something new for you to be late. Aren't you well?"

"Dissipation doesn't agree with you, I fear," said Mrs
Churchill. "You look quite pale this morning."

"Mamma!" exclaimed Josephine, in a tone mock-con-
fidential, just loud enough for every one to hear. "That
is unkind! Surely, you remember what happens to-day!"

"Come, come, that's not fair," said Phil. "I thought
you were more considerate, Joe. Let your cousin have her
breakfast in peace."

"Don't let me keep everybody waiting," I said, faintly.

"Well, if you'll excuse us," exclaimed Josephine, starting up. "We have all finished." Then with a wicked
look, "Mr. Viennet, you've been through your breakfast
some time. Don't you want to take a farewell promenade
on the piazza?"

Mr. Viennet bowed, and expressed his pleasure in rather
a low voice.

"Mr. Arbuthnot, you're not going to forsake me, are
you?" I asked, as the others rose.

"Of course not," said Phil. "I am always your very
good friend when you'll allow me to be."

Josephine little knew how much I thanked her for her
manœuvre; though done from motives the least amiable, it
was the kindest thing she could have thought of.

"Don't take that strong coffee," said Phil, noticing how my hand trembled, and substituting for it a cup of tea; then putting everything within my reach, he sent the servant away, and began reading the paper himself.

If Phil Arbuthnot should ever prove himself my worst enemy, I never could forget the considerateness of that morning. He was tender-hearted and kind as a woman, and great, strong man as he was, there was a delicacy of feeling and gentleness about him, that suffered with everything weak and suffering, and strove, at all costs, to give aid and comfort. And aid and comfort, prompted by such a heart, could not fail to soothe. In his eyes, women were sacred; their influence over him unbounded. If he only had been thrown with those who could have elevated and purified, instead of narrowing and lowering his nature, how noble and large-hearted a man he might have been. He had sacrificed his profession, his prospects in life, and all that elevates and nerves a man, to his love for Josephine. How far she accepted it, how she meant to requite it, there is no need to say. I think she liked him; I think that she felt for him a tenderness that no one else could ever awaken in her heart. He had been her lover ever since they were girl and boy together, and in those young days, perhaps, she had fancied that the happiest thing in the world, would be to marry Phil. But such sweet romance had been scorched and shrivelled by the first breath of the world. Josephine had renounced such folly early; she was wise and prudent beyond her years, and she had been trained in a good school. Some wondered that Mrs. Churchill could trust her daughter so constantly with a man of as pleasing an address as Phil; cousins were so apt to fancy each other. "I have perfect confidence in Josephine," said Mrs. Churchill, proudly. It was not misplaced; Josephine Churchill might have been trusted with Cupid in person, if he had not been a desirable *parti.*

"What time is it?" I asked of Phil, in a low tone,

after I had exhausted every device for prolonging my breakfast.

"Five minutes to ten," he answered, looking at his watch. "Shall we take a turn on the piazza, if you have finished?"

I followed him to the piazza. "It is too sunny for you," he said, as I screened my aching eyes from the light. "The parlor is pleasanter."

Ella was at the piano, playing some light air (very light, indeed, for the piano was not her forte), and chatting with Capt. McGuffy, who hung over her. Mrs. Churchill, Josephine, Grace, Ellerton, Victor and Mr. Rutledge were at the other end of the room.

"We shall miss you so much, Mr. Viennet," Josephine was saying, in a very charming tone. "Your place cannot be filled. Mr. Rutledge, cannot you manage to have him arrive at the station a few minutes too late?"

"Why didn't you suggest it a little sooner, Miss Josephine?" said Mr. Rutledge, with a smile, as he looked at his watch. "I think I hear the horses at the door now. Thomas will attend to your baggage—don't trouble yourself, Mr. Viennet."

"It is all ready, sir; I have nothing to do but make my adieux, and such painful work had better be short. Mrs. Churchill, I have many pleasures to remember during my residence in America, but none so great as those for which I am indebted to you. Will you accept my sincere thanks?"

I had not dared before to look at him, but I stole a glance at his face now. It was deadly pale, and showed but too plainly the pain and disappointment that he was trying to conceal.

The whole party now gathered round him; his parting with Josephine was very courteous, on her part very gracious; with Grace the same; a little less warm with Miss Wynkar, perhaps; but no one cared to revive old quarrels now

When he approached me, I gave him my hand, but my eyes were fastened on the ground. He held it for one instant, then dropping it, turned hastily away.

" Mr. Rutledge," he said, in a voice that trembled audibly, despite his manly efforts to control it, " I have to thank you for your hospitality. I shall not soon forget my visit here."

Mr. Rutledge's manner had less coldness than usual in it, as he bade his young guest good bye ; there was no lack of warmth in the adieux of the other gentlemen.

And I, cruel and cowardly, stood rooted to the floor ; I was afraid to acknowledge what I had not been afraid to promise ; I was letting him go without a word of kindness, when I might never see him again; when I was, in the sight of heaven, affianced to him, when nothing could absolve me from my vow, shrink and falter as I might. He had reached the hall, and stood for an instant in the doorway as I raised my eyes. They met his ; I sprang forward from the circle where I stood.

" Victor, I am not afraid they should know it now," I whispered, putting my hand in his.

I only knew the misery I had caused him, when I saw the change that came into his face, the light that hope lit in his eyes. He had but short grace to tell his love—a few brief minutes before we parted, perhaps for many years, yet nothing could have made me more certain of the depth and ardor of it, than those few moments did.

We walked once down the hall, then slowly back again,

" You must go now," I whispered, as we reached the door. Good bye !"

For a moment he stood as if it were an effort rending soul and body to leave me ; he held my hands tightly in his own, then, bending forward, pressed a kiss on my forehead, and was gone.

It was the seal of our engagement, that first kiss ; I stood in the sight of what was all the world to me, tacitly acknowledging what I had done. I was parting from the lover to whom they all fancied I was devoted, but it was shame, and not love, that brought the blood into my cheeks to meet his first caress. I did not move or raise my eyes till the sound of carriage-wheels died away down the avenue. Then the treacherous color receded slowly from my face, and left it white as marble. Conquering as best I might the giddy faintness that came over me, I walked steadily into the parlor, where the whispering and amazed group of ladies still stood. Not heeding Josephine's, "Well, my dear, we weren't quite prepared for this! We didn't know how far things had gone," I went up to Mrs. Churchill and said:

"I should have told you of this before, Aunt Edith. I have accepted Mr. Viennet."

"I should have been gratified by your confidence if you had chosen to bestow it. However, you have my congratulations," and she gave me her hand, and touched her lips lightly to my forehead.

"I suppose we must all congratulate you," said Grace, with a laugh. "But, really, it took *me* so entirely by surprise, that I shan't be able to collect my wits for an appropriate speech under two hours."

"I will excuse you from it altogether," I said, turning away to the door. I stopped involuntarily as I passed Josephine.

"If it is a matter of congratulation at all, I hope I have yours, Josephine," I said, holding out my hand.

"Of course," she returned, awkwardly, accepting my hand. "Of course you have."

I looked at her for a moment; it was so strange that I should be so miserable and she so blessed. We, "two daughters of one race"—the same blood flowing in our veins—the same woman's heart beating in our bosoms— why was it that I was forbidden every good, tempted of the devil, driven into evil, and she, unfeeling and light-hearted, smiled down at me from her secure height of happiness, wore carelessly the love that I would have died to win, played thoughtlessly with it in my jealous sight, and made a jest of what was life and death to me.

She did not understand my strange and wistful look, and, with a smothered sigh, I withdrew my gaze, and turned away. Perhaps her mother could have interpreted it better; perhaps, if she had chosen, she could have told her daughter I was not the happy fiancée I seemed; and perhaps, if she had chosen, she could have told her to whom I owed the greater part of what I suffered.

I mounted the stairs with a slow and heavy step; Mr. Rutledge passed me coming down. He did not raise his eyes nor look at me, but in the glance I had of his face it seemed to me darker and moodier than ever, and his step heavier and more decided. He went toward the stables, and in a few minutes I heard his horse's hoofs clattering down the avenue.

If my head had ached twice as madly as it did, I should not have dared to stay away from dinner. As I entered the dining-room, it was with rather a doubtful feeling of relief that I found only ladies there. The presence of the gentlemen always proved something of a restraint upon the vivacious tongue of Grace, and Josephine was never in a good humor when there was no one upon whom to exercise her charms. Indeed, the whole table presented a significant contrast to its usual animation. Toilettes had been deferred till evening, I found. Josephine and Ella took no pains to conceal their ennui, and Grace revelled in impertinence. The gentlemen—*i. e.* Phil, Captain McGuffy, and Ellerton—were shooting woodcock, and Mr. Rutledge had gone off on business, and it was possible, he had left word, that he might not return till late.

. "Let's have a glorious nap," said Josephine, as we left the table. "It will be time enough to dress just before tea-time. They will none of them be back sooner than eight o'clock."

Ella had been asleep all the morning, but she never ob-
jected to a nap; indeed, I believe sleeping was, next to the
pleasure of dressing herself, the principal *divertissement* of
her life. Josephine and Ella went to their rooms, Mrs.
Churchill followed them upstairs, Grace ran off to find "old
Roberts" and get the key of the locked-up bookcases in the
library, and I was left to myself.

It was a hot and sultry afternoon; not a breath moved
the motionless leaves in the park, not a ripple stirred the
lake; the insects hummed drowsily in the hot, hazy air, the
declining sun abated neither heat nor power as he neared
the horizon, but glared steadily upon the still parched earth.
Too languid and miserable to find a cooler place, I sat on
the piazza hour after hour, and watched listlessly the slowly-
declining sun, the inanimate and sultry landscape.

Even nightfall brought no relief. The sun withdrew his
light, it is true; but the sultriness that his reign had bred
continued to brood over the earth; no dew refreshed it, no
moisture wet the thirsty flowers. The stars, faint and dim,
hardly shed a ray of light through the thick air. It was a
night that, superstition and presentiment whispered, would
prompt dark deeds. Under cover of its weird-like gloom,
treachery and murder would steal abroad, and black sins
would stain the souls of some of the sons of men before the
light of day renewed the face of the earth.

None of us could help feeling the influence of it; dispirited and languid, the whole party dragged through the
evening with an unwonted lack of vivacity. Music and
dancing failed; the gentlemen pleaded fatigue, and the
ladies were very ready to accept the excuse, and at an early
hour we separated to our rooms. But I dreaded mine; I
dreaded the sleepless hours that I must count before the
dawning.

Once that night I slept, but it was a short sleep, and
worse than waking. The nightmare of my fate was less
horrible than the nightmare of my fancy, and, shuddering

with terror, I paced the floor to drive away the chance of its recurrence; I pressed my clenched fingers tightly on my breast to drive away the chill of that Phantom Hand, that had frozen my very soul.

Why had that long-forgotten terror come back to haunt me now?

CHAPTER XXX.

It was late on the following morning when I entered the breakfast-room; very fluttering and nervous, I anticipated the usual allusions to my pale looks, and Grace's amiable bantering, but quite a different scene from the one I had expected met me. Too much absorbed to notice my entrance, the whole group were clustered together, intent upon the newly-arrived paper. They had evidently devoured it, and now were commenting eagerly upon the news it contained, and referring constantly to it. Only Mr. Rutledge, with knit brow, leaning forward on the table, seemed to note my entrance.

"I never heard a more cool-blooded, revolting thing," said Phil.

"I suppose the whole country is alive with it now," remarked the captain. "The wretch can hardly escape detection, thanks to the telegraph, railroads, and police of this nineteenth century. The news, no doubt, has spread far and wide by this time."

"It will haunt me till the day of my death!" exclaimed Josephine. "I never read so horrible a murder."

"Oh," said Grace, coolly, "it's only because we knew him that it seems so dreadful. There are just as awful things in the paper every day."

"There has never been anything in this part of the country though, I fancy, that has caused as much excitement," said Phil. "Thomas tells me that the furore in the village is intense; the men do not think of going to their work, but stand in groups about, while most of them have

17

formed themselves into a sort of vigilance committee, and swear that the murderer shall be tracked. The poor doctor, you know, was quite a popular man, and such a thing as this is so unheard of, that the country-people are entirely beside themselves about it."

"What is it you are talking about?" I faltered, leaning on the back of a chair for support, and trying to be self-possessed.

"Oh! Why, have you just come down?" exclaimed Grace, delighted to find a fresh auditor for the awful tale that she seemed really to enjoy relating. "Why, you must know that last night, a man coming from Norbury, late in the evening, discovered the body of Dr. Hugh lying at the entrance of a wood about four miles from the village, stabbed in four or five places, and quite cold. His horse and gig were tied to a tree close by, and the footprints on the ground beside where the body was found, show that the poor wretch did not yield to his murderer without a desperate struggle. His hands were" ——

"You are making it unnecessarily horrible," said Mr. Rutledge, sternly, and starting forward, placed a chair for me, and poured out a glass of water.

"Why, she's going to faint!" exclaimed Ella Wynkar, staring at me with her dull, blue eyes, while Mrs. Churchill came forward ejaculating,

"What is the matter? Are you ill?"

"It is not at all strange that she should be shocked at hearing such a thing so suddenly," answered Mr. Rutledge for me. "You must remember, Miss Grace, we all had it more gradually: first my suspicions, then Thomas' report, then the morning paper; which is very different from hearing it all at a breath, and without any warning."

Mr. Rutledge tried to divert them from the theme, and save me from the faintness which his quick eye detected at each new disclosure or conjecture, but in vain. Nothing else could be thought or spoken of. How the murderer should be hunted down, what blood-thirsty and revengeful men were already on the track, how impossible was his escape; these were the pleasant topics of the morning Within those two hours I learned more self-command than all my previous life had taught me, for I had an awful dread at my heart, and I had to listen to these things, as if I were very indifferent to them.

Phil said, for the honor of the county, he supposed, Mr. Rutledge would do all in his power to ferret the thing out; and Mr. Rutledge rather reluctantly assented, and said he supposed it was his duty.

"And," added the captain, "from what you've said of some slight clue you thought you had to guide you, I suppose you may be of great service, and it's every man's duty to bring the perpetrator of such a deed to justice. By Jove! I wish I could help it along!"

"I suppose you are right," said Mr. Rutledge, with a sigh. "I am going to ride over to the court-house now. Thomas, has my horse been brought around?"

"He is at the door now, sir," said Thomas.

Mr. Rutledge, with a brief good-morning, left the room, and after a moment in the library, repassed the dining-room door with his riding-whip and hat in his hand.

I listened to his retreating footsteps in a kind of nightmare; I must speak to him before he started on his cruel errand; I must speak, and yet a spell sealed my lips, a horrible tyranny chained me motionless. That clue—what did it mean?—why did he look at me so strangely?—I knew but too well. I heard him pass down the hall slowly and pause at the door; in another moment he would be gone. I started from the room.

"Mr. Rutledge!"

He turned as I stood before him, white and trembling.

"What is it?" he said, regarding me with a kind of compassion. "What do you want to say?"

"I want to say—I want to ask you if you have no pity—

if you have the cruelty to want another murder—if there is not blood enough already shed. Don't listen to what those men tell you," I hurried on, "don't believe them, when they say it is your duty. It is not! It is your duty to be merciful. It is your duty to leave vengeance to God. It is your duty to leave the miserable and the sinful to His justice, and not to hurry them before man's !"

He looked down at me with a pity in his eyes that was almost divine. "You need not fear me," he said, turning from me; and descending the steps mounted his horse and rode slowly away.

"There are a few things," I overheard Kitty say to Frances outside my door, " in which I should be glad if my young lady was more like yours. Now there must be some comfort in dressing Miss Josephine, she cares about things ; but all my work is thrown away, sometimes I think. My young lady has no heart for anything, never looks in the glass after I've taken all the pains in the world with her, and is just as likely to throw herself on the bed after her hair is fixed for dinner, as if she had a nightcap on. For the last two days," Kitty went on in a low tone, for Frances and she were very good friends now, "for the last two days she has been so miserable, it makes my heart ache to see her. And as for the masquerade to-night! she don't care *that* for it I've worked my fingers to the bone to get her dress ready, and like as not, she won't stay downstairs ten minutes after she gets it on. The whole house is thinking about nothing else, everybody is in such spirits about it, the young ladies are just crazy with their dresses and the fun they're going to have, while she, poor young thing, hardly knows or cares what she's to wear, and stays moping in her room all day by herself."

"It's a hard thing to have one's young man away," said Frances in her soft voice, and with a little sigh that told she knew just how hard it was. Kitty didn't answer. I was afraid she would, and would tell her how inexplicable she found her mistress's moods. But Kitty was true to me, though she did love a little gossip, and let my *douleur* pass for what she very shrewdly suspected it was not, and soon reverted to the all-absorbing subject of the masquerade.

"Would you ever know the house!" she said, looking admiringly up and down the hall. "And doesn't the piazza look beautiful, and the hall. And just think how all those colored lamps will look when they're lighted. Really, I can't think what's got into master to take all this trouble, and turn the house inside out, to please a lot of young ladies that he doesn't care a straw for!"

Frances opened her eyes as if this were heresy. Kitty went on with energy: "Miss Josephine Churchill needn't flatter herself that she's ever going to be more at home at Rutledge than she is now. I don't know a great deal, but I know enough to know that."

"And I could tell you something perhaps," said Frances, "that might make you change your mind."

"I'd like to hear it!"

"Oh, but it wouldn't be right. I never talk about my young lady's secrets."

"But you might tell *me*," urged Kitty, artfully, "I've been so open with you."

"Come down to the laundry then, while I press out these flounces," and the two maids flitted downstairs to whisper over the secrets that their respective mistresses had fondly fancied were buried in the recesses of their own hearts.

And so each way I turned, there was a new dagger to stab me. No wonder that as Kitty said, I had no heart for anything, and only longed to be away and be at rest. Anxiety was added to the remorse and regret that I had first thought insupportable, and such an anxiety as made my nights sleepless, and my days a misery. No wonder that my white face, and the dark ring around my eyes bore hourly witness to the heaviness of my heart.

"'Why so sad and pale, young sinner?'" called out Grace that evening, as about an hour after tea we were dispersing to our rooms to dress for the all-important occasion. "I think you ought to appear as Mariana, and sing 'I am aweary, aweary;' don't you think so, Mr. Rutledge?"

"Miss Grace, I haven't given the subject enough thought."

"I would give worlds to know what you are going to wear, Mr. Rutledge!" exclaimed Josephine. "But I *know* I shall detect you instantly. I should know your step and carriage under twenty dominoes, and among a thousand people."

"Pretty high figures those, Joseph! Phil, I shall know you by your stride, and you couldn't disguise your voice if you practised a year, and that bow is 'Philip Arbuthnot, His Mark,' all the world over!"

"The best way to disguise our voices," said Capt. McGuffy, "is to speak French. I think we had all better agree to do it."

"Ella will not object," said Grace, "now Mr. Viennet is not here to criticise."

"Hush, Grace!" cried her sister maliciously. "How can you be so thoughtless? Why do you continually harrow up your cousin's feelings. By the way, this is the day the steamer sails, is it not?"

"No, yesterday," said Ellerton. "The list of passengers will be in to-day's papers. Has the mail come yet, Mr. Rutledge?"

"There is Thomas with it now."

Thomas deposited the package on the hall table and withdrew. I was standing nearest of the group to it, and putting out my hand, took up the "Times."

The others approached and with great interest examined the letters. "Why my dear!" said Josephine pleasantly, "I'm astonished that there's none for you! Not a word since he went away. That doesn't look devoted!"

The color went and came in my face, but it wasn't the taunt that I minded.

"Never mind!" cried Grace, "don't break its heart about him! It shall have another lover, it shall have the big Mason, so it shall!"

"May I trouble you for the 'Times' one moment?" asked Ellerton Wynkar, "I want to look over the departures."

"According to my cousin," I said, tightening my grasp upon the paper, "I have the greatest interest in them, and I must beg the privilege of reading the list first."

"That's not fair!" cried Grace. "How do you know but we have lovers sailing in the 'Arago' as well as you? I must have that paper," and, springing forward, she grasped my wrists.

She could have overcome me in a moment, for just then I was as weak as a child; but Mr. Rutledge, in his firm, quiet way, released my hands, and, holding Grace's tightly in his own, said:

"You had better make your escape with it to your room; I cannot insure you if you stay."

With a grateful look and a forced laugh I ran upstairs, locked myself in my room, and, tearing open the paper, glanced hurriedly up and down the columns for the list of the "Arago's" passengers. At last I found it, and skimmed eagerly through it. It was as I expected; I was not disappointed nor shocked; but my hand trembled so I could hardly cut the paragraph out. Ringing for Kitty, I sent the paper down, with my compliments to Mr. Wynkar.

It was nearly nine o'clock before Kitty came back to dress me. I had rung twice, but received no answer. When she did come, I saw in a moment that the delay had been caused by some unusual and exciting cause. She was nervous and uneasy, and started at every sound. Whenever I caught her eye, it dropped quickly before mine, and she hurried on with less than her usual care, the dress on which she had bestowed so much pains and regarded with so much pride

When I was dressed, I looked at myself with some surprise; I was, indeed, effectually disguised. Over my white tarletan ball-dress, I wore a domino of white silk, trimmed with heavy white fringe, and instead of the ordinary hideous black satin mask, a silver gauze before the upper part of my face, and a fall of white lace concealed my features entirely. The heels of my white kid boots were made very high, and that, together with the long sweeping dress, made me appear so much taller than usual, that that one circumstance would of itself have deceived almost any one. I noticed, after I was all dressed, and ready to go down, that Kitty was a long time in adjusting, to her entire satisfaction, the cord and tassel that confined the domino at the waist. Just as I was leaving the room, I chanced to look down, and saw that there was a narrow blue ribbon knotted to one of the tassels.

"What's this, Kitty? Take it off, please."

"That? O, it's nothing, Miss. The tassel was a little loose, and I fastened it up."

"But all the rest of my dress is white—this spoils the effect. You'd better take a piece of white ribbon."

"Oh! Miss" (a little impatiently), "how particular you've grown! I thought you wouldn't mind the bit of blue, and it's *so* late. The carriages have been coming this half hour."

"Well, no matter then. I'll go down."

Kitty preceded me, stealing an occasional look around, to ascertain that there was no one in sight, then beckoned me across the hall, hurried me down the private staircase and through a labyrinth of pantries, to a door that opened upon the shrubbery.

"This way," whispered Kitty. "Follow me."

CHAPTER XXXI.

"O purblind race of miserable men,
How many among us at this very hour
Do forge a life-long trouble for ourselves
By taking true for false, or false for true."
TENNYSON.

I FOLLOWED Kitty down the dark paths of the shrubbery, and, as far as I could tell, through the dazzling gauze of my mask, some distance across the park.

"Where are you taking me? There is no need of such precaution."

"O yes, indeed," she answered eagerly, "if you had gone right around the house and gone in, they would have known in a minute that it was somebody who lived there. Mr. Wynkar and the captain were on the steps, watching. I saw them."

She hurried me on till we reached a clump of trees too far from the lamps suspended to the branches of those on the lawn to be lighted by them; then pausing, she looked quickly around.

"Are you not tired, Miss?" she said, raising her voice. "Hadn't you better rest a minute here? We walked so fast."

"No," I answered, with slight impatience. "I want to go immediately to the house."

"Yes, Miss," she said, uneasily. "Just wait till this carriage passes."

It might have been fancy, but I thought I heard a step behind me, and starting forward, I called Kitty instantly to follow me. She could not but obey, and only left me where the lamps from the piazza threw too strong a light for her

17*   395 to venture. Whispering to me where I should find her if I wanted her during the evening, she slipped away, and I walked on.

The carriage reached the entrance, and the occupants of it alighted and disappeared within the awning before I arrived at it. There were several groups of masked figures on the piazza as I entered the inclosed walk from the carriage-way, and, mounting the steps, approached the door.

"How spectral!" whispered one. "And look at that black shadow following so close."

I turned involuntarily at this; a black domino whom I had not perceived had entered with me, and I hurried forward into the house a little abruptly, to escape his companionship, and, crossing the brilliant and beautifully decorated hall, I entered the drawing-room. There was a temporary lull in the dancing, and I paused a moment to reconnoitre before I advanced to Mrs. Churchill. She was unmasked, and was to receive the guests; she stood at the other end of the room, and it was rather a formidable thing to cross to her, but remembering to disguise my step, I walked slowly and with some stateliness over to where she stood, made my devoirs, and turned away; but half a yard behind me was my black shadow. All eyes were upon us.

"What a ghostly pair!" exclaimed a vivacious peasant girl from the folding-doors. "I shall not be astonished if, when the masks are dropped at supper-time, a skeleton should step out of that black domino, and preside at the feast!"

"And a nymph of Lurley out of that white drapery," said "General Washington," approaching and offering me his arm. We made the tour of the rooms, admired the flowers, discussed the dresses, and tried to find each other out. I soon discovered my companion to be Mr. Emerson of the Grove, a fine, dignified old gentleman, whom I had always admired. His unconscious interest in, and admiration for, a tall brunette, whose black eyes sparkled even through her mask, betrayed her immediately to me as his daughter, Miss Janet Emerson. The Misses Mason were flower-girls of course; their mamma, by virtue of her literary proclivities and immense fund of sentiment, appeared as a sibyl, and told fortunes untiringly; the younger Mr. Mason wore an English hunting-dress, and the elder one escaped my observation among the crowd of greater strangers in the-room. An Oxford student paid me marked attention, but discovering the unmistakable white eyelashes and feeble voice of my pet aversion, Ellerton Wynkar, I became discouragingly distant and severe, and he transferred his devotion to a pretty Greek dress, which I soon concluded must enshrine the indolent loveliness of my cousin Grace.

Beyond this, my penetration was entirely at fault; among the crowd of grotesque and graceful figures, I tried in vain to recognize any of our own party. There were half a dozen men of Phil's height, and as many of Mr. Rutledge's make; so many imitated the captain's military manner, that it was impossible to recognize the stork among the cranes. There were two Louis Quatorze costumes, that more than any others suggested Josephine and Ella, but I could not be positive; they were so exactly alike, that even when together one could not detect a shade of difference either in dress or manner. The powdered hair and masks, of course, concealed the diversity of color and complexion.

"Those two are the most distinguished-looking in the room," said General Washington, by way of small talk. "I suppose you have recognized them—Miss Churchill and her cousin."

"Which cousin?"

"The one who is engaged to the young Frenchman. Quite a pretty girl. I never saw her look so well as she does to-night."

"Which is Mr. Rutledge, do you know?" I asked.

"I have not made him out yet, but if you care to know

the surest way will be to stay here, in the neighborhood of
Miss Churchill : he will not be very far off !"

" Then let us sit here," and I sank down on a sofa.

" Your cavalier keeps a faithful watch upon your movements," said my companion.   " He has followed you from
room to room, and is just behind you now."

" Who is it that you mean ?"

" The black domino—the gentleman who came with
you."   .

And the black domino at that moment bent down, and,
in a low, smothered voice, asked me if I would dance.   I
declined very quickly, and turned away my head.

" Miss Churchill, will you dance this set with me ?" asked
a gentleman, in French, approaching me.

Disguised as the voice was, there was something familiar
in it.   I gave him my hand, and we took our places at the
head of the room.   It very soon became evident that he
had mistaken me for Miss Churchill, and I determined to
keep up the character.   It was not very difficult ; we were
exactly the same size, and I had always been a good mimic,
so that, in five minutes, I was coquetting, twisting my fan,
and taking off Josephine to the life.   It was not so easy to
find out who I was quizzing.   He was evidently a master
of the art of deception, disguised his voice, his step, his
manner, and was never off his guard an instant.   He did
not answer to anybody's description exactly, though I was
constantly convinced, by his familiarity with us all, that he
was " one of us."   I tried to bait him with allusions to all
our acquaintance, but he was too wary to rise to any of
them.

" How did you find me out so easily ?" I said, with a
laugh so like Josephine's that I was absolutely startled myself.   " I thought I was disguised beyond all detection."

" Not from me."

" Ah, you are so clever !" I said, putting my head on one
side, with an affectation characteristic of Josephine.   " Now

help me to discover some of the others. Who is our vis-à-
vis in the Spanish dress?"

" *You* should not have to ask."

" *Mais qui?*"

" Mr. Arbuthnot, *sans doute.*"

" Ah! my heart should have told me Phil! Which is the
captain ?"

" ' Ivanhoe,' there by the door, talking with the 'Father
of his Country.' "

" And oh! tell me, for I am dying to know, have you
found out my cousin ?"

" I do not think she is in the room."

' Impossible! Then she must be ill."

" Indifferent, more probably."

" Ah! perhaps. ' There is but one with whom she has
heart to be gay !' But has nobody been up to see what has
become of her ?"

" No one, I fancy."

" Had I better go ?"

" That's as you please," with a slight shrug.

" Well, I'll see, after this dance. Who is that black
domino, pray ?"

" That is more than I can tell you. He is the only man
in the room whom I have not detected. He has not danced,
nor spoken to any one, I think. I shall watch him closely
and be near him when he unmasks."

" Yes but that's rather uncertain. He may leave the
room before then.'

" That's very possible. He seems to be hovering near
us. Suppose, after this dance, you draw him into conversation, and try to make him out? He seems to avoid me,
and I am really very curious to know him."

" Very well, to gratify you, I will try to detect him;
but my cousin—will you take that duty off my hands ?"

" Yes, I will send a servant to inquire, and report the result to you."

" 'Thank you. How *kind* you always are! I should know that goodness of heart under twenty dominoes, and among a thousand people!"

My companion, bowing low, gave me a quick look from under the cowl of his monk's habit.

" You are too flattering," he said, and the dance ended.

The black domino was at my elbow, and nodding significantly to my partner, I turned abruptly to him, and said, still in imitation of Josephine's voice:

" Will you give me your arm? My partner has another engagement."

He bowed, and offered me his arm. His voice, when he spoke, was so low, and so studiously disguised, it was impossible to detect anything from that; his coarse black domino hung so long and amply about him, and the hood was drawn so tightly around his mask, that no one could possibly distinguish anything of his face, figure, or carriage. Before we had made the tour of the rooms, I began to repent my bargain. There was something in his manner that made me most uncomfortable. I determined not to give up my assumed vivacity, but it was like chatting with a ghost; and when I went with him into the punch-room, and raised a glass to my lips, bowing to him over it, it seemed like a " hob-and-nob with Death," and the laugh I laughed was a very faint and forced one, as we set our half-tasted glasses down. I was so uncomfortable at being alone with him, that I stammered hurriedly:

" Shan't we go back to the dancing-room?"

" Are you afraid of me?" he said quickly, and in a low tone, " can you not give me a moment from your pleasure?"

" Sir!" I said, shrinking back; " I haven't the least idea who you are."

" You can forget, it seems. I envy you the power!"

" You talk in riddles," I said, going toward the door. Another party entered the room, and my companion followed me out.

"What a grotesque scene!" I said, looking up and down the wide hall, where wreaths of flowers and lights and floating flags hung, and thronging across whose marble pavement were groups of fantastic figures. "I never was at a masquerade before. Is it not diverting?"

"Will you come upon the piazza?" asked my companion, not heeding my remark. "It is too warm here."

"No," I exclaimed, hurriedly, "I cannot, here is my partner."

The "friar of orders grey" obeyed my hasty summons, and I accepted his arm with very great *empressement*, stammering some excuse to the sable domino in the doorway, and walked down the hall.

"Well, have you discovered him?"

"No, I do not know him at all, he is very odd. I think he is a stranger. Not anybody, at all events, that any of us know well."

"I cannot understand it," he said, musingly. "I thought you would have been able to have obtained some clue. He seemed willing to talk to you."

"Only too willing!"

"Did he seem to recognize you?"

"I cannot tell exactly; he certainly thought he knew, but whether it were not a mistake on his part, I cannot say."

"He avoids me; I cannot make anything of him; I shall have to put some one else on the track."

"What of my cousin?" I asked.

"I found Kitty, who says she is not very well, but will probably be in the room a little before supper."

"Ah, thank you. You have no idea, I suppose, what her dress is to be?"

"Kitty gave me to understand, very quietly, that she would wear a rose-colored domino."

"There is a rose-colored domino just entering; do you imagine that is the fair *fiancée?*"

"Very possibly," said my companion.

"She is going to dance. Is that Phil with her?"

Phil at this moment asked my partner to be his vis ì-vis, so we were again drawn into the dance. By this time, half the people in the room thought I was Miss Churchill, and addressed me accordingly. In one of the pauses of the quadrille, as some one calling me by that name had turned away, the black domino, who stood a little behind me on my left, leaned forward and whispered:

"You cannot deceive *me;* it was not Miss Churchill who was to have a blue ribbon on her tassel."

I started; what intrigue was that Kitty about?

The dance was over; Phil and his partner left the room and turned toward the piazza.

"Shall we go into the fresh air?" said my companion, following them with his eyes. I took his arm, and we went on the piazza. The soft light of the colored lamps, the mellow music floating out to us, the cool air in our faces—I met with a gasp of relief and pleasure. Leading me to a seat rather more secluded than the others, my companion threw himself on the sofa beside me, and exclaimed, removing his mask:

"This is so unsupportably warm, I must take it off for a moment's relief, as I believe you know me. Well! Miss Josephine, how do you think our masquerade has succeeded? Are you satisfied with the result?"

"Perfectly," I said, feeling very guilty, and leaning back further into the shade. "It has been a delightful affair."

He rested his brow thoughtfully and sadly on his hand for a moment. "You are tired," I said.

"Miserably tired."

It was well for me he did not require me to talk; I should have betrayed myself if I had attempted it. His eyes were riveted on the pair who stood a few yards from us. Phil, bending down, was whispering in low tones to his companion in the pink domino. There was something in her attitude, as she listened with half-bent head, that I could not fail to recognize, and from below the edge of her domino, I caught a glimpse of yellow brocade. There was but one to whom Phil could talk in those earnest tones—but one to whom he could tell that tale. Josephine, I saw, must have gone upstairs, and put on the domino over her first dress, the more to puzzle some of her partners. Kitty had in some way become acquainted with her intention, and seized upon it to further the deception that she saw prevailed in regard to me. There was very little that escaped that clever jade. I wished, with a sigh, that she were less unscrupulous. In a few moments, the cousins passed where we sat, nearly concealed from them, walking slowly and talking earnestly.

"You cannot ask me to endure it longer; this suspense is misery," he said, with a quiver in his manly voice.

"Dear Phil," murmured the clear, low tones of his companion, "you must know my feelings toward you; I have never tried to hide them; but you know how it is—you know it would be madness for either of us to think of each other."

"Why would it be madness?" he urged. "Oh, Josephine! Why cannot you give up the ambition that separates us? Depend upon it, it has stood in the way of your happiness all your life."

It had been impossible to avoid hearing this conversation; my companion, starting up, looked after the retreating figures amazed and stern. In his haste, he had pulled down an American flag that had been draped over the sofa we occupied. I started up, and involuntarily raised my hand to replace it. The loose sleeve fell back from my arm, and in the strong light of the lamp overhead, the scar on my wrist caught his eye. With a quick, imperious movement, he seized my hand before I could withdraw it, and held it firmly in one of his, while with the other he raised my mask.

"You have deceived me," he said, between his teeth.

"You have deceived yourself, you are the victim of your own prejudices. You cannot say I did more than humor your decision!" I returned, quickly.

"You only acted a womanly and natural part, lied sweetly in every glance of your bright eyes, in every turn of your graceful figure, in every word on your red lips! I don't blame you; you are a woman."

"You are too cruel! you will repent this some day; it will be the bitterest thing you have to remember; the recollection of it will make you suffer as you have made me suffer."

"Never fear but I shall have enough to suffer, if the present is any earnest of the future for me! Your kindest wishes will be more than realized. For a proud man," he said, with a low, bitter laugh, flinging from him the hand he held, "for a proud man, I have had some humiliations that you would hardly believe if I told you! You could hardly understand them in your simplicity; your soft, woman's heart would bleed, perhaps, but it would heal itself too soon to allay in any great degree my wretchedness. Your morning-glory tenderness would droop before the fierceness of my pain, it would die in my hot grasp!—I will not ask your pity, but spare me your detestation. Save the aversion that your eyes showed then, for those who have deserved it better at you hands."

There was a sound of voices from within, a window near us was thrown open, and a group of people, laughing and talking, stepped out on the piazza. Hastily restoring my mask to its place, I turned away and entered the house through the window they had opened.

"You may have deceived one who is indifferent to you; you cannot deceive one who loves you," said a low voice in my ear, and the black figure I instinctively dreaded stood beside me. "For the sake of heaven, come with me, one moment!"

"Who are you?" I murmured, shrinking back.

He bent down and whispered a name in my ear, at which the color left my cheek, the light my eye, almost the life my pulses.

"Will you come?"

I bent my head without a word, and followed him out of the hall, down the terrace, through the winding paths of the shrubbery, across the garden; hurrying on to suit his fierce pace, but chilled to the heart with a terror that was no longer nameless.

CHAPTER XXXII

"O man! while in thy early years,
How prodigal of time!
Misspending all thy precious hours,
Thy glorious, youthful prime!
Alternate follies take the sway;
Licentious passions burn;
Which tenfold force give Nature's law,
That man was made to mourn."

BURNS.

THE spot to which my companion led me was a ruined summerhouse, not a stone's throw from the outer garden hedge. It was a lonely place in a sort of hollow, a low, dense orchard stretched dark on one side, while a little knoll, crowned with copse, rose between it and all view of the house and grounds on the other, and a little stream fell murmuring down from rock to rock through the ravine. Why it was so deserted and dilapidated, I had never exactly known; but from something Stephen had said, when I had questioned him about it, I had conjectured that it was associated with the shame and fall of her whose memory was even yet so painful, and that ruin and decay were welcome to hide the place from all eyes.

The night wind was moaning wildly down the little hollow; the ghastly moonlight flickered fitfully through the broken roof and moldering arches; the moss-grown, slimy stones rocked beneath my tread; steadying myself by one of the posts of the ruined doorway, I stood still and waited for my companion to speak. He had sunk down on a seat, but in a moment, raising his head, he loosed the hood of his domino, and, as it fell back, rose and turned his face toward me. With a faint cry, I put out my hands and

404

started back. In the haggard, bloodless face, the wild and troubled eye of the man before me, I could hardly recognize a feature of Victor Viennet's handsome face.

. "No need to start away and put out your white hands to keep me off," he said, with a laugh that made my blood run cold. "No need to press your pale lips together to keep back that cry of horror! I have risked my life—aye —sold it, rather—for this interview, and yet I would not lay my guilty grasp upon the hand you have promised to me, I would not touch the distantest fold of your white dress! There is no need to droop, and flutter, and clasp your hands, and pray me to be calm—don't turn your eyes on me with such a look as that! You try to say you love me yet ; wait till I tell you, wait till you know all, before you say you love me!"

"You need not tell me, Victor," I faltered, "I guessed it from the first."

"You guessed it from the first, and yet dared come here —alone—at midnight—with me ! No, you have not guessed it. Your girl's heart never framed the outline of such a sin, you will swoon but to hear its name !"

The night wind howling through the shivering trees, the restless brook moaning down the hollow, if ever their wild lament had ceased, would have heard, brokenly and incoherently, such a story as this :

In a quaint, secluded village, in some remote province of France, Victor Viennet's early childhood had been passed. It was a childhood so companionless that, but that he was happy and needed nothing save his sad mother's love and his wild freedom, one would have pitied him even then, before he knew the shame he had to bear and the sufferings it would bring. For months together no stranger's foot would cross the threshold of the lonely cottage ; the neighbors looked askance at the two pale women and the pretty boy, who had come so strangely and so stealthily into their midst, and rumor had been busy even there. The village children were forbid to play with "le petit Anglais;" they taunted and mocked him, and he, in his turn, spurned and hated them, and clung more entirely to his mother, who strove to interfere between him and every insult, every• harshness, and vexation. And but too well she succeeded in guarding him; when death came to unloose her arms from around him, he was left too sensitive and shrinking a piant to bear the first breath of the scorching simoon of scorn and ignominy that had been gathering up its strength so long. The fatal secret of his birth, that explained all, burst suddenly upon him while his childish heart was yet bleeding with his first grief. He learned that he must thank his dead mother for the brand of shame that he must bear through life; that for her, whom he had worshipped as an angel, there was on every lip a name of scorn. He learned that every man's hand was against him, as an outcast and a bastard; and all the strength of his nature became a strength of hatred; his southern blood turned to gall in his young veins. The home that had been his sanctuary, his city of refuge, was a desecrated and hateful place. The same fever that had struck down his mother, had laid her nurse and companion low. Tenderness and compassion had been blasted in the boy's heart; they had both deceived and wronged him; he owed nothing to the memory of the one, nor to the misery of the other; and without a look, he left her in her unconsciousness, and turned his back forever on his home, with the curse in his heart for which he had not yet learned the words.

Who needs be told the career on which the boy entered? Who but would sicken and turn away from the record of his houseless wanderings, his desperate shifts, his recklessness and wickedness. Who that could read with anything but sorrow of the scenes of squalid want, of cunning vice, of mad profligacy, through which he passed before his youth was yet begun. There could be but one result; all that was weak in him was bent to the service of sin, all that was

noble was turned to bitterness; the refinement of his nature
made him rise, but it was to no heights of truth and virtue;
ambition had taken the place of all noble aspirations, and
sustained him through ignominy, and reproach, and poverty,
helped him to trample on difficulties that would have daunted a less desperate man, and scruples that would have shak-
en a better one, aided him to free himself from the pollu-
tions that his wild boyhood had contracted, and to shake
off the trammels of the past, and crown himself with the
success that he had made his god. But through it all, there
lived a fear lest the forgotten stain of his birth should be
revived, the foundation stone be pulled from his fair fabric
of good fortune; and this morbid dread so haunted him,
that he came to hate the very sunshine and soft air of
France, to fear the very children in the streets, the strangers whose curious eyes he met in the thoroughfares of business. And with all the fearful and enslaved of the earth,
he turned his eyes toward the fair land that promises abso-
lution and new life to the sinful and miserable of other lands,
and denies its rich benison of hope and freedom neither to
the criminal who flies from justice, nor the miserable who
flies from memory. With three thousand miles of ocean
between him and France, perhaps he could shake off the
slavish dread that gnawed forever at his peace, and rise to
a position where he need not fear its sting. The untainted
air of that new land had never heard the whisper of his
shame, should never hear it; even in his own bosom, it
should die forgotten and unfeared.

But than his strong will, there had been a stronger. Within the first week of his arrival in America, he was seized
with a malignant fever, and from delirium and raving, sunk
to stupor and an almost death-like torpor, and for weeks
lay so. When at last he rallied and shook off the lethargy
that had so long dulled intelligence and feeling, it was to
find, that in the first hours of his delirium, he had betrayed
his secret and undone himself; and betrayed it to a man

whom neither honor nor pity could bind, but whose cunning
malice gloated over the power his discovery had invested
him with, and who would use it maliciously and unscrupu-
lously. It did no good to rave and curse his fate; all the
power of his strong will must go to the repairing of the error,
and to the hushing and pacifying this low man who held
him at such advantage. It seemed an easy enough thing at
first; the man was ready to promise silence and assure him
of his good will, and seemed to require nothing in return
but good fellowship and confidence. Anything would have
been easier for Victor to have given; his proud spirit re-
volted at such companionship and bondage, but at the first
sign of contempt or impatience, the glistening serpent
showed his sting, and chafed and despairing, the victim felt
the toils tighten around him. There was no escape from
his familiarity; he haunted and exasperated him, dogged
his steps, followed him into the company of men who could
not but wonder at the intimacy and draw their own conclu-
sions from his endurance of such a man.

With the exception of this cruel drawback, the new land
indeed proved an Eldorado to Victor. Friends thickened,
fortune smiled; he rose with hasty steps to success, social
and commercial. Only the sly gleam of Dr. Hugh's treacherous eye sent an occasional fear through the pride of his
heart, and kept it in a sort of check. But it did not humble him, it only galled and goaded him, and quickened his
determination to prove himself a man for a' that; it strengthened his haughtiness and self-reliance. In the course of a
year or two, however, circumstances somewhat changed;
Dr. Hugh left the city, and Victor breathed freer. Occasional letters still reached him, keeping him in mind, but
they ceased after awhile, and the young adventurer began
to feel secure; he was on the road to fortune, the only barrier to success was gone, and the happiness he had never
dared enjoy before, seemed just within his grasp. And just
then, just when the new hopes of love, and the nearly

crowned ambition, most demanded the hiding of the hated secret, chance threw him upon the only man who held it. No wonder that his cheek had blanched the evening that he came to Rutledge, when he found the doctor there before him. The doctor had not forgotten, the doctor had not lost sight of him, though he had lost sight of the doctor, and soon his stealthy hand was on the festering wound again, nd his old cunning at work to exasperate his victim, and with a new zest.

That Victor had been a successful man of business he had not minded; it only made his power over him the more desirable, and the remuneration for his silence greater; but that Victor should be the successful lover of one whom he had reason to regard with resentment and aversion, was too severe a trial for his love of malice to endure. Here was an opportunity for humbling the girl who had treated him with scorn and ridicule, and the proud man who endured him with but half concealed impatience. Victor Viennet should give up the woman he loved, and only buy a promise of continued silence at a heavy price. The girl should lose her lover ; in any case he promised himself that. If Victor refused to give her up, a whisper in his ear of what he knew of *her* secret, would damp his ardor and bring pride to weigh down the balance as he wished. And her pride, if even Victor's infatuation led him to prefer exposure and disgrace to separation, would never suffer her to marry a man, who, from the first she had never loved, now stripped of his name and honor. In any event that was secure to him. But he had overreached his aim when he drove Victor to resolve on such a sudden departure. Once in Europe, he might lose track of him; his vigilance at such a distance might be eluded, and all but his revenge would be lost; and chance had thrown into his hand the threads of a mystery that only time could unravel, that promised power over more than him ; but Victor's absence would ruin all.

Late on the night before his intended departure from
18

Rutledge, a note was handed to him from Dr. Hugh, de-
manding another interview before he sailed. Victor dared
not neglect or refuse the demand. It was too late now to
change his plans, and of all things he desired to conceal the
fact of his having any private business with Dr. Hugh, from
his host and the guests at Rutledge. Gnashing his teeth
at the humiliation of feeling himself at the beck and call of
this low villain, and cursing the fate that forced him to
stoop to such stratagems, he hastily returned a few lines to
the doctor, appointing to meet him the following day at
noon, at Brandon, the next station to Rutledge, distant
about twelve miles, intending to send his baggage on in the
train in which he should start, and remaining an hour at
Brandon with the doctor, should go on himself in the next
train. By this, he would avoid suspicion and meet the persecutor on neutral ground. He found no difficulty in leaving the cars unobserved, and repairing to the inn he had
appointed for rendezvous.

The bar-room was crowded with passengers for the cars
going west, so, an unnoticed guest, he awaited with growing impatience the keeping of his appointment. Half sus-
pecting that the man's object was to keep him back, and
make him lose the train, his impatience and vexation knew
no bounds, as the hour slowly waned and no one appeared.
The train came rushing through the town, paused a moment, and rushed on, and his last chance for that day had
passed. For one moment he had resolved to defy his persecutor, and escape him once and forever; but he knew
that before another sunset his secret would be published,
and what was this vexation to that ruin? As the crowd
hurried from the tavern to the cars, a horseman had
alighted at the door, and Victor shrunk back with a guilty
feeling of humiliation and fear as he recognized Mr. Rutledge. What a degrading bondage was this for a man of
honor—what a damnable humiliation! To be skulking
away from the man whom, a few hours ago, he had met as

his host and his equal. To be waiting submissively the
pleasure of a low villain, whose greedy cunning and mean
rascality marked him below the revenge of a gentleman.

"It shall end," muttered Victor, between his teeth, as he
screened himself from the sight of the new comer, who had
entered the bar-room. He was engaged for several minutes
in conversation with the bar-keeper, left a message for a
neighboring workman, paid a bill for the cartage of some
timber, and was about leaving the room, when his eye fell
upon a note that was lying on a table near the door; and
Victor's dark cheek mantled with shame and vexation, as,
taking it up, Mr. Rutledge read, in a tone of surprise:

"Mr. Victor Viennet. To be left at the Brandon
Shades."

"When was this brought here?" he inquired of the man
behind the bar.

"This morning, sir, I think," he returned. "A man from
your village came with it—a dark, thick-set fellow, if I'm
not mistaken; one of the hands from the factory."

"And no one has called for it—no one answering to that
name has been here?"

"Not to my knowledge, sir."

Mr. Rutledge knit his brow, and paced the floor uneasily.
The haughty curl of his lip, as he glanced again at the note,
made the blood boil in Victor's veins. It was almost impossible to keep back the defiant words that rushed to his
lips; but detection would be fatal now, and he remained
motionless, while Mr. Rutledge, crossing over to the bar-
keeper, said, in a lower tone:

"You will oblige me by noticing who comes for that
note, and by what way he returns. I will stop here on my
return from Renwick, before night."

The man promised obsequiously, and Mr. Rutledge left
the room. Victor only waited to hear his horse's hoofs die
away down the street, and to see the bar-keeper's attention
fully engaged with a group of jovial mechanics just entering

for their noon-day drink, to leave his place of concealment, and possessing himself hastily of the note, opened it carefully, and abstracting the contents, substituted a business circular which he had in his pocket, sealed up the envelope again, threw it on the table, and left the room by a side-door.

He had walked some distance down the street before he ventured to read the letter, which proved, of course, to be from Dr. Hugh, apologizing for the delay, but saying that it would be impossible for him to be at Brandon before four o'clock. At that hour he should hope to find Mr. Viennet at the Shades, as first named, etc.

"The Shades" was the last place where he desired to see him now, so he determined to walk forward on the road to Rutledge, and meet him on the way. It was a hot and dusty road, upon which the afternoon sun shone down un-. mercifully, but the heat and the dust were unheeded and indifferent to the over-wrought and exasperated traveller. The exercise and the fatigue of walking were in some measure a relief to his strained nerves, and without stopping to reflect, he hurried fiercely on, till eight miles of the twelve had been accomplished. Something familiar in the road had drawn his attention to his locality, and warned him of his nearness to Rutledge. It had been so lonely and monotonous a road before that, his attention had not been attracted to it; he had passed the last farmhouse three or four miles back, and only paused now, struck by the familiarity of the Hemlock Hollow road, leading off at the left. It was now only four miles to the village, and he stopped, resolved to await Dr. Hugh here.

It was no balm to his vexed and angry mood, to remember how near he was to what was at once dearest and most unattainable to him. It was no soother to his wounded pride, to feel that he was skulking like a thief around the place where for weeks he had been entertained as a guest; and as hour after hour dragged on, and no one approached down the lonely road, his impatience grew into a kind of frenzy, and before the glaring sun had sunk behind the woods, and the thick, dull twilight had crept slowly over the gloomy hollow, from an angry and exasperated, he had become a revengeful and desperate man.

It was in this mood that his persecutor met him. It was when all the venomous rancor that a long subjection had bred in his haughty nature, was roused to its utmost, that the interview for which Dr. Hugh had schemed, and planned, and lied, took place. Cold and cunning, plausible and imperturbable, he met a man with whose keenest feelings he had been playing for years, and who was even then lacerated to madness by insults and indignities that would have roused a tamer nature. Some fiend was blinding his eyes surely, and lulling him into security, that he did not feel a warning throb of fear as he rode into the lonely hollow, and through the dusky twilight discerned the waiting form of him he had wronged so deeply. Some luring devil put into his mouth the cold and sneering words with which he greeted him—the fool-hardy and contemptuous bravado with which he taunted him. Beyond any length he had ever gone before, he now dared, claiming his power over him, defying him to disdain it, and threatening him with instant exposure if he dared leave America.

And when Victor, driven to desperation, and quivering with passion, turned fiercely upon him and defied him to do it—from this hour he cared not whether it was known or not, the cunning fiend in the wretch's bosom prompted him to ask if he had grown tired of his pretty mistress so soon, that he gave her up so easily? Or did he flatter himself that the haughty girl, at whose feet he had been so long, would continue her hardly-won smiles when she knew him for a nameless, low-born adventurer, hiding the stain of his birth at the cost of his honor?

" You may tell it! You may proclaim it the length and breadth of the land! Who will believe you, low villain and known knave as you are, against the word and credit of a gentleman? Who will believe your paltry version of the delirium of a fever, that none but you heard—none but you interpreted? They will ask you for proofs—what then?"

"I will give them proofs. I will tell them more than you know yourself of the story of your birth, and prove it by more damning proofs than you have dreamed existed. You doubt me? You defy and mock the threat? Listen! At this moment I hold that about me that would prove the tale I tell to be as true as heaven, and would send you branded to lower depths of shame than you have ever known. I hold it but till you shall dare to thwart me, till you shall dare to to set a foot on foreign shores, and then the world—the woman that you love—the friends you trust —your gloating enemies—shall have the story, and shall see its proof!"

The words hissed through the dead, dull, twilight of the still night, and smote like livid fire on the brain of him who heard them—on his overwrought and maddened brain—and shot through every pulse, and tingled like wild-fire in his veins. The whispers of hell crept into his tempted soul; there was no light in the heavens above—there was none on the dark earth; the still night had no voice to breathe the things that should be done; hell had no torments worse than these, and these he might be free from with one blow! one cunning, short, sharp blow—one quick, well-aimed, unerring blow! It would revenge him—free him—restore him to peace—give him back his love.

If there is joy in heaven over one sinner that repents, what must there be of demoniac triumph in the vaults of hell, when another yields to sin—a fresh soul is lost! What mad exultation and unholy joy must have echoed in the regions of the damned, as the last cry of the murdered man died away among the whispering tree-tops and gloomy depths of Hemlock Hollow! and Victor Viennet pressed his blood-stained hand before his eyes to blot out the image that now neither time, nor sleep, nor anything save death could efface from his guilty vision.

A horror, of such fear as none but murderers know, fell upon him as he bent over that ghastly corpse, hardly still from the death-struggle yet—hardly cold in the life-blood that his hand had spilled. He had not feared his foe in life with such palpitating fear as now, when, with eager, trembling hands, he searched, unresisted, for the fatal proof that he had threatened him with. That found, he no longer strove to resist the impulse of flight, and through the blackness and stillness of that night, chased by such terror and such remorse as God suffers the dead to avenge themselves with, he fled from the sight of the dead and the justice of the living.

But the morning found him a baffled and a desperate man. The news had spread far and wide, the country was alive with it. A large reward had been offered for the apprehension of the murderer, and no boor within miles around but tried his best to earn it, and sharpened up his sluggish wits, and stood his watch, and scoured the woods, with incredible activity. It soon became apparent, though, to the wretched fugitive, that there was one on his track who brought more knowledge of the facts to the chase than his compeers, or, indeed, than he chose to own. One there was, who night and day dogged and hunted him with unflagging energy and terrible certainty, and from whom he knew he had no chance of escape if once he left the woods and high lands and took to the open country. There was only one hope, that of eluding and wearing him out, and back he plunged into the woods again, and night and day fought desperately against his fate. He had seen his pursuer pass almost within pistol-shot of him, and had recognized in him one who added the spur of malice to the sordid love of gold that animated the others. It was the dread of losing his game, and putting others on the track, that kept him from divulging what he knew, which was enough to fasten the murder upon the man to meet whom, to his knowledge, the doctor had started on the evening of his murder. And much more he might have told, of concerted plans to dog and waylay the young stranger, and to keep him in their power—of malicious watching, and intriguing, and vindictive hatred and cunning, and cruel purposes. But this he kept in his own vile breast, and, inspired by thirst for blood and love of gold, he pursued with deadly vigilance. the murderer of the man whose tool and accomplice he had been.

The third night of this unequal warfare was waning; the fugitive, worn out and hopeless, had resolved to end it; he had lost all privilege to hope, all right to love, and without these what was life worth?

The breaking dawn showed him that he was in the pine-grove that bordered Rutledge lake. He felt no fear at the danger of his nearness to detection; he had done with fear now; what malice his enemies had to wreak must bo wreaked on his dead body; and God have pity on the only one of all the world who would suffer pain or shame from his disgrace!

Parting the thick branches, he made his way down to the water's-edge. In the dim light of dawn, the lake spread calm and unruffled before him, but what was this that lay so dark and motionless among the reeds and lily-pads, not a stone's throw from the shore? Dark and motionless as the haunting memory of that corpse in the black Hollow; nothing but flesh and blood ever showed so dumb and horrible through the grey light—nothing but death ever lay so still as that. It was the stark and lifeless form of his enemy that he looked upon, and dying hope started up and whispered of reprieve; all might not be over yet, and suicide and temptation drew back chagrined. It looked almost like a mercy from the Heaven he had outraged that the only tongue that could have betrayed him had been stilled in death, and that not by his hand, and a dumb feeling of gratitude warmed his heart and melted him into something like repentance toward the Father and the Heaven he had sinned against.

Now flight was clear and almost easy; once safely beyond the neighborhood of Rutledge, there would be nothing to prevent his escaping to Canada; no suspicion as yet had been attached to his name, and no one need know that he had not fulfilled his intention of sailing at the time he had mentioned, till he was safely embarked from Halifax.

But then love stepped in, and pleaded for one last look— one last embrace—before the life-long separation that his crime had doomed him to; what could one day more or less endanger him? And Fate, baffled of his ruin at one hand, now lured him into this worse snare, and he yielded. Hiding himself through the day in the dense thicket that covered the opposite bank of the lake, he had ventured forth at twilight, and by bold manœuvre and sharpened cunning, had obtained an interview with Kitty. Not one girl in a thousand would have been capable of what he required of her—not one in a thousand would have been willing or trustworthy; but Kitty was as true as steel; her keen wits were equal to the task, and though she only guessed the truth, the rack and torture could not have won it from her. Before she dressed me for the evening, she had dressed Victor in the coarse domino that she had made since twilight for him, out of the black stuff that had lain so many years in the trunk upstairs, forgotten and unused since the last time that the household was in mourning. She had brought about the meeting and recognition between us, and now watched anxiously for us, no doubt, somewhere in the shrubbery.

We were both but too unconscious of the flight of the moments now so precious, when Kitty, with hurried hand, pushed aside the branches of the thicket, and sprang down the ravine.

"Fly, fly for your life, Mr. Victor! You are lost, if you

stop for a moment! The officers are at the house; they
say a suspicious person has been seen hanging about the
grounds, and master has given them permission to search
the outhouses and the premises, and they say the police are
swarming all around. My dear young lady, let him go!
Oh, that I should see you in such trouble!"

"But where shall I go!" murmured Victor, burying his
face in his hands. "I see no safety anywhere; the blood-
hounds are on my track. It would have been easy to die
this morning! Why did I shrink from it then?"

"Kitty!" I gasped, "can you think of no place—no-
where that we can hide him?"

"None! They will search the barn and stables. There's
not an inch of ground about the place they'll spare."

"And the house; have they a warrant for that?"

"They have searched the house, they had gone nearly
through it before I knew anything about it; I was watching for you outside."

"Then, Kitty, the house is the safest place, if they are
out of it; and, if we could only get him there, there is *one
room* where he would be safe!"

Kitty started with a keen look as she caught my meaning.

"Heaven help us! If we only could—I can think of
one way—if you wouldn't be afraid "——

"No, no, I wouldn't be afraid of anything," I said, laying my hand in Victor's. "Speak quick."

"Mr. Victor must give me his domino, and you and I
must watch our chance and go boldly in at the front door;
there's no other way, there are people all over the hall and
piazza, and plenty saw you go out together, and will notice
if you come back alone; there has been a great deal of suspicion about the black domino, and master, I know, is on
the look-out for him, and very likely will try to find out;
and no harm's done, you know, if I'm found in it; and then
soon as I'm in the house I'll slip upstairs, and throw down
the pink domino that Miss Josephine has taken off by this

time, and Mr. Victor will wait for it at the west corner of house, where it is more retired than anywhere else; he'll put it on where it's dark there, in the shade of the trees, and join you on the piazza, where you'll wait for him, and then try to get him upstairs while they're at supper. I'll have the keys ready and get everybody out of the way. It's the only thing we can do—there's not a minute to lose!"

It was desperate enough, but I saw no other way. Whispering a courage and confidence I did not feel to Victor, I hurried off his domino, and Kitty threw it over her dress. There was no time for fear; I did not stop to think, or I should not have shaken off Victor's grasp so hastily as I did, when we reached the shrubbery, nor have parted with so hurried an adieu, only imploring him to be calm and cautious, and not to lose a minute in gaining the west corner of the house.

"Alas!" murmured Kitty, as we hurried up the steps, "there's a hundred chances to one we don't see him again! It'll be just God's mercy and nothing else, if he gets into the house. There goes the constable now, and the men "——

"Which way?" I gasped.

"Down toward the garden. Heaven help him! If he only sees them in time! Take my arm, Miss, and come in; we can't stop now to see whether they meet him; they're watching us on the piazza."

I needed all the support of Kitty's arm as I entered the hall; the glare of the lights made me sick and faint, and she hurried me to a chair.

"Don't wait a minute to attend to me," I murmured, "hurry upstairs."

"It won't do yet; everybody is looking at us; I must sit down and talk to you awhile."

A gentleman, Mr. Mason, approached me, and began to rally me upon keeping up my incognito so long, the rest of the maskers, he said, had consented to reveal themselves.

"Say you won't unmask till supper," whispered Kitty.

I mechanically repeated the words. Others came up to talk to me, there was evidently some curiosity felt about me; I knew that I was not recognized. I can hardly tell how I found answers to the questions put to me; the questioners must have been satisfied with very vague and senseless responses, if mine satisfied them. Kitty, at once prompt and self-possessed, relieved me, and kept up her own part, disguising her voice, and answering readily.

Unable to control my agony at the delay any longer, I exclaimed suddenly: "I feel faint, won't you (turning to the black domino) won't you get the bottle of salts I left in the dressing-room?"

Her height and step nearly betrayed her; and Mr. Mason catching sight of a woman's foot as she ran up the stairs, proclaimed the fact, and excited a general exclamation of wonder.

"Never saw a character better sustained—everybody had thought it a man all the evening."

I listened for the opening of the window in the west room overhead, then for Kitty's step as she stole out. I I heard it through all the din of music and of voices. Then came a dreadful suspense; how to get rid of the people, how to get on the piazza, I could not tell. Victor might even now be waiting for me, a moment more might be too late; the officers might at any instant return. Just then supper was announced, and, "now you have promised to unmask, now you must tell us who you are," exclaimed the gentlemen.

"Not while you are all here," I exclaimed, "I will not take off my mask to-night unless you all go to supper and leave me."

It was long before I rid myself of my admirers; the last one was dismissed to bring me an ice, and the instant I was alone, I stole out on the piazza and round to the appointed spot, and sheltering myself from sight, waited with a throbbing heart the appearance of the rose-colored domino. But the throbs sunk to faint and sickening slowness as minute after minute passed and no one came; dull, slow, torturing minutes that seemed to count themselves out by the dropping of my life's blood, each one left me so much fainter and more deathlike than before. Reason and endurance began to give way under the intense pressure, the laughter and merriment from within rang hideously in my ears, the gaudy lamps and glaring lights swam before me, I clung to the balcony for support; it seemed to reel from my grasp, and staggering forward, I should have fallen, but for the arm of some one that approached, and hurried to my side. He pushed back my mask and in a moment the fresh air in my face revived me, I raised my head and cast an agonized look down the walk that led to the shrubbery, and this time it was hope and not despair that followed the look.

"Pray leave me," I said imperiously to my attendant, "I am well now, I had rather be alone."

It was only when he turned to leave me that I saw it was Mr. Rutledge; the figure that approached down the walk claimed all my thoughts. It faltered a moment irresolutely on the steps.

"Courage!" I whispered putting my hand in his. "Follow me to this window, and we will cross the parlors, they are nearly clear."

I knew that the spirit of the man I led was broken hopelessly, he who had been so brave and reckless! At every step he wavered and held back; "I cannot," he murmured shrinking as we reached the hall, now filling with the gay throng from the supper room and library and the adjoining balconies. I hurried him forward, nerved with a new courage; I braved the inquisitive eyes of the crowd that thronged us, I had a bold answer for all their questions, a repartee for all their jests, and so I fought my way to the foot of the stairs.

"Go up," I whispered to Victor, pushing him forward,

and turning, I kept back with laugh and raillery the knot of people clustered round the landing-place.

"You shall be mobbed!" cried Grace. "We all unmasked half an hour ago. No one has a right to invisibility now!"

"I am just going up to unmask, but you will not let me."

"Will you promise to come instantly down?" asked Mr. Mason.

"Instantly."

"Will you dance the next set with me?" asked Ellerton.

"With great pleasure."

"Then it's but fair we should leave her," said Phil, and they moved away. Kitty, as I reached the upper hall, made me a hasty gesture to turn out the light at the head of the stairs. I obeyed, and in a moment the lights at that end of the hall were all extinguished, and only one left burning dimly at the other extremity.

"Quick!" whispered Kitty. "Mrs. Roberts is in her room. I have the key."

We hurried toward her, groping along the dark passage. The heavy wardrobe moved from its place with a dull, rumbling sound; the key grated in the unused lock.

"Quick! quick!" whispered Victor. "There is a step on the stairs!" There was a cruel moment of suspense as the key refused to turn; Victor held my hand in his with a grasp of iron; a low cry of despair burst from Kitty, as the step on the stairs mounted quickly. It was a matter of life and death indeed; discovery seemed inevitable now.

"Push, push it with all your might," I cried in an agony, "perhaps it will give way!"

"Thank heaven!" murmured Victor, as it yielded to her desperate strength. In less time than it takes to speak it, the door closed upon him, the wardrobe was pushed back to its place.

"What is the meaning of this?" said the stern voice of

the master at the head of the stairs. "Why are the lights put out? Who is there? Answer me."

Kitty thrust me into the nearest room, and advanced to meet her angry master.

"It's me, sir—Kitty; and I was just come up myself to see what had made it so dark up here; I think, sir, that the north windows there have been left open, and the wind has come up strong from that way, and the draught has put them out. It was very careless of Mrs. Roberts not to look after it," she continued, busying herself in relighting the lamps.

"Kitty," said Mr. Rutledge in a voice that I knew had more terror for the girl, than any other in the world, "your falsehoods are very ready, but they can never deceive me, remember that. Tell me promptly who put the lamps out."

"The fact is, master," she said dropping her eyes and looking contrite as she approached him, "my poor young lady has had a fainting-fit down stairs, and she wanted to get to her own room without anybody recognizing her, so I turned the lights out, for several of the young gentlemen were waiting about the stairs to see what room she'd go to."

"That lie is even more ingenious than the first. It is useless to question you further; you do not know how to speak the truth even when it is the best policy. Bring that light and follow me."

"Don't scold Kitty," I said, faintly, coming forward. "It was my fault, I wanted the lights put out. I thought it would do no harm, just for a moment, but I beg your pardon."

Mr. Rutledge turned abruptly away with a curling lip. "Mistress and maid together are too much for a plain man like me. I accept whatever interpretation you choose to put upon it." And he strode angrily down the stairs.

"Take off your domino and go down quick!" exclaimed Kitty.

"Oh Kitty! How can I? I can hardly stand, I am so faint."

"No matter," she said, inexorably. "Everybody will be wondering if you don't come, and there's been enough already! Take this, Miss, and do be brave, and don't give way."

She poured me out a dose of valerian; I swallowed it, submitted unquestioningly to her as she smoothed my hair, and arranged my dress and sent me downstairs. After that it is all a misty sort of dream; I danced and laughed with a gaiety that startled all who had seen the recent listlessness of my manner; I was daring, coquettish, brilliant; I hardly knew what words were on my lips, but they must have been light and merry, for the others laughed and whispered: "What would absent friends say to such high spirits!" and arch and coquettish I turned away to hide the pang their words awoke, and danced—danced till the last guest had gone and the tired musicians faltered at their task, and the weary members of the household eagerly turned to their own rooms. Once in mine, the unnatural tension of my nerves gave way; Kitty laid me on the bed, and for hours, I fancy, thought it an even chance whether I ever came out of that death-like swoon or not.

CHAPTER XXXIII.

"I lived on and on,
As if my heart were kept beneath a glass
And everybody stood, all eyes and ears,
To see and hear it tick."

E. B. BROWNING.

"MR. RUTLEDGE, sir!" exclaimed the captain, vehemently, bringing his hand down on the table with a force that made the glasses ring, "it's my opinion that there's a black mystery to be unravelled yet about that murder. It's my opinion that all our ears would tingle if we knew the truth. Certainly, in some inexplicable way, this place is connected with it. The man lurking about the grounds, the footprints across the garden-beds, the cravat found at the old summer-house—all seem to point out this neighborhood as his hiding-place."

"I cannot see that exactly, Captain McGuffy," returned his host. "I acknowledge that there is a mystery, and a dark one, yet to be cleared away from the matter; and that the murderer may have taken a temporary refuge in the woods near the house, is a possible, though not an infallible deduction to be drawn from the circumstances you have mentioned. The fact of garden-beds defaced with footprints on such a night as that of the masquerade, can hardly excite any surprise; and as to the suspicious-looking person lurking about the grounds all day, why, none of the three witnesses who swear to having seen him, can at all describe his appearance or occupation. A drunken loafer from the village sleeping off the effects of a night's carouse in the shelter of our woods, is a much more simple interpretation of it, to my mind."

The captain shook his head. "I cannot agree with you, sir ; I cannot think that that cravat, blood-stained and soiled, was left in the summer-house by any village loafer. Village loafers, sir, do not, as a general thing, wear such cravats, nor stain them with anything darker than the drippings of their lager-bier."

"I know you'll all laugh at me," said Ellerton Wynkar, "but, absurd as it is, I can't help thinking I've seen that cravat worn by ――. Good heavens! what's the matter now! Mrs. Churchill, your niece is going to faint!"

"Oh no!" said Grace, coolly passing me a glass of water. "Only turning white and looking distractingly pretty, then rallying a little, and looking up and saying faintly, 'I'm better, thank you,' and regaining composure gradually and gracefully. That's the programme. We're quite used to it by this time. When I have a *fiancé* who must go to Europe, I shall be perfected in the art of graceful grief if I attend properly to the example I have now before me."

"There's one art you're not perfected in at all events," said Phil.

"What's that, bonnie Phil ; what's that?"

"The art of feeling," said her cousin, shortly.

"Grace is thoughtless," said her mother, and entered into an apology so elaborate, that Phil was really distressed, and felt that he had been most unkind and unjust. He gave his hand to Grace, and said, with an honest smile :

"I didn't mean any reproach, Gracie, only you know you *are* a tease!"

"But, sir," continued the captain, unable to relinquish the subject that most interested him, "do you really feel that everything has been done toward the clearing up of this mystery that lays within your power? Don't you think that if some stronger measures were taken, some more detectives placed on the track, the thing might be ferreted out? It's aggravating to one's feelings to think that the villain may be within pistol shot of us, and get clear after all."

"It makes me so nervous," said Ella Wynkar, "I can't sleep at night, and Josephine makes Frances barricade the doors and windows as if we were preparing to stand a siege."

"It's truly horrible," said Josephine, with a shudder. "I wouldn't go half a dozen yards from the house alone for any consideration."

"Yes, Joseph, you are a coward, there's no denying it. Mr. Rutledge, what do you think of a girl of her age looking in all the closets, and even the bureau drawers, before she goes to bed at night, and making Frances sit beside her till she gets asleep?"

"I really think," said Mr. Rutledge, rising from the table, "that you are all alarming yourselves unnecessarily. Every precaution has been taken to insure the arrest of any suspicious person, and there is no danger of any abatement in the zeal and activity of our rustic police. The woods and neighborhood are swarming with volunteer detectives, and till the offer of the reward is withdrawn, you may rest assured that their assiduity will not be. I think the young ladies may omit the nightly barricading, and excuse Frances from mounting guard after eleven o'clock. I should not advise your walking very far from the house unattended, but beyond that, really, I think you need not take any trouble."

"And really *I* think," muttered the captain, as we moved into the hall, "that he takes it very coolly. Upon my word, I didn't think he was the man to let such a thing as this be passed over in such an indifferent way."

"God bless him for it!" I thought in my heart.

"Stephen is waiting at the door to speak with you, sir," said Thomas to his master. Stephen's face expressed such a volume of alarm and importance, that we involuntarily stopped in the hall, as he answered Mr. Rutledge's inquiry as to his errand.

"The body of a man, sir, has just been found in the lake.

It has evidently been there a day or more. The men are down there, sir; I came immediately up to let you know."

Mr. Rutledge gave a hurried glance at me, as he said quickly:

" Possibly one of the laborers. I will go down with you at once."

Capt. McGuffy, with an I-told-you-so nod to Phil, snatched his hat, and, followed by the other gentlemen, hurried with Stephen toward the lake. The ladies, in a frightened group, clustered together on the lawn and watched them from a distance.

How well I could have told them who it was, and how long the bloated, disfigured corpse had lain floating among the reeds and alder-bushes at the head of the lake! How their ears, indeed, would tingle, if they should know the quarter part of what I knew. How sleepless and terrified Josephine's nights might well be, if she knew that a single foot of brick and mortar was all that separated her from the execrated murderer, with the horror of whose crime the country rang. How doubly aghast she would be, if she knew that the murderer was none other than the guest she had herself invited to Rutledge—the brilliant and clever man whose admiration she had vainly striven to obtain—the affianced husband of her cousin! What if they knew all this? What if my brain should give way under the pressure of this dreadful secret, and I should betray all! Sometimes I really thought I was losing my reason; the knowledge that I held the life of another in my own weak hands, made them tremble more; the keeping of the secret was wearing my very life away; sleepless nights and wretched days were doing their sure work with me, and the terrible excitement within, shone out in my eyes and burned in a crimson spot on each white cheek, throbbed in my quick pulse and sapped the strength and vigor of my being. I could have wrestled with and overcome fear and timidity, if they had

been all; I could have been brave and strong, if I had had
but his sin to cover, his crime to hide; if I had been true,
if my own heart had been pure of sin, I could have borne it.
But it was the weight of remorse, added to all the rest, that
crushed me to the dust. It was remembering how great a
part I had had in Victor's sin, that took all courage out of
my heart. If I had not deceived him, and allowed him to
believe I loved him—would he not now have been safe?
From those first beginnings of pride and resentment, I
traced my sin in regard to him. Whenever they had got a
foothold, the soothing flattery of Victor's love had crept in,
to allay and lull the pain they caused. And I had not
remembered to pray in those hours; I had trusted to
myself, and gone on sinning. Just so far as I had been
estranged from duty, and grown cold to holy things, just so
far had I gone forward in the path which had now brought
me to such terrible bewilderment. Whenever I had
prayed and repented, his influence and the temptation
of his presence had been weakened or withdrawn; whenever I had listened to the whispers of wounded pride or
determined resentment, his voice had been at my ear, his
love laid at my feet. When little Essie's death had drawn
my thoughts awhile toward heaven, and made me realize
the littleness and impotence of pride and wrath, and the
insignificance of things seen, the power and eternity of
things unseen, he had been forgotten and indifferent; but
so soon as I had allowed the return of worldliness, so soon
had I found myself snared in hypocrisy and deceit toward
him. The little sins of every day, they had tempted me on
to where I now stood. It was so easy to look back and see
it all—how one slight omission of duty had led to another—
how one moment of indulgence had weakened self-control—
one disregard of truth had grown into the tyrant sin
from which I could not now release myself; struggle
as I might, I was helpless in its grasp. Every step but
plunged me deeper; every word was but a fresh deceit.

I saw Victor that evening for a few moments ; Kitty had watched long for a safe chance to admit me. Mrs. Roberts, contrary to all precedent, had taken her knitting and seated herself in one of the hall windows, declaring that it was the coolest place in the house, and there remained the whole afternoon. There was nothing to induce her to do it but the obstinate instincts of her nature, to which she was ever true. She may have had some lurking suspicion that there was "something going on" upstairs, and though entirely ignorant of its nature, she could not doubt its evil tendency, believing as she had reason to, that Kitty was concerned in it. She had encountered that young person on the stairs after dinner, with a surreptitious plate of confectionery and fruit from dessert. Kitty had readily answered upon demand, that it was for her young lady; and Mrs. Roberts had very tartly remarked that in *her* time, young ladies thought it best manners to eat as much as they wanted at the table, and not take the credit of being delicate, and then have extra plates of good things brought up to their rooms. Kitty could hardly brook the implied taunt, but she had to swallow it. She hovered anxiously around all the afternoon, inventing all manner of excuses to get Mrs. Roberts away, but to no avail, and it was only after dusk, when she had at last withdrawn to order tea, that Kitty eagerly beckoned me to follow her to the door of the hidden room, that had always had such a mysterious awe in my eyes.

As I crept through the narrow space between the wardrobe and the door, I grasped Kitty's hand with an involuntary shudder. "Don't go away," I whispered.

"No, Miss. I'll stay just outside the door and watch, and you must come the very minute I tap at it, for Mrs. Roberts will be back as soon as ever she has given out the things for tea. I won't go away, don't be afraid, Miss."

The twilight was too dim for me to distinguish anything

as Kitty closed the door softly behind me, and I groped my way into the room. "Victor!" I said, in a whisper, as no sound met my ear.

A dark figure between me and the faint light of the window, started forward as I spoke, and, in another moment, my hands were grasped in hands as cold and tren bling. Did it give me a shudder to remember the work those hands had done in the grey shadowy twilight, one short week before? I tried not to think of it. I tried to remember it was the man who loved me—who had risked his life for my love. But crime and remorse had strangely darkened and changed him. There was a wild sort of despair in his very tenderness—a fierce recklessness when he spoke of the future; I tried in vain to reassure myself and soothe him, but I quailed before a nature, beside the strength of whose passion, all that I had known or seen of despair and desperation faded into insignificance. A weak man can sin weakly, and bewail it feebly and with tears : a strong man, who is hurried into crime by the very intensity and strength of his nature, turns fiercely upon the remorse that besets him; the very gall of bitterness is his repentance— blood and curses are the tears he sheds.

Tenderness and confidence shrunk back affrighted from such contact; I trembled in his grasp, and he caught a suspicion of my fear. I never shall forget the agony of the gesture with which he released me, and turning away, buried his face in his hands. I started forward, and tried, in faltering accents, to assure him of—what? The words died on my lips. At that moment there was a hurried tap at the door, and Kitty's voice whispered :

"Quick!"

"There is your release!" he exclaimed, bitterly. "You have done your duty; draw a long breath, and hurry back into the light and freedom of the outer world. Quick! I must not keep you."

"You are wrong," I murmured, "I must go, but it is

just as dark and miserable outside to me, as it is here for you. Don't fancy, Victor, that there is any pleasure for me now."

"You need not remind me of that!" he exclaimed, sinking down, and bowing his face on the table before him. "You need not remind me of that! I know I have dragged you down with me in my fall, and it is the cruellest thought in all my cruel anguish; but you shall be freed—be sure you shall be freed!"

"Why will you talk so strangely, Victor? What have I done to make you doubt me now? I would die to serve you—I have no other thought than how to save you from the danger that threatens "——

Kitty shook the door impatiently, and implored me to come out.

"I must go, Victor," I whispered. "Will you not speak to me? Good night."

I bent over him, and touched my lips to his forehead, and then groped my way hastily to the door. He did not move or speak, and I turned back irresolutely, to beg him for a word of forgiveness, but Kitty, opening the door, caught me by the hand, and pulled me out.

"They are all asking for you; Miss Josephine has been upstairs for you, and when she came down and said you weren't in your room, master looked so white, and started up so frightened, that the others all caught it of him, and began to call you and hunt all about for you; and I couldn't let you know, for old Roberts was marching up and down the hall, and keeping her eyes all about her. She's gone into her room a minute—now's your chance; run right down the private staircase—there's nobody in the butler's pantry—go out on the piazza, and so around to the front door. Quick! She's coming back!"

I should have done anything Kitty told me to do at that moment. It was lucky for me she was the clear-headed, ingenious girl she was. I ran downstairs, and hurried round the piazza. At the hall door I paused a moment, and leaned against one of the pillars, to recover myself before I entered. Some one hurrying out of the house brushed against me. An exclamation of surprise and relief escaped his lips, and looking up, I saw Mr. Rutledge.

"Where have you been?" he asked, abruptly.

The suddenness of the question, and my miserable nervousness, overcame my self-possession entirely. I struggled in vain to speak, but ended by putting my face in my hands, and bursting into a flood of tears.

"You are not well," he said, kindly, taking my hand and drawing me to a seat. "You are very unhappy. I cannot bear to see you suffer so. Will you not tell me what it is, and let me help you?"

"No one can help me—no one can do me the least good."

"You think so, perhaps; but you do not know how far I might. You do not know how much I would sacrifice to see you happy again. If you will only confide to me the anxiety that I see is killing you, I will promise to further your wishes, and to endeavor to relieve your mind, at the cost of anything to myself except my honor."

I shook my head. "You cannot help me—no one can."

"If it is only grief at parting with your lover," he went on, quickly, "I cannot do you any good; but if it is what I fear for you, I can perhaps advise you—perhaps materially aid you. Trust in me for this; show the confidence in me that you have hitherto refused, and you shall see how well I will serve you—how unselfishly and unreservedly I will try to restore you to happiness."

Pity can make the human face almost like the face of an angel; there is no emotion that is so transforming. When pride, self-will, and selfishness, resign their sway, and pity, heaven-born and god-like, dawns, all that is mean, and coarse, and earthly, seems to fade before it, to grow dumb and quiet in the calm radiance of its risen fullness. Such pity beamed on me now, but its healing and tenderness came too late,

"As on the uprooted flower, the genial rain."

"You are very kind," I murmured; "but there is nothing anybody can do for me."

He rose sadly. "I will not torment you, then. Will you come into the house? If you desire to go to your room, I will manage your excuses for you."

With almost inaudible thanks, I hurried into the hall and upstairs. My aunt came up in the course of the evening, but Kitty represented me as "just going to sleep," and I was spared an interview.

"Kitty!" I exclaimed, starting up, long after she had fancied I was soothed to sleep, "how—how will it all end? What is to become of him after we go? It was decided yesterday that we leave in two days' time, and you know it will not be safe for him to think of escape till the excitement has died away in the country. Poor Victor! What is to become of him?"

"Don't fret," said Kitty, soothingly, "even if you have to leave him here, there'll be no more danger for him than if you stayed. Mr. Rutledge is going too, you know, and the house will be shut up, and it will be safer, if anything, than now. I'll write you every day of my life, and tell you how things go on. And, depend upon it, the worst of the danger is over. Since this body has been found in the lake, people will begin to content themselves that there's no use in looking further for the murderer—that he did it and then drowned himself in despair. Michael hasn't brought up the news of the inquest yet—he's waiting in the village to hear it; but I've no manner of doubt what it'll be. Everybody knows he and the doctor had dealings together, and that, with the character he bears, will tell against him."

"You don't suppose he had any papers about him that might do Victor harm?"

"If he had had, they wouldn't be of any use now ; they've been in the water too long to serve any purpose, good or bad. No, Black John, as they call him, will have to bear the credit of the crime he was hunting poor Mr. Victor to death for. There ain't many that he didn't deserve to take the credit of. Everybody knows that he was nothing slow at all manner of wickedness, and it seems the likeliest thing in the world that he should do the devil's work ; and, mark my words, before a week is over, there won't be man, woman or child in the country round, that won't curse Black John as Dr. Hugh's murderer. It won't do him much harm now, poor wretch ; a few curses more or less won't make much difference to him where he is now, I suppose."

"Had he a wife ?"

"A drunken, half-crazy thing. She spends her time between the poor-house and the grog-shop. She'll never mind about her husband, beyond howling for an hour or two when she first hears it, if she happens to be sober. Now, Miss, don't think any more about it, but try to go to sleep. You'll be quite worn out."

And Kitty threw herself upon her mattress by my bed, where she now slept, and, faithfullest and tenderest of attendants, never left me, day or night.

CHAPTER XXXIV.

"Nor peace nor ease, the heart can know,
    That, like the needle true,
Turns at the touch of joy or woe,
    But, turning, trembles too."

GREVILLE.

"Things seem to be taking a new turn," said the captain, meditatively, over his coffee the next morning. "I own I thought we were at the bottom of the mystery, yesterday, but this woman's testimony seems to set us all adrift again, and we're no nearer a conclusion than we were a week ago."

"What woman's?" asked Ellerton, who had just come in.

"The man's wife," said the captain.

"What man's?" demanded Ella, who generally arrived at a subject about ten minutes after it had been introduced.

"Why the man who was supposed to have murdered the doctor, Miss Ella, and whose body was found in the lake. We were all mightily relieved yesterday, and thought the murderer had found his reward, and were only sorry that he'd cheated the hangman. But in the meantime his wife turns up, and brings a lot of things to light; swears that on the night of the murder he was at Brandon, on an errand for the doctor, and brings the landlord and barkeeper of the 'Brandon Shades' to testify to his remaining there till after eleven o'clock. She also states that the doctor and her husband were on good terms, and that the doctor often employed him in a confidential way; that there was a person who, she knew, bore malice against the doctor; she had overheard a conversation between her husband and Dr. Hugh, in which"——

436

"But her testimony goes for nothing," I interrupted, eagerly. "She is well known to be half crazy, and hardly ever sober. Her testimony can't be worth a straw—nobody would listen to her for a moment."

"I don't know about that; her story hangs together, she's sober enough now, and will be kept so till they have done with her. She says that the doctor came to their shanty late the night before the murder, and called John out; she crept to the keyhole and listened. She lost a good deal of what they said for a little while, they talked so low; then John raised his voice, and said with an oath, he'd take down the villain's pride for him a bit; he wondered the doctor had stood his cursed ugliness so long; for his part, he'd put a bullet through him to-morrow, with pleasure. The doctor hushed him, and said, 'Not so fast, John, not so fast, wait awhile; we must get a little more out of him before we send him to his long account. We'll settle up old scores with pleasure, after we've no further use for him. Attend to this little errand for me to-morrow, and don't let him slip, and that'll be the first step toward a reckoning.'"

"Well, but I cannot see," said Mr. Rutledge, "what it all amounts to, even if the woman's testimony is received, which is more than doubtful. She didn't hear any names. Nobody has any doubt but that the doctor had plenty of enemies, and that her man John was a scoundrel, and I cannot see what else her evidence goes to prove."

"It goes to prove that there was *somebody* with whom the doctor was not on good terms, who has not appeared on the stage as yet, and of whom we want to get hold. It goes to prove, my dear sir, that the man John was sent to Brandon on a matter in some way connected with this person; and, to my mind, when we shall have found out who that person was, we shall have found out who was the murderer of Dr. Hugh!"

"But," said Phil, "what do the barkeeper and landlord

of 'The Shades' say? Don't they know who he came to meet, and for whom he waited till eleven?"

"John, it seems, 'kept dark,' lounged around the bar-room, and spoke little to any one, as was his manner, but went often to the door, and seemed to wait for some one. The barkeeper thinks, but is not sure, that it was he who was there once before during the morning, with a letter which he left, directed to a gentleman whose name he has forgotten, who never called for it."

"Ah!" cried Phil, "now we shall get at it, I think. What became of the letter?"

"The letter," interrupted Mr. Rutledge, "the letter that was left there that morning "——

I crushed the newspaper that lay beside me with my nervous hand; I smothered the cry that trembled on my lips, but my eyes burned on his face. He avoided them and went on.

"The letter which was left there by some one, who, it is conjectured, only *conjectured*, may have been this man, was addressed to some person not at all known in Brandon, and who never came for it. It was opened and examined, and proved to be only the business circular of some importing house in New York. So all idea of tracing anything from that was given up, and the letter thrown aside."

"Strange," said Phil, thoughtfully. "I should have thought something could have been made out of it. In a small place like Brandon, where everybody knows every-body, I should have thought that the circumstance of a strange name on a letter left at a little tavern would have excited some interest."

"Brandon is a railway station, you know, and conse-quently there are strangers always coming and going."

"Do you remember the name on the letter, sir?"

"Some foreign name, I think. Captain McGuffy, do you remember it?" said Mr. Rutledge, indifferently.

"I don't think I heard it," returned the captain. "And

I really have the curiosity to want to know something more about that letter, though all the legal gentlemen, I know, have decided against its usefulness in the case. I must remember to ask Judge Talbot to let me look at it," he continued, taking out his memorandum-book and making an entry. "Phil, don't you feel like taking a drive over to Brandon with me, this morning, and seeing if there's anything new to be learned?"

"Captain McGuffy," I exclaimed, "don't you want to do me a favor? I am perfectly wild to have a ride on horseback this morning, and you know you promised to give me some lessons in 'cavalry practice' before we left, and there is only one day more. What do you say to a canter over to Windy Hill this fine morning?"

The captain fell in with the proposition very readily, and Mr. Rutledge suggested that it would be a very good arrangement for all of the party to accompany us, in the carriage and open wagon, and to make our farewell call, also, to the Emersons.

"To-morrow may not be fine," said Mr. Rutledge, "and perhaps we had better secure to-day."

The rest were agreed, and we hurried off to dress; as the two places were far distant from each other and from Rutledge, it was necessary to start as soon as possible. In my dread lest Phil should decline being of the party, and should ride over to Brandon by himself, I called out to him to know if he would not accept an appointment in my regiment? He laughed, and accepted; and unheeding the flaming battery of Josephine's eyes, I ran up to put on my habit. There was another lady's horse in the stable, besides the one I should use, but Josephine and Ella, though dying to ride, would neither of them volunteer to accompany me.

"You are too nervous to ride, Miss," said Kitty, as she buttoned my gloves. "See how your hand shakes. Why will you go? You are not fit."

"I must; there is no help. Tell him why I go, Kitty

and that I will be back as soon as I can, and you must manage to let me see him in the course of the after-noon. And be sure you make him understand about my going."

Glorious Madge! I had never expected to mount her again. I had never expected to burden her with such a heavy heart. What a contrast to the daring young rider of a few short months ago. Madge Wildfire was as eager and untamed as then, but not so her mistress. Her mistress, the fire quenched in her eye, the pride of her free step humbled, the courage of her spirit broken, trembled at the very beauty of the animal she rode.

" You are not fit for this," said Mr. Rutledge, in a low tone, as he put me in the saddle. " You had better give it up. It is not too late; let one of the others take your place."

" No, thank you. I shall be better for the ride."

" Captain McGuffy, you must remember your pupil is rather inexperienced," he said, uneasily, as the captain mounted and rode up beside me. " Madge has not been used for some time, and she is feeling very fine."

" No danger," said the captain, as, followed by Phil, we trotted rapidly down the avenue. There must have been a touch of human intelligence and sympathy in Madge; she was burning to be off on a mad race across the country; she was fairly throbbing with impatience; my weak grasp upon her bridle she could have thrown off with one toss of her arched neck; but, quivering with life and fire as she was, she restrained her pace to suit my fears, and minded my slightest touch, with more than human gentleness. By degrees, I came to realize this, and reassured and embold-ened, I sat more firmly and rode less timidly. The cool air of the morning braced and strengthened my nerves; I could hardly have believed that I could have felt so differ-ently in so short a time, and every foot of ground we put between us and Rutledge, seemed to distance just so far my anxiety and wretchedness. My companions amused themselves, and thought they were amusing me, by reminiscences of military adventures, frontier experiences, and camp life ; which served to keep them occupied, and give me time to rest and recover myself. When we rode into the lodge gate at Windy Hill, I was indeed so much better for my ride, that even Phil noticed the change in my expression.

"You ought to have ridden every day while we have been here. You must ride to-morrow by all means."

We were the first of the party to arrive, and had been seated in the parlor some minutes, enjoying the prattle of the Misses Mason, before the others drove up. All were made hugely welcome. One is surest of appreciation, socially, in a visit to a lonely country place, where visitors are at a premium, and where there are pining young daughters, and unemployed young sons, and a hospitable head of the family, to swell the note of welcome. All these elements of hospitality we found at Windy Hill; never were guests more welcome, and the only doubt seemed to be, whether we should ever be allowed to go. Lunch did not suffice, we must stay to dinner. Mason *père* said it should be so, and Mason *fils* ordered the carriage away, and the horses taken out. Mrs. Churchill pleaded our toilets, but was overruled. Mr. Rutledge advanced the necessity for our visit at Beech Grove as an obstacle. That should be no objection. After dinner the young people should join us, and we could all go together. There being really no reason why we should not accept this hospitality, it was at last decided we should remain. The morning slipped away very fast; there was a great deal to be seen about the place ; fine views and pretty walks on every hand, outside, and a library and picture-gallery full of interest within. New merchandisable interest, that is. The Masons had just returned from Europe, and had brought with them whatever had been procurable for money, unbacked by taste or judgment. The result was, a good many pictures in rather questionable taste, but framed and hung unexceptionably; a great deal of so-so statuary, engravings bought by the portfolio, and "gems of art," bearing about the same relation to high art, that the contents of some jeweller's show-case, in Chatham street, bears to the Koh-i-noor. My particular friend, the younger Mr. Mason, attended me through the library and picture-gallery; and though the names of the pictures and the prices of the books seemed to be the items that he was most familiar with, I could not but admire the grasp of mind that could master and retain such dry statistics. By the time that dinner was announced, I felt that we had earned it, so much listening, looking, admiring had we done.

Dinner at the Masons' was never a brief meal; the master of the house had known too much of short commons in his boyhood, and eighteen-penny lunches at second-rate eating-houses during his clerkship, not to place a full value upon the luxuries of the table; and on the present occasion nothing was wanting to make it an elaborate and elegant repast, honorable to guests and entertainers. It was five o'clock before we left the table, and fully six before we were in the saddle. The ride to Beech Grove occupied another hour; a mere call, of course, was impossible. We were quite as cordially, though rather less enthusiastically, welcomed by Mr. Emerson and his black-eyed daughter; the horses were again sent away, and we were told to consider ourselves prisoners for the evening. Not a very dreary and insupportable prison, certainly, we were condemned to. Beech Grove was a lovely spot; the house, about one-third the size of the one we had just left, was a gem in point of architectural beauty and tasteful decoration. Cultivation and refinement spoke at every turn—choice pictures, rare books, exquisite bronzes, were the natural and unobtrusive furniture of the rooms; one was not called upon to admire by anything more demonstrative than quiet enjoy ment and ease. It was the atmosphere of the place that one was to revel in; and no obligation existed to analyze its component parts.

The realization of the speedy termination of our pleasant intercourse, at least for the present, gave a very natural charm to the evening, and made it a very prolonged and happy one. At least, to those of us who had not forgotten how to be happy; for me, I could hardly remember when I had not been wretched, so agonizingly long and miserable had the past fortnight been, and so strongly had it marked itself on my memory. I looked with a kind of wonder at the light-heartedness of my companions. Was it possible I had ever found anything to laugh at in such things as called forth their merriment, or anything to stir my anger in their puerile slights and taunts? Grace was vexed by my indifference, and tried, with no contemptible ingenuity, to irritate me; and Josephine and Ella too, resented my determined appropriation of their beaux. I was too listless though, at last they found, to make it pay to tease me; so, by degrees, they dropped off and left me. Even Mr. Mason, it was evident, was beginning to think that he had overrated my spirit, and the captain, that my overtures of the morning did not mean quite so much, after all, as he had flattered himself. Miss Emerson, who was a nice, bright girl, not in the least afraid of herself or of any one else, and with whom one felt intimate after half an hour's acquaintance, ran up to me and asked me *sotto voce*, if it didn't bore me to death to have that man talk to me; she was sure I looked tired, and she meant to relieve me; so, with some clever excuse, in a few minutes she hurried me off to the library, made me lie on the sofa while she sat beside me, and chatted with me in her peculiarly piquant and amusing manner. It was very nice and comfortable to be treated so; but I could not help wondering what her other guests would think of her for absenting herself from them so much. It was a matter of very little moment to Miss

Janet, however, what any one but "papa" thought of her, and she was sure of a tender judgment from him always; but at last it seemed to strike her that even he might consider it rather negligent to leave the parlor so long, so springing up, she said:

"I must go back to those people; but remember, you are not to stir; or, yes, you may sit here by the table, and look over these engravings. You are not fit to be dragged about making visits; they're a set of heathens to make you go. I know you hate it. What *is* the matter, really, now?" she said, abruptly, stooping over me, and fixing her black eyes on my face. "You don't look like the same girl latterly. If I hadn't known you before, I should have thought you were tiresome and mopish and had no spirit. I like you better than your French cousins, and I wish you'd come and stay with me. Won't you? I'll make papa coax Mrs. Churchill to let you stay after they go."

I shook my head and sighed.

"You look as if it were no use to talk about it; but I don't give it up, though I must go to the parlor. I shall come back and look after you every little while, and I'm going to send some one to entertain you while I'm gone."

"Oh! I'd rather not—I'd rather be quiet"——

Miss Janet shook her head with a very pretty determined shake.

"You shall have somebody that won't bore you—somebody that I like and that you like; the only man here, in point of fact, worth talking to, except papa;" and she ran off.

I leaned back in my chair and tried to be patient; since we left Windy Hill every minute had grown longer than the last. I had been in a fever of anxiety about the effect our absence might produce on Victor. I knew his morbid bitterness would construe it into a willful thing on my part, and that the neglect would seem unpardonable and cruel.

The evening had seemed interminable, and no one dreamed of going yet.

In a few moments I heard Miss Emerson's voice in the hall, and Mr. Rutledge's in reply. " Of course, since you desire it, I will do my best to be entertaining ; but you know you have not told me who it is I am to devote myself to."

" O, you shall see for yourself; go in the library, she is there, and be sure you amuse and please her, for she's my particular favorite," and with a laugh and a nod, she left him in the door.

Mr. Rutledge started a little, and did not look very much pleased when he recognized me ; but there was no help, so he sat down beside me at the table.

" Miss Emerson told me she should send some one to entertain me. I didn't know she meant to send you."

" Is there any one you would prefer ? Mr. Arbuthnot, the captain, or your heavy adorer, Mr. Theodore Mason ? You need not hesitate to tell me. I will resign in favor of any one you name."

I was too miserable to be angry at his tone ; with a languid movement of my hand, I answered :

" If you are willing to stay, sir, there is no one I should like so well."

" It is not often you allow yourself in anything so gracious as that. I will stay with pleasure. But Miss Emerson says I must entertain you—I must be agreeable. Now, though I dare not, for my life, disobey anything so blackeyed and imperious, still I haven't the first idea how to proceed, and unless you give me a hint, I am certain I shall fail. What shall I talk about ? What do young ladies like, literature or gossip—people or things ?"

" My tastes haven't changed, Mr. Rutledge; you used to find no difficulty in talking to me—at least, I never supposed it cost you much effort, and you always succeeded in entertaining me; so if that is honestly your object to night, I do not think you need be at a loss."

"What did I use to talk about, when I amused you, if ever I was so happy? If you would give me a sugges-tion"——

He turned his eyes full on me, as I answered:

"When you first used to talk to me, you seemed to think me a very foolish, frightened child, and were very kind and gentle. Then, after you had found out I was old enough to understand you, and clever enough to appreciate you, you used to talk to me about your travels, and the people you had met, the countries you had seen. Sometimes you would talk to me about books, and make me tell you what ones I liked, and after you were convinced, I was prejudiced and enthusiastic enough to make it worth your while to oppose me, you would amuse yourself by contradicting and thwart-ing me. Then you would suddenly change and be kind— oh! so kind!—and treat me as if I were fit to be your friend and your companion; you would tell me about the world that I had only dreamed of then; you warned me of its danger, its heartlessness and treachery; you counselled me, and talked as if you really cared what became of me; you told me the world was full of coldness and unkindness, but oh! you did not tell me half you might have told me about that. Then, sometimes—not often—you would tell me some slight thing about yourself; you looked sterner and colder than ever when you did; your eye would flash, and your lip would curl—some unseen chain would gall you when you thought of the Past; something that came with its memory humbled you, you hated it, you hated your-self; but I liked you—I liked you better then than when you were talking to please me, or to instruct me, or to please or instruct other people; you were involuntary then—you were yourself—and though I liked you in those days whatever you did, I liked you best of all when you talked of yourself."

"Then I will talk of myself now; I have promised to en-tertain you, and you have told me how to do it. They are

dancing in the parlor now, and the music and the laughing
will screen us from them; you can listen at your ease, and
be entertained without fear of interruption. I believe you
when you say you like to hear me talk of myself, because it
pleases me to believe it, and men, you know, will go great
lengths to believe anything that suits their vanity.

"But first, you will not mind anything that I may say—
you will not shrink and blush? Remember, it is a man's
life, and not a woman's, that you are to hear about—a dark
life, and not a prosperous one—and to make it vivid to you,
I must show you the blackness of the shadow and the depth
of the gloom; you must know what the trial has been before you can know what grim strength was needed to
endure it—what coldness and sternness, as you call them,
to keep down the pain within. You are a child no longer;
you know something of what suffering is, so I can tell you
with some hope of pity, if you will listen and not be dainty
—if you will forget all about yourself, and think only of
what you hear. Can you be such a listener? Such only
are worthy of confidence. I never found one before, but I
will try you. Do you hear the rumbling of that distant
thunder? How strangely it mixes with the music across
the hall! There is a storm coming up; we cannot go home
for two hours yet, and they will not tire of dancing even
then "——

There was a keen, piercing flash of lightning.

"Does it make you nervous? You used to be afraid in
thunder-storms."

"I don't mind the lightning any more than the flare of
the candle to-night, Mr. Rutledge. Why don't you go on
with what you promised to tell me?"

"I will not begin by telling you about my childhood; a
happy childhood is a thing to be enjoyed once in reality,
and forever in memory, but not to be talked about; no one
but the man himself can see the least pathos or delicious-
ness in the details and recollections of his nursery days; to

others they are weariness and folly; to him they are the sweetest pages in his memory; but he must not hope to find there is any other than himself who can see any interest in them. Perhaps his mother, if God spares her to him—perhaps the woman whom he has taught to love him, and to whom he is all the world—perhaps his young children, before they have learned their perfect lesson of egotism and selfishness—may listen as if the story were their own; but I have found no one to whom I could be egotistical and not be wearisome; I have found that most people like to hear about themselves, and I have not thwarted them.

"But you shall hear of what I have told no one else."

CHAPTER XXXV.

——" Of all sad words of tongue or pen,
The saddest are these: ' It might have been!'"
WHITTIER.

AND I did hear it; I heard during the slow gathering
and heavy bursting of that summer storm, the story about
which my imagination had been so busy, and of which I had
so longed to be assured; I heard from Mr. Rutledge's own
lips, of his happy childhood, his hopeful boyhood. He described himself as he was then, as if he were describing
some one else, some one who had died and left the light of
day; for it was nothing else but death that passed upon
him, a death to hope and faith, a death to tenderness and
trust, a death to all but stern endurance and sufferings that
make life worse than death. If he had not been just so en
thusiastic and full of hope, he could not have been so dashed
down to despair; but because he had never dreamed that
there could be anything but truth and purity and honor in
those he loved, just so cruel and fatal was the awakening
from the dream. He told me of his brother, the handsome
Richard; with a soul too refined and delicate for the rough
world he had to do with, a temperament that recoiled with
pain from all that was coarse or common, a pride that was
so intuitive that it could hardly be overcome, so unconscious that it could hardly be called a sin, so fostered that
he, at least, was not to blame for it. To him it was not
matter of exultation that he was rich and well-born and
high-bred; it was only his native air, his place in life, his vital breath, without which he must have died. Never overbearing and imperious, his reserve saved him from familiarity, his gentleness from aversion. Ah! Rutledge had

449

then a worthy heir, noble, handsome, high-toned enough to fill even his proud father's ambition.

And then he told me, and it cost him a keen pang to speak her name, of Alice, his beautiful sister; of the adoration with which he had looked up to her, the pride which every one of the narrow home circle felt in her loveliness and grace. He had believed she was almost an angel; he had never looked above her for purity and truth, and in one cruel moment he had to learn that she was false and sinful, that she had fallen below the lowest, that "she had mixed her ancient blood with shame," that the darling and pride of every heart was now the disgrace and anguish of every heart.

The story that he told me did not sound at all like this; I could no more tell it as he told it, than I could paint one of Church's pictures. I could, perhaps, describe, so as to make intelligible, the picture or the story, but it would be as impossible for me to render faithfully, in every delicate tone and touch, in the masterly strength and vivid power, the one as the other.

I listened with every pulse; my heart stopped, spellbound, before that story; not even my own life could have had more interest to me than his; and vaguely—but oh! how bitterly—it began to dawn upon me, that once I might have had the power to have made the past forgotten in the present, to have won him to believe in love and truth once more; that in my fatal choice I had not doomed myself alone, that three souls, instead of my own sinning one, were writhing now under the curse of my folly and deceit. Alice Rutledge's name had perished forever from the records of the good and pure; where would mine be, when the secrets of all hearts should be revealed? Not among the good, with a lie on my lips, a life-long hypocrisy to be carried in my heart; not among the pure, cherishing yet this unconquered passion, while in the sight of Heaven I was breaking a vow only less sacred than the one I must make before the altar. But it is her story and not mine I am to tell.

If human love and care could suffice to keep any soul, under the pressure of a strong temptation, Alice Rutledge might have been safe; yet environed and hemmed in with affection, she fell; honor, pride, filial love, were powerless to keep her back. The only principle that can save man or woman in the hour when the powers of darkness have leave to try them, she lacked, and lacking that, fell hopelessly from the earthly paradise which alone she had lived for or regarded. The fair, frail daughter of a godless house, the child whose glance had never been directed to anything higher than virtue and honor, to whom no principle more binding than that of morality had been taught, whose frailty had never been strengthened by any aid more powerful and enduring than the yearning fondness of the hearts that doted on her; what wonder that when the powers of hell assaulted her, no strength could stand against them that was not divine, no work stand in that day, that was of wood, or hay, or stubble, no work that had not Heaven's own seal to resist the devouring flame!

All that the wit and knowledge and virtue of man could teach, Alice Rutledge had been taught; but the only lesson that could have done her any good in that day, she had never learned. The lesson that she should have lisped at her mother's knee, that should have been implanted before any earthly desire had taken root in her flexile soul, had never been given to her. The "sign to angels known," had not marked her baby-forehead, holy hands had not overshadowed her before the strife began, all her goodness and strength were of the earth, earthy, and the prince of this world won an easy victory over them. When temptation came, it found her careless, secure. How was it a possible thing for her to fall? Why need she renounce what was but a pleasant dream, as innocent as it was secret. She was promised to one whom she had meant to love; she had, perhaps, loved him at first, but with a shade too much of

awe to make it perfect love, and the weakness and timidity
of her nature made her shrink involuntarily from what was
higher and stronger, and cling to what was lower, and nearer
to her own level. And so she yielded, little by little, to the
fascinations of an intercourse that, had she listened to it,
even her own weak heart would have told her was a sin
She was bound by betrothal, her tempter was bound by
marriage; if the glamour of destruction had not been over
her already, she could have seen the madness of such an intimacy, the sure perdition that such a violation of right,
even in thought, must lead to. But it was the very impossibility and security that ensnared her, that blinded those
around her. Richard's dearest friend, the most desired and
welcome guest at her father's house, the most accomplished
and refined gentleman she knew, how could she see in him
the traitor that he was? She, almost a child in years and
inexperience, and he, a man of the world, with the world's
worst principles, and withal, so wily, so eloquent, so impas-
sioned, was it strange that before she dreamed of danger,
she was snared beyond redemption. The destruction of
her principles had been so gradual, the instilling of his so
artful, that the work was nearly done before the lost girl
saw her peril. Then, no one can tell the struggles of her
tempted soul; duty and reason against sinful love and guilty
passion; but who can question for a moment which way the
balance turned? There was none of whom she could ask
counsel. She had deceived and outraged all she loved, so
shamefully, by the very thought of what now tempted her,
that it was worse than death to betray in the least her misery. The one to whom at last she turned, was the one least
fitted to direct her; her companion, governess and friend
was only less worldly and thoughtless than her charge; she
loved her with all her heart, would have sacrificed anything
to serve her; she never dreamed of the danger she was in
till too late; terrified, she strove to bring her back to rea-

son, but in vain. Alice's was the stronger will, and she
weakly yielded to it, and became the reluctant too in the
hands of the seducer.

In one awful moment it burst upon the proud old man that
his name was branded with disgrace, his daughter fled, his
love outraged, his honor stabbed a deadly blow; all that he
had lived for lost; all that he had hoped for blighted.

In that household there was such amazement and wrath
and desolation as are horrible but to imagine. Love outraged most cruelly, friendship betrayed most vilely, all that
was pure turned into sin, all that was true turned false. In
one short hour, the pride of that ungodly home was humbled
to the dust, its fair name stained with shame, its very life's
blood oozing from that cruel wound. "Therefore revenge
became it well?" Therefore the agony that nothing else
could allay, should seek to dull itself in vengeance, should
hunt to the very death the shameless traitor? Should hurl
blighting curses on the head of her who had brought this
ruin on her home?

But God stayed the impotent wrath of man. He took
the vengeance that alone is His, in His own hands; the
curses that the outraged father called down on his erring
child, clustered, a black and ghastly troop, around his own
dying bed, and shut off the last ray of mercy. Before a
hand could be raised to deal vengeance, death struck down
the father, and but few days and nights of anguish and
solicitude had passed before his heir lay dead beside him,
and the life of the boy who alone of all survived, lay trembling in the balance. For a long while it seemed uncertain
whether God had not forgotten the race that had so long
forgotten Him; whether He had not turned away His face,
and they should all die and turn again to their dust; whether the memory of them should not be rooted off of the
earth, and their name perish from among the children of
men. For a long while, the boy lay between life and death,
but when at last life conquered, and he came back to the

changed and desolated world, it was with but little gratitude for the boon that had been granted him, with almost
a loathing of the life that had been spared to him.

It is not necessary to the purposes of my story nor will it
further its elucidation, to repeat the history of the years that
followed. It is sufficient that they were years of misan-
thropy and misery, almost of infidelity. Travel, change,
society, neither attracted nor soothed him; the life he led
it suited no one to join him in, and in the midst of the
world he lived unmolested by it and regardless oi .t. At
last—what need to tell when or how—there came an awakening; he saw the truth he had been so long shutting his eyes
from, he saw God's mercy and his own sin, and rousing
from his apathy he bent himself to the work that lay before
him. We know what that work was, and how well he fulfilled it; from the misanthropic recluse, he became the
Christian. I knew all this, and much more, that he did not
tell me.

"The story has been too long already, I will leave you now,"
said Mr. Rutledge with a sudden change of voice; "I have
finished my office of *raconteur*, you have listened well;
almost I could swear to having seen a tear glisten in your
eye, almost I could take my oath you have not once thought
of yourself and your young lady sensibilities, but have been
absorbed to forgetfulness of them all by the story of one
who is almost a stranger to you, quite a stranger, indeed,
you said not long ago."

" I did not mean that when I said it, Mr. Rutledge, I
repented of it a minute afterward. And I want to say to
you now—I am sorry from my heart for that, and the many
other hypocrisies you know I have been guilty of. You
don't know all, you would despise me if you did; if you
knew how cowardly I have been, and how deceitful. I have
not meant it; I have said a hundred things that I have cried
for afterward, that I never would have said if I had not
been too proud and too angry to have controlled myself.

But believe me, I am miserably sorry now. Will you forgive me?"

He leaned forward for a moment on the table, and shading his eyes with his hand, fixed them on my face. "Forgive you?" he said in a low, clear tone, "Forgive you? no—not yet—you must not ask it yet! When I have conquered *my* pride and *my* passion, you may ask me to forgive you, but not now—not now!"

"Aunt Edith, do you want me?" I faltered, starting up. Mrs. Churchill moved from where she stood beside the doorway and entered the room.

"You have been absent a long while," she said in a soft voice, "we have been wondering where you were. Mr. Rutledge, how have you managed to amuse my listless and *distraite* young niece so long? Have you been studying a map of France with her, or poring over a chart of the Atlantic? For such pursuits are all, I believe, that have any interest for her now."

"Miss Emerson, who sent me to entertain the young lady, did not confine me to those topics," he answered, rising, "and I have ventured to go beyond them. She will pardon me, I know, if I have not succeeded in my attempts to interest her." And Mr. Rutledge bowed and withdrew.

"I have a few words to say to you," said Mrs. Churchill, with muffled hatred in her low tones. "You have withdrawn yourself from my confidence, and from my affections; but remember, you cannot withdraw yourself from my authority. It is perfectly useless for you to attempt to deceive me; from the first night you came under my roof, I have known you thoroughly. You are a care and a vexation to me daily; your coquetry, your vanity, your boldness, I have hitherto tried to see unmoved, knowing I was unable to influence you; but where influence fails, authority may step in. And authority, for your own sake, for the sake of the man you are engaged to, for my own dignity, I shall use to prevent the recurrence of such evenings as this."

" The authority you hold, Aunt Edith," I returned with a
steadiness of tone and manner she was quite unprepared
for, " the authority you hold over me, I beg to remind you,
is very limited. Don't fancy I am unacquainted with the
circumstances that have placed me in your care. I know
every word of my mother's will, I have known it from a
child. My fortune is placed at my own disposal after I am
eighteen ; till then I am recommended—*recommended*, Aunt
Edith, to your care, and naturally devolve on you, but I
know that I am free : I know that after next December I
am my own mistress, and till that time, no one has any
right but that of seniority and affection to dictate to me.
So we understand each other, Aunt Edith, you say rightly,
and why waste words ? You cannot influence me ; you
have lost the only power you ever had over me. I came to
you an affectionate, trusting child ; you did not care to win
my affection, you took no pains to make me trust in you.
I threatened unconsciously to interfere in the plans you had
for Josephine, and you, without a scruple, sacrificed me to
her : you sacrificed my happiness, my peace, to the ambition
you had for her ; you have misled, thwarted, tortured me
to make the path clear for her ; you have done what in the
sight of heaven will one day be a millstone round your neck
to sink you to perdition ! Oh ! if I had but seen it all as
clearly a few short weeks ago, as now I see it, you would
not have had your triumph as near as you think you have
it now ! But because I was a foolish, trusting child, it was
not hard to deceive me ; because I looked to you for direction, you had the power to mislead me ; because I had strong
feelings it was all the easier to ensnare me. Let me say
what I have to say now ; this is our reckoning—I never
want to have another explanation ; we have understood each
other perfectly since we came to Rutledge, this plain talk
we scarcely needed, and let us end it. As long as I can
endure to stay with you, just so long will I stay, and not a
moment beyond it. As long as I must stay, you must bear

the vexation and the trial of my presence, but you may be sure, your release will not be very distant. I am not bound to you nor to your children by one tie of gratitude or affection, and those that restrain me of custom and convenience, don't cost much in the snapping!"

"All this tirade has wandered very far of the mark. I began to give you a caution and a command which my duty required me to give, and your duty required you to heed; and you fly angrily off on some unmeaning invectives which are very harmless because of their unmeaningness; if it were not the case, I should call you sternly to account for your words, and make you retract them."

"Unmeaning or not, Aunt Edith, they are sown in your memory, and nothing can root them out. They will bear bitter fruit some day, I promise you. They will yield a rich harvest, when the early growths of ambition and worldliness have died down, and left you only the withered husks and stalks of remorse and regret to satisfy your hunger withal. And now unless you want to publish this, will you go into the parlor and let me follow you?"

"I have something more to say to you"——

"There comes Miss Emerson; if it is anything that will bear being said before her, pray continue."

"Ah! Is it not delightful!" cried our pretty hostess. "Mr. Rutledge and the other gentlemen have been out, holding a post-mortem examination of the storm, and they have decided that it has left so black a state of heavens and so wet a state of roads that it is impossible to think of your going home to-night, so you will have to stay till to-morrow, *bongré malgré.* And I am so charmed. Ah! *you* are not, though, I see plainly enough, you want to go back to that tiresome Rutledge. What can it be, Mrs. Churchill? What is the matter with her. Though to be sure, the pale cheeks are gone now; I think I prescribed well. Mr. Rutledge must have said something very exciting all the

20

while he was in here, to have given you such a bright coloɪ and such flashing eyes."

"A very little excitement brings that result, Miss Emer. son. She has not learned much self-possession or self-control yet; we must excuse her."

"Oh! by all means. I am only glad she looks brighter than when I left her. But will you come into the parlor? Miss Josephine is going to give us one more song before we go to our rooms."

Josephine's song was gay and brilliant, her voice was rich and full, but they failed to drive the dreary echo of Victor's last words out of my mind, that deepened and strengthened as the night advanced : "You shall be freed! Be sure you shall be freed !" The lights shone clear and soft on the gay groups that peopled the rooms around me ; but instead of them, I seemed to see, far nearer and more distinct, the deserted chamber at Rutledge, where the guilt of the Past and the crime of the Present, kept awful watch together.

CHAPTER XXXVI.

"My care is like my shadow in the sun,
    Follows me flying, flies when I pursue it;
Stands and lies by me, does what I have done,
    This too familiar care does make me rue it.
                                QUEEN ELIZABETH.

LATE breakfast, long lingering at the table, delay in or-
dering the horses, lengthened adieux, all combined to re-
tard our starting for home on the following morning. I had
stood ready on the piazza, waiting for the others to come
out, for fifteen minutes; every new delay increased unbear-
ingly my nervousness. "Spare that innocent vine," said
Phil, arresting my riding-whip. "You have beaten that
cluster of roses to fragments." "Will they never come!"
I ejaculated. "It is so tiresome to wait for all those adieux.
Can't we start?"

"Certainly," said he, signalling the man who held our
horses. "We can ride forward; they will soon overtake us,
and McGuffy can accompany the carriage as far as the cross-
road. He is going to Brandon, I believe, this morning."

I stepped back. "After all, it would hardly be polite to
go, as he was of the riding party. There they come from the
greenhouse. They must be ready now."

At last, we were mounted, and our companions arranged
for the drive, our last good byes said; but the understanding was, as we parted, that the whole party of Masons and
Emersons should adjourn to Rutledge for the evening, where
a grand finale, in the shape of a supper and a dance, should
wind up the festivities of the season. The pretty Janet
whispered, as I went down from the saddle to exchange a
parting word with her, "I have not given up the visit yet

459

papa promises to take Mrs. Churchill by storm this evening, and you must consent."

As we rode along, I gave a sigh to the impossibility of this ; nothing could give me pleasure now, but this seemed more like it than anything else. To be quietly with Janet, and to learn to love her, and to unlearn the terrible lesson of the last few weeks, looked almost like peace. But I knew too well what my aunt's answer would be, as she was to be appealed to, and without throwing off the mask of deference that I still preserved and wished to preserve, I could not resist her decision. I well knew the programme sketched out for me, for the rest of the summer: in the thrice empty dreariness of Gramercy Park I was to be immured, while the others whiled away the pleasant weeks at Newport and Nahant. The Wynkars, Capt. McGuffy and Phil had consented to make their plans agree with the Churchills, and Mr. Rutledge had promised to join them in the course of a fortnight. He had made his arrangements to leave home on the same day that we did, and accompany us part of the way ; business in the western part of the State would occupy him for some ten days ; but, at the end of that time, he proposed rejoining the party at Newport. Nothing had been said to me about my plans, but I knew from something that escaped inadvertently, that the subject had been canvassed, and it had been decided that the income allowed me would not warrant such an expense, and that, with Frances, I was to be dropped at home, while mamma's maid should serve also for Josephine and Grace for the remainder of the summer. I should have loathed the gaiety of Newport, the crowd and the excitement would have been insupportable to me ; but the prospect of being smothered in that silent, dark house in the hot city, hateful with memories of my recent illness, and with trials that I could never forget, was even harder to anticipate. But I had to submit. What a future for seventeen.

"Wait till December," whispered Hope, just stirring his

wounded, drooping wings, just trembling with a faint life
that for days had seemed extinct. "Yes," I thought, with
a bitter sigh, "in December I shall be of age, it will be a
glorious thing to be my own mistress! To begin the world
when I've lost all interest in it—to do as I please when
there's nothing on earth that pleases me—to be free from
restraint and authority, and from all human love and care!
To be *independent!* God help me! What a glorious thing
it will be. All hope points to December!"

But my release, such as it was, was nearer than December. I might have spared myself the hateful anticipations
with which I blackened the fresh summer morning. I had
not seen any further into futurity than the rest of the human
family, who fret about their fate and look whole years
ahead, and put the misery of a lifetime into the present,
and torture themselves about what they know is, and fear
is to be, till the flood of God's judgment comes and sweeps
all away, and leaves them bewildered in the midst of a
strange desolation and a new terror.

"Phil," said Capt. McGuffy, as we rode slowly along
through the loveliest, freshest country, washed by last
night's rain, and gleaming in the morning sun—of which I
had not seen one beauty, in my absorbing anxiety—" Phil,
may I trust this young lady to you, if I leave you at the
cross-road? I want to ride over to Brandon for half an
hour before dinner."

"Oh, Captain McGuffy!" I exclaimed, startled out of
future fears by present dangers, "why do you take that
tiresome ride this morning? It will be sunny and disagreeable before you get back to Rutledge; wait till after
dinner."

The captain still leaned to the idea of accomplishing it all
"under one head," and having the rest of the day at home;
I didn't dare to press the subject, but seeing my only
chance lay in engrossing their attention to the exclusion
of their memories of the Brandon project, I worked

faithfully to accomplish my design, and succeeded in a
great measure. Before we had gone another half mile, I
had enticed the captain into the enthusiastic description of
a bull-baiting in Mexico, at which Phil and he had
"assisted," and into the recollection of which they both
seemed to enter with great ardor. We were on the top of
Ridgway Hill—the road for a good mile stretched away at
its foot, while on the left, branched off the Brandon turnpike.

"Heaven send they may forget it!" I ejaculated, bending forward to renew my questions about the bull-baiting.
The carriages were coming close behind—the bull-fight soon
began to flag.

"Phil," began the captain again.

"Capt. McGuffy," I cried, "Madge is fairly beside herself this morning, I can hardly hold her; we have been
creeping all the way from the Grove, what do you say to a
race, a bona fide race, and I'll ask no favor. It's a clear
road from here to Rutledge, and he's the best fellow who
clears the park gate first!"

"Done!" cried the captain, catching fire from my eyes;
and before another minute, we were off on the maddest
race I ever ran or hope to run. For a while, the three
straining beasts were nearly neck and neck, the th
dilated nostrils and fiery eyes were nearly on a line; the
gradually, very gradually, Madge's black head gained an
inch or so upon them, an inch or so, and then we were a
foot in advance. Phil drove the spurs into his horse—he
sprang forward, but soon fell back in no—the captain urged
Vagabond on with lash and oath; I did not move the
loosened bridle on Madge's neck—steady and unswerving
she kept the road, each spring as even and as sure as if
measured and done by rule—no relaxing of the eager
neck—no gasping in the even breath. I only saw, with a
heartfelt sigh of relief, that the Brandon turnpike lay
unnoticed far behind us, and Madge might take us

she liked : but when I dashed through the park gate, half a dozen yards in advance of Phil, and the captain in a fury with Vagabond, perfectly blown, quarter of a mile in the rear, I was quite helpless and weak from excitement.

"I don't know which to be proudest of, the young lady or the mare," said Stephen, as he lifted me down. "I wouldn't have missed seeing you come in for considerable money."

I hurried into the house and upstairs, leaving Phil to make all explanations and apologies: Kitty had seen me, and followed close behind me.

"Well?" I asked, breathlessly, as she closed the door.

"Nothing, Miss, nothing has happened. Do lie down and rest; you look fit to drop."

"But he is well? What did he say—has nothing happened?"

"Nothing has happened. I only saw him for a moment yesterday. Mrs. Roberts kept me close at marking linen all the rest of the day and evening; and this morning I had only a few moments to speak to him when I went in, for her door was open a crack, and I didn't dare to stay: you look so tired—won't you let me undress you?"

"But how did he seem? what did he say about my being away?"

"Oh!" returned Kitty, rather uneasily, "he asked why the house was so quiet, and whether you'd got back yet: he looks a little pale and badly, but I'm sure that's natural enough. Anybody would get pale and gloomy shut up day after day in that awful room, among all poor Miss Alice's books and pictures and things, all looking so dusty and dismal; it gives me a shudder only to go inside the door."

"But he doesn't know anything about her; you've never told him anything about the room?"

"I didn't mean to, Miss; I had no thought of opening

my lips about it; but he made me tell him—he wouldn't be satisfied till I had told him every word I knew about the family troubles. What put it into his head to ask, I think was something he had come across in a French book he had been reading; it was a little note that had marked the place. He held it in his hand as I came in, and he looked so white and strange, I was almost frightened. Oh, so many questions as he put me! so eager as he was! He seemed to look so through and through me with those black eyes of his, I didn't dare to keep back anything I knew. And then he asked me about master; if he had really loved his sister—if he had grieved for her, and tried to find her out, or if he held her memory in contempt—if he tried to forget that she had ever lived, and hated to hear her name."

"You didn't tell him that he did, Kitty?"

"How could I help it, Miss? You would not have had me tell him *a lie.* I had to tell him how it was. I had to tell him that her name was forbidden here—that no one dared for their lives to breathe a word about those times to the master—that her picture, and all that belonged to her, was put out of sight forever—that her room was shut up and hid as much from the living, as the poor lady was herself in her lonesome grave beyond seas. And he clenched his hand till the blood sprung under his nails, and his very lips were white like the wall; he said so low I could just hear him, 'but he shall not forget!' I am no coward, Miss, but I confess I was right glad when I got outside again."

All that wretched day I watched for a chance to see him. Kitty, nearly as anxious as I was myself, hovered around to try to clear the way for me, but in vain. No other day had the upper hall been so favorite a resort. Josephine had ordered her trunks to be put out there, and Ella's also, and Frances was packing them. Ellerton and Grace, lounging on the stairs, watched the operation, Mrs. Churchill sat with

. ner door open. 1 cannot possibly describe the misery it gave me to know what danger might arise from this delay. I knew too much already of Victor's morbid jealousy, to imagine it was not brooding now over this long neglect. The hours were leaden-winged and fiery-footed; each slow passing one seemed to burn into my very soul.

Kitty wiped away frequent tears as she busied herself about my packing; there were no tears in my eyes as I walked quickly up and down the room, or lay, face downward on the bed, trying to stifle thoughts that I could not endure.

"There's dinner!" said Kitty, ruefully. "And there's no hope of any more chance after it. Mrs. Roberts is at her eternal knitting in the hall window, and Frances won't stop packing these four hours yet. But don't you worry, Miss; I'll manage it, somehow. Go down to dinner, and *don't* fret!"

Of course not, why should I? What was there in my circumstances to occasion it? Nothing, of course; and nothing, either, to fret about in Josephine's taunts and Grace's sauciness, in the cold eyes of my aunt, in Ella's supercilious scorn; nothing to fret about when the captain talked of the murder and the evidence, the state of the public mind, and the state of his own private mind, in regard to it; when Ellerton talked about the news from town, and the letters he had just received from some of his inestimable chums there resident, and of the inexplicable nature of the fact that none of them had spoken of meeting or seeing Victor before he sailed, and of his own conviction that it was very strange we had heard nothing from him since he left, *very* strange.

"Oh!" cried Grace, "that's the way, they say, with these foreigners, adventurers, may be. You mustn't be astonished, my dear (turning pleasantly to me), you mustn't be astonished if you shouldn't hear from him 'never no more.' These French meteors, they say, sometimes flash through society in that way, and dazzle everybody, then sink into their native night again. And you know it is just possible our Victor may be of that order; but, of course, I don't want to distress you, only it's as well you should be prepared."

" Grace, hush! you are a saucy child; but really it *is* odd that we have never heard a word from him since he left."

"Did you expect to, Josephine? I didn't suppose you had made any arrangements to correspond. I am sorry I didn't know how deep your interest was, I might have relieved your mind before. Mr. Viennet is very well. I have heard from him more than once since we parted."

An exclamation of surprise went round the table; I was overwhelmed with questions and reproaches.

"You might have told us, really, now I think," said Ellerton.

" Why did you not ask me, then ?"

" Why, we thought you'd tell, to be sure. We didn't know how sacred you considered his epistles."

" What sort of a journey did he have ? What day did he get in town ?"

"He didn't say much about his journey. I fancy from something he said that he met with some detentions."

" Didn't he send any messages to anybody ?"

" None that I remember."

"Ungrateful rascal !"

" He succeeded, I suppose, in getting a state-room? He had some fears that he would be too late."

" He didn't say a word about it."

" Absurd! what did he talk about, then ?"

" Not about his journey, nor his stateroom, nor you, Josephine; but you know there are more things, and as interesting, in heaven and earth, to us both, strange as it may seem to you."

" *Pardon !* I had forgotten !"

" You won't hear again before the Persia is in, will you ?"

"That will be in three weeks, will it not?"

"Yes; that will be after we are at Newport. To whose care do your letters come addressed?"

"Really, Mr. Wynkar, you are too kind. Your interest is so unexpected!"

"Let us all drink to his *bon voyage*," said the captain, filling my glass.

"*Avec plaisir*," cried Josephine, and Phil said heartily, as he poured her out a glass:

"Victor's a good fellow; he has my best wishes on land or sea."

"And mine," said Mr. Rutledge, very low.

Why was there a hush around the table as that toast was drank? Why did a sort of shade creep over the careless mirth of the company? Not surely because they guessed that he whose health they drank was within hearing, almost, of their words, nor because they knew how fallen and how wretched he was; but because, perhaps unconsciously, the gloom on their host's face, and the misery on mine, damped for a moment their gaiety and confidence.

"The last day at Rutledge!" murmured Josephine, with a pretty sigh, as we left the dining-room. "I cannot bear to think of it. I never had so happy a fortnight in my life. Shall any of us ever forget this visit?"

"It doesn't seem as if we'd been here a week," said Ella, "does it?"

"A week! It seems to me a year!" I exclaimed, involuntarily.

"That doesn't speak well for your enjoyment, at all events; Mr. Rutledge will never ask you to come again. Will you, Mr. Rutledge?"

"I am afraid, Miss Wynkar, that it will be out of my power to enjoy the honor of any one's society here for a long while to come. I am going abroad in the course of a month, and "——

"You, Mr. Rutledge!" exclaimed more than one voice, and Josephine's color suffered a shade of diminution.

"It is a sudden determination, it is not, sir?" asked Phil.

"No, I have been thinking of it for some weeks, but I have not till recently had much idea of the time I should start."

"Mr. Rutledge does not look upon crossing the Atlantic for a few months, as any way more formidable than going to town for a night, he has been such a traveller," said Mrs. Churchill, with admirable composure; but *I* knew the effort that it cost her. "You do not think of being absent long, I suppose?"

"It is uncertain; I shall make my arrangements to be gone for about two years, but something may occur to detain me longer, in which case I can easily settle all things here by letter. I have trusty persons in my employ, and I think there is no chance of my presence being necessary at home for a long while to come."

"I envy you," said Ellerton; "I wish I could run off for a year or two."

I saw Josephine's lips move, but she could not command her voice, and, bending down, she caressed Tigre with a nervous hand. I could not but pity her; I had not realized before how much her heart had been set upon this match; and wounded pride is next in sting to wounded love.

The gentlemen lit their cigars, and talked of Mr. Rutledge's plans; we all lounged idly about the north end of the hall; the doors were all open, and a fine fresh breeze came in. I had been listening anxiously to a faint sound overhead, *where* I knew too well; a hasty stride from one end to the other of the room above us.

"Hark!" cried Grace, "what's that? I heard the same sound this morning."

Every one stopped talking, and listened.

" The house is haunted, you may depend," said Josephine. " There have been strange noises next my room
for the last three nights."

" That's a peculiar sound. What do you make of it, Mr.
Rutledge?" said Ellerton, walking toward the stairs.

" It is nothing," he returned, advancing that way too.
" Some of the servants are up there now, perhaps; I will
go and see. Don't trouble yourself, Mr. Wynkar."

" I'll go," I cried, starting forward. " Perhaps it's Kitty,
she may be waiting for me."

Ellerton paused and listened; Mr. Rutledge passed up
before him, followed closely by Tigre. I brushed past
Ellerton and kept close to Mr. Rutledge. Mrs. Roberts
was standing at the head of the stairs.

" Mrs. Roberts," said Ellerton, " we're investigating an
unusual noise up here. Can you account for it?"

Now, Mrs. Roberts never could abide the insinuation
that anything might possibly be going on of which she was
ignorant; if she had nosed anything herself, she did not, as
we have seen, lack zeal in ferreting it out, but it was impossible to put her on a new scent; she refused to acknowledge
any other sagacity than her own. So, on the present occasion, as she had heard no noise, she utterly scouted the
idea, and assigned some trifling cause for it; the girls, she
said, had been in the attic, clearing out an old store-room;
probably that was what Mr. Rutledge had heard. Ellerton
hurried down to inform the ladies of the explanation, and
Mr. Rutledge, crossing the hall, was going toward his
dressing-room, when Tigre, who had been exploring the
neighborhood, now rushed whining along the hall, with his
nose to the floor. The attention of all was attracted to
him; he darted under the wardrobe, and began scratching
and growling earnestly at the door of Victor's hiding-place.
I followed Mr. Rutledge's quick glance from my face to
the wardrobe, and, starting forward, I tried to call off Tigre.

"Come here, sir! Come here, I say!" But he was too intent upon his discovery to heed me.

"He is a little nuisance," said Mrs. Roberts. "I never approved having him allowed to come upstairs."

"Tigre, what are you after, sir?" said Mr. Rutledge, as he walked down the hall toward him.

"Oh, nothing, I'm sure, sir, nothing!" I cried, following him. "Don't scold him. Tigre, come out, you rascal! come out, I say!" and I stamped vehemently on the floor.

"He will not mind you," said Mr. Rutledge, in a low voice. "He will obey his instincts, and persevere till he has reached the object of his search."

"He isn't searching for anything," I exclaimed, dropping down on my knees and stooping till I could see under the wardrobe. "If I could only reach him. Tigre—you torment—if you don't come, I'll whip you, *so!* Here, here, *poor* fellow! Come here, my pet!"

Tigre desisted a moment from his whining, and wavered in his determination. I thrust my arm under the wardrobe, seized him, and drew him, yelping, out; then, springing up, ran across the hall, and almost threw him into my room. Mr. Rutledge watched me silently with a contracted brow, and crossing over to his own room, shut himself into it.

Not a very faithful index, certainly of the real feelings of men and women, is to be obtained from their outward and visible emotions. A very gay party, no doubt, the visitors who came that night to Rutledge, thought they found there. They little guessed how unhappy and disappointed a man their courteous host was, nor that Mrs. Churchill, serene and charming, was looking in the face the failure of the hopes of years, nor that the pretty Josephine's smiles were in ghastly contrast with the bitterness of her spirit; nor that Phil, who knew her face too well to be deceived by them, was smarting under the realizing sense it gave him of her ambition and worldliness.   And if they had guessed the interpretation of *my* gaiety!

There were just enough of us to make the dancing spirited, and to keep every one on the floor.   We had before always danced in the parlors, but some evil spirit prompted Grace to propose that we should try a double set of Lancers in the hall.   Everybody, encouraged, doubtless, by their attendant evil spirits, seemed to think nothing could be more delightful than the hall, and urged the moving of the piano out there; and there we adjourned.   I tried not to remember how plainly we could be heard in a certain room at the end of the hall above; how the laughing and the music would grate on the jealous ears there. If he caught the tones of my voice, he would not know that I laughed because I must keep pace with the captain's jokes, and encourage him in punning and joke-making, to keep him from the hideous topic that he always turned to when left to himself; and to drive away the suspicion that sharpened Mr. Rutledge's eyes, and to keep Mr. Mason my admirer, and no more.

"Like the lady of ' Old Oak Chest ' memory, ' I'm weary of dancing,' " I cried at length, " let's amuse ourselves some other way."

" Play hide-and-seek, like that ancient party?" asked Phil, throwing himself on the lowest step of the stairs.

" That's not a bad suggestion!" exclaimed Grace.   " This is just the place for such an adventure.   I don't mean that I want anybody to be smothered in a chest exactly, but lost for a little while, and hunted for, you know.   It would be so jolly."

" So it would!" echoed Ellerton.

" And there's no end of capital hiding-places about the house, so many odd rooms where you'd never expect them; and acres of attic, beyond a doubt!"

" Come!" cried Josephine, " we're all ripe for adventure. Let's have a game of hide-and-seek."

.

"Delightful!" cried the youngest Miss Mason.

"I'm ready for anything," said Phil, getting up and shaking himself.

"I'm afraid you will not find any oak chests," said Mr. Rutledge, discouragingly.

"Oh! yes, we will," cried Grace, "chests, and crannies, and closets, and wardrobes, and trap-doors without number. A regiment of soldiers might be hid away in this house and nobody the wiser."

Everybody was in the spirit of it now, and it was useless to oppose.

"Who shall hide first?" demanded Grace.

"Oh, your cousin, of course!" cried the captain. "She proposed the game."

I was voted in by acclamation.

"And you must take somebody with you, it will make it more exciting, but you must hide in separate places," added Grace.

"Very well; the captain must go out with me, and you must all go into the parlor, and promise, on your honor, to stay there five minutes by the clock, and then we give you leave to find us."

"We promise," said Ellerton; "but remember, you are to hide somewhere in the house, and to surrender yourselves in half an hour if you are not found before."

"Always provided," said the captain, shutting the parlor-doors upon them, "that we're not smothered in some old chest in the meantime."

CHAPTER XXXVII.

> " Sweetest lips that ever were kissed,
> Brightest eyes that ever have shone,
> May sigh and whisper, and *he* not list,
> Or look away, and never be missed
> Long or ever a month be gone."

" WHERE shall we go?" said the captain, in a whisper,
as we paused in the hall irresolutely.

"What do you think of the dining-room, behind the tall
clock for one of us?"

The captain shook his head.

"They'll look there the first thing; it will not do. But
in the second story, there's a huge old wardrobe that I've
noticed at the north end, that would be a capital place for
one."

"Yes, I know where you mean, but I think it's locked,
and we haven't the key, and it would take too long to hunt
up the housekeeper and get it. There's the lower part of a
bookcase in the library empty. Captain McGuffy, if you
only could get into it! Not even Mr. Rutledge knows
about it. Mrs. Roberts only cleared the books out of it last
week, and you'd be as safe as possible. Do try if you can't
arrange it, and I'll go somewhere upstairs; I know a place."

Captain McGuffy consented, and we hurried to the library. The hiding-place was not so large as I had fancied,
but still my companion agreed to risk it. He doubled up
like a jack-knife; it was perfectly wonderful to me how he
ever got his long limbs into so small a compass.

"Are you comfortable?" I asked, smothering a laugh.

"Don't shut the door tight," he whispered, hoarsely. "I
can't stand this long."

I had no time for more lengthened condolences, but hurried off to dispose of myself. The second story was entirely clear; the servants were all downstairs; Mrs. Roberts was busy about supper. I resolved to hide behind the linen-press outside her door; but first, I thought, if I were quick, I could go one instant to Victor's door, whisper my excuses, and promise to come back when they were all gone. It was rather a dangerous thing to do, but the moment I heard the parlor-door open, I could fly to my hiding-place; I dared not lose this chance.

Moving aside the wardrobe with some effort, I tapped low at the door. Again—and no answer. "Victor," I whispered at the key-hole, "come to the door one moment;" but not a sound from within.

Apprehension of I do not know what new danger overcame my prudence, and I wasted the few precious seconds I had to spare in irresolution. When it was too late to effect my escape, I heard the door of the parlor burst open, and Josephine's voice crying, "Allons!" They separated to all parts of the house, Grace, Janet, and Ellerton flying up the stairs. There was but one thing for me to do: I hurriedly pulled the wardrobe after me into its place, opened the door, entered, and closed it stealthily behind me. Only when I was in it, did I realize the folly of what I had done. The room was as dark and silent as the grave; such a silence and such a darkness as would have chilled a stouter heart than mine. I whispered Victor's name—there was no answer. Had he fled, then, and was I alone in this horrid room—shut up in it for hours perhaps? No! I would risk all and grope my way out, no matter if I encountered them all. I could endure this no longer. All Kitty had told me—all I ever fancied of the ghastly terrors of the room—crowded into my mind, and, starting forward, I attempted to find the door, but in my bewilderment and the utter blackness around me, I must have turned away, instead of toward it. My outstretched hand struck against an icy surface; I screamed and started back, my foot slipped and I fell, striking my temple heavily against some projection. The fall and the blow stunned me for awhile; then returning consciousness suggested all that they had mercifully absolved me from. Alice Rutledge's neglected, dishonored room—Alice Rutledge's sin-troubled spirit haunting it—the curses that had been spoken in it—the agony that had been endured in it—the years of silence that had passed over it—and now, a murderer's hiding-place—a murderer with crime fresh upon him. And oh! the horror of that crime! It seemed almost as if it had been me instead of Victor who had done it. My brain seemed reeling —had I not been there—had I not seen—heard—that of which I never lost the memory—or was it only haunting me from another's lips? Was *that* avenging ghost here, too—within the limits of this dreadful room? Was that a touch of human hand upon my breast?—was it fancy, or— or—was that a breath upon my cheek? A thousand horrid whispers—hollow laughter—dying shrieks—filled the air; within these accursed walls, it was weird and unearthly all; without, I heard, but as through triple dungeon walls, the voices of those I had left behind; I heard their steps overhead, their searching, high and low, in every nook and corner for me; I heard them call my name, and pause for answer. I tried to call, but a nightmare stifled my voice. As one might feel who had buried himself yet living—who had pulled the coffin-lid down on his own head, and heard the devils eagerly filling the grave up and laughing at their work—and at each new shovelful of heavy clay had felt the distance between him and life grow shorter, and felt the weight press heavier and heavier, and the horror and the darkness grow tighter and tighter around him, and the remorse, and the helplessness, and the terror—so I felt that hideous night, and so I feel whenever I remember it.

The house quieted, I heard the carriages drive away, then the faint good-nights, and the closing of the many doors.

and all grew into repose. That was cruel; they had forgotten me—they had given me up easily! But I would
make them hear—I would get out of this sepulchral place,
and I started to my feet. Just then the handle of the door
turned, and a ray of light streamed across the room. It
was Mr. Rutledge who entered; but the sternness and
whiteness of his face repressed the cry of joy with which I
had started forward. The light, though, had put all the
ghastly train to flight, and I breathed freer as I looked
around and saw that he and I were alone in the room. He
closed the door, and pressing his hand for a moment before
his eyes, looked up and around the apartment. I suppose
he had never been in it since it had been closed upon the
flight of his sister, and since his father's curse had doomed
it to desolation. I followed his glance around the dim and
dusky walls—the familiar pictures—the disordered, time-
stained ornaments—the tall, canopied bed—the open wardrobe. A low groan escaped his lips, and sinking on a chair,
he bowed his head in his hands upon the table. Some
sound from me at last aroused him, and looking up, he
said:

"I knew I should find you here. What evil spirit
brought you to this place! Are you alone?"

"Yes," I faltered, coming to him, "I am alone. Take
me out, for the love of heaven! I have been in such terror
—Victor is not here—I have"——

I stopped, with an exclamation of alarm. I had betrayed
my secret.

"It is better that he has gone," he said, but without any
surprise; "it could not have been kept up much longer. I
hope, for your sake, he may be safe. Flight would have
been better a week ago. I could have managed it, but you
would not trust me. Did you really think," he continued,
rising slowly from his seat, and looking at me with an expression compounded of bitterness, and tenderness, and
sadness, "did you really think I did not know you were

hiding your lover in my house—that you were dying a
thousand deaths in the midst of this careless crowd? Why,
child," he said, laying his hand on my shoulder, and looking
into my eyes, " I know every expression of this face better
than I know my own. I know its flashes of fear, its white
mantle of despair, and its crimson glow of love, too well to
be deceived. If I had needed confirmation of my suspicions
on the morning after Dr. Hugh's murder, that Victor Viennet was the guilty man, I should have had only to have
looked in your face. And from that dreadful day to this, I
have read there each event as it has come to pass. I have
helped you in your lover's cause, though you did not know
it. I have worked day and night to mislead his persecu-
tors, to allay the suspicions and blind the eyes of the author-
ities ; and I have nearly succeeded. There is very little
danger now, if he is prudent and dexterous in his flight.
Do not tremble so ; you need not fear for him. By this
time he is probably beyond the only part of his journey
that was attended with much risk."

I burst into tears ; it was so hard to hear him say all this,
and talk to me as if I had nothing to be miserable about,
now that Victor was safe. Ah! this was but the beginning.
A life-time lay before me full of such hours as this.

"It is a heavy fate, poor child," he said, compassionately.
" I would have saved you from it if I could."

" You don't know half how heavy !" I sobbed. " If you
did, you wouldn't think it a sin for me to pray to die."

" Take the harder penance, and submit to live. Death
doesn't always come for the asking. God has sent you a
terrible trial, but he will help you through it if you will only
keep that in mind."

" No, no. God did not send it. I have brought it
on myself—it is all my own deed! Oh! if you only
knew "——

" I do know. I know you are disappointed in the man
you love—that you have found weakness where you fancied

strength : but I know that, woman-like, you still love, if possible, more tenderly than before your idol was shat. tered, and that you are shrinking now from the prospect of a long and uncertain separation. I pity you, believe me, I pity you ; but these are griefs that time has a cure for. Do not talk of despair till you have felt what it is to be unloved and unblest—to be without an interest on earth, with but a slender right to hope in heaven—to be thwarted in all you undertake, balked of all you desire—till you have seen another and an unworthier hand take down your crown of life, and wear it careless in your sight."

" Perhaps I know all that as well as you," was on my lips, but I only hid my face and turned away. He did not understand the gesture, and said sadly, after a pause :

" Why are you so wretched ? I have assured you there is little danger, and what is there so insupportable in the separation of a year or two ? Or is it something in the manner of parting ; were you unprepared to find him gone ? Did he leave no good bye ?"

" No," I said, glad to have some excuse for my tears ; " I never dreamed of his going—it is too unkind ! And I shall never forgive myself either ; when I saw him last, there was some misunderstanding, and I have not explained it to him ! He has gone away in despair and in anger ! Oh, I shall never, never forgive myself !"

" You may overrate the cause," said my companion, " perhaps he may have found it more prudent to fly now, and could not wait to see you. Look about the room, there may be a letter somewhere, or he may have left one with Kitty."

" Kitty knows nothing of it, and I do not see any letter."

" What is that little package—beyond you—there on the table ?"

I seized it, and, bending eagerly over the light, read my name upon it. My hand trembled so that I could hardly open it. Within the first paper there was a letter; my eyes glanced hurriedly over it, but from another wrapping something dropped, one sight of which served to make me grasp the table for support, and drop the letter on the floor.

"What is it?" cried my companion, starting forward, and picking up my letter, leading me to a chair.

"Read it to me—I can't—I don't understand," I faltered, putting back the letter in his hand. He looked at me hesitatingly a moment, then read it aloud:

"I promised you freedom. Well! I have been a coward not to have given it to you sooner; but when you read this, there will be such a gulf between us, that you may well grant a little pity to the cowardice that only feared death as a separation from you—that only clung to life as sweetened by your love.

"It is trite to tell you of my love—to tell you to be happy—to say I forgive the coldness that you strove to hide—and to ask forgiveness for the pain I have given you. You know all this—better, much better than at this dreadful hour I can tell you—and though you can never know in its fullness the agony that the parting inflicts on me, there is no need that you should realize it: I have done enough to make you miserable already. Forget all this black dream; it will soon be over, and be again the happy girl I found you.

"But one thing more. Would you know who it is to whom you had affianced yourself—to whose life you had promised to unite yours—whose name you had promised to bear? It is a good name—*mon ange*—an ancient name—an honorable! Ask your proud host if it is not; ask him if there is a better in the country, or one that a woman need be prouder to bear. It is no new name to your ears; it is *Rutledge;* the only name I have any claim to, though, perhaps, my host would say that was but a slender one: did his sister lose the ancient and honored name she was born

with, when she lost her honor, when she stepped down from
her high place, and stooped to sin? Or did she drag down
that name with her in her fall? Did it cling to her, like a
robe of mockery and scorn, only making her shame the
greater; did it descend with the heritage of infamy, to the
child of her shame? Or did it die with her, and has her
neglected grave the only right to bear the record of it?
Ask our host—he can tell you more of it than I. But tell
him I am not inclined to dispute it with him: I am not as
proud of the name as he; tell him I loathe—I execrate it!
I could almost wish to live to show him my contempt for it
—to show him what a low wretch could share with him his
inheritance and his pride. If he doubts it—if he questions
whether the same blood runs in our veins, show him the
only souvenir I have to leave you—the picture of my father.
Ask him if he remembers Alice Rutledge's lover. He will
not need more damning proof; it came to me like a message
from the dead—it may go to him as such. Tell him that a
murderer wrenched it from his victim's dying grasp; that
it has struck awe to his guilty soul at every glance; that it
has hurried him on to perdition. But if he longs to be
more certain, show him these two letters; one that I have
worn next my heart for years—the other, that I found between the leaves of a forgotten book in this ghastly room.

"The God whom you believe in bless you, and, if he has
the right—forgive me!

"VICTOR."

"I don't understand—what does he mean—where has he
gone?" I said, wildly, pressing my hand to my head. "I
am so bewildered, I can't think. Oh! don't look so awfully!
There must be some mistake. You can't believe that—that
—oh! heaven help me!"

My companion did not speak; my eyes searched his
blanched face in vain for comfort—a wild impulse seized me;
I grasped the candle in my hand, and, with a hasty look

around the apartment, hurried to the bed and drew aside the curtains.

I did not swoon or cry; I did not even drop the candle from my hand, nor loose the grasp with which I held back the curtains; but, with glazed eyes and freezing veins, gazed steadily at what lay before me.· Pale with the unmistakable pallor of death, one arm thrown above his head, the other buried in his bosom, his dark tangled curls lying distinct against the pillow, his manly limbs rigid—a crimson stream that had stained his breast, and was creeping down upon the bed, gave awful proof that Victor and I had indeed parted forever — that my wretched lover lay dead before me.

Brought so suddenly to my sight, there was nothing in that moment of the remorse and the lingering tenderness that after the first shock nearly deprived me of reason; it was only horror—staring, ghastly horror—at the sight of his dead body—at the thought of his lost soul; the words that rang in my head, and the first that struggled to my lips were: "God have mercy on his soul! God have mercy on his soul!" Dead—without a prayer—dead—by his own hand — cast out forever from God's mercy — a wailing, · damned, lost soul through all eternity. I stood as if turned to stone; my companion, in an agony of grief and consternation, had thrown himself on his knees beside the bed; his iron fortitude broken down before this awful judgment that, laying bare the anguish of the past, had interwoven itself so strangely with the present; the unerring retribution that had worked out this end to sins so long ago committed.

But no sob or cry came from my lips; no tears dimmed my riveted eyes. I heard the broken words that burst from him as in a dream, and neither knew nor felt that there was anything in this world but blank horror—hopeless consternation—till from a slight movement of the candle, I caught the shine of a trinket that the unhappy man had

21

worn around his neck. Bending forward, I saw in a moment
what it was. A little ring of mine, and a link of the broken
bracelet, worn on a chain next his heart while living, now
wet with blood, was lying still above the heart that beat no
more. At that sight a passion of tears came to my relief.
His tender and devoted love, the miserable return I had
made, the unkindness of our parting, my shameful injustice
and deceit, the cruelty of his sufferings, all rushed over me
and shook me with a tempest of tears and sobs. I threw
myself beside him on the bed, and covered his cold hand
with tears and caresses; wild with pain and remorse, I laid
my cheek against his on the pillow, and implored him to
forgive me, to speak to me but once, to say I had not killed
him; with incoherent passion I called heaven to witness
that I really loved him—that I would have been true to
him—that I would have died for him—that I had nothing
else to live for or to love.

It was long before, worn out by excess of weeping, I
yielded to my companion, and was led faint and almost
unresisting from the room. With a few words of pity, he
left me in my own apartment, reluctantly turning away from
me, so wretched and so lonely. But I shook my head; I
did not want any one, I had rather be by myself.

"No one can do you much good, it is true," he said sadly.
"God help you!" and he left me.

I stood motionless for some minutes after the door closed
upon him. Then, stung by some fresh recollection and by
the added terrors of solitude, I paced rapidly up and down
the room, and flinging myself on my knees by the bedside,
I prayed incoherently and passionately for Victor—for myself—for pardon and for death. I could not endure one
thought or one occupation long: before I rose from my
knees my resolution was taken; my brain would have given
way if I had not had some necessity for exertion, some
design to carry out. And strange and sudden as my determination was, I doubt whether I could have done anything

wiser and better. There was one uncontrollable longing uppermost—to escape from this place, to hide myself forever from all who had ever known me here.

Stealthily and hurriedly, for Kitty was sleeping in the dressing-room, I went through my preparations. They were not many; there were some letters to be burned and one to be written, some clothes to be selected and made up into a package, a trinket to be clasped round Kitty's arm, and a coin slipped in her hand, and I was ready. I looked at my watch; it was half-past three, the faint grey dawn was just streaking the eastern sky, I must go. Where should I put my letter? I sat down and hurriedly wrote the address, then with a momentary indecision, the first that had marked my rapid movements since my resolution was taken, I opened and read it over:

"You will not be surprised when you find that I have gone away. You can understand, if you will think a moment about it, and try to realize what I should have to endure in concealing and controlling my feelings, that it is the only thing I could do. My life with Mrs. Churchill has grown so intolerable that I had before this resolved it should not continue. And now is the best time to do what at any other moment would be painful, but which at this, is only a relief. Inquiries and investigations as to where I go, will be just so many cruelties; will you do this last of many kindnesses, and help to cover my retreat, and keep them from any attempts to find me? It would kill me to have to face any of them now; will you not trust me enough to help me to the only comfort possible to me now, solitude and rest? You are ingenious, you can divert them from it, if you try; it is not as if they had any instincts of affection to guide them in finding me out. You need not let them know that I did not project the pastime of last night to accomplish a premeditated flight. If you ever had any kindness for me, do not try to find me out yourself, *do not let them.* You may trust me when I promise you I will do nothing rash, nothing that you would not approve if I could tell you. I promise you that I will remember my religion and my womanhood, and spend what length of life God sentences me to, as penitently, patiently and reasonably as He will grant me grace to do. If you will show this proof of confidence and friendship, you will never repent it.

" God knows, you have little reason to trust in me : but I am changed—I am much changed—I will not deceive you now. If you will believe in me this once, and shield me from exposure, and leave me in peace where I may choose to go, I will pledge you my word that as soon as I shall ascertain that you have sailed for Europe, I will write you fully and truthfully where I am, and what I intend to do, and will from that time make no secret of my place of abode and my plans.

" There is another thing—but I need not ask it of you. You, for your own sake are concerned to keep this cruel secret that I have so long been hiding, a secret still. It passes now from my hands to yours. Perhaps I should be insensible to disgrace and ignominy ; they cannot harm *him* now : but oh ! shield me from them, save his memory from shame. Do not let the world know of it till that day when the secrets of all hearts shall be revealed ; when God shall commit all judgment to His Son, who is more merciful than man—more compassionate and more just.

" You have helped me hitherto, though I did not know whose hand was smoothing my way ; do not give up now, despairing. Kitty and Stephen will be faithful, no one else need know the secrets of that dreadful room.

" I am not so selfish as you think. I do not forget that you are only less miserable than I am, as you have only grief and not remorse to bear. Heaven send you the peace I have no right to ask for myself."

I folded my letter quickly and sealed it ; then with one

more look at Kitty, and one hurried glance around the familiar room, I put out the candle, took the package from the table and stole out. Where should I put my letter? It must be within reach of no other hand than his; no one must know that I had written to him. The hall—no words can tell its gloom, the early dawn just turning its darkness into spectral dimness. If inevitable detection had been the result, I could not have helped the hurried, incautious steps with which I crossed it, and listened at Mr. Rutledge's door. Within the inner room I heard a step pacing restlessly up and down, but no other sound. He was awake, then; I stooped, and softly tried the handle of the door. It was locked; he would be the first to open it; so I slipped the letter under it, and springing up, fled down the stairs and through the hall, without a look behind, with no thought but that of escape, no fear so strong as that of detection. I had forgotten everything now but flight.

It was Heaven's mercy and nothing else, as poor Kitty would have said, that no one was aroused by the loud sliding of the bolts, that required all my strength to move; I hardly stopped to pull the heavy door to, after me; I should not have heard, if the whole household had been in pursuit, for the wild throbbing of my heart, the maddening pressure on my brain, the choking fear, kept me insensible to sight and sound. I flew on, through the shrubbery, across the unfrequented, dark orchard; my feet tangled in the rank, wet grass that lay in the field beyond it, my light dress tore to fragments in the thicket that bordered the western extremity of the park; but on, till the thickest of the forest sheltered me; then sinking exhausted and panting upon the ground, I hid my eyes and shuddered at the terrors I was flying, and the dismal blank, and dread uncertainty of what was beyond.

CHAPTER XXXVIII.

" Vous qui pleurez, venez à ce Dieu, car il pleure.
   Vous qui souffrez, venez à lui, car il guerit. •
   Vous qui tremblez, venez à lui, car il sourit.
   Vous qui passez, venez à lui, car il demeure.
                        ECRIT AU BAS D'UN CRUCIFIX.

THE years that have passed since that night, have been long and strange years. At first they were too strange and hopeless and blank to be borne without repining; I knew but too well the curse that turns life into a burden and a dread, and makes the wretched soul cry in the morning, " would God, it were evening," and in the evening, " would God, it were morning !" I knew what it was to dread solitude, and yet to shrink from the reproach of any human face ; to hate life, and yet to fear death; to know to the fullest the terrors of remorse and the bitterness of repentance.

I have passed through this howling wilderness, passed through it once and forever; it lies black and horrible behind me; when I look back, I cross myself and murmur a prayer ; but beyond—thank God's good grace—lies a plain path; over it shines the steady star of faith, the cold, clear light of duty fills the sky, the still air breathes peace; the promise is faint of the life that now is, but of that which is to come, of the bliss that never tires, the joy that never ceases, the majesty of the Glory that fills the heaven beyond the dividing limit of that horizon, I can dream and hope, till the dream fills my soul to satisfaction, and the hope grows strong as life itself.

The daily routine of my life is easily described, and the occupations that served to soothe and sustain me will not

take many words to paint. The refuge I had sought upon
my flight from Rutledge, was not distant; Mr. Shenstone's
compassion was the first I asked; he heard, fresh from its
occurrence, the awful story of Victor's death, the not less
awful story of his life. I needed no truer friend than he;
and though it opened anew the recollection of his own early
trial, I did not suffer from the association it awoke; he was
only tenderer and kinder.

Mr. Rutledge regarded my request. Whether he suspected my retreat or not, I could not tell, but in the confusion and excitement that ensued upon the discovery of my
flight, I have reason to believe he influenced the direction of
the search that was instituted, and did not thwart the general idea, that I had fled to the city to rejoin Victor, who,
it was soon learned, had not sailed when he had appointed.
All was mystery and confusion, but this idea saved me from
pursuit here, and gave something for suspicion to fasten and
feed upon, and out of which to build up an effigy, to receive
the maledictions and reproaches of the world. All this was
less than indifferent to me; while they were searching for
me with venom and wrath, and bemoaning my iniquities
with dainty horror, and execrating my hypocrisy, and settling my fate, and clearing themselves forever of any further
part or lot in me, I was much nearer the other world than
this; so near indeed, that when after long weeks of hovering between this and the unseen, I gradually awoke to the
knowledge that I was still to stay in life, I had so far lost
my interest in it, that it gave me hardly a moment's concern
to find that Mrs. Churchill had discovered my place of retreat, and had written in almost insulting language to Mr.
Shenstone, forbidding my return to her, and casting me off
forever. Mr. Shenstone seemed sadly distressed to communicate this to me; the languid smile with which I received
it, reassured him.

"She could not have done me a greater favor, sir; she
has saved me the trouble of saying that I would not

return to her, and she knew it very well. She is glad to be rid of me, and hurried to spare her dignity the rebuff that she knew it would receive as soon as I was able to put pen to paper."

But there was a harder task to perform; my promise to Mr. Rutledge was yet unfulfilled. I understood from Mr. Shenstone that he had sailed for Havre a fortnight after I had left Rutledge, and I dared no longer delay my promised communication to him. A very brief and simple letter told him all that was necessary. In the course of the winter there came an answer to it, short but kind, with nothing wanting in consideration and interest, characteristic and manly, yet with a shade of formality and restraint, differing from all phases of our former intercourse; ever so slight a shade, it is true, but it made me put this his last letter away, with the same feeling that I think I should have had, if I had just turned away from my last look at him in his coffin. He was dead to *me*, at least.

Occasional letters, indeed, came from him to Mr. Shenstone, generally with some mention of my name; Mr. Shenstone always showed them to me; they brought back old times, and made me restless and vaguely sad for a day or two, then the *dead* feeling would come back, and all would be the same as before. As time wore on, the letters grew almost imperceptibly shorter and less explicit; he was travelling—he was here—at such a time he should be there —such places pleased him—such spots were changed since his former visits; then would follow some general directions about the farm—remembrances to Mrs. Arnold and to me—kind inquiries into Mr. Shenstone's own health—renewed assurances of friendship—and so the letter would end.

Of my aunt's family I rarely heard. They went abroad the year after we parted; I saw occasionally by the papers their residence at Paris, or their journeying in Italy; and Grace's marriage with a Frenchman of good family came to my knowledge through the same means. Why Josephine still lingered unmarried I could only conjecture. Phil Arbuthnot returned to America after spending a year with them in Paris, and I believe has never rejoined them.

So much for these once prominent participators in my interest, and now of myself. In the home I had chosen I was soon as necessary as I was occupied; Mrs. Arnold saw life and usefulness receding from her now with less pain, that she saw one younger and stronger, able to take up the duties that she had reluctantly laid down. There was no chance for time to hang heavy on my hands; besides the occupations of the house, there were unnumbered calls upon my energies in the parish. Mr. Shenstone was no longer young, almost an old man now, and though his energy never flagged, his strength did, and I found many ways of relieving him, and inducing him to save himself and depend on me. I have no doubt he saw it was the kindest thing he could do for me, and so the more willingly yielded the duties to me. No one that sets himself or herself earnestly at work, with a sincere desire to do right, and to atone for the past, but will, sooner or later, feel the good effect of such effort; his languor will yield before the invigorating glow of exercise, his nerves will regain the tone they had lost, his pulse will beat with something of its old vigor; he will, though never again the same man, be once more a man, be free from the corroding melancholy that threatened to be his ruin, and be ready to look on life with steadier, wiser eyes than in his youth. Such reward work brings; no matter how plain and coarse and unattractive the work may be, no matter if, in itself, it has no interest and no charm, the will, the duty, the spirit in which it is done, will give it its interest and its charm, and will bring it its certain reward. —Youth can hardly see this, misery cannot at first acknowledge it, but none ever faithfully and patiently tried it, without finding the truth of it.

There is a lonely grave in the very heart of the pine for

est, unmarked by cross or stone, above which no prayers
but mine have ever been said, which the dark moss covers
thickly, and around which the trees sound their everlasting
dirge. I have not learned to be tranquil there; years more
of faith and prayer may take the sting out of that sorrow,
and bring me to leave it utterly in His high hand who seeth
not as man seeth. If prayer could avail, after the grave
had shut her mouth upon any of the children of men, if
fast and vigil, tears and penance, could mitigate the wrath
decreed against them, I might hope, I might stand by that
desolate mound with a less despairing heart. I have tried
to realize that God's ways are not as our ways, that nothing is impossible with him, that His mercy is as incompre-
nensible as is His power; and that our puny prayers, however they may chasten and purify ourselves, are not needed,
and not efficient in influencing His sentence on our brothers'
souls.

There is enough to do among the living. "Let the dead
Past bury its dead." There are souls yet unsentenced to
be prayed for and to be gained, there are children to be
brought to baptism and to be led aright, there are dark
homes of poverty and sin to be invaded with the light of
truth and love; there is doubt to be won to faith, ignorance
to be enlightened, sluggish indolence to be roused, God's
church to work for, His honor to be extended, our most
holy faith to be spread and reverenced; there is no need to
languish for want of work, or to waste tears and prayers
upon that which is already in the hands of Almighty Love
and Almighty Power.

Yes; I believe I was, through it all, happier than Mrs.
Churchill, haggard and worn in a service whose nominal
wages are pleasure and ease; and than Josephine, wasting
her youth in the pursuit of an ambition that had rewarded
her as yet by nothing but vanity and vexation of spirit. A
gay hotel in Paris, and a secluded country parsonage—on
the one hand wealth, the pleasures of society, the admira-

tion of the world, on the other seclusion, the annihilation
of every hope that had its root only in this earth, the love
only of the poor, the aged and the suffering, yet I would
not have exchanged their gaiety for my peace, their prosperity for my adversity.

"What should we do without you, child?" said Mr.
Shenstone, kindly, one day as I was leaving him. "What
should we do without these young eyes and this young
zeal? I am afraid the village would begin to tire of its old
pastor, and to fret about his old ways and his new negli-
gences, if we had not this fresh enthusiast to throw herself
into the breach, and to save both flock and pastor from dis-
couragement and disgust. You have assimilated yourself
strangely to those you have fallen among. Tell me truly,
my dear child, are you never weary of this dull life—never
tired of the companionship of two solitary, sad people, old
and spiritless? We are apt to forget—you cheer and comfort us—we must depress and sadden you."

"You? Oh, Mr. Shenstone! You know to whom it is
I owe it that I have conquered depression and sadness.
You have done everything for me; may I do nothing for
you? It is little enough, surely, but it is my greatest
pleasure."

"If it is—then go," he said, with a sad smile on his
wan, furrowed face. "Go and fulfill the duties that God
has taken out of my hands, and I will try to be patient and
stay at home in idleness. I will try to remember,

'They also serve who only stand and wait.'

But God knows, it is the hardest kind of service!"

Every day lately had been adding to his languor; I
watched with anxious foreboding his slow step and altered
tone. It was the twenty-fourth of December, and I knew
that the contrast of his present inactivity at this holy season,
to former diligence, must be a keen trial to him with his
stern rules of duty. I left the house with a sigh, and went

out into the clear, still air of the winter afternoon, with the energy of youth and earnestness in my veins, and thought, wonderingly, of the different grades of trials, the "anguish of all sizes" that God's elect must pass through,

"Till every pulse beat true to airs divine.'

It must be hard, indeed, to "stand and wait," to feel that energy and strength are going before life goes, and that there is nothing left to do, only to endure. Such a trial, it seemed to me, would be the worst of all : as long as there is work there is a panacea, but take away that, and the burden grows intolerable. God spare me that! And I hurried on through my many duties with double thankfulness that they were so many.

The short winter afternoon was all too short for them— it was almost sundown when I started to cross the common on my return from a distant cottage. There was but one thing more to do to-night; the school-children were waiting for me to go into the church and practice their Christmas-hymn with them, and it was late already, so I quickened my pace. I found my young pupils waiting for me around the gate of the churchyard ; they hailed me with acclamations, and clustering round my skirts, followed me into the church. They were too well taught to continue their chattering there, even if they had been unrestrained by my presence, but I could not but believe the scene must have struck them with some reverence, thoughtless and trifling though too many of them were. The lowering sun streamed in through the stained glass of the western windows, and lit up gorgeously the sombre church, illuminating the joyful Christmas words above the altar, touching cross and star and tablet with soft light, and laying rich and warm upon the glossy wreaths that were twined round font and chancel, desk and pillar. Coming from the cold air and wintry landscape, into such a mellow, warm, green sanctu-ary, where there seemed no winter and no chill, I could understand the feeling that checked the children's mirth so suddenly, and made them look wistfully and silently around; and when their sweet, young voices followed mine in the Christmas-hymn, and when the organ yielded its full tones to my touch, arch and rafter, pavement and aisle seemed to stretch away into infinity; the light that filled the church was the glory of heaven; the sweet music, the voices of the angels; and time and earth seemed to fade and recede, and floating down that path of glory, I could almost have touched the open gates of heaven— almost have mingled in the white-robed throng within. The chains of sin and sense fall off—the sounds of warfare die away—the terrors of the conflict with the hosts of hell are all forgotten; if one's soul could follow in the wake of one's longing at such a moment as this, death would indeed be conquered—the king of terrors be cheated of his prey.

The glory had faded from the west, and dullness and gloom had crept into the church before the young choir dispersed. It seemed as if the very spirit of music had possessed the children; hymn after hymn, anthem and carol, and never tired or flagging. As at last I rose to go, and bent forward to shut the organ, one of them whispered eagerly:

"There's somebody been below there in the church! I hear steps going down the aisle; and hark! The door just opened and shut again."

"No matter," I said, a little startled. "Some one has heard the music, and come in to listen. Follow me quietly, children: it is almost dark; we have stayed too late."

The little group separated at the church door; bidding them good-night, and taking by the hand the child whose way lay partly with mine going home, I took the path toward the village. It gave me, I confess, a little uneasiness to see how faint the daylight was, and the conjecture—

who could have been in the church so long and so silent, recurred again and again uncomfortably. It was too late to trust little Rosy to go home alone, so, though it took me a full half mile beyond my own road, I kept on with her; and beguiling her with a Christmas story as we went, soon succeeded in forgetting foolish fears, *malgré* the twilight and the lonesome road. At last we reached the little gate of Rosy's home, and stooping to kiss her as I left her at it, I was turning away, when a carriage drove quickly past toward Brandon. It was a strange carriage, and it gave me a sort of start; I could not quite recover my composure for some minutes; but then strangers came so seldom through the village at this season, it was not very wonderful after all that I had been startled. However, I reflected, it was not improbably some one on the way from northward, detained by the freezing of the river, and hurrying on to catch the evening train from Brandon; and with that, dismissed the subject from my mind.

When I reached home, I hurried into the study, anxious to explain to Mr. Shenstone the cause of my long absence, and to make amends for it by enlivening his evening. I found him alone; Mrs. Arnold had not been able to leave her room for several days, and the study was in darkness, and tea had not been thought of.

"Why, how dismal you look, sir!" I exclaimed, as I came in. "I beg you will excuse my staying till this hour; but the children were so in love with their own voices, that I could not get them away; and that little gipsy of a Rosy had to be escorted all the way home. Kitty should have brought you lights, sir; shall I ring?"

"No, not just yet; I am in no hurry. Sit down; are you not tired? I have wondered at your being so late. You have missed a visitor."

"A visitor? No! Why, who?"

"One whom I little expected to see, and much less expected to have had so short a visit from. I confess it has quite startled and unsettled me, seeing him so unexpectedly and for such a moment. But he could not stay over night, and the Brandon-train leaves at half-past six, he says. He was sorry you were away."

" Mr. Rutledge has been here ?"

" Yes."

" And gone ?"

" And gone."

———•••———

CHAPTER XXXIX.

" Be not amazed at life. 'Tis still
The mode of God with his elect,
Their hopes exactly to fulfill,
In times and ways they least expect."

COVENTRY PATMORE.

THE winter passed heavily away : no change for the better relieved our fears for Mr. Shenstone, and, before spring, poor Mrs. Arnold died, and left me alone with the burden of care and dread. All that time is like a sad, slow dream ; I cannot tell the days apart as I look back upon them—the one fear that grew daily colored all events alike. It was like no other approaching death that I had ever seen. I knew he was longing for his release ; but what would be release to him would be my sentence of banishment — my separation from the only friend I had, the severing of the only tie I knew.

Still it seemed vague and far off, and the warm spring days came slowly on, and crept into June, before either he or I knew how very few he had yet to live. The doctor had at last to tell me what every one else knew—that Mr. Shenstone could not live a week. I do not think that he himself, though knowing well that the time was at hand, had been aware how very near it was. I knew it was not too near for his desires; but one earthly care vexed the holy calm of his death-bed.

"I must see Arthur before I die. Write to him again, and beg him to come quickly. He could not have realized what I meant him to understand when you wrote last, or he would have been here before."

I wrote again urgently, and told him in the plainest words what the necessity for his coming was, and how anxiously Mr. Shenstone desired an interview before he died; that it was the one ungratified wish that disturbed his last moments; the letter was hurriedly dispatched, and yet day after day passed and no answer came. It was cruel to see the momentary eagerness with which the dying man's eye lighted up at each new sound without, and to hear the faint sigh with which he sank back at the fresh disappointment.

I had my own interpretation of this silence; but I dared not tell him. Through the winter his letters had been irregular; it was now some weeks since any had come; I did not feel a doubt but that he had gone abroad again, and, in the hurry of departure, had omitted to write. Something that Mrs. Fielding (the pretty Janet Emerson, married and living at New Orleans, but on a visit to her old home, who had found me out and come to see me a month or so before) had said, confirmed my suspicions.

"I heard from Paris a week or so ago," she said, "that your cousin, Miss Churchill, and Mr. Rutledge are really to be married. Upon my word, you must excuse me; but it is a shame. I grudge him to her. Ah! *méchante*, if you had made the proper use of that evening in the library that I gave you, she would not have had him."

I had not told Mr. Shenstone this; nor dared I tell him that there was hardly a hope that his friend was still in America. A week had elapsed since my letter had been sent; the end was surely approaching—we could not shut our eyes to that. That morning, Mr. Shenstone had, with great pain and difficulty, refusing my assistance, himself written a few lines to Mr. Rutledge, and, sealing it, had committed it to my hands, charging me to deliver it to him as soon as he should come. From the moment that that was done, he had put off all care, and given himself wholly up to the exercises of religion and the preparations for death. Of my future he had never spoken much. God would direct my lot mercifully, he was sure ; he left me, his sole earthly care, with faith, to God's protection. He desired that for the present I should remain, with the two servants, in the house, till some other home presented, or till the parsonage was required for his successor.

It was a holy, religious day ; such peace as soothed the last hours of his life told well for the service in which he had spent it. It was not like death—it was like the coming of a blessing that had been long prayed for. We had with him received the sacrament, and heard the faint words that told his triumph and his hope, and stood waiting around him, almost following him to the courts of heaven, almost forgetting with him, the world in which our path still lay; when through the window, open to the sunset of a June evening, there came the sound of a hurried arrival.

"It is Arthur," murmured the dying man, faintly, turning his eyes on me. "Go and bring him to me."

I hurried to the door and down the path. "You have not a moment to lose," I said, without a word of preparation or salutation. "He can hardly live an hour, and he desires to see you."

"Good heaven ! Has it indeed come to that !" he exclaimed, following me up the stairs. I left him at the door ; for half an hour they were alone together, then Mr. Rutledge opened the door and called me hastily to come in. I obeyed ; but only in time to receive the last blessing of the dying saint, and, kneeling in unspeakable sorrow by his bedside, to feel his hand rest tenderly on my head, with a silent benediction, even after his departing soul had carried its supplication and its intercession to the very presence of the Divine Benefactor.

Two days had passed since the funeral; there was no more anxiety to engross, no more watching to employ me; the blank idleness that is the earliest pain after a great loss, was just then creeping over me with its worst power. There was nothing more to do—the house was settled to its ordinary ways, and I sat alone in my little room in the deepening twilight, with a sadder sense of my loneliness than I had had before. It was not time yet for me to think of what was to become of me; I had a right to rest a little before I faced any greater change, yet harassing thoughts of my homelessness and desolation crowded on me to make my present trial heavier. There was no one on earth I had a right to call my friend, save only the humble ones who could offer me nothing but gratitude and affection, and who were as unable to direct and help me, as I was to direct and help myself. It was long before I could summon courage enough to say that I must decide upon some change, and to resolve that it must be done now. There was no right and no propriety in staying longer here than till I had arranged some other home; indeed for some reasons this was the last roof that I should stay under now. But my resolves came quick when they did come—I saw that the sooner I began my new life the better; it would be like another death if I waited till a few months hence before I left this dear home; now, in this time of change and restlessness, I could best bear the pain. To-morrow, I had resolved, I would go out and try to find some cottage or some rooms, where, with Kitty to attend me, I could make the best of my slender fortune, and remain quietly at least for the present, when a knock at the door aroused me. The servant said: "Mr. Rutledge is in the study, Miss, and desires to see you for a few moments."

"Ask him to excuse me to-night," I began; but no, it was as easy now as it would ever be, so telling the woman to say I would be down in a moment, I shut the door and tried to prepare myself. There was a good deal to help me to be calm; some pride and some humility—a prayer—and the remembrance of my sorrow—and the gulf that lay between the present and the past; and I went downstairs quite self-possessed and quiet.

The study was so dusky I could hardly see my visitor's face as he rose to meet me. I longed to keep the dusk, but said:

"Do you mind twilight, sir? My head aches a little, but if you prefer it, I will send for candles."

"Not at all," he said, sitting down opposite me in the window. "I am sorry to hear you are not well. Kitty told me, when she admitted me, that it was doubtful whether you could come down; but I fancied you would not have the least hesitation in declining to see me if you were not able."

"I did think, sir, when you were first announced, that I would beg you to excuse me; but I remembered that possibly you might be returning to the city to-morrow, and this might be my last chance of seeing you, so I made an effort to come down."

There was a moment's pause, which I broke by saying:

"I wanted to see you, sir, about the change in my plans, which, as Mr. Shenstone's nearest friend, you would, perhaps, be kind enough to sanction."

"It was about that that I came this evening."

"You are very kind, sir, and so I may go at once to the subject. You know, of course, of Mr. Shenstone's legacy; that, with my own property, is sufficient to provide very comfortably for Kitty and myself. I propose making my arrangements to leave here within a fortnight, keeping Kitty with me; but for the other servant, Mary, I would ask your advice. She has been some time in the family, and is a faithful person. Would it be best to leave her in the house till it is otherwise occupied, or to provide a place for her, and close the house? You know, as I shall have

the packing up and settling of all at the last, it is necessary
I should know your wishes."

"I do not quite comprehend. I had understood from
Mr. Shenstone that it was his wish that you should remain for the present here. Did he not express the same to
you?"

"He did, sir, but it was a mistaken kindness. I had
rather go now; and I do not think there can be any wrong
in disregarding a request which he only meant as an indulgence and a respite, and would not have insisted on if he
had known my reasons."

"Can I know them?"

"They are so many, sir, it would not be worth while to
trouble you."

"Am I wrong when I fancy that one is, that the house
belongs to one from whom you would not endure an obligation?"

"You put it too harshly, sir; but in truth I do not like
obligations."

"You would incur none, then, let me assure you, by remaining here. The house will be unoccupied; I should be
glad to have some one in it, and there is, I fear, little
chance of having the parish permanently suited with a
clergyman before fall, and even after that, there is no necessity of retaining this as a parsonage; there are one or
two houses nearer the church, which would, indeed, be
more convenient."

"Thank you, sir, but it will be impossible. You do not
estimate the difficulties. I cannot stay here: and perhaps
you will be kind enough to tell me what to do about the
arrangement of the books. Shall they be packed, or are
they to remain on the shelves? And here, sir, is the key
of the private drawers in that book-case, that I was to give
you when you came."

My voice faltered as I delivered my kind friend's last
message. There was a long pause, then Mr. Rutledge said:

"These things are very trying to you now; there is no need that you should distress yourself by attending to them at once. Leave them till later."

"No, sir, it is better that they should be all arranged before you go. I do not mind the effort of undertaking it at once."

"But how do you know I am going? Why will not a few weeks hence do as well?"

"Why, sir, as I told you, I should prefer that everything were settled, the papers arranged, the house vacated, before you go abroad. It may make no difference, but it will be more agreeable to me."

"I am not going abroad; I do not intend to leave America again. Can you not be contented to let things rest as they are at present, and to let me, in some degree, take the place of him you have lost? Consider, you are homeless and friendless—you have no one to direct or guide you "——

"I have considered this, sir, more fully, perhaps, than you have. There is not a circumstance in my fate that I have not weighed. Indeed, I do not need so much pity; your attention has just been called to it, and so it sounds new and dreadful to you for a woman to be left so alone. But I am used to the idea, and I do not mind it. People will be kind to me, no doubt, and I shall do very well."

"Then you are resolved to go away from here?"

"Within a fortnight, sir."

"And you refuse all offers of assistance from me, of all kinds?"

"Why, sir, you know it would be useless to trouble you, when I do not need any; but I hope you understand that I am very grateful for your goodness."

"I understand it fully, and that you decline any further demonstration of it. But if you have no scruple against telling me where you intend to go, perhaps it would be wiser to do it, as some cases may occur which you cannot foresee, in which it would be safer for you to have the judgment and advice of one whose age and experience place him above you in knowledge, of the world, at least."

"It would be impossible for me to tell you, sir, for I do not know in the least where I shall go. You know I have not had time to arrange my plans definitely—it is only two days—since—since—I have had to think about them."

"And you will not take more time, and put off any change for a few months—you will not let me advise you?"

"Mr. Rutledge, you are trying to make me seem rude; I have but one answer to make, and it sounds so ungracious you are not kind to oblige me to repeat it."

"I will not; I believe I understand how you wish it to stand; and perhaps you are right. It is not necessary to detain you longer," he continued, rising, "there is nothing of importance left to say, I believe. About the books and furniture, I should prefer having them left for the present in the house; I will not trouble you to do anything but to send the keys, when you leave, to my house. Mrs. Roberts will take charge of them. The papers I can look over at my leisure. In regard to the servant you spoke of—I will mention her to Mrs. Roberts, and will see that she is provided with a situation. Is there anything more?"

"Nothing that I remember at this moment, sir. You are very kind; I shall endeavor to leave everything in the order you would wish."

"I do not doubt it; I hope you will be able to bear whatever you intend to put upon yourself, but you will do well not to overtask your strength or fortitude just now; you are not at present fit for exertion. But I forget"——

I rose, and held out my hand; he went on: "You know you have always my best wishes; there is no need for me to say that."

"I know it, sir," I replied, with what steadiness of voice I could. "I wish I could tell you how"—— but the words choked me. He did not relinquish my hand, but with a sudden change from the cold tone of his last words, he exclaimed hurriedly, and with a smothered vehemence:

"You wish you could tell me what? You wish you could tell me what I already know—could tell me that you pity me—that you are sorry for the pain you give me? That you know how much it costs me to say a final farewell to you—and that you are sorry—sorry. No! You need not wish to do it; I can spare you that. I came to you to-night to see if time, and sorrow, and necessity had not helped me in my suit; to try, for the last time, whether there was any chance of winning you; I came to tempt you by the fortune and the luxury I could offer you, just to endure my love, and to repay, by ever so cold a kindness, the devotion of years. I came, misled by a hope held out by one who loved us both too well to be an impartial judge; and I find you colder, more distant than ever, and that the hope I have been trying to extinguish so long is only rekindled to be quenched at last utterly!

"Foolish girl!" he went on, in a lower tone, "how little you know what you throw away. How vain to cling so fondly to a memory. Believe me, it will not be wronging the dead—I little thought I should ever stoop to ask it, but only try to love me—only consent to give me your esteem and consideration, and I will take the risk of teaching you to love me. Is it nothing to be loved as I have loved you? To be the first, and last, and only choice of a man who has had so many to choose from? Have you no vanity that can be touched—no pride? If you had, I could allure you by the promise that you should be proud of the position you would hold; those who have slighted you should look at you with envy—those who "——

"Oh, Mr. Rutledge do not talk of those things now—I

have given them up forever; I shall never care again for the world—but—there is something else—I"——

"You relent!" he murmured, eagerly. "You will con sent to forget the past—you will"——

"I must tell you one thing first; I must tell you some-thing that I have told to no one else. Heaven have mercy on me if it is a sin, or if I am betraying what I should still conceal. I never felt the love you think I did. I deceived him and you; but as I have been bitterly punished, and bitterly penitent, so Heaven forgive me for it! Between him and me there was another love, that began before I ever saw him—that is not ended yet—that has never known change or wavering."

"And that love?"

Within his arms, my face hidden on his shoulder, I could whisper the answer to that question, and the confession of the folly, and deceit, and pride, that had so long kept me from him.